PLUGGED IN

PLUGGED IN

How Media Attract and Affect Youth

Patti M. Valkenburg
Jessica Taylor Piotrowski

Yale UNIVERSITY PRESS
New Haven and London

Yale University Press books may be purchased in quantity for educational, business, or promotional use. For information, please e-mail sales.press@yale.edu (U.S. office) or sales@yaleup.co.uk (U.K. office).

Set in Galliard Old Style type by IDS Infotech Ltd., Chandigarh, India.
Printed in the United States of America.

Library of Congress Control Number: 2016953447
ISBN 978-0-300-21887-9 (cloth : alk. paper)

A catalogue record for this book is available from the British Library.

This paper meets the requirements of ANSI/NISO Z39.48-1992 (Permanence of Paper).

10 9 8 7 6 5 4 3 2 1

FOR PAUL AND JOHN

CONTENTS

Preface ix

1 Youth and Media 1
2 Then and Now 10
3 Themes and Theoretical Perspectives 28
4 Infants, Toddlers, and Preschoolers 44
5 Children 63
6 Adolescents 78
7 Media and Violence 96
8 Media and Emotions 116
9 Advertising and Commercialism 137
10 Media and Sex 158
11 Media and Education 175
12 Digital Games 195
13 Social Media 218
14 Media and Parenting 244
15 The End 267

Notes 277

Acknowledgments 313

Index 315

PREFACE

In the past decades, a dazzling number of studies have investigated the effects of old and new media on children and teens. These studies have greatly improved our understanding of why youth are so massively attracted to media. And they have also shown how children and teens can be affected by media, in positive and negative ways. *Plugged In* provides insight into the most important issues and debates regarding media, children, and teens.

Plugged In discusses the dark sides of media, such as the effects of media violence and pornography. But it also discusses their sunny sides, such as the countless opportunities of educational media for learning, and the potential of social media for identity development. Each chapter gives an overview of existing theories and research on a particular topic. This general literature review is occasionally illustrated by our own research findings. The book covers research among infants (up to 1 year old), toddlers (1–3 years), preschoolers (4–5 years), children (5–12 years), and teens or adolescents (12–19 years). Within these general age groups, we sometimes refer to subgroups, such as tweens (8–12 years), early adolescents (12–15 years), and late adolescents (15–19 years). We use the term "youth" to refer to both children and adolescents.

Plugged In is based, in part, on *Responses to the Screen* (Erlbaum, 2004), by Patti Valkenburg. Additionally, it draws on her Dutch book published in 2014 by Prometheus. But whereas that book focused primarily on Dutch data, this one internationalizes and updates both the research and the examples of media and tools. Incidentally, doing so was less difficult than we anticipated, because the preferences of youth in Western countries are remarkably homogenous. For example, a cartoon or digital game that is popular in the United States is very likely to be popular in most other westernized countries.

We see this book, like Valkenburg's earlier ones, as an informative device for anyone interested in the study of children, adolescents, and the media. We are grateful that Yale University Press gave us the opportunity to publish an open-access book whose online version is free to students and researchers all over the world. We hope you enjoy reading the book as much as we enjoyed writing it.

PLUGGED IN

1

YOUTH AND MEDIA

> My dear, here we must run as fast as we can, just to stay in place. And if you want to get somewhere else you must run at least twice as fast as that.
> —Lewis Carroll, *Through the Looking-Glass* (1871)

Over the past few decades, there have been several thousand studies about the effects of media on youth. And yet, somewhat paradoxically, we still have much to learn. In part, the gaps in our knowledge are due to dramatic changes in young people's media use. In the 1990s, children and teens spent on average four hours a day with media; these estimates have now skyrocketed to an average of six (for children) and nine hours a day (for teens).[1] As a matter of fact, today's children and teens spend more time with media than they do at school. And indeed, some of us are less concerned about what youth are learning in school than about what they are picking up from their many hours with all those screens.

Along with the significant growth in media use, the gaps in our knowledge are caused by the sweeping and rapid changes in the media landscape. New media and technologies are developing and replacing one another at a dramatic pace. Social media tools that we studied not long ago now seem as old as Methuselah. In 2015, virtually all teens had Facebook accounts, yet even a juggernaut like Facebook has to continually do its best to stay ahead of the competition and not lose its users to newer, more attractive interfaces such as Snapchat, Taptalk, and so forth. Indeed, the truth of the epigraph from *Through the Looking-Glass* is compelling: in the new media landscape, we must run as fast as we can, just to stay in place.

The changes in the media landscape are due not only to the development of new media but also to the repurposing of traditional media. Youth, and adults too, are watching television differently from the way they did in previous decades. They are watching more programs online, recording more programs to watch later, and often using a second screen while they are watching so that they can comment on a show, avoid advertising, or stay in contact with other people. No longer are they watching a series like *Pretty Little Liars* or *Gossip Girl* when it is scheduled to air. Now they watch the program when they feel like it, and sometimes for hours at a stretch by "binge viewing" with streaming services such as Netflix or Apple TV, on their television, tablet, or smartphone. And although most teens are still interested in the news, more than adults sometimes think, watching the evening news on TV and buying the (paper) newspaper is a thing of the past. Teens have become "news grazers": the vast majority (93 percent) pick up the news from a variety of on- and offline sources, depending on which is most convenient at the moment.[2]

The commercial environment surrounding youth is experiencing major changes, too. Traditional TV advertising has lost its dominant position. The discrete thirty-second commercial is no longer the best way to reach young people. Instead, advertisers are being forced to create and implement other, often more covert forms of advertising, such as product placement and advergames. Today's James Bond will gladly order a Heineken, and *Mad Men*'s Don Draper a Canadian Club whiskey, which, according to its makers, has boosted the sales of whiskey among teens. And thanks to cross-media marketing, *Dora the Explorer* has become more than a TV series; there are Dora apps, Dora games, Dora toys, Dora quilt covers, and Dora websites in dozens of languages.

Then there is the world of games. In the 1990s, gaming was considered the domain of teenage boys, but it has increasingly become mainstream for young and old, male and female. Ten years ago, a mention of video games brought with it images of a home computer or a console player such as Nintendo or PlayStation. Games such as *Street Fighter, Super Mario Bros,* and *Counter-Strike* are probably among the first to come to mind. When we think of games today, our first thoughts are likely to be *Pokémon GO* or *Candy Crush*—games that can be played with smartphones or tablets. Touch-screen technology and the Internet have profoundly influenced what gaming looks like.

We see now that even very young children are playing games with their parents' smartphones, and that the gender divide is changing as girls find their own game spaces in virtual worlds such as *Club Penguin* and *Neopets.* Virtual gaming worlds, in general, have spiked in popularity: the game *Minecraft* is among the highest-grossing apps of all time. This increased access to gaming on touch-screen platforms, combined with a reliance on freemiums (that is, apps that are free to download and rely on advertising and "in-app purchasing"), has provided formidable competition to traditional console game manufacturers.

Academic Interest in Youth and Media

In parallel with these wide-ranging changes in the media landscape, the topic of youth and media has acquired greater significance in academia, drawing interest from more and more scientific disciplines. Within psychiatry and pediatric medicine, there are countless studies of the effects of media use on aggressive behavior, attention-deficit-hyperactivity disorder (ADHD), and obesity. Neuroscientists are researching whether media use causes changes in brain areas responsible for aggressive behavior, spatial awareness, and motor skills. Sociology is studying the dynamics of youth cultures and teenage behavior in online social networks.

Research on youth and media requires an interdisciplinary approach integrating knowledge and theories from several disciplines. After all, to understand the effects of media on children and adolescents, we need to know theories about media in general as well as about cognitive and social-emotional development in youth, since it is this development that largely shapes their media use and its effects. We need to be familiar with theories about a child's social environment, such as family, friends, and the youth culture, since factors in these environments predict the nature of media effects to some or a great extent.

Two major interdisciplinary fields have been studying youth and media since the 1960s: cultural studies and media psychology. Both fields are part of communication studies. Cultural studies, which falls within the critical tradition of communication studies, originated with the Frankfurt School in the 1940s. This field is concerned with the meaning of popular culture in daily life, and it primarily uses theories and methods from the fields of literature, history, sociology, and anthropology. Empirical methodology is typically qualitative and inductive in nature (for example, in-depth interviews or focus groups). Cultural studies researchers focus on questions that fit within the critical tradition, for example, whether children and teens have the same access as adults to media and technology, or how particular minority groups, such as homosexuals or ethnic groups, are portrayed in popular culture aimed at youth.

The second interdisciplinary field, and the one to which our research belongs, is media psychology. Research in this field gained momentum in the 1960s with Albert Bandura's famous studies on the effects of television violence.[3] Media psychology concerns itself with the use, power of attraction, and effects of media on the individual. It typically relies on quantitative, deductive research methods, such as experiments, surveys, and longitudinal research. Media psychologists, like researchers in cultural studies, make use of theories from different disciplines. They work mainly in communication studies, but also in psychology and education.

Interdisciplinary research on youth and media has had a spectacular evolution in the last few decades. In the early 1990s, only a handful of quantitatively oriented empirical scientists were interested in youth and media. Most of these scientists focused on television's negative effects on, for example, aggression, reading, doing homework, and creativity. Some were interested in the positive effects of educational programs such as *Sesame Street*, but this research was less common. Today, hundreds of academics all over the world work on a variety of topics in the area of youth and media. They are looking at an increasing number of new questions. Are teenagers becoming narcissistic from self-presentation on the Internet? Does gaming lead to gaming addiction? How widespread is cyberbullying? What does Internet pornography do to children and teenagers? How does one cope with the thousands of educational apps for toddlers and preschoolers in the Apple Education Store? How can we teach youth to handle the temptations they are bombarded with in ads, games, and social media?

Although many social trends have contributed to the dramatic growth of this academic interest in youth, three trends have played particularly impressive roles. The first is the commercialization of the media environment around youth. In the United States, where television has been commercial since its inception, research on children and commercialism began in the 1970s. By contrast, in the Netherlands there was no commercial television, and hence no research on its effects, until 1989, when the first commercial station was launched. Children's channels then sprouted like mushrooms, and before long no fewer than 113 commercials were aired during a popular Saturday-morning television show. This dramatic uptick in advertising to children was seen across many industrialized countries and led to the beginning of empirical research on youth and commercialism. For example, researchers began to ask about "host selling," in which famous children's heroes or hosts could freely advertise unhealthy children's products on their own programs. Though this type of advertising was initially permissible, empirical research soon demonstrated the ethical concerns associated with this approach and ultimately played a key role in the banning of this practice in countries throughout the world.

The end of the 1990s witnessed a second important change in the media landscape that required an empirically based scientific standpoint: the development of media for the very youngest viewers, children between one and two years old. Launched in 1997, the BBC blockbuster *Teletubbies* opened the eyes of commercial conglomerates like Disney and Fox International, which soon realized that this "diaper demographic" was potentially lucrative. As a consequence, they set their sights on an even younger audience—babies as young as three months—with Baby Einstein and Baby TV. The rise of baby media led to new and heated debates among the public, especially in the United States. Was it really a good idea to plop such young children in front of the boob tube?

To respond to these concerns, in 2001 the American Academy of Pediatrics published a policy statement calling on parents to keep children under age two away from TV screens. This somewhat conservative recommendation largely resulted from a lack of scientific knowledge about very young children's media use. But it was often interpreted as suggesting that media use for children under two is harmful—a sentiment that continues to pervade much of the discourse about toddlers' media use. This controversy between pediatricians and commercial interests spurred new youth and media research on this topic. As we discuss later in this book, research so far has not found any evidence that developmentally appropriate media content is harmful to very young children. But inappropriate media, and background media not aimed at very young children, have been shown to negatively influence children's concentration and their ability to play imaginatively.[4] Today, researchers remain interested in the effects of television on this youngest demographic, although their interest has expanded to include games and, since 2010, apps.

The dawn of the new millennium saw a third trend, one that has irrevocably turned the field of youth and media on its head: social media. The concerns raised by social media were broader than those raised by television and games. In addition to fears about exposing children to violence, sex, or frightening content, social media raised concerns about online social interaction. Would social media cause children to grow up lonely, socially inept, and sexually out of control? Would social media stimulate online bullying? The first research on the social effects of the Internet was published in the United States in 1998. The study did not actually investigate the effects of the Internet, because at the time of data collection hardly any participating families had access to it. At that time, the Internet was primarily the domain of early adopters, and only a small percentage of children were online.[5] Public debate about the Internet heated up only around 2002, when access rates rose dramatically and the majority of American and European youth were online. Shortly thereafter, researchers began to seriously investigate youth's access to the Internet. The results of these studies revealed a more nuanced picture than many expected, which led researchers to ask more questions about social media, including their influence on self-esteem, social skills, online sexual risk behavior, and cyberbullying.

In the last few years, the subject of youth and media has branched out more than ever. Although most empirical research in the 1990s was done among preschoolers and children, the rise of new media has brought two additional age groups into the picture: toddlers, as a result of baby media, and teenagers, as a result of social media. This broadened age range has helped the field become more interdisciplinary. This is because, particularly for the last two age groups, it is nearly impossible to understand the effects of media without also understanding their developmental level and their social environment, both of which can have a sizable influence on the size and nature of media effects.

Along with studying children and youth from a wider age range, researchers have broadened their research foci. They no longer primarily study the potential risks of media for youth but, more than ever, also recognize the potential opportunities of media. For example, in addition to asking whether early media use may be detrimental to brain development, contemporary researchers try to determine whether early use of educational apps may bolster learning. In the same vein, researchers studying online peer interaction are interested in not just cyberbullying, but also whether social media may provide a place for teens to practice and develop their social skills. This broader approach, reflecting the negative and positive opportunities of media, recognizes that media are an integral part of youth's lives. And thus, the best contribution researchers can offer is to identify ways to ensure that these media are healthfully incorporated into their lives.

In parallel with this rapid growth in the variety of ages and topics studied, the academic area of youth and media has become more institutionalized. In 2007, the successful interdisciplinary *Journal of Children and Media* was launched, which specializes in both cultural studies and media psychology. A few months later, the International Communication Association (ICA) started a special division called Children, Adolescents, and the Media, which provides an important forum for researchers in cultural studies and media psychology to exchange ideas and research. With several hundred members, this division has grown into one of the largest within the ICA. Last, we have seen the success of several academic research centers around the world. For example, the University of Amsterdam's Center for Research on Children, Adolescents, and the Media (CcaM), with which we are both affiliated, has experienced enormous growth and is considered the largest research center of its kind. With more than twenty researchers studying topics including media multitasking, game addiction, cyberbullying, and the opportunities of digital media, CcaM and centers like it have become interdisciplinary hubs for empirical research on the complex relationship between youth and media.

Public Debate

Today, stories about youth and media make the news headlines virtually every day. The news stories have four common characteristics. First, they are more often about the negative than the positive effects of media. "If it bleeds it leads" and "good news is no news" seem to be the mantras of journalists writing on youth and the media. Second, news stories often focus on extreme incidents, such as cyberbullying cases and online sexual predators. Third, journalists frequently quote clinical experts such as pediatricians and psychiatrists as a means of lending expert credibility to the topics. Yet these clinical experts often speak from their daily experience with atypical kids, who do not represent the average child or adolescent. Finally, journalistic coverage of youth and media issues often misses the nuance of research findings, opting instead for a clean, simplistic, and often alarming sound bite.

These mechanisms mean that popular science books with negative messages tend to attract significant public interest. Books such as *iBrain,* by the American psychologist Gary Small, *Digital Dementia,* by the German psychiatrist Manfred Spitzer, and *Alone Together,* by Sherry Turkle, appeal to the moral panic that our children are losing their innocence, sense of decency, memory, or ability to maintain social relationships because of their use of new technologies. Worrying about the effects of new technologies has been with us for millennia. Enthusiasm about technological progress goes hand in hand with fear or even aversion of the same progress. This was true in the age of Socrates, who in the year 360 BCE expressed his concern (put into the mouth of the Egyptian king Thamus) in a dialogue with Phaedrus that written language would lead to memory loss in his students. With the aid of the written word, Socrates opined, students would no longer have to do their best to remember something all by themselves, and would appear pseudo-wise rather than truly wise: "[Writing] will produce forgetfulness in the minds of those who learn to use it, because they will not practice their memory. Their trust in writing, produced by external characters that are no part of themselves, will discourage the use of their own memory within them. You have invented an elixir not of memory, but of reminding; and you offer your pupils the appearance of wisdom, not true wisdom" (275a–b).[6]

The negative spin that youth and media research often receives in the news can give most people the idea that media primarily have negative effects on children and adolescents. But this is not the picture that emerges from empirical research on youth and media. Instead, this research reveals neither a dystopian paradigm, in which all media are problematic for youth, nor a utopian paradigm, in which youth universally benefit from media. To quote danah boyd: "Reality is nuanced and messy, full of pros and cons. Living in a networked world is complicated."[7] Media effects are not simple—not all media are the same, not all children are the same, and not all environmental contexts are the same. Some research has shown that media can affect certain children in certain situations negatively, while other research shows the reverse. In this book, our goal is to present a nuanced picture of the complex relationship between youth and media. Relying on research that has been conducted throughout the Western world, we aim to provide an accurate account on the role of media—both traditional and new—in the lives of youth today.

2

THEN AND NOW

> The White Rabbit put on his spectacles. "Where shall I begin, please your Majesty?" he asked. "Begin at the beginning," the King said gravely, "and go on till you come to the end: then stop."
>
> —Lewis Carroll, *Alice's Adventures in Wonderland* (1865)

This book begins in the second half of the eighteenth century. This is a logical starting point, since it was then that the first children's media—books—appeared. Previously, children were not considered children in the sense they are today, and if they could read, they read books for adults. This changed gradually after the publication of Jean-Jacques Rousseau's influential book on child rearing, *Émile, ou De l'éducation*, in 1762. As society's ideas about childhood and parenting began to shift, so did our ideas about which media are appropriate for children. In this chapter, we describe how society's ideas about youth and media have been subject to swings of the pendulum since the seventeenth century. In addition, we compare the current generation with previous generations. Why are children and teens more self-aware and intelligent than ever? Why has youth culture become so dominant in society? Why do children display adult behavior at younger and younger ages? And lastly, what is media's role in these developments?

The Child as Miniature Adult

Although the subject of youth and media has captured the public's interest for several decades, children's media are relatively new phenomena, as is the concept of childhood itself. In fact, until the second half of the eighteenth century, there were hardly any specialized media for children nor was there a clear delineation between childhood and adulthood.[1] Children were essentially seen as miniature adults and were treated as such. For example, children's clothing did not differ from that of adults. Until the age of five, both boys and girls wore a kind of dress that made toilet training easier.[2] After that, girls wore bodices and boys wore knee breeches. Contemporary attitudes to childhood can be clearly seen in portraits of children from this time, in which not only their clothing, but even their faces are depicted as those of adults (see figure 2.1).

Children and adults also read the same texts in this period (if they could read): the Bible, chapbooks (inexpensive books containing ballads and popular tales), and sometimes the newspaper. Writers of the time unabashedly covered subjects such as poverty, disease, and death as well as drunkenness, sexuality, and adultery. Newspapers published political and military

Figure 2.1. Children as miniature adults: a seven-year-old Mozart painted by Pietro Lorenzoni (1763). (Internationale Stiftung Mozarteum)

news as well as terrifying reports of natural disasters, cholera, and witch trials. Children would regularly accompany their parents to the market square to attend public beheadings and physical punishments. For many families, this was an enjoyable family outing, during which people fought for the best view of the proceedings. Rather than being "brought up," children were simply confronted with current events, no holds barred.[3]

The Vulnerable Child

The view of children as miniature adults changed in the second half of the eighteenth century. Thanks, in part, to ideas promulgated by the seventeenth- and eighteenth-century Enlightenment, especially those of Locke and Rousseau, children became a vulnerable audience—worthy and deserving of protection. Newspapers, which until then had essentially served as cheap textbooks, disappeared from the classroom, and the ABC books from which children had learned the alphabet were supplemented by children's books. The philosophers of the day felt that the content of newspapers was not suitable for children. Other instructional materials, such as the Bible and books of fairy tales, were adapted for the experiential world of the child. Indecent passages such as the Bible story of Daniel and Susanna, in which Susanna is spied on by two men while she bathes, were censored so as not to torment children's souls. Fairy tales such as "Little Red Riding Hood" and "The Frog Prince," which originally included nudity and sex, came to be considered harmful to children's moral development, and were thereafter sanitized.[4]

This censorship was perfectly in line with the new ideas of the eighteenth century and the Enlightenment. Rousseau, for example, reasoned that man is good and unspoiled by nature, and that individual differences are the result of environmental factors. Children's social environments could have a positive, encouraging effect as well as a negative and corrupting influence. Similarly, according to Locke, a person is born as a tabula rasa (literally, a "clean slate"), which becomes filled with experiences and impressions through one's senses. Those raising and teaching children have a crucial role to play in the process—it is their responsibility to write wise lessons on this clean slate. As a result of the Enlightenment perspective, citizens were increasingly expected to keep their sexual and aggressive urges under control. Gradually, they began to be embarrassed about the physical aspects of life. For example, parents stopped cuddling each other and fondling their children, because it was thought to expose children to adult temptations and thereby sully their innocence.[5]

The Emerging Notion of an Innocent Childhood

Rousseau was one of the first to proclaim that children should be raised in freedom and also protected from the distorting influences of the adult world. In *Émile,* he advocated that a period in a child's life be focused on upbringing—not confrontation. This upbringing, he believed, should give children the opportunity to discover themselves without being distressed by the cares and fears of the adult world. Rousseau believed that children were not passive receivers of stimuli from their environment, but instead active researchers who determined how their identity and development took shape. He believed that as childhood became more joyful and carefree, children would, as adults, be less mistrustful and aggressive.

Despite the idea of childhood as a carefree and joyful phase between infancy and adulthood, such a childhood long remained the privilege of the aristocracy and the wealthy bourgeoisie. For children of working-class parents, it was normal to work long days on farms, in the textile industry, or in glass or shoe factories. Most children (and their parents) did not benefit from printed media: most were illiterate, and even if they could read, books and newspapers were expensive. Working-class children had such a short life expectancy that raising them was primarily aimed at teaching them to cope with pain and to prepare them for an early death.

These conditions began to change in the early twentieth century. With the introduction of social legislation such as laws banning child labor and requiring school attendance, the phenomenon of a carefree childhood began to permeate all classes of society. Children were protected en masse from the reality of daily life. Subjects such as childbirth, death, sex, and money were not discussed with them. Printed media for them were primarily moral stories cleansed of taboo subjects. Misbehavior in children's books was innocent mischief. Strict, clear rules prescribed what children of certain ages should and should not know about. Harsh punishments for disobedience softened, since they were seen as contradicting the increasingly popular picture of the sweet and vulnerable child.

The Miniature Adult Returns

In the second half of the twentieth century, the pendulum began to swing back, and the paradigm of the vulnerable child was increasingly questioned. In particular, by the late 1960s, people began to feel that it was wrong to present children with an illusory safe world and, instead, felt that children should be presented with reality so that they would be aware of the true state of the world around them.[6] This view was fueled, in part, by the rise of youth-driven emancipation movements such as the hippies, who protested bourgeois propriety and demanded a place of their own in society. It was also fueled by the rising commercialization of youth culture through music, fashion, and media, all of which ensured that young people acquired an ever-more prominent place in society.

In the 1970s, formerly taboo subjects such as sexuality, death, and divorce once more became acceptable in media aimed at youth. This trend was well illustrated by children's literature from the time, in which a new genre was created: the realistic problem book. Children's literature, according to the experts of the time, had to be relevant to today's world. As a result, a profusion of newly published books dealt with social issues such as homosexuality, incest, divorce, racism, drug use, and incurable diseases.[7] Children's books also began to include an antimoralistic aspect, exemplified by the mischievous creatures in the books of American author Dr. Seuss. Comic books featuring unsavory characters drinking in dimly lit bars became popular, as did comic books that featured strong, independent children as main characters (Tintin, for example, the titular hero of the famous Belgian comic book series).

Criticisms of the Miniature Adult

The idea that the child should squarely face the adult world was not without consequences. Starting in the 1980s, influential child psychologists and cultural critics observed (at about the same time) a number of significant changes in the social order (that is, the more or less predictable relationships between individuals and social institutions). One of their main arguments was that children were being treated too little like children and that, as a result, childhood itself was threatened with erosion. The child psychologist David Elkind was one of the first to express this view, in *The Hurried Child: Growing Up Too Fast Too Soon* (1981).[8] He argued that children were being hurried through childhood, becoming adults too fast and too early. The "pseudo-sophistication" that comes from forcing youth into situations for which they are not emotionally prepared, he argued, could lead to stress, insecurity, depression, and aggression.

Just as child psychologists began bucking the trend against taking a "miniature adult" approach to childhood, similar ideas were coming from communication studies. The cultural critics Joshua Meyrowitz and Neil Postman, for example, each noted that childhood as a phenomenon was disappearing.[9] According to the authors, children were being exposed to information that adults had kept secret from them for centuries. Both authors observed a firmly entrenched "homogenization" of youth and adults: children and adults behaved more alike in their dress, language, gestures, and preferences for media content. As a result, the boundary between children and adults had become obscured or, as Meyrowitz argued, may have disappeared altogether:

> Today, a walk on any city street or in any park suggests that the era of distinct clothing for different age-groups has passed. Just as children sometimes dress in three-piece suits or designer dresses, so do many adults dress like "big children": in jeans, Mickey-Mouse or Superman T-shirts, and sneakers . . . Children and adults have also begun to behave more alike. Even casual observation suggests that posture, sitting positions, and gestures have become more homogenized. It is no longer unusual to see adults in public sitting cross-legged on the ground or engaging in "children's play."[10]

This homogenization of children and adults, critics argued, put undue pressure on the parent-child relationship. According to Postman, the structure of the family and the automatic authority of parents were severely weakened because parents lost control over what information reached their children.[11] Moreover, as parents became more apt to admit their mistakes and shortcomings, their relationships with their children became more democratized. According to Meyrowitz, formal roles can be maintained only by deliberately and bilaterally withholding personal information. When this no longer happens, formal relationships are demystified and formal behavior disappears—and along with it, children's "natural" belief that their parents always know better.[12]

Television Viewing as Cause

These scholars—Elkind, Postman, and Meyrowitz—argued in some way that the emergence of television played a key role in changing parent-child relationships in the late twentieth century. For example, Elkind believed that the emergence of television reinforced bonds between parents and children more than any other previous media. In his view, parents and children were likely to watch the same shows and identify with the same lead characters and role models, thus ultimately homogenizing the experiences of adults and children. Postman pushed this argument further by suggesting that the emergence of television effectively took childhood away. Whereas print media created childhood by segregating reading material appropriate to each phase of life, he argued that television integrated these phases. These arguments were based on the insight that print media are largely inaccessible to children under six, given their inability to read, whereas such inaccessibility does not hold for television.

Indeed, studies from the dawn of the television age demonstrated that children's use of television was different from their experience of earlier forms of media such as books and radio. In 1951, when television was new, children's television preferences were already anything but limited to children's programs.[13] According to a study by Wilbur Schramm and his colleagues in 1961, six- and seven-year-olds spent about 40 percent of their viewing time watching adult programs, and twelve-year-olds no less than 80 percent.[14] Thus, this early research suggests that children's exposure to adult programming began with the dawn of television. Watching television turned out to be a different activity from reading or listening to radio, both of which segregated age groups more than television did.

"Drip-Drip" Effects of Television

While Elkind, Meyrowitz, and Postman used the homogenization argument to explain how television altered notions of childhood, Meyrowitz offered a second explanation. He argued that it was not the broad accessibility of television but rather the representations of reality in television that influenced this change. According to Meyrowitz, the dominant portrayal of children in television was of outspoken, autonomous, headstrong, and worldly-wise beings who were smarter than their silly parents and other authority figures. Television thereby created a distorted reality that undermined the authority and prestige that historically characterized parents: "It is now difficult to find traditional adults in films or on television. In the age of the 'anti-hero,' adult characters—including many of those portrayed by Diane Keaton, Burt Reynolds, Chevy Chase, and Elliot Gould—often have the needs and emotions of overgrown children. Not only are adults often outsmarted by children in today's motion pictures, but children are sometimes portrayed as more mature, sensitive, and intelligent."[15]

Theories about the effects of media, especially from sociology, have pointed out that media are indeed capable of influencing the social order. These theories dealt less with the effects of media on the individual than with broader concepts and ideologies at work within a society. The theories postulated that the influence of media on the social order was rarely immediate, and if it occurred, it did so cumulatively, over a longer period. Such theories are sometimes referred to as "drip-drip" theories, using the analogy of water hollowing out a stone drop by drop.

One of the most cited sociological media effect theories is the cultivation theory of George Gerbner.[16] In the late 1960s, Gerbner and his colleagues began with a series of content analyses that proved how sharply the reality shown on television differed from everyday reality. They demonstrated that compared with reality, television was more violent, included more men than women, and showed more traditional gender relationships. The same group of researchers likened the power of media to that of religion. As in religion, the continual repetition of patterns in the media (myths, ideologies, facts, and relationships) "serve[s] to define the world and legitimize the social order."[17]

According to Gerbner and his colleagues, television and other media cultivate such a powerful shared culture that they are capable of leveling differences between the elite and the rest of the population. Anyone, regardless of socioeconomic status, who comes into frequent contact with media sees the same distorted view of reality. Gerbner called this phenomenon, in which media contribute to the wiping out of differences between social groups, "mainstreaming." Drip-drip theories such as Gerbner's cultivation theory offer an explanation for how television, through its presentation of a distorted reality, contributed to the homogenization of parents and children.

Changes in Family Communication

Drip-drip theories typically acknowledge that the environment in which media effects occur also play a part in the process. While media are a significant cause of change in the social order, rarely are they the only one, or largest one. Thus, while the emergence of television likely contributed to changing notions of childhood, several other sociocultural factors may have strengthened this process. One particularly relevant factor has been a shifting balance of power in the family. Unlike the traditional "top-down" family communication style of the 1950s, today's parents negotiate with their children about what they may and must do, and both parties have a say in the outcome. Parents feel it is important to involve their children in family decisions so that they can learn to make choices and develop their identities. The parental motto has changed from "behave yourself" to "be yourself." Parents are more indulgent, feel guilty more often, and want the best for their children. They want to be "cool" parents, more their children's friends than authority figures.

Interestingly, although these changes suggest that youth have the autonomy and empowerment that characterize adulthood at an increasingly early age, these same youth are delaying the responsibilities of adulthood, such as joining the labor market, being in a permanent relationship, having children, and more. The classical moratorium phase, as Erik Erikson called it—in which the young person is experimenting with his or her identity and is not taking any real responsibility—has thus become longer.[18] This particularly seems to be the case among those youth whose families can provide them with continued financial support.[19] For example, between 1968 and 2012, the percentage of American young people age 25–34 still living with their parents reached its highest ever rate (22 percent).[20] In Italy, where more than half of those 18–35 still live at home, governmental policy is being drafted to stimulate this group of "*bamboccioni*" (big babies) to leave the parental home.

This process seems to be reinforced by the "privatization" of media use, which offers individual family members the opportunity to withdraw to their own personal spaces for entertainment and communication with people outside the family. Together, these developments constitute the paradox of childhood. Even though children today, with their outspokenness and grown-up looks, may indeed seem like miniature adults, as they did before Rousseau, and even though they have a strong need for autonomy earlier than they did before, their need for a carefree childhood seems stronger than ever.

Rapid Technological Changes as Cause

Like television and changes in family communication, the rapid technological changes of the past decades may have also contributed to our notions of childhood. In the late 1960s, the anthropologist Margaret Mead predicted that the young would eventually have a dominant role in society.[21] Although Mead could not know precisely what contemporary parent-child relationships would look like, she hypothesized that they would change drastically and irreversibly after the 1960s. And her visionary predictions came true. We now see that youth culture has become the dominant culture in society. Parents seem to be conforming to their children's fashion choices, behavior, and language. Being young is the norm and becoming old is to be avoided, as the Dutch writer Anna Enquist observed: "People dress like children, being old is reviled, and youth is glorified."[22]

Mead's predictions about the changes in youth culture were based on her observations of three types of cultures: post-figurative, co-figurative, and pre-figurative.[23] In each culture a different age group functions as a role model. In a post-figurative culture such as a traditional society (and in the West until the 1950s), parents, with their wisdom and life experience, are the most important models. In such cultures, children are expected to follow in the footsteps of their parents and grandparents. Differences between older and younger generations are seen as temporary, age-related effects. In a co-figurative culture, seen in the tumultuous 1960s, adults and children orient themselves primarily to their peers. In the event of rapid technological changes, a post-figurative culture often changes into a co-figurative one. Since parents did not experience this type of change during their childhoods, they can no longer function as role models for the young. This forces young people to turn more to those of the same age. A co-figurative culture is temporary, according to Mead, a transition leading to a pre-figurative culture.

In a pre-figurative culture, youth are the dominant role model and they determine what happens. Mead predicted that the co-figurative society, in which she found herself at the time of her publication, was at the point of making the transition to a pre-figurative one. This step would result in a rigorous and irreversible change in the relationships between parents and children. As prescient as Mead was about this era, she could not have suspected how drastic the consequences of the rapid technological changes would be for the individual, family, and society.

And now, as we sit in this pre-figurative culture, youth may indeed be in a more dominant position than they used to be. Compared to earlier generations, they more often have a say in family decisions, they are more accustomed to being the center of attention, and they have more money to spend on their needs and wants. This is due, in part, to their parents' higher levels of income and education, in comparison with previous generations. Moreover, parents are having fewer children than in previous generations, leaving a greater portion of money available to youth. There are also more divorced parents and single-parent families. In these families, children take on independent roles earlier than before. And more than ever before, there are families in which both parents work outside the home. As a result of all of these factors, parents are more indulgent with their children, and will do a great deal to ensure that their children lack nothing.[24]

Commercialism as Cause

While the emergence of television and other sociocultural factors have influenced our modern view of childhood, commercialism—particularly the recognition that youth represent a major market—also played an important role in establishing this view. Widespread marketing aimed at the young dates from the 1950s, when advertisers used marketing techniques to promote comic books and films to teenagers. Yet marketing to kids and teens as we know it today took off only in the 1980s.

In this new world of kids and teen marketing, the paradigm of the assertive child prevails: children are kids, and kids speak up, and they are clever, autonomous, and shrewd. They are spoiled and difficult to please, and they unfailingly see through any attempts to cheat or manipulate them.

According to Stephen Kline, kids and teen marketing has been able to flourish primarily because it has always taken children's imaginations, heroes, and humor seriously, as well as their extreme sensitivity to peer pressure. More than any other social institution, the commercial world has recognized that children's preferences are deeply rooted and must be taken seriously.[25]

The tendency of children to dress and behave more like adults has been intensified by marketing aimed at children. In the 1990s, the marketing world came up with a term to describe this phenomenon: KGOY (kids getting older younger). The "tween"—defined as children eight to twelve years old—is one exemplar of this KGOY phenomenon. While already reaching children in childhood and adolescence, marketers realized they could do a better job of attracting youth who were "between" childhood and adolescence. Referred to as tweens, this group—in part because of this commercialism—is no longer interested in toys such as Barbie dolls, as they were a generation ago. Instead, tweens prefer products with a social function, such as music, clothing, makeup, and social media, in which the focus is on the development of social relationships (see figure 2.2).

Just as the tween is emblematic of the KGOY phenomenon, a second striking change, also partly set in motion by marketing, is that children up to three years old have become a new, separate demographic. This trend began in the 1990s, when media researchers and the marketing world discovered that this age group has its own highly specific preferences and that its members are astonishingly brand aware.[26] Before the 1990s there was hardly any commercial interest in infants and young toddlers. One important trigger of this change was the huge success of the BBC's *Teletubbies,* launched in 1997, which quickly became a blockbuster hit. Although they may not have suspected beforehand, the show's producers instigated a veritable revolution in the toddler media landscape. The successful merchandising of *Teletubbies* marked the real start of infant and toddler marketing.

With the mega success of *Teletubbies,* advertisers and TV producers quickly discovered an important new demographic, one having its own distinct preferences and exercising an enormous influence over its parents. Other initiatives followed at about the same time, such as Baby Einstein and Baby TV, aimed at even younger infants and their parents. Special

Figure 2.2. Kids getting older younger: tweens as consumers. (Corbis)

marketing congresses organized around this time came with teasers along the lines of "Interested in reaching the youngest generation and their parents? Then don't miss the meeting place for this sector!" Like tweens, infants and toddlers became an age group worth taking seriously.

Are Children Different from the Way They Used to Be?

It should now be clear that over the last few decades, childhood has undergone a paradoxical metamorphosis. On the one hand, children seem to get older younger (the KGOY phenomenon). On the other hand, they defer all sorts of responsibilities traditionally associated with adulthood, such as having a partner and children, until later in life: kids getting older later (KGOL). An important question is thus whether young people have essentially changed compared to those from previous generations. Many publications about the Net Generation, Digital Natives, Generation Me, or the Millennials would assert that children are different now—but is this really true?

The idea in these publications is usually that the youngest generation differs in a fundamental way from previous generations, because its members have been steeped in technology their entire lives, have grown up in an individualistic and materialistic society, or have had a democratic or permissive upbringing. As a result, either they are blessed with talents that older people, as digital immigrants, have difficulty comprehending, or they experience serious problems, for example, because they have not learned to deal with setbacks as well as previous generations. These publications sometimes carry a desperate cry for change in education or parenting. But what do the data suggest? Are children today really different from those in previous generations?

Especially in the last decade, published studies have compared physical, cognitive, and psychosocial characteristics of children and adolescents from different generations. The answer, as it turns out, it somewhat mixed. For some characteristics, there have been changes over time. For others, however, children remain quite similar. What is particularly striking, however, is that all these physical, cognitive, and psychosocial "changes," whether or not they have actually taken place, have been discussed, at least partly, within the context of media use.

Physical Changes: Accelerated Puberty

Physically, youth today are different from those in former generations. They are larger, and they reach puberty earlier. Data from northern Europe, for example, show that the average age of puberty for girls went from just under fourteen in 1980 to twelve and a half in 1990. Similarly, U.S. researchers demonstrated that while the average age of the onset of puberty in girls was around fourteen in 1920, it decreased to thirteen in 1950, and by 2000 it was around twelve.[27] In 2013, the average onset of puberty was around age eleven for girls, and about one to two years later for boys. That said, research into the onset of puberty is difficult to compare because there is no fixed definition of the onset of puberty. One study defines puberty for girls as beginning with the growth of breasts, while in another it is the first menstrual period. What is clear in any case is that children have entered puberty at an increasingly early age, although its causes are still unknown. Most researchers ascribe it to better nutrition and health, and sometimes to the increase in various chemicals in our diet.

While it is true that today's youth are physically different from those in previous generations, correlations between media use and these physical differences have not been found. For example, in the 1930s, when movies were the rage among adolescents, concern arose that children would reach puberty earlier because of seeing sex and romance in commercial films. A large-scale research project from 1933, known as the Payne Fund Studies, looked at whether adolescents who went to the movies tended to reach puberty earlier than those who did not. This was found not to be the case.[28]

Cognitive Changes: Increased Intelligence

Today's children are more intelligent than children of the same age in previous generations. This increase in intelligence is called the Flynn effect. James Flynn was one of the first researchers to observe that children's IQ scores had risen steadily since the beginning of the twentieth century. In one of his studies, Flynn compared the scores on intelligence tests from 1952 to 1982 in fourteen countries, including the United States, Germany, France, and the Netherlands. In virtually every one of the countries studied, he observed a significant increase in IQ scores over this period.[29] The increase in intelligence turned out to hold true mainly for fluid intelligence, which involves visual, logical, and problem-solving abilities, and less for crystallized intelligence, for which specific knowledge is required (for example, "What is the capital of Argentina?").[30] Although IQ scores have increased for several decades, the rise in fluid intelligence seems to have reached a ceiling in the last few years.[31]

According to Flynn, these increases could have been caused only by environmental factors. There is no reason to think that our genes changed in such a short time span. Although better nutrition and health are most commonly mentioned as causes, Flynn argues that they can explain only the changes in the first half of the twentieth century. It is unlikely that people's diets were better in the 1960s than now, says Flynn. Plausible causes for these changes include smaller families and the new parenting style, which may be more stimulating to children. And interestingly, it is often believed that media may play a role in the increase in fluid intelligence. According to Flynn, we have more "leisure, and particularly more leisure devoted to cognitively demanding pursuits." As a result, "things our predecessors never dreamed of, such as radio, TV, the internet, and computers occupy our leisure," which may explain this increased intelligence.[32] Later in the book, in the chapter on digital games, we discuss evidence that shows how playing video games is related to the fluid intelligence of youth.

Psychosocial Changes: Self-Awareness and Narcissism

Just as the current generation is assumed to be physically and cognitively different from previous generations, it is also said to have more self-esteem, more self-awareness, and a higher degree of narcissism. These three qualities are related to one another. Self-esteem is the degree to which we value ourselves. Self-awareness—or rather, public self-awareness—is our understanding of how others perceive us. People with high self-awareness can predict well how others will respond to them. If self-esteem and self-awareness are both high, they can turn into narcissism. Narcissists have an inflated self-esteem. They are vain, and they overestimate their own talent and achievements. They can also become arrogant and aggressive if they do not get their way.

There are indeed indications that the current generation has more self-esteem, is more self-aware, and is more narcissistic than previous generations.[33] The differences found between generations are often modest, however. Moreover, cross-sectional studies comparing the scores on personality tests of older and younger generations often have difficulty disentangling generational effects from age effects: older people's norms about the appropriateness of disclosing aspects of themselves might, for example, differ from those of younger people, or they might see themselves or the world differently from the way that younger people do, and thus also respond differently to personality tests.

What the research statistics cannot demonstrate is whether the differences found between generations are good or bad. We may legitimately wonder whether a small amount of narcissism might be functional or adaptive. Self-confidence, self-awareness, and a healthy measure of narcissism are important for success in many professions, including the arts and sciences. Society itself has also greatly changed. What we used to consider bragging is now common practice (for example, the "selfie" culture on social media). And it is precisely the emergence of social media that has led many scholars to blame it for this increase in self-esteem, self-awareness, and narcissism. Whether this blame is justified is discussed in chapter 13.

Psychosocial Problems

Although self-esteem, self-awareness, and narcissism are most frequently mentioned in discussions of generation shifts, the literature on psychosocial problems points out that depression and behavioral problems such as ADHD and anxiety are occurring more frequently than before.[34] Interestingly, however, the data indicate that it is not that these problems per se are occurring more frequently—instead, what has often increased is the number of children being treated for depression or other psychosocial problems.[35] Indeed, if anything has changed, it seems that criteria for diagnosis have been broadened.[36]

As with other psychosocial changes, many people have questioned what the role of the media environment might be in the rise of these health problems. For example, about thirty studies have investigated whether the use of fearful media enhances anxiety,[37] and nearly fifty studies have examined whether there is a link between media use (television, films, games) and ADHD symptoms.[38] Together, these studies have yielded small but significant effects of media use on anxiety and ADHD symptoms. The small size of these effects is due to the great individual differences in children's susceptibility to the effects of media as a source of anxiety and ADHD symptoms. As is shown in the following chapters, although most children are not extremely susceptible to the effects of media, a minority of them are, and these children deserve our full attention.

Conclusion

So what is the truth? Have children changed over time? Yes, research partly confirms what many people already know: children have indeed changed. Youth today are more intelligent and self-aware than their ancestors, and they have more self-confidence. It is also important to see nuances in these developments. Reports that young people are happy or are doing well, as well as reports emphasizing the numbers of problem youth, can easily overlook individual differences. This caveat applies also to the many "generation books" stating that the new generation is narcissistic, or that the new generation is particularly media savvy because they are digital natives. It often turns out that the differences between generations are much smaller than those within a generation.

It should be clear from this chapter that just as youth have changed physically, cognitively, and psychosocially over time, views of childhood have also dramatically changed. Because of the emergence of television, rapid technological changes, and commercialism, there is no longer a dominant view of children and adolescents. Instead, various views can be placed on a scale between two extremes: the paradigm of the vulnerable child and that of the empowered child. In the paradigm of the vulnerable child, children are seen as passive, vulnerable, and innocent beings who must be protected from the evil coming their way (including the media). Diametrically opposed to this view is the paradigm of the empowered child—the child who has a strong need for autonomy and is able and ready to handle life's stresses. These views, and those lying along the scale, represent the paradox of childhood today—that is, the view that children need protection and yet their autonomy must simultaneously be supported. This paradox, while complicated, highlights the idea that childhood is not just a developmental phase of life, but also a social construction influenced by historical, social, and economic factors.

3

THEMES AND THEORETICAL PERSPECTIVES

> For *some* children, under *some* conditions, *some* television is harmful. For *other* children under the same conditions, or for the same children under *other* conditions it may be beneficial. For *most* children, under *most* conditions, *most* television is probably neither particularly harmful nor particularly beneficial.
>
> This may seem unduly cautious, or full of weasel words, or, perhaps, academic gobbledygook to cover up something inherently simple. But the topic we are dealing with . . . is not simple. We wish it were. . . . Effects are not that simple.
>
> —Wilbur Schramm, Jack Lyle, and Edwin B. Parker, *Television in the Lives of Our Children* (1961)

Taken from one of the first studies on the role of media in children's lives, the chapter epigraph reminds us what we know to be true: not all youth are equally susceptible to the influence of media. Yet despite this truth, the idea that media and technology have large effects on all children and teens often prevails in contemporary discourse. In this chapter, we review media effects theories from the early twentieth century onward. We clarify what we do and do not know about the influence of media on youth. When are media effects large, and when are they small? And what do "small" and "large" effects mean, exactly? And which children and teens are especially susceptible to media effects, and why?

How It All Began

In the 1920s, the prevailing notion was that the mass media had a significant and uniform influence on the public, regardless of age. The mass media—specifically, radio and film—were rapidly gaining in popularity at the time. Radio brought popular music into the home, and that led to considerable concerns among parents and educators. Jazz, the pop music of its day, was thought to be so sexually arousing for men that young women were cautioned not to date a jazz fan without a chaperon, and certainly never to get into a car alone with one.[1]

There were even more concerns at the time about the possible negative influence of motion pictures on youth. In 1930, approximately 65 percent of the U.S. population attended the cinema weekly.[2] Motion pictures gave people, especially youth, a new form of entertainment, which at the time had few rivals.[3] While elite families may have had a piano along with a radio and books, for the vast majority, such luxuries were out of reach. Movie theaters offered an affordable and welcome form of entertainment for young people. But parents and educators began to worry about the influence of this affordable entertainment. Were motion pictures affecting young people? And if so, how?

The Hypodermic Needle Perspective

During the heyday of motion pictures, communication theories typically suggested that media effects were immediate, direct, and uniform. These theories, which have retrospectively been coined "hypodermic needle," "stimulus-response," or "magic bullet" theories, were not well documented at the time. For example, no one has been able to trace an original reference to an author who coined or developed these theories. Yet they are important because they represent a starting point for research and more solidly conceived theories about the effects of media on audiences. Some researchers continue to use the old hypodermic needle theories as a caricature with which they can compare their own, more advanced theories.

Today, the hypodermic needle perspective is considered naive and obsolete—not least because it clashes with contemporary notions of human nature in which human beings are seen as active explorers who define their behavior and values in interaction with their environment. Still, it is easy to understand how people in the early twentieth century believed that media had large and universal effects. This belief fit in with general notions of human nature at the time, which were heavily influenced by Darwin's theory of evolution. Darwin rejected the idea of man as a rational, thinking creature. He believed that human and animal behavior alike were driven by unconscious instincts that evolved over time and were uniform within a species.[4]

Darwin's view of humankind resurfaced in the social and behavioral sciences during the early twentieth century, which were then strongly dominated by psychoanalysis and behaviorism. Both schools of thought believe that much of our behavior is determined (that is, beyond our control). Psychoanalysts maintained that human behavior was determined by unconscious instincts and sexual drives formed in infancy and early childhood. Behaviorists saw human behavior as uniform and involuntary reflexes to cues and reinforcers in the environment: the stimulus (in the environment) was followed by the response (the behavior). What happened in between, in the mind, was a "black box," and irrelevant.

Although the hypodermic needle perspective has come to be widely criticized for its lack of nuance, it received some support in the early twentieth century—suggesting that audiences may well have been more gullible, sensitive, and vulnerable to media influence than those of the present day. For example, during the First and Second World Wars and the interwar period, propaganda rapidly became a fact of modern society, and it led to enormous effects. In fact, growing concern in the United States about the impact of Nazi propaganda led to the establishment of the Institute for Propaganda Analysis (IPA) in 1937. The purpose of IPA was to educate citizens about the increasing amounts of propaganda and to help them recognize and deal with it. At the time, Adolf Hitler and his minister for propaganda, Joseph Goebbels, had great success with their radio and film propaganda.

Gullible Audiences

People's experiences with the film industry provided some support for the hypodermic needle perspective. For example, the urban legend goes that a showing of the 1896 silent film *L'Arrivée d'un train en gare de La Ciotat* (*The Arrival of a Train at La Ciotat Station*), in which a life-size train arrives in a station, caused sheer panic among the adult audience.

The first time this film was shown, viewers supposedly screamed and ran away in panic, believing that a real train was heading toward them. It is doubtful that the audience actually responded this hysterically.[5] What is certain, however, is that the new and unfamiliar technology of cinematography left a deep impression on people. Audiences had not yet learned to read the cinematographic codes of audiovisual media. They were unfamiliar with the language of close-ups, scene changes, fade-outs, and so on. Because they were unable to interpret them properly, misunderstandings easily arose. Such strong audience reactions are unimaginable today.

Interestingly, research conducted in the 1950s supported the idea that inexperienced audiences were more susceptible than their worldly peers to the effects of media. Researchers at the time showed a group of adults in Africa—all of them first-time moviegoers—a film about a plague of insects. The film had several close-up shots of the insects. The viewers were exultant, relieved that they lived in a region safe from such enormous bugs.[6] Even today, young viewers who have no or little understanding of cinematographic techniques can easily get frightened when shown close-ups of insects. This same unfamiliarity with visual codes makes it entirely plausible that films scared audiences in the early days of cinema. Media literacy might be both a skill that people acquire throughout their lifetime, and something that is handed down from generation to generation.

Over all, however, whether audiences were in fact more sensitive to media effects in the early twentieth century than they are today is impossible to establish. Researchers could neither confirm nor deny the hypodermic needle perspective, because they lacked the tools to study the effects of media. Quantitative research methods were in their infancy, and statistical methods made their entrance into the social sciences only in the 1930s.[7] In fact, the first empirical studies exploring the effects of motion pictures on children and teenagers—the Payne Fund Studies—were not published until 1933.

The Payne Fund Studies

The popularity of motion pictures reached its peak in the late 1920s. The first "talkies" had just been released, signaling a breakthrough in mass communication. Almost every teenager went to the movie theater at least once a week. There they became acquainted with a world far removed from their own reality. The movies depicted handsome, stylishly dressed gangsters driving fast cars, drinking liquor, and lounging in bedrooms with their girlfriends. In the meantime, parents watched their children imitate the clothing, attitudes, and behavior of cinema idols. This Pied Piper effect of the movies began to worry them, and as a result there was a widespread demand for information about the effect of movies on children and adolescents.

This demand led to the Payne Fund project, one of the largest-ever studies on the influence of motion pictures on children and adolescents. Initiated by William Short, director of the Motion Picture Research Council, this project consisted of twelve studies conducted between 1929 and 1933.[8] Short was convinced that motion pictures strongly influenced the behavior of youth, and that empirical research was necessary to confirm his view. In 1927, he convinced American philanthropist Frances Payne Bolton to award him a sizable research grant to investigate the influence of motion pictures. He also involved several leading researchers of the day, including the film specialist Edgar Dale, the sociologist Herbert Blumer, and the psychologist Louis Thurstone.

Despite their massive scale, the Payne Fund Studies, as the series came to be called, are infrequently cited in contemporary literature. Yet they offer a wealth of information about young people's relationship to motion pictures in the 1930s, and many of their findings are still surprisingly relevant. They are now in the public domain, and many are available free of charge (see, for example, the Internet Archive's Open Library).

Content and Effects of the Motion Pictures

The Payne Fund Studies captured a range of aspects associated with motion pictures, such as the specific content of movies and the effects of this content on youth. In terms of content, for each of the years 1920, 1925, and 1930, Edgar Dale analyzed 500 motion pictures. In an attempt to classify these films, he identified ten major themes: crime, sex, love, comedy, mystery, war, children (about or for), history, travel, and social propaganda. Most movies could be classified under three major themes, referred to by Dale as the "Big Three": love (30 percent), crime (27 percent), and sex (15 percent).[9] It seems that the main themes of motion pictures have not changed much in the past century.

At the same time, Herbert Blumer studied the effects of motion pictures on teenagers by analyzing what they mimicked from films, and how often. He used "motion picture autobiographies" and interviewed teens and emerging adults (ages 12–25) about what in the movies inspired and influenced them. More than a thousand young people from differing backgrounds participated in the study, including reformatory inmates. Blumer found that movie heroes' clothing and mannerisms were imitated most often. In addition, many respondents drew inspiration from the way film stars kissed and courted each other. Finally, boys—and especially the reformatory inmates—regularly copied the criminal behavior depicted in motion pictures. Below are several excerpts from these autobiographies:

> I copy all the collegiate styles from the movies. In 'Wild Party,' starring Clara Bow, she wears a kind of sleeveless jumper dress which attracted my attention very much. Nothing could be done about it. My mother had to buy me one just like it.
> *Female (16) high-school junior*

> Well, the movies taught me how to live that 'fast life.' And how to go on wild parties with men. How to long for clothes and good times. It just made me want to lead the life that I saw in some of the movies. Fast life and easy money. The movies also teach one how to be popular.
> *Female (19) sexual delinquent*

> The movies in my childhood were the principal cause of my downfall . . . I saw how the bad guy in the movies got money and cops could not catch him. Sometimes I wanted to help the bad guy get away . . . When I saw the movies, I sometimes did just as the bad guy did. Yes, it tempted me to crime and I wanted to be a bold guy and take the part of the bad guy in our games.
> *Male (22) sentenced for burglary, inmate of reformatory*

> The sex pictures are ones a lot of us go to, just to get excited. Afterwards we go to a house of prostitution and satisfy our desires.
> *Male (22) sentenced for robbery, inmate of reformatory*[10]

Still other researchers focused on the effects of film on learning, attitudes, emotions, and behavior, sometimes employing what were then considered unconventional methods. For example, researchers showed children, teenagers, and young adults sad, frightening, and erotic films, both in the laboratory and in movie theaters. They attached their film-watching subjects to equipment that measured their physiological responses. Compared with teenagers and adults, children had stronger physiological responses to almost every category of film except erotic ones. Erotic films led to physiological arousal among children only after they reached ten years of age.[11] This study is particularly remarkable when one considers that most empirical research on how children (and adults) process media content did not emerge until the 1970s.

The Hypodermic Needle Perspective Begins to Crack

What were the main conclusions of the Payne Fund Studies? Given the size and scope of studies, it is difficult to expect unequivocal results from this work. Indeed, each study and resulting report offered its own set of interpretations. The age of the child, for example, emerged as an important factor for predicting susceptibility to the effects of movies. In addition, the movies had stronger effects on less intelligent children, children from lower-income households, children whose parents neglected them, and children who had a greater inclination toward criminal behavior. One of the key findings of these studies is that motion pictures do not exert a strong and universal influence on all children. While the results undoubtedly unnerved many people at the time, particularly the autobiographies showing how criminal teens were inspired by motion picture idols, the concluding summary presents a remarkably balanced accounting across the twelve studies: "That the movies exert an influence there can be no doubt. But it is our opinion that this influence is specific for a given child and a given movie. The same picture may influence different children in distinctly opposite directions. Thus in a general survey such as we have made, the net effect appears small."[12]

Taken as a whole, then, the results of the Payne Fund Studies produced no evidence to support the hypodermic needle perspective. But does that mean that their results changed prevailing ideas about the effects of movies on children in American society? The answer is no. The critical responses in the media at the time indicated little consensus among societal groups about the power of the media. On the one hand, parents and practitioners held that the Payne Fund Studies supported the idea that motion pictures posed a serious threat to youth, and especially delinquent youth. On the other hand, fearing censorship and regulation, many journalists heavily criticized the studies.[13]

Despite all the criticism, the Payne Fund Studies represent an important milestone in the history of media effects research. After their completion, several decades would pass before researchers once again examined the influence of the mass media on children and adolescents. The Second World War was looming, pushing any worries about media effects well into the background. It was only after the advent of television, in the 1950s, that researchers once again began to take an interest in the subject.

More Cracks: The War of the Worlds *Study*

Several years after the publication of the Payne Fund Studies, another research project chipped away at the hypodermic needle perspective. Although it did not focus specifically on children, it is relevant nevertheless. The 1940 study, conducted by the social psychologist Hadley Cantril, examined the audience's response to the infamous *War of the Worlds* radio broadcast.[14] Aired in October 1938, this radio play, directed and narrated by Orson Welles, was an adaptation of H. G. Wells's famous novel of the same name. The radio play "reported" news of an alien invasion in North America. The broadcast described how Martians were destroying parts of New Jersey. Welles wanted the radio play to be as realistic as possible. He presented it as a live newscast of developing events, including interviews with fictitious government officials and faked eyewitness accounts of the invasion. To the astonishment of all concerned, the broadcast caused approximately one million listeners to panic (see figure 3.1 for an example of the numerous news articles that appeared about the upheaval that the radio play caused). Many listeners telephoned their neighbors and relatives to warn them about the invasion. Many fled their homes, bundling the children and Grandma into the car and heading for the hills, convinced that what they had heard on the radio was actually happening. In the days following the broadcast, the radio station was inundated with complaints about the play's effect on listeners.

Daily---1,800,000
Sunday-3,150,000

DAILY NEWS
NEW YORK'S PICTURE NEWSPAPER

FINAL

Vol. 20. No. 109 New York, Monday, October 31, 1938 48 Pages 2 Cents

FAKE RADIO 'WAR' STIRS TERROR THROUGH U.S.

Story on Page 2

"War" Victim

Caroline Caution, WPA actress, listening to this radio in West 49th St., heard announcement of "smoke in Times Square." Running to street, she fell, broke her arm.

"I Didn't Know". Orson Welles, after broadcast expresses amazement at public reaction. He adapted H. G. Wells' "War of the Worlds" for radio and played principal role. Left: a machine conceived for another H. G. Wells story. Dramatic description of landing of weird "machine from Mars" started last night's panic.

—Story on page 2.

Figure 3.1. *New York Daily News* article from October 31, 1938, about the upheaval caused by the radio play *War of the Worlds.* (*New York Daily News* Archive/Getty Images)

In his study, Cantril examined why the broadcast sowed panic in some but not all listeners. After all, sixteen million people had listened to the radio play, but "only" a million had panicked. In and of itself, this finding disproves the hypodermic needle perspective. If this perspective were correct, then everyone should have been frightened by the broadcast. Cantril and his research team conducted 135 in-depth interviews with listeners, some who had panicked and others who had not. The researchers discovered that those who had panicked tended to be religious. They had taken the invasion as a sign from God and thought that the end of the world was at hand. Compared with the non-panickers, those who had panicked more often suffered from low self-esteem and emotional instability, and showed less ability to think critically and size up new situations accurately. The environment in which people learned of the "invasion" also played an important role. People who tuned in to the station after a telephone call from a frightened acquaintance tended to be more fearful, a phenomenon often referred to as emotional contagion. When people witness others responding emotionally to something, including a media broadcast or event, they tend to experience the same emotions. Cantril's study demonstrated once again that the nature and size of media effects hinge largely on the user's personality and the social context in which the particular medium is being used.

Many publications covering the history of media effects research posit that the universal media effects perspective held sway until the late 1950s, and that this perspective began to change only when conditional (or limited) media effects theories gained credence. But the results of the Payne Fund Studies and Cantril's *War of the Worlds* study show that the hypodermic needle perspective was the subject of debate long before the 1950s. Empirical evidence against this perspective had begun to mount in the 1930s and 1940s. In fact, in 1948, Bernard Berelson succinctly summarized the conditional media effects perspective as follows: "Some kinds of communication, on some kinds of issues, brought to the attention of some kinds of people, under certain kinds of conditions, have some kinds of effects."[15]

Historical accounts of media effects theories often claim that it was Joseph Klapper's book *The Effects of Mass Communication* (1960) that led to the abandonment of universal media effects theories and their replacement by conditional media effects theories. But Klapper was not responsible for this paradigm shift. Although his work marks an important milestone in the history of media effects research, Klapper's pivotal contribution was that he thoroughly reviewed and summarized previous research. Like his predecessors, most notably Elihu Katz and Paul Lazarsfeld, Klapper recognized that the effects of media are limited.[16] His selective exposure theory argues that people can attend to only a limited number of messages out of the constellation of messages vying for their attention, and that only those messages people select have the potential to influence them. Klapper argued that people have a tendency not only toward selective exposure, but also toward selective perception, selective interpretation, and selective retention.

According to Klapper's theory, people tend to favor information that reinforces their existing preferences and behavior. They actively seek out such information and tend to ignore conflicting information. Thus, the media are more likely to bolster existing attitudes and behavior than to cause people to change their behavior. This insight built on evidence acquired in the Payne Fund Studies in 1933: "The movies tend to fix and further establish the behavior patterns and types of attitudes which already exist among those who attend most frequently."[17] Selective exposure—the tendency to gravitate toward media content that is consistent with our beliefs, attitudes, and preferences—is still one of the main assumptions of contemporary media effects theories.

Contemporary Media Effects Theories

The conditional media effects perspective remains the prevailing paradigm in the field of media psychology. In the past two decades, researchers have acknowledged that youth, like adults, are not mere passive and involuntary recipients of media effects. New media effects models have arisen, for example, Michael Slater's reinforcing spiral model,[18] Albert Bandura's social cognitive theory,[19] and Richard Petty and John Cacioppo's elaboration likelihood model.[20] Another much-cited model is Craig Anderson and Brad Bushman's general aggression model, which focuses on the media's influence on aggressive behavior, but can be useful for understanding other types of media effects as well.[21] In 2013, Patti Valkenburg and Jochen Peter merged these media effects theories into a new model, termed the differential susceptibility to media effects model (DSMM).[22]

Media Use as Cause and Effect

Many studies examining media effects assume that media use can bring about changes in knowledge, beliefs, emotions, attitudes, and behavior. According to such studies, media use is a cause, and it triggers a process of change or influence in the media user. But media effects are not that straightforward. As Wilbur Schramm and colleagues lamented in the 1960s: "Effects are not that simple," even though "we wish they were."[23] Modern media effects theories see media use not only as a cause of changes in a media user, but also as an effect. In other words, although these theories support the idea that media use can bring about changes in media users, they identify the media user, and not the media, as the starting point for that process.[24] Media use is seen as an outcome of a number of factors related to the media user, for example, the user's age, his or her motives, interests, earlier experiences, and his or her family or peer group. All these factors predict media use (for example, the content that a user selects or the frequency of its use). In other words, our media use is the result of who we are, what we want or strive for, and with whom we keep company.

This idea of modern media effects theories is elaborated on in the DSMM, in which three global factors are argued to predict youths' (and adults') media use. The first factor, disposition, reflects every person-based trait that could influence a person's media use, including gender, personality, temperament, intelligence, motivations, and cognitive schemas. For example, we know that children with an aggressive temperament tend to favor depictions of violence in media. We similarly know that personality traits such as sensation seeking and empathy, as well as certain moods, are strong predictors of media use.

The second factor that predicts media use is age or developmental level. In fact, as we show later in the book, age or developmental level is one of the most important predictors of media use and preferences. Toddlers, for example, typically prefer media with a slow pace, familiar contexts, and simple characters. But these specific preferences rapidly evolve during childhood to a preference for a faster pace, adventurous content, and more sophisticated characters. And by adolescence there is often a significant shift toward the use of social media, and an interest in media entertainment that humorously presents irreverent or risky behavior.

The third and final predictor of media use is the social environment of the media user. These social influences can act on micro (for example, family, peers), meso (school, church), and macro levels (cultural norms and values). For example, parents can forbid or stimulate exposure to certain films or games. Similarly, peers can implicitly or explicitly encourage or discourage one another's media use. After all, every teenager wants to do or see what's cool. And finally, schools or governments can forbid or encourage access to certain media content.

Media Effects Are Conditional

The second assumption underpinning contemporary media effects theories is that media effects are conditional in nature and not universal. Just as the Payne Fund Studies concluded that the same motion picture could influence children in different ways, recent brain research has similarly confirmed that individuals can respond in entirely different ways to the same stimuli. Richard Davidson, for example, has shown that activity in certain brain areas can vary by a factor of thirty in people exposed to the same emotional pictures.[25]

If media use influences children in different, and even opposite, directions, the net effect of media use on their knowledge, beliefs, attitudes, and behavior can never be large. That was the conclusion of the Payne Fund Studies. A wealth of research published since then has confirmed, over and over, that media effects established in large and heterogeneous groups of children are only small to moderate. Notably, these small-to-moderate effect sizes are also common in research examining the influence of other environmental factors, such as parenting style, on children's beliefs, attitudes, and behavior.[26] Indeed, numerous studies in the past decades have shown that human beliefs, attitudes, and behavior are the result of a complex set of dispositional and environmental influences. And because media and parenting styles each represent only one of many influencing factors in a child's environment, and because both can have different effects on different children, their influences can never be very great if they are assessed among large and heterogeneous groups of children.

The small-to-moderate media effects found in heterogeneous groups are by no means unimportant ones. Such media effects usually suggest that the influence of media use pertains to smaller groups of children. For example, it has been estimated that 5–10 percent of children are vulnerable to media violence as a source of aggression.[27] Although our knowledge about who these children are is currently growing, we still do not know precisely which children are susceptible to media violence effects. To develop such an understanding, we must study individual susceptibility to media effects, a strand of research rapidly gaining momentum in media effects research.[28]

Interest in individual susceptibility to environmental influences is growing in a number of other research disciplines as well. In medicine, for example, "personalized medicine" is on the rise; in education, advances in information and communication technology are leading to personalized learning strategies. And in developmental psychology, there is the orchid-dandelion hypothesis. According to this hypothesis, most children are like dandelions, able to thrive in almost any environment imaginable. A smaller group of children, the orchids, have the potential to outshine the dandelions, but only if they grow up in an appropriately stimulating environment. Without that environment, they will wither away.[29]

These differential susceptibility perspectives have something in common. They all explore the interaction between disposition and a single environmental factor, for example, a medication or a parenting style. Promising as such models may be, many are still too simple to explain the complex nature of human behavior. The future lies in assessing more complex models that examine the relationship between disposition and a number of environmental factors simultaneously.

Toward Personalized Media Effects

The DSMM is a complex model of the kind discussed above. It allows us to investigate the interplay between disposition and environmental factors, and to identify which children are especially susceptible to media effects. The three factors that predict children's media use (disposition, developmental level, and social environment) are particularly important in this regard. Besides predicting children's media use, these three factors can also influence the effects that media have on children's knowledge, beliefs, attitudes, and behavior. These three factors therefore play two conceptual roles in the media effects process.

We can explain the double role of dispositional, developmental, and social context factors more clearly by discussing some examples of each. As for disposition, it has been shown that children with an aggressive temperament are more likely to prefer violent entertainment than their nonaggressive peers. This means that an aggressive temperament predicts these children's media use (role 1: predictor). Other studies have shown, however, that children with aggressive temperaments are also more likely to be negatively influenced by media violence. In other words, an aggressive temperament can also intensify the effect of media use on aggressive behavior. A variable that changes the effect of one variable (media use) on another (aggressive behavior) is known as a moderator. In this particular case, an aggressive temperament may strengthen the effect of media use on aggression (role 2: moderator).

The other two predictive factors, developmental stage and social environment, can similarly moderate the effects of media use on certain outcomes. For example, by the time children reach puberty, they become more interested in sexual media content (role 1: developmental level as predictor). But at the same time, teens at this age are more vulnerable than other age groups to the negative effects of sexual media content because they are relatively inexperienced and struggle with putting such content into perspective (role 2: developmental level as moderator). Last, in the social environment, parents play an important role in the media their children use (role 1: social environment as predictor). Moreover, through the use of media-related parenting strategies, parents can also increase the positive effects of educational media and mitigate the negative effects of violent media (role 2: social environment as moderator).

Media Effects Are Reciprocal

Finally, contemporary media effects theories agree that media effects are reciprocal. In other words, media use may have an effect on (some) children, but these effects in turn may influence how children subsequently use media. Studies have shown, for example, that some children become hyperactive or aggressive after exposure to media violence. But there is also convincing evidence that aggressive or hyperactive children watch violent forms of entertainment media more often than other children. Similarly, the relationship between a child's developmental level and media use is often reciprocal. Developmental level is one of the key predictors of children's media use, but media use can also have a positive or negative effect on a child's development. When we refer to media effects, then, we must realize that children—by shaping their own media use—also, in part, shape their own media effects. This notion has important implications for parents, who, especially in the case of young children, can exert a strong influence on their children's media use. Media-specific parenting is a topic to which we return in chapter 14.

Conclusion

Contemporary media effects theories generally agree that media effects are conditional and reciprocal. In the past decades, there has been a shift in the focus of research. In modern media effects theories, there is less emphasis on whether media effects exist, and more interest in the underlying mechanisms of media effects, and in identifying who is particularly susceptible to such effects. The arrival of Web 2.0 has increased the size and scope of these questions. We need to understand the effects of media on recipients of media, and to ask how sending or creating media messages may affect the senders. We therefore expect that the future of media effects research will be characterized by increasingly complex models that are sensitive to the increasingly complex experience known as media use. To return again to Schramm and his colleagues: "Effects are not that simple," even though "we wish they were."[30]

4

INFANTS, TODDLERS, AND PRESCHOOLERS

> When the first baby laughed for the first time, its laugh broke into a thousand pieces and they all went skipping about, and that was the beginning of fairies.
>
> —James M. Barrie, *Peter and Wendy / Peter Pan* (1911)

Anyone who has ever worked with or spent time with young children knows that infants, toddlers, and preschoolers differ considerably in their media preferences. Although some of these young children take little or no interest in television, smartphones, or tablets, most find them endlessly fascinating. In this chapter, we discuss how media preferences evolve from birth through early childhood. The focus is on two age groups, infants and young toddlers (up to 2 years old) and older toddlers and preschoolers (2–5 years). For both age groups, we describe a number of specific developmental characteristics and predict how they influence these young children's media preferences. At what age do infants begin to take an interest in media, and why at that age? Why are toddlers so fascinated by smartphones and tablets? Should very young children even be using media? What is the "pink frilly dress" phenomenon and how does it influence media preferences? And finally, why exactly is development such a strong predictor of media preference?

Child Development and Media Preferences

Although many factors can influence children's media preference, one of its most important predictors—particularly in the early years—is developmental level. Generally speaking, child development can be divided into two categories: cognitive development and social-emotional development. Cognitive development encompasses all age-specific changes associated with the way children acquire and process information in their environment. Cognitive development, in part, helps us understand how well children are able to pay attention and comprehend media content. While numerous theories have been developed to explain children's cognitive development, Jean Piaget—considered by many to be the founding father of developmental psychology—proposed four successive stages of cognitive development from infancy to adulthood.[1] His stage-based paradigm remains among the most widely used theories of cognitive development. And it is the point of entrance we take in this book to help us understand how children's cognitive development predicts their media preferences.

Like children's cognitive development, their social-emotional development helps us understand their media preferences. Social-emotional development concerns our ability to express and recognize emotions such as happiness, sadness, jealousy, and shame; to form interpersonal relationships; and to develop an identity (answering the question "who am I?"). Social-emotional development closely hinges on cognitive development. For example, we would not feel shame, jealousy, or other emotions without knowledge and understanding of the world in general and of interpersonal relationships in particular. And empathy, our capacity to share another's emotions, would be difficult to feel if we did not understand the situation and person whose emotions we were sharing.

The notion that children's cognitive development and social-emotional development are strong predictors of their media preferences first arose in the 1970s, when television researchers became interested in the cognitive effects of educational television shows. At the time, media researchers based their work on a reactive model of television viewing, which postulated that striking program features, such as sound effects, rapid action, and quick changes of scenery, influenced how closely children paid attention to educational broadcasts. The idea was that if producers successfully incorporated these features into their programs, they would automatically gain children's attention and foster their comprehension and retention.

The reactive model came under increasing fire in the 1980s and beyond, particularly in response to studies by Daniel Anderson and colleagues, who—inspired by Piaget's perspective on cognitive development—showed that striking program features had less influence on children's attention than assumed. Their studies instead showed that children took little or no interest in programs that they had trouble comprehending. Much research thereafter has confirmed that media's ability to hold a child's attention depends largely on the child's comprehension schemata and, thus, his or her level of cognitive development.[2] By the late 1980s, when developmental psychologists had become interested in emotions, researchers began to recognize that social-emotional development is also a crucial predictor of media interest.

Today, we understand that cognitive development and social-emotional development play independent and interdependent roles in predicting children's media preference. Moreover, we know that the relationship between media use and child development is reciprocal. Just as development exerts a strong influence on children's media use and preferences, media use also influences the cognitive and social-emotional development of children. This reciprocal perspective is one that we take throughout this book.

Moderate Discrepancy Hypothesis

Why, precisely, are young children interested in media content? Many researchers believe that the concept of optimal stimulation level goes a long way toward explaining this interest. According to this concept, children prefer content that they can at least partly fit into their cognitive and social-emotional frame of reference. They equally avoid content that diverges too much from that frame of reference, because they perceive such content as either too easy or too difficult to grasp. This idea, known as the moderate discrepancy hypothesis, predicts that children will pay the most attention to media content that diverges only moderately from their level of cognitive and social-emotional development.

Studies have shown that children are much more likely to pay attention to media content that does not diverge too much from their existing knowledge and emotional experiences, and that they avoid content that does.[3] The moderate discrepancy hypothesis thus offers a reasonable explanation of why children's media preferences change throughout childhood. After all, the perceived difficulty or simplicity of media content changes dramatically as children grow older. Content that is moderately discrepant and therefore interesting to a two-year-old is often too simple, and thus boring, to a child of six. As is made clear throughout this book, the moderate discrepancy hypothesis can be used to explain the many changes in children's media preferences as they grow.

No Two Children Are Alike

In this chapter, we differentiate between two age groups in childhood, zero to two years (infants and young toddlers) and two to five years (older toddlers and preschoolers). Dividing childhood into age categories has its limits, however, since individual differences among children in the same age group might thereby be underestimated or even ignored. No two two-year-olds are alike, after all. We know that from birth, children can respond quite differently to the same experience. Development is driven not only by a biologically programmed, fixed process of maturation, but equally by children's temperament and social environment. As the Swiss philosopher Rousseau discerned more than two centuries ago, a child's environment can be positive and stimulating, but also negative and corrupting.

Although children in the same age group can differ considerably from one another, average preferences are a reasonable starting point. Anyone who wishes to communicate effectively with children has to start somewhere. We can appeal to children of a specific age only if we know their average, age-specific preferences and their general perceptions of the world. That is why in the following sections (and throughout this book), we describe the most important cognitive and social-emotional characteristics of each of the two age groups and then predict how these characteristics influence their media use and preferences. That said, it is important to keep in mind that the characteristics of media use and preferences described here represent "average" behaviors, and so we encourage researchers and practitioners to consider the role of relevant individual differences whenever feasible.[4]

Birth to Two Years

Even as newborns, infants have a strong desire for sensory experience, whether it involves their sense of touch, hearing, or vision. Piaget called the period from birth to two years the sensorimotor stage because it is then that a child's sensory and motor skills become integrated.[5] In plain English, we might refer to this as the "looking and grabbing" stage. A child in this stage of development wants to touch whatever she or he sees, and look at whatever she or he touches.

Some sensory preferences of children appear to be innate, whereas most others are shaped early in childhood. Some of children's flavor and scent preferences, for example, seem to be inborn, as are some rhythmic and musical preferences. Infants as young as three months show a preference for music—orienting their head toward all kinds of music, including lullabies and Mozart preludes.[6] Newborns favor the human voice above all other sounds, especially when speech is slow and high-pitched and intonation is exaggerated—in short, the form of speech parents generally adopt when speaking to their infants. Research has shown that four-month-olds prefer to listen to a recording of this "parentese" rather than to a recording of someone speaking with standard intonation.[7] Children's preference for speech with a variable pattern of intonation persists for the first few years. It is thus not surprising that entertainment media using this form of speech is successful with this age group.

Although newborns can hear reasonably well, their sense of vision is initially underdeveloped. They can see colors and motion, but the images are blurry. Objects more than half a meter away are out of focus. Their vision will not match that of an adult's until they are about eight months old. This may explain why infants prefer high-contrast images. In the first few months of life, infants focus mainly on high-contrast areas of the face such as the eyes and hairline, directing their attention to objects that they can see best, meaning those with bold contrasts.

From very early on, infants prefer looking at human faces. In fact, they prefer to look at faces more than at any other stimulus. They also pay more attention to attractive (that is, symmetrical) faces than to unattractive ones. They have a preference for brightly colored moving objects (although the colors should not be too bright), especially if they also make noise (rattling, whistling, or jangling). They can distinguish colors immediately after birth, and by the time they are one month old they can differentiate between all colors in the spectrum.[8] It is no wonder that toys and media entertainment targeting infants and toddlers tend to be brightly colored.

Interest in Television and Commercials

Children below the age of two spend nearly an hour a day viewing or using audiovisual media (television, DVDs, games, tablets).[9] Interestingly, the age at which infants and toddlers start using media has fallen in the past decade; the current age is now estimated to be between three and five months. Developmentally, this age makes sense. By this age, vision has significantly improved, and children are thus able to follow moving objects on the screen. Moreover, around this age, the "social smile" emerges—the process of smiling when children hear or see something that they perceive as appealing. It is also around this age that infants begin to orient themselves toward situations that interest them, including media content. Nevertheless, research by Alissa Setliff and Mary Courage shows that children differ enormously in how much interest they take in audiovisual media. In their study, sixty six-month-olds were offered appealing moving toys while a television was on in the background. In the ten minutes that the television was on, children looked up from their toys an average of 23 times. The differences between children were immense. Some infants looked up from their toys only twice in the ten-minute period, whereas others did so almost constantly, up to sixty-one times.[10]

Given young children's attraction to bright colors and high contrast, it makes sense that they are most attracted to programs with colorful fantasy characters such as *Teletubbies* or *Big Bugs Band*. Perhaps surprisingly, very young children are often attracted to commercials. Given the structure of a commercial, this actually makes a good deal of sense. The first year of life is characterized by what some researchers refer to as the investigative-orienting system of attention. In other words, children's attention in the first year is directed mainly at objects that are novel or surprising. And commercials, with their striking auditory and visual features (also called orienting features), are exactly the type of content that is attuned to young children's system of attention. By the second year of life, as children's attention becomes guided less by such orienting features and more by their own cognition, they become less attracted by novelty and more by objects that have real meaning for them.[11]

Do Stories Matter for the Very Young?

People often think that watching television is a passive activity, but this is a misconception—certainly where very young children are concerned. Most people would agree that playing a game on a computer or tablet is not a passive activity, but children are also verbally and physically active when they watch television. They imitate what they see, and sing and dance along with television characters. They also do their best to understand the content and fit it into their conceptual frameworks, for example, by asking frequent questions about the content they are watching.[12]

Children usually say their first real words at about age one. Those first words are the same in almost every language. They reflect the universal preferences of one-year-olds, for example, people (mama, papa, grandma), animals (dog, cat), toys (ball, dolly), food (milk, cookie), and transportation (car). At the same time, one-year-olds feel the need to verbally label the things that they see or play with: 40 percent of children up to the age of two will call out the name of a television character while watching a show, or say aloud the names of objects that they see on the screen. They start to do this at fifteen months, the same age when they first imitate words or songs from a program, and sing or dance along with media characters.

Although very young children respond actively to media content, they usually do not yet understand story line. Children under eighteen months are just as interested in a video clip that mixes up beginning, middle, and end as they are in a clip with a coherent story line.[13] In other words, infants and young toddlers are drawn to orienting program features, but they do not require meaningful context. That is why long stories are inappropriate for this age group, and why so much popular content for this audience lacks a narrative—it is simply not necessary.

Interest in Tablets

Although the majority of research on very young children and audiovisual media has focused on television, many infants and toddlers today are absolutely mesmerized by smartphones and tablets, as parents today are acutely aware. An ABC News report in 2013 demonstrated rather persuasively that most toddlers seem to prefer a tablet to a pile of colorful toys. One toddler in the news story even preferred a tablet to his own mother![14] As with television, infants' interest in tablets seems to emerge between three and five months of age; current estimates suggest that more than a third of American parents allow their infants and young toddlers to play with a tablet, and other countries are showing similarly fast rates of adoption.[15]

When thinking of the developmental attributes of infants and toddlers, it is easy to see why this technology is so appealing. First, tablet screens are high contrast and are held closer than arm's length, bringing them into the infants' developing field of vision. Second, from a content perspective, the numerous "baby apps" available typically rely on colorful moving objects and characters and equally engaging sound effects—which appeal directly to children's investigative-orienting system of attention. The tablet's biggest plus, however, is that the software gives infants and young toddlers instant feedback. That is what fascinates them most, probably for the same reason that they enjoy switching lights on and off repeatedly or insist on playing with the remote control. Young children enjoy what they see as "magical" effects in their surroundings. Anything that changes because of an action on their part has their undivided attention.

This magical appeal of tablets for infants and toddlers can be explained by the moderate discrepancy hypothesis. In 1993, Erik Strommen—who could not have anticipated the immense popularity of tablets in the new millennium—predicted that for very young children, the touch screen was the only suitable interface.[16] A touch screen diverges only moderately from infants' and toddlers' motor and cognitive development, a phenomenon not experienced earlier in the history of digital media. It offers very young children everything they could possibly want: motion with interesting sounds, high-contrast images, new and constantly changing experiences, and instant feedback that fosters a sense of control.

"Under Twos" and Media: The Debate

Any discussion about the role of media among very young children would be incomplete if it did not acknowledge that such media use is controversial. In fact, many parents have mixed feelings about young children's enthrallment with media content. And researchers and health care providers worldwide have prominently voiced concerns about this issue. In response to these concerns, health departments in the United States, Australia, and Canada now officially discourage screen media use for children under the age of two, and the French banned television stations from airing programs that target children under the age of three.[17]

Although the debate about whether very young children should use media rages on, estimates of young children's media use continue to rise. In 1971, the average age at which children began watching television was about four years old.[18] As discussed earlier, today it is around four months.

The question, of course, is who is right? Should very young children be discouraged from interacting with any media? Is there reason for concern? Or are there opportunities to be gleaned from media?

Research into the benefits and drawbacks of media use among very young children is scarce but promising. On the one hand, some studies suggest that media use at very young ages can be detrimental to healthy activities, such as playtime and parent-child interaction. Studies have also yielded evidence for a "video deficit," which means that very young children learn better from a real-life model than from a model on a screen. On the other hand, more recent research has convincingly shown that the video deficit can be mitigated, for example, when the media content is repeated or when a parent actively explains the content. And numerous studies have shown that developmentally appropriate educational media can support both cognitive learning (for example, numeracy, literacy) and social-emotional learning (friendliness, sharing, acceptance of diversity), particularly when parents are involved with the content their children consume.[19]

With the quick adoption of touch screens by this young audience, there is likely to be an influx of studies designed to address this question. For now, it seems fair to say that limited exposure to content that is sensitive to the developmental level of this young audience may be, at minimum, unimpactful and, at best, supportive of children's cognitive and social-emotional development. We discuss this issue in greater detail in chapters 11 ("Media and Education") and chapter 14 ("Media and Parenting").

Two to Five Years

From age two onward, children deal with media entirely differently from how they did before. Piaget called the period between two and six the preoperational stage. This stage is characterized by symbolic thinking—the ability to use a symbol to stand for something that is not there. Such a symbol can be a drawing of a specific event, or a box that the child uses as a boat. Children must develop symbolic thinking in order to engage in the activities of the preoperational stage, such as imitation, drawing, and pretend play. Piaget called children's thinking in this stage *pre*operational because unlike operational thinking, which characterizes middle childhood, preoperational thinking is not yet logical or tied to the law of cause and effect.

Stories Now Matter

Between eighteen and twenty-four months of age, children become increasingly interested in narratives. No longer drawn primarily by orienting features, they begin to pay attention to (short) stories from beginning to end, and are eager to know how things will turn out. As their interest in narratives grows, their understanding of television program content makes an equally huge leap forward. Their vocabulary expands rapidly in this period. A two-year-old knows a few hundred words, but by the time she turns six, her vocabulary will have grown to approximately ten thousand words. Unsurprisingly, this newly acquired vocabulary brings with it an interest in audiovisual narratives.

Using an in-home observation study, Patti Valkenburg and Marjolein Vroone documented this shift in attention from orienting features to meaningful content by observing the viewing patterns of children ages six months to five years who were shown an array of program content (adult news, *Sesame Street, Teletubbies,* and *The Lion King II*).[20] Results showed that at around two and a half years of age, children begin to appreciate stories. This could be inferred, for example, from the nature and frequency of their questions. At that age, almost half the children asked questions while watching in order to help them better understand the events in the programs.

This study confirmed that children's preferences for media content change rapidly during early childhood. For example, the scenes of *Teletubbies* (a show designed explicitly for young toddlers) that attracted the full attention of those up to two years old disappeared almost entirely from the list of favorite scenes of the five-year-olds. The only scene that continued to attract considerable attention in both age groups was one in which a piece of "Tubbie toast" suddenly flies through the air. But sudden movement of this kind always captures the viewer's attention, regardless of his or her age, because it stimulates the orienting reflex. Both adults and children react in this manner to a sudden movement, a flash of light, or a loud noise, even before they can identify what it is. Young children, older children, and adults do not differ that much regarding the kinds of stimuli that grab their attention, but they do differ in the ones that hold it.

Blurry Boundaries: Fantasy and Reality

During the early childhood years, toddlers and preschoolers can be deeply awed by certain fantasy characters. Yet at the same time, if the fantasy characters become too grotesque, children can easily become frightened of them. This is due to the development of their symbolic thinking, their imagination, which undergoes a powerful transformation at this age. The first expressions of symbolic thinking begin when children are about eighteen months old. At that age, they can pretend that a banana is a telephone, for example. Once they reach three or four, their imaginary games become more complex and social in nature. They are able to think up and develop complex scenarios; play house, doctor, or fireman; and pretend they are traveling to uninhabited islands and distant planets. Piaget believed that children in the preoperational stage were incapable of separating fantasy from reality. More recent research, however, suggests that children as young as three can distinguish reasonably well between fantasy and reality, although it is easy to get them to doubt themselves.[21] The following conversation between a mother and her three-year-old daughter illustrates this superbly:

> MOTHER: "What shall we have for dinner?"
> KATIE: "Daddy."
> MOTHER: "That's a good idea, yes, with ketchup."
> KATIE: "Let's have Mommy for dinner."
> MOTHER: "With ketchup?"
> KATIE: "Yes."
> MOTHER: "But then Mommy would be eaten all up. I'd be all gone if you had me for dinner."
> KATIE: (looking upset) ". . . It's just pretend."[22]

Toddlers and preschoolers generally know when they are fantasizing. Nonetheless, they have more trouble than older children with "reality monitoring" (that is, with distinguishing imagined from real actions). Even when children know that a movie such as Disney's *Frozen* is "just pretend," they may still feel terrified while watching it. The boundary between fantasy and reality in this age group is clearly permeable, as the following conversation between two three-year-olds shows:

"Pretend there's a monster coming, OK?"
"No, let's don't pretend that."
"OK, why?"
"Cause it's too scary, that's why."[23]

Thus, it seems that toddlers and preschoolers do understand the difference between fantasy and reality, at least in their own play. But at what age can they tell whether media content is fantasy or reality? That ability grows gradually between the ages of three and ten. Up to about age four, children generally believe that everything in the media is real. Two- and three-year-olds may even think that television characters live inside the TV set. If they see an egg breaking on television, they may run to the kitchen for a paper towel to clean it off the screen.[24] According to Dafna Lemish, this response generally disappears by the time children are about two because by then they have learned that the screen always feels the same (cold and flat).[25] But in our work, we have found that some three-year-olds still walk up to the screen, for example, to wave at a beloved television character or to kiss or grab it (in vain).[26]

Children's struggle with separating fantasy from reality in the media influences their media preferences. First, fantasy characters are often just as engaging as real-life ones. Children first start identifying with media characters around age three. But because all characters are real to them, they can identify just as easily with an animal or a fantasy character as with a real-life one. They are also deeply affected by special effects and stunts, such as a hero disappearing in a puff of smoke. Because toddlers and preschoolers do not understand the cinematic tricks behind such events, they are much more susceptible to their effects. By the time they are three years old, children know when they themselves are pretending, but they are unable to apply their knowledge of fantasy and reality when watching fiction. Symbolic thinking improves steadily in toddlers and preschoolers, but because their thinking is not yet bound by the laws of logic, everything is possible in their minds. That is why young children are so awed by certain fantasy characters, and that is why they are also more easily frightened by them.

Simple Is Successful

Media content for young children is generally populated by uncomplicated, colorful, friendly dolls and puppets. Up to age five, children are visually oriented toward information in general and media characters in particular. When describing their favorite media characters, children often fixate on simple physical traits, such as big eyes and long hair, without integrating these traits into an overall picture. Young children often pay little to no attention to what the characters are doing, or why.

The tendency to focus on simple physical traits of a media character instead of on his or her behavior once again reflects children's level of development. One of the most distinctive qualities of children's thinking between the ages of two and five is their tendency to focus on the immediately perceptible features of an object, product, or person, and to ignore information that is less explicitly perceptible. This phenomenon is called perceptual boundedness.[27] Cynthia Hoffner and Joanne Cantor clearly demonstrated this tendency in an experiment in which they had three groups of children (three- to five-year-olds, six- to seven-year-olds, and eight- to nine-year-olds) watch a film with a female protagonist. The researchers manipulated the protagonist's appearance (ugly or attractive) and behavior (kind or cruel). The three- to five-year-olds were more likely than the older children to say that the ugly character was cruel even if her behavior was kind. They were also more likely to find the attractive woman kind even if her behavior was cruel. Older children, on the other hand, were more likely to judge the protagonist by her behavior rather than her appearance.[28]

Closely related to perceptual boundedness is the concept of centration. According to Piaget, this is the tendency in young children to focus their attention on one visually striking feature while ignoring other, less striking visual attributes.[29] A good example can be found in a study reported by Daniel Acuff and Robert Reiher, in which a group of young girls were given three dolls. Two of the dolls were very expensive, with beautifully modeled faces and advanced mechanical effects. The third doll was much more cheaply made, with a coarse face and no mechanical extras. It did have a large red sequined heart sewn on its dress, however. To the astonishment of the researchers, almost all the girls preferred the cheap doll with the red-sequined heart.[30] This is typical behavior for toddlers and preschoolers. As they evaluate a product, they focus on a single striking feature, limiting their ability to take in multiple details simultaneously, including details that reflect quality. This is especially the case when children are presented with a product or stimulus for the very first time. After repeated exposure, they develop a better eye for details. This is why children like to watch their favorite movies over and over again. Every time they watch them, they discover something new.

Familiarity Is Fun!

Children between two and five years of age prefer to watch television shows that offer them a familiar context with situations that they recognize and that happen close to their own home. They enjoy watching shows that feature other toddlers and preschoolers, or simple, friendly fantasy characters. They also take a special interest in objects and animals that they know and can label verbally, such as a dog, a cat, or a bear. It is no wonder, then, that many picture books, apps, and television programs for toddlers concern situations in and around the home.

Children's preferences for the familiar can be attributed to their nascent ability to process information. From two to five years of age, their memory span (that is, the list of numbers or words that they can retain in short-term memory) doubles in capacity, and the speed at which they process information increases proportionally. Despite these cognitive advances, much information is still too complex for young children. Why is this? Compared to older children, they have fewer experiences to which they can relate new information. In the literature, it is sometimes said that young children's responses are stimulus driven, whereas older children's responses are more schema driven. Compared with their younger peers, older children have more knowledge to help them select, encode, organize, and process new information.

It is no wonder, then, that young children need more time than older ones to interpret and understand media content, and that they prefer watching slow-paced television shows that involve a lot of repetition. Repetition provides them the opportunity not only to overcome centration (discussed above), but also to "master" the stories. Just as adults might need to read a difficult text a few times before they can grasp it, toddlers and preschoolers find support by watching the same scenes over and over again.

Self-Conscious Emotions: Jealousy, Pride, and Empathy

Ever since Darwin's treatise on emotions in man and animals, we have differentiated between the emotions present from the beginning, in infancy, and the emotions that develop later in childhood. According to Paul Ekman, the first category consists of six basic emotions: enjoyment, surprise, anger, fear, sadness, and disgust. What these six basic emotions have in common is that they first appear early in infancy, their onset is quick and unbidden, and they give rise to universal facial expressions that are similar across cultures.[31]

Between the ages of two and three, children develop more complex feelings, known as self-conscious emotions. These include shame, jealousy, pride, empathy, and guilt. Self-conscious emotions appear only after children develop a sense of self-awareness, which generally starts at around twenty-two months.[32] To feel self-conscious emotions, children must understand that there are norms and rules. After all, a child can feel an emotion such as shame only if it knows that it has done something wrong. To experience self-conscious emotions, children also need to have reached a certain level of social-emotional development. For example, they need to understand why someone might be sad or disappointed, or why a person might love someone else. Only then will they be able to feel empathy or jealousy.

The moderate discrepancy hypothesis predicts that children will prefer media products that reflect their own experience as closely as possible. Media products that are successful with this target group therefore key into their social-emotional development. Toddlers and preschoolers identify closely with media characters and want to see those characters expressing emotions that they recognize in themselves. But the perceptual boundedness of this age group requires emotions to be portrayed visually and straightforwardly. Complex emotions, for example, crying while happy, are generally confusing. In the following example, a teacher tells Cathy (age four) about a surprise party that someone threw for her:

> CATHY: "Why did you cry? Were you sad?"
> TEACHER: "No, I was happy."
> CATHY: "Did you get hurt?"
> TEACHER: "No, but sometimes when you are really happy you cry too."
> CATHY: "Oh." (said with a puzzled look).[33]

With Development Comes Gender

As almost any parent can tell you, a girl between the ages of three and seven may at some point adamantly refuse to leave the house unless she is wearing a pink frilly dress. In the United States, where store shelves are crammed with pink princess dresses and blue Spiderman suits, people refer to it as the Pink Frilly Dress Phenomenon (see figure 4.1). Almost every child goes through a phase of wanting to wear "real" girls' or boys' clothing. Boys avoid wearing anything that has even the slightest hint of femininity, and girls reject any apparel that smacks of masculinity. Two-thirds of three- and four-year-olds and 44 percent of five- and six-year-olds become extremely rigid about gender-specific behavior at a certain period.[34]

How do boys and girls develop such distinct preferences? Are they born with different tastes, or do the differences appear when they are older?

Figure 4.1. The Pink Frilly Dress Phenomenon, commonly seen among three- to seven-year-old girls. (Shutterstock)

Researchers agree that until they reach twelve to eighteen months, infants scarcely differ in their preferences for toys and entertainment. Both find dolls, cars, and trucks equally enjoyable. Nor do they differ in their television, video game, or picture book preferences. Animated or cartoon characters might just as well be gender-neutral in entertainment targeting young toddlers, and in fact they often are.

But these gender-neutral preferences changes very quickly. Researchers have discovered gender differences in children's toy preferences in toddlers as young as fourteen months old. By the time children are three, the observable differences are more apparent. At that time, boys and girls avoid playing with toys that they consider appropriate for the opposite sex. They become interested in different activities and prefer same-sex playmates. Known as gender segregation, this process takes place across social environments and cultures. Groups of boys and girls have different standards of social interaction, and those standards have a significant influence on children's socialization.[35]

Why does behavior start out as gender-neutral for the first eighteen months or so of a child's life, but change thereafter? There are several different explanations, none of them mutually exclusive. Biological or biosocial explanations suggest that gender differences are rooted in genetic and hormonal differences between men and women and that society merely exaggerates those differences.[36] Second, gender differences can be ascribed to differences in the way boys and girls are reared. From birth, parents expect different kinds of behavior from their sons and daughters, and they express those expectations in their communication with their children. For example, they speak to boys and girls differently, dress them differently, and give them different toys.

The third factor in gender segregation is behavior compatibility. This happens at around eighteen months, when boys and girls start to diverge in their interests and preferences and find that members of the opposite sex often do not like what they like. That is why boys would rather play with other boys, and girls with other girls.[37] Time and again, studies have shown that boys prefer aggressive play, such as roughhousing, imaginary fights or battles, and rowdy sports. Girls, on the other hand, generally prefer play that requires fine motor skills, such as dressing and undressing dolls, designing jewelry, and other handicrafts.

Gender Differences in Media Preferences

The budding differences between boys and girls quickly become obvious in their media preferences. From the preschool age, boys and girls pay attention to different aspects of entertainment, including action, sports, competition, adventure, violence, and romance. Preschool boys have a stronger preference than girls for sports, action, and violence, both in books and in screen media. They also generally like scary scenarios, for example, ones featuring dinosaurs or aliens from outer space. They are interested in male fantasy heroes with supernatural powers, in sports stars, in knights and soldiers, and in doctors and policemen. Girls are more interested in nurturing themes and in relationships between people. They prefer contexts that feature castles, dance studios, schools, and farms, and that tend to focus on models, dancers, fairies, and princesses.[38]

In addition to content preferences, gender dramatically influences character preferences. Bradley Bond and Sandra Calvert were interested in understanding children's favorite media characters as well as when children "break up" with these characters. In their work, they found that around two years of age, children's favorite characters were not highly masculine or feminine. For example, girls often noted a preference for *Sesame Street*'s Abby Cadabby—described as an inquisitive, rambunctious little girl. Likewise, boys noted a preference for Thomas from *Thomas the Tank Engine*—a rather docile, altruistic character with a gentle, childlike personality. By the age of five, however, the majority of children had "broken up" with these favorite characters and had come to prefer much more feminized or masculinized characters, such as Disney's Tinkerbell (a physically attractive, graceful fairy) or Pixar's Lightning McQueen (an overly confident, competitive, bold character).[39] It seems, then, that children's preferences for media content—including media characters—become more gender stereotyped as their own gender identity becomes more rigid. These differences between boys and girls fade away during elementary school, but return with a vengeance once puberty hits. We look at this in more detail in the next two chapters.

Conclusion

As children grow and develop, their response to certain media or media content changes—sometimes even radically. Cognitive development and social-emotional development are among the best predictors of these changing media preferences in childhood. And while individual differences play a role in explaining the specific types of media that young children enjoy or dislike, development provides a useful starting point for assessing the types of media content that are likely to be "moderately discrepant," and thus appealing, for children of different ages.

This chapter shows that development helps explain the shift between very young children's stimuli-driven processing to older toddlers' and preschoolers' schema-driven processing. Further, content preferences (for example, fantasy content, repetition, slow pacing, narrative, familiar contexts) map closely on children's cognitive and social-emotional development. And finally, at least among "under twos," children's media use remains the subject of a relatively contentious debate. While some argue that media use in early childhood is likely harmless and, depending on content, potentially helpful, others have fiercely opposite opinions—taking a decidedly vulnerable view of very young children.

As has often been seen in the history of media and technology, the truth is likely somewhere in between. What the debate about toddlers' screen media use more generally does, however, is to highlight that studying the effects of children's development on their media preferences is only part of the picture. Just as children's development plays a role in predicting their media use, children's media use can play a role in predicting their development. Later in this book, we discuss the thousands of studies on the positive and negative effects of media use in detail—thinking through the other side of the reciprocal relationship between development and media use.

5

CHILDREN

"There ought to be one fairy for every boy and girl."

"Ought to be? Isn't there?"

"No. You see children know such a lot now, they soon don't believe in fairies, and every time a child says, 'I don't believe in fairies,' there is a fairy somewhere that falls down dead."

—James Barrie, *Peter and Wendy/Peter Pan* (1911)

As children leave the preschool phase and enter elementary school, they undergo an enormous surge of development. If we hope to understand the media they are interested in, it is crucial that we understand how they perceive the world. Without this knowledge, any attempt to reach this age group will be futile. To that end, in this chapter we highlight how children 5–12 years of age perceive the world—connecting this development with their media preferences. Since five-year-olds and nine-year-olds look at the world very differently, we divide this age period into two groups: young elementary schoolchildren (5–7 years old) and preadolescents (8–12). For both groups, we discuss the most significant developmental changes and connect these changes with media preferences. For example, what is the "spinach syndrome"? What sort of humor do children in both age groups prefer? Why do children recognize bad acting only at around eight years? Why does collecting become important to children in this period? And when and why does the peer group emerge as a key context?

Young Elementary Schoolchildren

The period from five up to eight years of age is generally considered a transitional time. Piaget believed that children between these ages were still in the preoperational stage. And in fact, many of the characteristics exhibited by toddlers and preschoolers carry over into this period. Physical growth continues, but more slowly and with less spectacular spurts than before. Children in this period are still perceptually bounded in that they pay more attention to the external features of an object or person than to information that is less explicitly perceptible. By the time they are nine, however, this tendency has largely disappeared. The same is true of centration (that is, their tendency to focus on the visually salient features of a product or person and their inability to take in multiple details at once). Although most children just entering formal school (around five years of age) still engage in centration, the tendency decreases during this transitional period, and by about nine years of age they are adeptly able to take in multiple details at once. Children's comprehension of more complex narratives also continues to develop during this period. For example, their comprehension of movies that integrate multiple subplots or use sophisticated production techniques (for example, flashbacks) rapidly increases.

Most children this age still have trouble distinguishing realistic from unrealistic media content, but as with their perceptual boundedness and centration skills, their ability to separate fantasy from reality improves. Although children no longer believe that everything they see in movies is real, they still have doubts. This is the age when their unconditional belief in Santa Claus begins to waver. They no longer believe in him, but they are not absolutely certain either. They now know that Big Bird on *Sesame Street* is a person dressed in a costume, and they are starting to see that unrealistic stunts and special effects on television would be impossible in real life. Occasionally, a child will go a step further and believe that everything on television is fake, even realistic content. What most children find difficult at this age is to distinguish fiction (soaps, comedies with real-life actors) from reality. For example, they think that actors in a television sitcom have the same occupations in real life, and that onscreen families are real families offscreen. The latter is something that many nine- and ten-year-olds also still believe.[1]

Nevertheless, children in this phase undergo a number of changes that justify placing them in a separate age group. Perhaps the biggest change is the beginning of formal education. With formal school entry, they become slightly less dependent on their parents, particularly with regard to their playtime and media use. Thanks to formal education, children in this age group begin to read on their own, and they possess a vocabulary that is large enough to allow for detailed communication with adults. Their attention span dramatically increases. For example, while a three-year-old can concentrate on a single activity for a maximum of twenty minutes (and even then is easily distracted), a five-year-old can concentrate on a favorite activity for up to an hour. As a result, they can watch longer media content (for example, feature-length films) and can concentrate on games for quite some time.[2] They also have a better sense of structure and rules than they did previously. For example, if they are given a new board game, their first aim is to learn the rules.

Media play an important role in the daily life of this age group. In our data from a large sample of Dutch children, for example, we found that young elementary schoolchildren spend an average of slightly more than two hours a day watching television or movies, playing games, or reading. Of this time, television dominates: children spend nearly seventy minutes a day watching it (online, on a DVD, or in some other format). Children of this age begin to incorporate electronic games (about thirty minutes a day) into their media diet, and spend a similar amount of time reading books or comic books (twenty-five minutes), either on their own or with their parents reading to them.

There is little difference in the amount of time that boys and girls spend on media, although boys spend slightly more time (thirty minutes) than girls (twenty-two minutes) per day playing electronic games. This is not particularly surprising, since it is more likely that content preferences would differ by gender than by media exposure amounts. These patterns of media use are not exclusive to Dutch children. Indeed, similar patterns have been found for children of this age throughout many industrialized countries; estimates suggest that these children spend roughly two hours a day with media, of which the greatest portion of time is typically spent with television or films.[3]

Humor in Media: "Why Are Frogs So Happy?"

Toddlers and preschoolers typically enjoy innocent, physical, clownish humor. From age five upward, thanks to their rapid linguistic development and growing ability to interact with others, they begin to show more interest in verbal humor such as riddles, word games, and mislabeled objects and events. Riddles such as "Why are frogs so happy?" "Because they eat whatever bugs them" are thought to be hilarious by children at this age. Moreover, they begin to appreciate humor based on conceptual incongruities, for example, an exaggeration or a distortion of a familiar situation or event (for example, "What do you get when you mix a cow and a duck?" "Milk and quackers!").[4]

Although young elementary schoolchildren are not yet capable of engaging in the kind of fast-paced, humorous exchanges that typify adolescence, it is common to see them take an interest in naughty, socially unacceptable types of humor. Children as young as three imitate "dirty" words, but from about age five they start to use them more consciously and incorporate them into their humor. Jokes about human excrement will make many a child howl with laughter, explaining why books such as *Walter the Farting Dog* and *Everyone Poops* are international best sellers.[5]

Educational Media Begins to Bore

At around five, media preferences begin to shift. Young schoolchildren often begin to express a stubborn preference for violent, action-packed adventure programs, often to their parents' great aggravation. These children prefer content that is faster and more complex, relies on less friendly characters, and uses more adventurous contexts, such as unexplored islands or alien planets. At the same time, children lose interest in educational television for preschoolers such as *Sesame Street* and *Dora the Explorer*, boys somewhat sooner than girls.[6] Researchers have suggested that this shift from interest in educational to entertainment content reflects the so-called spinach syndrome: while toddlers like almost everything, five-year-olds reject anything that is supposed to be good for them.

Why are young elementary schoolchildren strongly attracted to fast-paced and action-packed entertainment? First, compared with their toddler and preschooler counterparts, children in this age group have dramatically improved cognitive-processing abilities, and so the slow (often educational) content they once preferred becomes boring. As a result, they search for more challenging (that is, faster and more action-packed) entertainment to meet their newly developed cognitive needs. Moreover, this type of entertainment offers them all the things that they love: action, physical humor, and moving "toys" in the form of cartoon or animated characters.

Another explanation is that the action and (occasional) violence in such entertainment programs can function as rebellion against the restrictions that adults impose on children. In particular, superheroes allow children to escape their everyday restrictions. By identifying with superheroes, children can pretend that they too are big and strong, and the feeling this gives them is pleasurable.[7] This is because children take vicarious pleasure in the behavior of someone they admire and would like to resemble, but could never actually imitate. This process of wishful identification allows children to feel strong and powerful at a time when they are struggling with everyday problems that they cannot immediately resolve.[8]

A final explanation for the success of action-packed entertainment is that the events in this content often involve a group of peers or friends. Remember the moderate discrepancy hypothesis, whereby children are mostly attracted to media content that is moderately discrepant from their own experiences? Whereas peers are important in early childhood, peers and the corresponding social interactions among them become indispensable for young elementary schoolchildren. Thus, it is not surprising that as peers become increasingly important in daily life, children express an increased interest in peer and social interaction in media content. This particular interest continues to grow throughout preadolescence and adolescence.

Children in this transitional period begin to appreciate a different type of media character. They often start to gravitate toward so-called binary characters, which are, for example, extremely good or evil or extremely masculine or feminine. Adults often reject these characters as too stereotypical, and by many accounts, they are stereotypical. But children in this age group—and many older children—greatly enjoy entertainment with characters that present the world in binary contrasts. They often will use such portrayals to help them interpret the world around them and to help inform their gender identity.[9]

"When It Comes to Toys, Girls Will Be Girls and Boys . . ."

Speaking of gender identity, children in this transitional period typically become acutely aware of their gender roles, developing very rigid ideas about what members of their sex can and cannot do.[10] As boys and girls spend more and more time in separate groups, they feel pressure to conform to behavior that the group sees as gender appropriate. Toy manufacturers, media developers, and advertisers know how to key into these notions. Experience has taught them that the most successful products for children in this age group are gender specific. "When it comes to toys, girls will be girls and boys will be boys" is their motto.

In any children's toy store today, the striking degree of gender-role stereotyping is easily seen in the "pink" and "blue" sections of the store.[11] Similarly, anyone watching commercials targeting children can see how well advertisers know that gender roles are rigid during this period. For example, in one study, researchers analyzed over six hundred commercials targeting youth. The analysis was designed to evaluate the types of "appeals" commonly used in commercials (that is, the approach used to attract and influence consumers). Results showed that commercials offer boys an entirely different world from the one they offer girls. For example, whereas 76 percent of the commercials aimed at boys showed action and adventure, only 12 percent of the commercials for girls did. Thirteen percent of the boys' commercials were about sports; none of the girls' were. On the other hand, in the girls' commercials, the top appeals were about nurturing, physical attractiveness, friendship, and affection for animals; not one of these themes was featured in any the boys' commercials.[12]

Boys' and girls' gender-specific preferences at this age are clearly illustrated by their media preferences. For example, table 5.1 shows the top ten favorite games of boys and girls. The data come from one of our current longitudinal studies. Though the study follows Dutch children, these popular games, as many will recognize, are not specific to the Netherlands. Indeed, the majority of games on this list also appear on top ten lists across most Western countries. For example, at the time of this writing, *Minecraft* is the second best-selling video game worldwide, followed closely by *Super Mario Bros.*

What is striking about this table is that four of the ten favorite games appear on the lists of both girls and boys—namely, *Minecraft, Subway*

Table 5.1. Top ten favorite games among Dutch five- to eight-year-olds, by gender, 2014

	Boys	*Girls*
1	*Minecraft*	*Subway Surfers*
2	*Skylander*	*Dora*
3	*Super Mario*	*Minecraft*
4	*Lego*	*Pou*
5	*Mario Kart*	*Candy Crush*
6	*Angry Birds*	*Mario Kart*
7	*Fifa*	*Super Mario*
8	*Subway Surfers*	*Just Dance*
9	*Wii Sports Resort*	*Barbie*
10	*Cars*	*MovieStarPlanet*

Source: Unpublished data from a study by Patti M. Valkenburg, supported by a grant from the European Research Council

Surfers, Mario Kart (different versions), and *Super Mario* (different versions). Closer inspection of the table, however, reveals a number of obvious gender-specific differences in boys' and girls' preferences. For example, dressing up dolls (*Barbie*), dancing (*Just Dance*), creating your own movie star on a pink planet (*MovieStarPlanet*), and taking care of an adorable pet (*Pou*) remain activities preferred by girls. Although *Dora the Explorer* appeals to some boys, she is mainly a girls' idol and is likely to remain so. Racing, action, and sports games such as *Cars, Skylander,* and *Fifa* remain all-time favorites among boys.

Preadolescents

Whatever we call eight- to twelve-year-olds, whether preadolescents, preteens, or tweens, this group differs from their younger counterparts in numerous ways. According to Piaget, they are concrete-operational thinkers. This means that their thinking is based on a system of rules and logic, and—unlike younger children—they understand that the order of events can be reversed. For example, younger children typically struggle with what Piaget called "conservation tasks." Imagine you have two glasses—one tall and the other wide. A younger child, upon seeing you pour water from the wide glass to the tall glass is likely to say that the tall glass now has more water—even though nothing has changed. The younger child is struggling with transformation, and instead judges the final outcome (the perception of the water being higher) rather than the process.

Contrast this with eight- to twelve-year-olds, whose cognitive development has significantly advanced. These children understand this transformation process and can easily explain that the amount of water has not changed, only the size of the container has changed. There is one proviso to this newfound logical thinking. Children at this age can apply their logic only to concrete objects or events. This limitation is how they differ from children over the age of twelve, the formal-operational thinkers, who can think logically not only about concrete phenomena but also about abstract concepts.

Eight- to twelve-year-olds are capable of "decentering." Whereas younger children tend to focus on the most striking aspects of an object or a piece of information (referred to as centration in chapter 4), these children use their newfound logical abilities to scrutinize, down to the last detail, every product that attracts their attention. If a preteen is given a new pair of shoes, he or she will dissect and evaluate every aspect of the shoe, from the laces to the logo.[13] Their growing critical faculties and their concrete-operational thinking drive them to compare everything in their surroundings against standards of genuineness and authenticity.

Children of this age become more critical not only of their parents, friends, and family, but also of commercials, games, and television programs that are not action packed or newsworthy. They are no longer as impressed by special effects and fantasy characters, and think that such features cannot compensate for a boring story. In addition, children at this age are able to divide their attention between many different activities, and nearly 30 percent of preadolescents use other media while watching television.[14]

Collect Them All!

As children in this age group develop an eye for detail and quality, they start to enjoy collecting or saving.[15] Think about your own experience as a child of this age. What did you collect? Most often, preteens report collecting paraphernalia about sports (for example, baseball cards), media heroes (for example, Pokemon cards, Disney Infinity cards), or toys (for example, Beanie Babies). Why do tweens feel such a need to collect things at this particular age? Children of this age are concrete-operational thinkers. Besides having an eye for the details of objects that they collect, they feel a pressing need to follow rules and to order and categorize their surroundings. By saving and collecting objects, they can practice all sorts of new concrete operations, for example, grouping, ordering, classifying, and categorizing (see figure 5.1). Unlike younger children, they are capable of grouping objects by more than one criterion at a time (for example, shape, color, length, and thickness).

Younger children also tend to collect things, but they typically just want to have as many toys around them as possible. As they get older, they begin to collect objects because they feel a need to distinguish and differentiate these objects. They wish to exercise their newly developed concrete-operation skills, and at the same time they are naturally interested in the

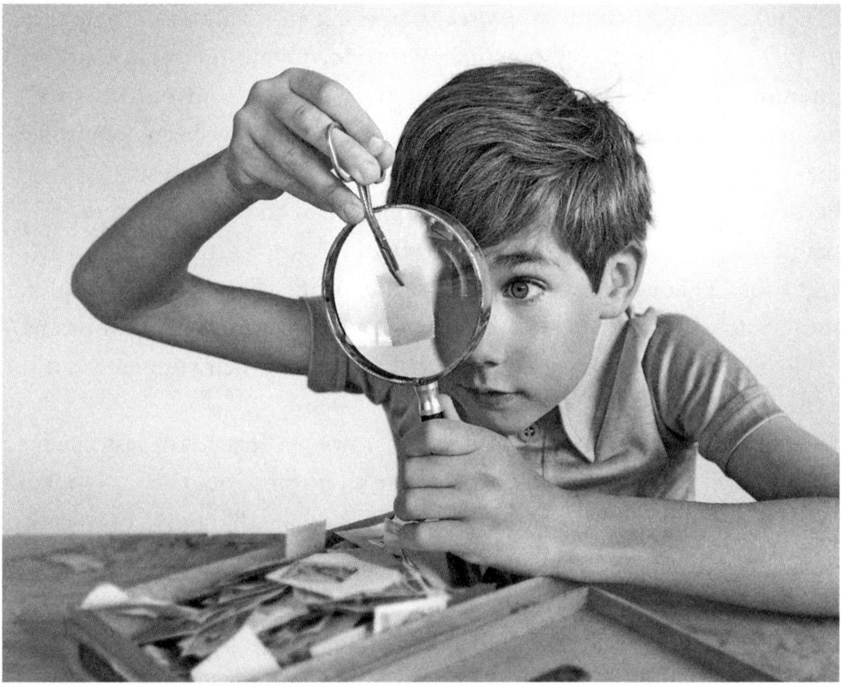

Figure 5.1. By saving and collecting, children can practice and enjoy grouping, ordering, classifying, and categorizing. (Mieke Dalle/Getty Images)

social opportunities that collecting offers them, for example, trading objects with classmates and playing games.

When it comes to media content, then, it makes sense that so much of the media content popular with this audience includes some aspect of collecting. For example, virtual gaming worlds such as *Club Penguin*, *Minecraft*, and *Webkinz* dramatically increase in popularity among members of this age group.[16] A close examination of these games shows that collection is a key attribute in all of them. In *Club Penguin*, children can adopt different Puffles to care for, and they can collect a variety of clothing for their personalized character. In *Webkinz*, children are invited to collect as many animals as possible—each with its own games and activities. It is also not uncommon for toy and media conglomerates to market associated products to this audience. In fact, the phrase "collect them all!" seems to be almost commonplace in advertisements for this audience.

Magical Realism

Unlike younger children, preteens fantasize more about realistic situations. They take a sincere, sometimes disproportionate interest in real-world phenomena, looking for realism in toys, books, and entertainment programs.[17] Because most of their fantasy characters have been demystified, they come to identify primarily with real-world human idols, such as sports heroes and movie stars. Interestingly, girls tend to be more interested in realism than boys, who generally remain longer attracted to fantasy scenarios. This gender difference helps explain why girls tend to prefer shows such as *Zoey 101* and *Victorious* (shows featuring preteen drama), while boys tend to enjoy the superhero cartoons of their younger years for a bit longer.

Realism is a broad concept at this age, however. It is not necessarily true that children no longer enjoy fantasy per se, but instead, they are looking for realistic fantasy. In other words, children will still enjoy content that happens in a fantasy setting, but they want the characters' experiences to follow the rules of logic.[18] The Harry Potter series is a good example of this. The Harry Potter novels are what we would call "magical realism." The situations described in the books and movies are entirely fantastical, but they also reflect the real world of preadolescents. The main characters are early adolescents with true-to-life emotions, and their experiences of love, competition, jealousy, and so on are convincingly depicted. This is similarly true of other popular realistic fantasy programs such as *Aaron Stone* or *Wizards of Waverly Place*.

Production Quality

Children grow progressively more social from about age seven. From then on, their social-emotional development increasingly influences their media preferences. One very important characteristic of preadolescents is that they are much better able than their younger counterparts to recognize and understand other people's emotions. Four-year-olds can explain whether playmates are happy, sad, or angry, but they rely mainly on visible cues, for example, facial expressions. As they get older, however, children increasingly depend on less visible information (that is, by focusing more on motives and contextual information) to help them interpret other people's emotions. They also start to understand that people can have more than one emotion at once, and that they can hide their feelings or even feign them.

Given these more advanced social-emotional skills, combined with their heightened interest in details and realism, it makes sense that preadolescents recognize and loathe bad acting (for example, unconvincing displays of emotion on television or in a commercial).[19] In addition, children can be highly critical of entertainment and commercials that lack realism, as when an actor's behavior is implausible or a product is presented in a fantasy context. Whereas the production quality of media content was not necessarily crucial for younger children, preadolescents place a high value on it.

Identification with Media Characters

Children's ability to look at the world from another person's perspective increases during the preschool and early elementary school years. Piaget regarded children under the age of about six as "egocentric" in their thinking. He meant not that young children think only of themselves, but rather that they do not see things from the perspective of others (their thoughts or feelings). Piaget came up with the term "egocentrism" to describe certain aspects of children's language. Toddlers and preschoolers sometimes have a habit of talking without intending to communicate anything. They repeat something that they have just heard, or talk to themselves. Piaget referred to this type of language use as egocentric. Examples of this talk can often be heard at the playground when youngsters play "together" by playing independently and talking next to each other.

As they go through elementary school, children gradually become more skilled at seeing things from another person's perspective. Children learn to consider others' points of view simultaneously and to anticipate how they will respond in different situations, although this skill is still developing. As their ability to understand other perspectives improves, children's understanding of human relationships changes. Whereas a preschooler often assumes that every social interaction with an available playmate makes that playmate a "friend," by the time they are about eight, children grasp that they and their peers might have similar but also different interests, and they start to look for friends who are psychologically similar to themselves.[20]

Children's growing capacity to see things from different perspectives influences not only how they deal with people in their real-life environment, but also their preferences for characters in media. While preschoolers tend to focus on physical similarities when it comes to character preference, preadolescents are more attentive to the psychological or social aspects of a character's personality. In particular, more than ever before, preadolescents enjoy watching actors that are not only physically but also psychologically similar to themselves. By watching such actors, they have the opportunity to observe events and situations that might be relevant to their own lives. It is therefore no surprise that preadolescents tend to identify with same-sex characters, particularly when these characters share similar psychological characteristics. Finally, they often prefer actors of at least their own age, and teenagers and adults even more. According to preadolescents, these older performers are more attractive because they are involved in more interesting and exciting activities, and tend to be better actors than children.[21] This sentiment reflects not only their increasingly critical view of media content, but also their increased interest in realistic content.

The Need to Belong

As children's social-emotional development increases in complexity, so does their interaction with peers. This is logical. As preadolescents become better able to understand the perspective and emotions of others, their ability to interact with and share similar experiences with others also increases. We see that during preadolescence, peer groups become stable alliances that share common interests and explicit norms of behavior. While some children become sensitive to the opinions of other children before the age of six, this sensitivity heightens significantly during the preadolescent period.

Children become highly committed and loyal to the group to which they belong. They are mindful of how to behave, and they become sensitive to current trends. They do everything possible to avoid being ridiculed by their peers, for example, by avoiding the "wrong" clothes or media content. During this period, many children develop a strong aversion to entertainment that they regard as "childish." When they are with their peers, they sometimes take special pains to distance themselves from the younger age groups for whom such programs were created. And as we discussed earlier, they become primarily interested in media products featuring characters of at least their own age or older—particularly content that highlights peer situations.[22]

Gender Differences

Preadolescent boys and girls differ in important ways when it comes to their entertainment preferences, but the differences are less stark than earlier in childhood. Boys continue to have a stronger preference than girls for action and violence, as they did in early elementary school. They generally like sports, science fiction, action, and adventure, and enjoy watching cartoons more than girls. Boys of this age still appreciate masculine action heroes, although they more often prefer heroes of flesh and blood. Watching adult television makes boys in particular feel "cool" and grown-up.

Girls generally have a more negative response to scenarios featuring action, violence, and horror, probably because—as they report—they are more likely to feel scared. In one of our studies in the Netherlands, we asked children about positive and negative experiences on the Internet. Girls described violence and pornography as negative experiences, whereas some boys regarded these same experiences as positive. We also asked children what elements they would include if they were producing a new entertainment program for kids. Only the girls spontaneously responded that they would not want to include sex or violence in the program.[23]

During this period, girls typically place greater value on a clear story line and—as mentioned earlier—are more attracted than boys to realistic dramas that depict developing relationships between characters. Girls prefer stories about families and attractive characters such as actresses, film stars, and pop idols. Compared with boys, for example, girls are more likely to seek out actors and actresses that they know, to spend more time looking for information about television shows and characters, and to want to watch a show from beginning to end.[24] But it is a fallacy to think that only girls are interested in entertainment focusing on interpersonal relationships; if that were true, some online role-playing games would not be as popular among boys as they are. In many instances, the focus in these types of games is predominantly on story lines and character development.

Conclusion

This chapter took a detailed look at the cognitive development and social-emotional development of children. Given the significant changes that occur during this period, we divided this audience into young elementary schoolchildren and preadolescents in order to allow for a more detailed look at how development predicts media preferences. We discussed that between five and eight years of age, interest in educational media is replaced by an interest in faster and more complex and action-packed content. Moreover, children in this age group exhibit highly gendered media preferences—reflecting the statement that "when it comes to toys, girls will be girls and boys will be boys."

Importantly, as children leave this transitional period, they enter preadolescence—a period characterized by a more sophisticated cognitive and social-emotional development. This enhanced developmental level leads to an interest in more complex and realistic content, and it can also make them more critical of poorly produced media content. They are interested in media characters that are psychologically similar to themselves, and in social situations with which they can identify and learn from. The media content and toys of their former years are no longer "cool," and they quickly try to find their footing as soon-to-be adolescents.

Yet despite all their "adult" preferences, preadolescents are still children in many respects. Although they are reluctant to admit it, approximately a quarter of ten- and eleven-year-old girls still play with Barbies.[25] They want autonomy, but have a distinct preference for operating in the safe environment of same-sex groups. And while most have a budding interest in sexuality, they are mainly taken up with belonging and having lots of friends. No longer children, and not yet teens, they are truly “tweens”—working to find their footing in a complex world.

6

ADOLESCENTS

> Our youth now love luxury. They have bad manners, contempt for authority; they show disrespect for their elders and love chatter in place of exercise; they no longer rise when elders enter the room; they contradict their parents, chatter before company; gobble up their food and tyrannize their teachers.
>
> —Socrates, 469–399 BCE

Complaints about adolescent behavior have existed since the invention of writing, and perhaps even before. Adolescence, the period between childhood and adulthood, brings about spectacular changes in the human body and brain. These changes have a huge influence on adolescents' behavior and their interest in media. Studying these developmental processes helps us understand how best to appeal to younger and older adolescents. What, for example, interests young teens (ages 12–15) and how does this differ (or not) from what interests their older teenage peers (16–19)? What specific developmental characteristics typify these age groups, and how do these characteristics influence their media use and preferences? Why do teens enjoy sarcasm and fast-paced, humorous banter in media? Why do social media have such a "Pied Piper effect" on adolescents? And finally, how does teens' developing autonomy influence their media preferences?

Generation Digital

Anyone who has anything to do with adolescents knows that they are massive users of media. They are among the most avid consumers of television and music, and the fastest adopters of digital technology—particularly social media.[1] Although estimates vary by country, current data suggest that teens spend about six hours a day interacting with screens. This total includes nearly two hours spent chatting with friends via media such as WhatsApp, texting, or Snapchat, as well as more than an hour a day spent on social media sites such as Facebook, YouTube, and Instagram. In other words, the time that adolescents spend using social media—more than three hours a day—has now surpassed the amount of time they spend on entertainment media, for example, watching shows, series, or movies on television or online (97 minutes) or playing electronic games (75 minutes). They spend the least amount of time reading books or comic books (35 minutes).[2]

Although reports about adolescents' media use usually present information as though teenagers reflect one homogenous group, the truth is that adolescence is a period of significant developmental changes. After all, a thirteen-year-old differs enormously from an eighteen-year-old. Admittedly, it is not easy to divide the period of adolescence into segments. Individual differences in this period are at least as large as they are in childhood. Moreover, physical development, cognitive development, and social-emotional development often do not occur synchronously. While there seems to be no perfect recipe for segmenting this group, we divide adolescence into two age groups: early adolescence (ages 12–15) and late adolescence (ages 16–19). There are two reasons for this decision. First, puberty is thought to begin at approximately eleven years of age and to conclude around fifteen. Since puberty reflects significant physical, psychological, and social changes, segmenting adolescence in a way that is sensitive to pubertal changes is reasonable. Second, this segmentation decision is pragmatic: much of the research on teens and media use seems to focus on one or the other of these two groups—affirming the underlying developmental differences of both groups.

Early Adolescence

Puberty, the period between the ages of eleven and sixteen, is characterized by intense physical changes that, in turn, affect adolescents' emotions and cognition. In the brain, the hypothalamus begins sending signals to the pituitary gland, announcing the start of puberty. The pituitary gland in turn causes girls' ovaries and boys' testicles to release sex hormones, including estrogens in girls and androgens in boys. In girls, the estrogens cause them to have their first menstruation, and the androgen increase in boys eventually leads to their first ejaculation. These hormones are responsible for the intense state of sexual arousal that young teens may experience, as well as their fascination with all things related to sex and sexual attraction, both in their immediate environment and in the media.

A number of other important physical changes also take place at this time. For example, girls develop breasts; boys' voices deepen, and they add muscle. Both sexes experience an increase in sebum production that may lead to oily skin and acne. Moreover, both boys and girls undergo an impressive growth spurt, accompanied by weight gain. Girls accumulate more fat around the hips, and boys at the waist. On average, girls experience this growth spurt between the ages of ten and fourteen, whereas boys experience it slightly later (between the ages of twelve and sixteen).[3]

Changes in the Adolescent Brain

Besides the noticeable physical changes that puberty brings, there are other, less obvious changes that have major consequences for the way teens think and behave, and for what interests them. These changes take place in different regions of the brain and in different ways. The human brain is made up of gray and white matter. Gray matter, which consists of the cell bodies, dendrites, and axon terminals of neurons (nerve cells), is responsible for information processing. White matter, made up of the axons themselves, consists of the pathways that connect neurons to one another. If we compare the brain to a computer network, the gray matter would be analogous to the individual computers, and white matter to the network cables that connect them.

During childhood, the volume of gray matter increases significantly in many regions of the brain. Around the start of puberty, however, gray matter starts to decline in volume. This increase and subsequent decrease of gray matter can be plotted as a bell curve. The decline in gray matter, known as "pruning," is said to indicate that the brain is beginning to function more efficiently. The "use it or lose it" principle applies here: neurons that are used will survive, and those that are not will disappear.[4] Unlike gray matter, white matter increases in volume throughout late childhood and adolescence.[5] This increase is mainly responsible for the faster and more efficient communication between the different regions of the preadolescent and adolescent brain, which helps explain a good deal of adolescents' thinking and behavior.

One major misconception about the adolescent brain is the idea that the prefrontal cortex, which is located at the front of the brain and plays an important role in self-control and planning, matures only toward the end of early adulthood, at around age twenty-five. Previously, the "immature" prefrontal cortex was thought to explain all sorts of "immature" behavior on the part of adolescents, for example, their trouble keeping appointments, their sometimes unstructured thought patterns, and their risk-taking tendencies. In part because of widespread media reports about the pubescent brain, society has generally accepted this notion.

In 2012, however, Eveline Crone and Ronald Dahl reviewed the 150 studies that supposedly delivered the evidence for this theory.[6] Their research showed that the prefrontal cortex of adolescents is actually not structurally immature. If teens are motivated to learn, their prefrontal cortex is decidedly active. If they want to create a website or learn to play a game, they can spend hours and days on end trying to master all sorts of complex new tasks. In other words, the maturity of their prefrontal cortex appears to depend on their motivation to keep their appointments, to structure their thoughts, and plan their activities.

Abstract Thought and Metacognition

In part a result of their advancing brain development, early adolescents no longer take the world for what it is. They are quick to find something implausible. They also question and criticize all manner of authority, including their schools, teachers, and, especially, parents. Anyone who has ever parented a teenager will likely let out an exasperated sigh when they reflect on the challenges and resistance experienced during the teenage years. Although frustrating to many adults, this behavior is in line with Piaget's formal-operational stage of development. Formal-operational thinking refers to thinking that is both logical and abstract.

In chapter 5, we discussed concrete-operational thinking. That too is logical thinking, but it is limited to concrete problems. For example: "Karen is bigger than Susan but smaller than Diane. Which of the three is biggest?" Unlike younger children, early adolescents, thanks to their more advanced brain development, are capable of solving this word problem without requiring the concrete phenomena—the three girls—to be present. Moreover, early adolescents can reason hypothetically and think about what could happen in specific situations. They thus can engage in systematic problem solving.

Teens' increasingly advanced way of thinking has significant implications for their behavior and interests. They think more clearly than preadolescents about the future and take those thoughts into account when making decisions. They start taking a sincere interest in or grow worried about major global issues, such as the conflicts in the Middle East, the financial crisis, or global warming. They become able to compare situations and use their comparisons in arguments. For example, in their disagreements with parents, it is common to hear comparisons used as behavioral justification: "No way I'm doing the dishes! When Cindy was studying for her exams, she didn't have to do them!"

In addition to adolescents' increasingly abstract thinking and problem-solving skills, their metacognitive skills improve significantly during this period. Once early adolescents have acquired metacognition, the ability to evaluate one's own thoughts, they are better able to summarize what they have learned or what another person's train of thought might have been. They can not only indicate what they know, but also say why they know it. As a result of these metacognitive skills, they are capable of introspection (that is, the ability to reflect on their own thoughts and emotions).

Not surprisingly, while their metacognitive skills are increasing, their social cognition—their ability to interpret and anticipate others' desires, emotions, and motives—is also improving. This newfound metacognition, combined with improved social cognition, brings with it many internal struggles. In particular, they may begin to worry more about what others are thinking of them, becoming much more self-conscious and concerned about how they appear to others.

Keep It Fast, Compact, and True to Life

Early adolescents can be extremely critical consumers of media entertainment. Earlier in this book, we discussed the moderate discrepancy hypothesis, which suggests that children and teens are most interested in media content that departs moderately from their level of cognitive and social-emotional development. This hypothesis continues to apply in early adolescence. Entertainment programs should not diverge too much in content or structure from their cognitive skills. Their advancing brain development means that speed and variety are the norm in this age group.[7] This may explain why apps such as Snapchat (a time-limited photo messaging application) and Vine (a six-second video creation application) have become so popular with this age group—they privilege speed and variation above all else.

The pacing of media entertainment that targets this age group has quickened in recent decades. But it is not clear whether this new, fast-paced media entertainment environment is changing teens' preferences for fast-paced entertainment or whether this entertainment environment is just catering to what today's teens gravitate toward. The influence is probably reciprocal. Interestingly, adolescents' desire for speed and variation has accompanied a quickly growing trend toward media multitasking. Whereas only 16 percent of adolescents used different media simultaneously in the 1990s, today that percentage has nearly doubled.[8]

Beyond variety and speed, early adolescents are looking for plausible content in entertainment media content. This interest begins during preadolescence with an increasing interest in realistic fantasy (for example, Harry Potter). With adolescents' growing ability to engage in abstract thinking and their increased social cognition, their demands for plausible media content are even stronger. Story lines should be logical, characters should fit within the context of adolescents' social and cultural background, and historical and situational factors should be true to life. Compared to their younger peers, early adolescents prefer increasingly complex content—including content that relies on more abstract ideas and problems—but this, too, should be plausible. They also begin to prefer characters that are more psychologically complex, such as Damon Salvatore from *The Vampire Diaries,* or Spencer, Hanna, Aria, and Emily from *Pretty Little Liars.*

Keep Me Laughing: Irony, Sarcasm, and Wit

Children's sense of humor changes when they reach puberty. Early adolescents become interested in complex forms of humor involving irony, sarcasm, and cynicism. This is a logical development, since more complex humor requires the ability to size up both a situation and the motives of those displaying that humor—in other words, the metacognition and social cognition that accompany adolescent development. A teacher who winks and tells Monique, "Wow, you've really studied hard," when Monique has given all the wrong answers in class can only mean this ironically. If the same teacher says to her, this time without winking, "Just keep this up, Monique, and you'll really go places," then Monique knows the remark is sarcastic and not meant kindly.

In addition, early adolescents begin to prefer spontaneous, witty forms of humor to the ready-made jokes and riddles popular with children. Off-the-cuff wit is an important popularity factor in peer groups, especially among boys, who tend to engage in more verbal sparring than girls do.[9] Girls are more likely to giggle with one another than boys, something that appears to bind them as a group. Girls are also more inclined to laugh passively at the humorous antics of boys whom they like.[10] Boys, on the other hand, like girls who laugh at their humor. This reciprocal confirmation helps stimulate the forming of heterosexual romantic attachments.

This preference for complex humor is seen in early adolescents' media preferences. For example, popular shows such as *South Park* and *Tosh.o* frequently rely on sarcasm and irony to entertain their audiences. Early adolescents (particularly boys) seem to particularly enjoy entertainment content that pairs absurdist and irreverent humor with more adult concepts or taboos (for example, the portrayal of sexuality in *Napoleon Dynamite*). That said, despite this preference for increasingly complex humor, early adolescents still find slapstick and other physical displays of humor entertaining, as in shows such as *Wildboyz*.

Make It Extreme: Vampires, Sports, and Horror

As children move into early adolescence, they show an increased interest in horror movies, vampires, and high-risk sports, for example, BMX biking and BASE jumping. Why might this occur? One primary explanation is again associated with their brain development. Recall that during this period, there is an increase in the activity of neural axons. These axons use dopamine, a neurotransmitter that sends signals between neurons and is commonly associated with the pleasure system of the brain. In particular, dopamine is thought to co-occur with feelings of enjoyment and to reinforce a tendency to do (or continue to do) certain activities. Dopamine also plays a role in the desire to embark on new or exciting adventures.[11]

It is not entirely clear how the dopamine system works in adolescence. Given the challenges associated with brain research in humans, most of what we know about the dopamine system comes from research among adolescent animals. While many researchers assume that dopamine activity is higher in adolescents than in children or adults, others think that base dopamine levels are lower in adolescence than in childhood and adulthood, but that levels skyrocket when adolescents have or anticipate having an exciting experience.[12] This is thought to explain why adolescents often feel listless and bored unless they experience new or exhilarating things. When they do, their dopamine levels shoot up, causing them to feel their emotions with great intensity. Whatever the case, most neuroscientists agree that the dopamine system in adolescence differs from that in childhood and adulthood.

The changes in the dopamine system during adolescence may lead teens to act more impulsively than children or adults and to show a greater tendency toward risk taking. This is particularly true when teens are in the company of peers, whose presence kicks the brain's reward system into high gear.[13] Adolescents—compared with children and adults—are much more likely to focus on the positive, exciting side of an activity and less on the risks involved.[14] This is thought to reflect a mismatch between their much-improved cognitive functions and their (in)ability to see the "bigger picture" when necessary. Although many of teens' cognitive skills are well developed, the same cannot be said of their intuition (that is, their gut feeling, their ability to understand something automatically, without the need for conscious reasoning).[15]

Given this imbalance between their advanced cognitive functioning and their still-developing intuition, combined with their highly active dopamine system, it is not surprising that risk-taking behaviors increase dramatically in frequency during the adolescent years—reaching an all-time high toward the end of puberty. This is a time when youth are trying different sport stunts (on skateboards or bikes, for example) as well as experimenting with drugs, smoking, and alcohol. For teens, the rewards from these activities (the thrills) greatly outweigh the risks, particularly when they are in the presence of their peers.

Early adolescence is also a time when teens exhibit an increased interest in thrilling media content—for example, vampires (for example, *True Blood, Twilight*), extreme sports or stunts (*Careless Teens, Jackass, Scarred, Nitro Circus*), and horror movies (the wildly popular *Scream* slasher movies)—since this content depicts the excitement, sensation, and adventure that they are craving. And with the emergence of social media comes an upsurge of risky behavior online—for example, sexting (sharing sexual photographs on the Internet)—with a peak coming around fifteen years of age (also see chapter 13).[16]

Social-Emotional Development

While cognitive development is a core aspect of the adolescent years, teens' social-emotional development is just as significant. One of the crucial goals of adolescence is the development of autonomy—defined as the capacity to make independent decisions and care for oneself. To gain autonomy, teens have to develop three key social-emotional subgoals. First, they need to develop a stable identity, a reasonably firm sense of who they are and who they would like to become. Second, they must develop a sense of intimacy, which refers to close relationships in which partners are open, caring, and trusting.[17] In adolescence, teens must acquire the skills needed to form such close relationships. Finally, they need to discover their sexual identity. They have to get used to and learn to handle their sexual desires, and learn how to engage in mutual, honest, and safe sexual relationships. All three of these developing social-emotional subgoals intersect with teens' media use and preferences—particularly digital media.

Identity: Learning from the Media

Much has been written about adolescent identity, and numerous terms describe more or less the same processes. We assume that identity consists of at least two aspects: self-concept and self-esteem.[18] Our self-concept is how we see ourselves: who we are and who we want to become. Our self-esteem is the extent to which we value this self-concept. To develop a stable self-concept and positive self-esteem, teens need to experiment with their behavior in order to find out what those in their social environment (peers, adults) appreciate or dislike about them. To learn about "appropriate" behavioral options, teens typically observe not only peers and adults in their physical environment, but also their media idols. It is logical, then, that many teens appreciate entertainment programs that feature social relationships, romance, or love. For example, popular MTV reality programs such as *Girl Code, True Life,* and *Jersey Shore* frequently feature content about friendships, romance, and love. Similarly, popular scripted programs such as *Gossip Girls, Glee,* and *Awkward* often focus on the development and maintenance of friendships and romantic relationships—including the challenges associated with such relationships.

During this period of identity experimentation, teens can be moody, and their self-esteem may waver. Early adolescents tend to be more troubled by day-to-day fluctuations in self-esteem than older adolescents, since they are more likely to base their self-esteem on how people in their environment react to their behavior and appearance.[19] The egocentrism seen in toddlers and preschoolers re-emerges in this period, but manifests itself in new ways. For example, teens often feel as if everyone is looking at them, as if they are performing for an attentive audience. David Elkind refers to this form of egocentrism as the "imaginary audience." Teens often believe that their experiences are unique and that no one feels, or has ever felt, the way they do. "No one understands me!" is an oft-heard lament at this age. Elkind calls this form of egocentrism the "personal fable."[20] Because teens frequently feel different from everyone else, they often experience a sense of invincibility. Combined with their dopamine-related sensitivity to rewards, this sense of invincibility can exacerbate their tendency to engage in risky behaviors.

Teens' increased self-focus means that they can become incredibly preoccupied with their appearance. They see that their bodies are growing, that they are becoming gangly and moving clumsily, and as a result, they may feel uncomfortable or even awkward in their bodies and social situations. Girls want nothing more than to live up to the feminine "ideal," and boys desperately want to be tall and broad shouldered. If boys and girls believe they fall short of these ideals, they become uncertain and insecure about their appearance.

Given these gendered ideals, it is perhaps not surprising that at the onset of adolescence, differences in gender-specific preferences return with a vengeance. Indeed, both boys and girls prefer entertainment with noticeably gender-specific characters.[21] Girls want to see feminine girls, and boys want to see macho boys. Much as they do in their physical social environment, they derive social lessons and solutions to their problems from entertainment programs. Girls want to know how popular actresses solve their problems, and boys similarly want to see how tough-guy actors handle their concerns. Like tweens, they prefer movies and shows featuring somewhat older, socially successful actors whom they admire and can identify with. This is certainly nothing new. Almost a century ago, when the movie industry emerged, young teens fell under the sway of motion pictures—with nearly 70 percent of them acting out scenes that they had seen in a movie.[22]

Although entertainment media provide teens with many examples of potential identities to practice with, social media have provided them with many new opportunities to experiment with their identities. As early adolescents work on building their self-concept and self-esteem, they find social media irresistible.[23] Two things are important for adolescents trying to develop a stable self-concept and self-esteem: the approval of their social environment and the possibility of influencing that environment. Social media offers teens both. They can tinker endlessly with their self-presentation on the Internet (as with selfies). They can decide which photographs they will upload and how many; they have more time to think about what they will and will not communicate; and with a great deal of practice, they can optimize the feedback that they receive on their profile.

Today, approximately half of teens sometimes experiment with their identity on the Internet, with girls doing so more frequently than boys. Adolescents experiment with their identity online mainly to gauge other people's reactions to their online behavior. They are typically more flirtatious online than offline, and indicate that they are less inhibited when communicating online than offline. Boys and girls do not differ in the frequency with which they experiment with their identities online, but they do differ with respect to the nature of that experimentation. Girls pretend to be older and beautiful more often than boys, while boys more frequently pretend to be macho.[24] We return to this topic in more detail in our chapter on social media (chapter 13).

Intimacy: WhatsApping with Friends

Once boys and girls enter puberty, they spend more time with peers and less time with their parents. They develop a seemingly compulsive need to communicate with their friends, in person or through their tablets and phones, and preferably from early in the morning until late at night. Close friendships in adolescence play a crucial role in helping youth develop their identity and practice the skills needed for intimacy. For most teens, friendships provide an important opportunity to evaluate their physical changes and experiences, particularly with friends who are similar to them. Close friends serve as an important sounding board for comparing experiences, identifying standards and values in the peer group, and learning which behaviors are and are not acceptable.

Before age thirteen, teens typically hang out in same-sex groups and generally consider members of the opposite sex "dumb" or "irritating." That soon changes. Early adolescents often have one or two best friends or buddies and also belong to a group of friends—known as a clique—who interact frequently both online and off. Cliques are usually made up of two to ten members (five or six on average).[25] Girls typically organize themselves into cliques at around age eleven, boys at about thirteen. Although cliques perform the same function for both genders, girls are more likely to use them to share intimate information, whereas boys tend to focus more on games and sports.

Cliques are usually inspired by subcultures. Unlike cliques, subcultures are considerably larger. Their members share certain interests, for example, a preference for particular musical genres, fashions, or politics, but they do not necessarily communicate with or even know one another. Subcultures first emerged in the 1960s, initially fueled by dissatisfaction with the establishment, for example, the hippies and yippies of the sixties and the punk rockers of the eighties. Subcultures in the new millennium are seemingly less rebellious, conspicuous, and outspoken than those in the past. But that does not mean that subcultures are less important than before for identity development.

Since the advent of the Internet, adolescents have had more opportunities than ever to validate their opinions and behavior against peer group standards. That is perhaps why their clothes, behavior, and music styles need not be as conspicuous as those of their counterparts from earlier generations. Subcultures traditionally evolved in the wake of spectacular new musical genres, and we still see subculture formation among teens who identify with a specific performer or entertainment program. For example, Justin Bieber's fans are known as "Beliebers," Taylor Swift's fans are "Swifties," Lady Gaga's are "Little Monsters," and the devotees of the television series *Glee* call themselves "Gleeks."

Early adolescents usually have a strong desire to conform to the standards of their cliques and subcultures. They are no longer interested in toys, and they avoid products that they perceive as being marketed to children. Their strong desire to conform to the standards of their clique and subculture makes them extremely brand conscious. And they are especially interested in products and media that have a social function and that express their identity, including music, social media, games, books and magazines, sports apparel, movies, concerts, dancing, and partying.

Sexuality: Love, Sex, and the Media

One of the key tasks in developing autonomy during adolescence is to begin to understand and become comfortable with one's sexuality. Sexuality does not suddenly emerge with the onset of puberty, but puberty does mark the first time that young people are both physically able to reproduce and cognitively advanced enough to think about it.[26] It makes sense, then, that puberty marks a time when sexual development is most intense. Unlike sexuality in childhood, sexuality in puberty is closely associated with self-consciousness ("What if he rejects me?") and the ability to think hypothetically ("What's the best way for me to act now?"). For most early adolescents, sexuality is closely associated with falling in love and romance.[27]

For the vast majority of early adolescents, puberty marks the first time that they become interested in having a boyfriend or girlfriend. In these first "puppy love" relationships (typically around twelve or thirteen years of age), sexuality plays little or no role.[28] Instead, couples often hold hands and perhaps kiss. These initial relationships typically do not last more than a few weeks. More than anything, they serve as an identity experiment meant to boost adolescents' social status and, to a lesser extent, provide early "practice" for later sexuality.

Given teens' efforts to develop and understand their sexuality, it makes sense that they look to the media for advice about sexual situations and sexual behaviors. They particularly seem to seek out television and movie content that features sexual scenes or sexual innuendo. For example, in addition to content that combines sarcastic humor with sexuality (for example, the *American Pie* series), teens show increased interest in reality television that places sexuality at the forefront (*The Bachelor*, *Temptation Island*). Moreover, relationships and sexuality figure prominently in most drama series and movies (*Gossip Girls*, *Glee*, *The Vampire Diaries*). This is nothing new, though. In fact, a look at the most popular teen programs as of the 1970s shows that sexuality has long been a key ingredient of such programs.[29]

Although sexuality in television and film has largely remained a staple in teens' media diets, the emergence of digital media has brought about an entirely new way to access sexual content. In fact, a sizable number of teens regularly use the Internet to obtain advice about sex or to discuss moral, emotional, and social issues related to sex.[30] The Internet provides them with a (perceived) safe space, not only to talk about sex with their friends but also to actively look for sex and pornography. For example, our work in the Netherlands has shown that almost 50 percent of thirteen-year-old boys and nearly 20 percent of thirteen-year-old girls report deliberately searching for sex and porn online.[31] Similar estimates have emerged in other industrialized countries.[32] And with the emergence of selfie culture, the Internet seems to supports teens' need for social comparison: nearly 74 percent of teenage boys and 82 percent of girls have looked for sexy or seminude photographs ("sexy selfies") of their friends in the past year.[33]

Online sexual exploration seems to be even more important for certain minority groups, such as homosexual youth. For these groups, online communication can serve as a relatively safe way of exploring sensitive issues such as homosexuality, bisexuality, or transsexuality—sexual identities that are often still subject to taboos. The Internet provides these minority groups with the chance to experiment and prepare for the process of coming out publicly.[34] Homosexual adolescents may indeed benefit from websites such as ItGetsBetter.org and TrevorProject.org.[35] And more recently, we have seen the emergence of special dating apps for homosexual youth and adults (for example, Grindr), although too little is still known about the benefits and drawbacks of these apps.

Late Adolescence

Late adolescence (sixteen to nineteen years old) is the period that follows puberty. The physical changes continue, but they are less noticeable, and their impact on self-concept and self-esteem is milder than during early adolescence. While early and late adolescents share many preferences, they also differ in several important ways. One important cognitive change in late adolescence is the rapid improvement of so-called executive functions, which refer to the cognitive functions needed for effective, efficient, socially adapted behavior. Executive-functioning skills are present during the preschool years, but they continue to improve during late adolescence. In comparison to early adolescents, late adolescents are better able to control their impulses, allowing them to focus and concentrate on tasks longer.

Another important change in late adolescents is their improved ability to grasp the broader context of a problem or decision. Whereas early adolescents struggle to see the bigger picture as they argue and weigh alternatives, late adolescents have less trouble identifying the important facts about a situation and the effects of that situation on other things. Late adolescents also have little trouble putting their ideas into words. Furthermore, along with advancements in executive function, late adolescents develop intuition—something many experts consider necessary for making good decisions. As a result, they are less inclined than their younger counterparts to pursue immediate, dopamine-fueled rewards, and are more likely to start thinking about the future and possible careers.[36] Indeed, starting around sixteen years of age, adolescents' preference for risk taking begins to decline.[37]

Among late adolescents, media preferences are in a transitional state. While they still share many of the same preferences of early adolescents, they also share many of the preferences of young adults. For example, they continue to feel attracted to fast-paced media and still show some interest in television and music targeting teenagers (although this starts to fade). But their understanding of humor is more advanced and mimics that of adults. No longer are their cognitive development and social-emotional development the main predictors of their appreciation of humor; other factors, such as educational level and cultural background, come to play an important role. Late adolescents are able to grasp all forms of adult humor in advertising, public information campaigns, or entertainment, including word play, hints and sexual innuendo, and parody. By the end of adolescence, teens are primarily reading magazines, watching television programs, and buying products meant for adults. Therefore, the best way to reach late adolescents is to address them as the mature people that they are soon becoming.

Too Old for Conflicts, Too Old for Facebook

While peers remain crucial during late adolescence, the relationship between teens and their parents often improves during this time. In late adolescence, teens start to have a bigger say in family decisions. They can persuade their parents by using adult arguments. As a result, their parents come to view them more like fellow adults. While early adolescents also try to secure a more powerful role for themselves in the family, their attempts are often awkward and unsuccessful. They may pester their parents, for example, or go head-to-head with them. By late adolescence, however, the relationship between teenagers and parents has often improved and become more intimate. Parents are more likely to talk to their nearly grown children about adult matters and may also ask them for help and support.

Late adolescents still feel a tremendous need to communicate with peers. By this period, many friendships have developed into full-fledged, intimate, and caring relationships that resemble those between adults. The quality of their friendships becomes increasingly important. It is crucial to late adolescents that their friends understand them and that they can count on one another. Unlike early adolescents, who use the number of friends on a social networking site as an important marker of status, late adolescents are less interested in racking up as many Facebook friends as possible. Now, their friendships help them grasp the meaning of intimacy; they learn to disclose themselves appropriately (not too intimate, but not too distant either). They also come to see that friendship involves give-and-take, and that loyalty and trust are paramount.

By the end of adolescence, teenagers are somewhat less under the sway of cliques and crowds—although there are significant individual differences in this regard. For some youth, cliques continue to play an important role until they are well into their twenties and even beyond. In general, though, peer pressure and cliques are not as intense or influential as they were during puberty. Instead, late adolescents tend to be more focused on communicating with individuals than with their group. Moreover, romantic relationships—and the influence of these relationships on behaviors—begin to take precedence.

There Is a First Time for Everything

During early adolescence, teens move toward autonomy by working to discover their identity, developing intimacy, and beginning to understand their sexuality. This process continues among late adolescents, who are still working on stabilizing their identity and self-esteem.[38] In doing so, they still experience a strong need for introspection, that is, a need to examine their own experiences and emotions. For many teens (particularly girls), this need for introspection leads them to keep a diary or a blog—both of which can be a good channel for analyzing experiences and feelings. Indeed, research has shown that blog writing during adolescence is associated with improved self-esteem.[39]

One of the largest differences between early and late adolescence is associated with sexuality. Whereas early adolescents are beginning to discover their sexuality and perhaps may have their first "puppy love," it is during late adolescence that most teenagers have their first sexual experience with another person.[40] While their level of sexual activity primarily depends on the onset and course of puberty, other factors also play a significant role. For example, low-educated adolescents tend to engage in sexual activity at a younger age than high-educated ones. Religious adolescents, on the other hand, have their first sexual experience at a later age than their nonreligious peers.[41] In all situations, these first sexual relationships are often deeply emotional. Everyone remembers the passion of his or her first love affair. It is the stuff of many song lyrics, and the fodder for many Internet articles on how to get over one's first love.

Conclusion

This chapter explains the important role that cognitive development and social-emotional development play in adolescents' media use and preferences. The broad period of adolescence can be divided into two age groups, early (ages 12–15) and late (ages 16–19) adolescence. We highlighted how the significant changes in brain development, particularly during early adolescence, lead to an increased interest in content that is fast and complex, relies on complex humor, and features riskier content such as extreme sports.

Moreover, we highlighted how adolescents are charged with tackling three social-emotional tasks: developing an identity, learning about intimacy, and discovering their sexuality. As we have shown, these three developmental tasks have major consequences for behavior and preferences in early and late adolescence. For example, they are the reason early adolescents want to communicate constantly with peers, feel a need to belong, and seek information and validation for aspects of their identity from peers or from idols or heroes in the media.

This triple social-emotional developmental challenge also explains why early adolescents spend so much time on social media and with entertainment media. Social media offer young teens ample opportunity to communicate endlessly with peers. In addition, more than ever before, social media provide early adolescents with the opportunity to discover and validate their identity, including their sexual identity. Entertainment media also help them in this respect. Media heroes and idols have long taught adolescents how to behave and how to deal with problematic social situations such as relationships, bullying, and falling in love.

Late adolescents have some of the same preferences as early adolescents, such as a liking for fast-paced entertainment programs, but in other respects they begin to look much more like young adults. Their sense of autonomy and self-control increases considerably, and their media preferences are more mature. They are less concerned with accumulating as many friends as possible, but instead start to focus on the quality of their friendships and romantic relationships. It is a period typically marked by one's first sexual relationship, and it is thus a crucial time for stabilizing one's identity and establishing oneself as an autonomous person. This autonomy means that efforts to reach this audience through traditional "teenage approaches" are often unsuccessful. Instead, in this somewhat transitional period, it becomes increasingly important that media producers treat this audience as the autonomous individuals they are striving to become.

7

MEDIA AND VIOLENCE

> No one is suggesting that video games are the only reason they went out and committed those horrific acts, but was it a tipping point? Was it something that pushed them over the edge? Was it a factor in that? Perhaps. That's a really big deal.
>
> —Jim Steyer, CEO, Common Sense Media, 2012

No topic in the field of communication has been more heavily investigated than media violence and its effects on aggression. Every time a child or teenager committed an act of violence in recent years, the debate about the effects of media violence on aggression flared up again. Can children and teens indeed become aggressive, or even criminal, from seeing violence on television, in movies, or in games? And if so, are some children and teens particularly vulnerable to media violence effects? This chapter reviews the latest findings on the effects of media violence on aggression and criminal behavior. We first discuss key studies that investigated the effects of media violence on aggression. We then discuss the most important theories of why and how media violence may stimulate aggression. Finally, we reflect on how and why some children may be more—and others less—susceptible to media violence effects.

Copycat Crimes

The quotation by Jim Steyer that serves as the chapter epigraph concerns the tragic history of Adam Lanza. In December 2012, Lanza shot and killed twenty schoolchildren and six adults at Sandy Hook Elementary School, in Newtown, Connecticut, and then turned his weapon on himself.

Following these events, some news media suggested that Lanza had used the first-person-shooter game *Combat Arms* to practice "head shots." Lanza's criminal deed was labeled a copycat crime, that is, a crime inspired by a similar crime in the past or in media.

Copycat crimes have a history as long as the media. It is said that the publication in 1774 of Goethe's *The Sorrows of Young Werther*, in which unrequited love drives the main character, Werther, to kill himself, led to a surge in suicides among readers. Newspaper reports in 1888 about the horrific murders of London prostitutes by the mysterious serial killer Jack the Ripper inspired a string of copycat crimes.

In more recent decades, a number of alleged copycat crimes committed by youth were said to have been inspired by violent films or games. In 1993, two ten-year-olds from Liverpool murdered two-year-old James Bulger in broad daylight. The movie *Child Play 3* was thought to have inspired their horrendous deed. In 1999, the world was shocked by the shootings at Columbine High School in Littleton, Colorado. Two boys, ages seventeen and eighteen, murdered twelve fellow students and a teacher. Their crime was said to have been inspired by the computer game *Doom*.

In 2002, a nineteen-year-old at a high school in Erfurt, Germany, shot and killed fourteen teachers, two students, a police officer, and himself. The first-person-shooter game *Counter-Strike* was held responsible for his crime. The 2007 shooting spree on the Virginia Tech campus by Seung-Hui Cho, a twenty-three-year-old student, was ascribed to this game, too. In the Netherlands, Tristan van der Vlis killed himself in 2011 after carrying out an assault attack at a shopping mall. Some newspapers reported that a game he was fond of playing, *Call of Duty: Modern Warfare 2*, showed a gruesome resemblance to the bloodbath he caused.

Are Copycat Crimes Evidence of Media Effects?

In each of these horrific incidents, commentators suggested a link between violence in the media and the extreme behavior of the young perpetrators. Each of them either frequently viewed horror movies or played violent games, and each was said to have been inspired by the violence depicted in these films or games. Both suggestions are plausible. Many youth do indeed watch horror movies and play violent games. But did media violence actually cause these adolescents to commit murder?

To establish causality between media use and crime, the circumstances must meet at least two criteria. The first is that the person's exposure to media violence must predate his or her criminal behavior. The second is that all other possible explanations for that behavior can be excluded. The incidents described above appear to meet the first criterion: the perpetrators had all played the game or watched the movie before they committed their horrific crimes. That said, in each case, we cannot exclude significant alternative explanations for their behaviors. The boys who murdered James Bulger, for example, were problem children who had been severely neglected. One boy's father was extremely violent. Both boys and their siblings spent their days and nights on the street and hardly ever attended school.

The other perpetrators were either loners or had grown up in unusual and distressing circumstances. For example, Cho, the Virginia Tech shooter, had an anxiety disorder and was completely alienated from his family and friends. Personal circumstances like these are important alternative explanatory factors to consider. In fact, criminal behavior is usually the result of a complex combination of factors, including, for example, genetic predisposition, neglect, and exposure to violence in early childhood.[1]

All in all, although it is plausible that media violence inspired the perpetrators, we cannot exclude alternative explanations for any of these crimes. That is why these incidents do not prove that exposure to media violence causes criminal behavior. In addition, these incidents underscore why it is difficult to conclude whether and when media violence leads to deleterious outcomes. Exposure to media violence among delinquent youth often co-occurs with a multitude of other risk factors, whose effects are incredibly challenging to disentangle.

Research on Media Violence and Aggression

In the case of copycat crimes, it is typically suggested that there is a relationship between media violence and criminally violent behavior. Criminally violent behavior should not be confused with aggression or aggressive behavior. The lion's share of research on the effects of media violence has focused on aggression or aggressive behavior. "Aggression" in these studies refers to aggressive thoughts and feelings, for example, the desire to punch someone or to take revenge. "Aggressive behavior" refers to a display of physical or verbal behavior (for example, fighting, cursing, or bullying) meant to hurt someone. By all estimates, more than six hundred studies have so far been published concerning the effect of media violence on aggression or aggressive behavior.[2]

By contrast, there have been approximately thirty studies of the effects of media violence on criminally violent behavior.[3] While criminally violent behavior is illegal behavior, and therefore punishable by law, aggressive behavior is not illegal—unless it becomes extreme. Thus, the boundary between aggressive behavior and criminally violent behavior is not always clear. Criminologists define criminally violent behavior as behavior "that transcends normal aggression and causes physical harm to others in a manner that is designated as illegal in the criminal code."[4]

Even fewer studies have looked at the effects of media violence on indirect aggression. Indirect aggression (also called social or relational aggression) involves aggression in which harm is delivered covertly, "behind the back." Examples of indirect aggression include spreading rumors, damaging possessions, and trying to get others to exclude a peer from a social group. It has been estimated that teen television entertainment commonly depicts more indirect than direct aggression.[5] And while interest in the effects of viewing dramatized indirect aggression has increased rapidly in recent years, to date only a handful of studies have investigated the effects of such content on teens' indirect aggression.[6]

In sum, most research on the effects of media violence has focused on direct aggressive behavior. Thus, the following discussion largely focuses on the empirical evidence regarding the link between media violence exposure and direct aggressive behavior. These studies are broadly divided into three categories: experiments, correlational studies, and meta-analyses. Where relevant, we consider criminal behavior and indirect aggressive behavior as well.

Laboratory and Field Experiments

There are two types of experiments, laboratory experiments and field experiments. In a typical laboratory experiment concerning the influence of media violence on aggression, half the study participants, the experimental group, watch a violent movie or play a violent game. The other half, the control group, watch a neutral film or play a neutral game (or neither) in the same setting. The researchers then measure aggression by observing the subjects, for example, during their play with dolls or other children. Sometimes researchers use other measurement instruments, for example, a knob or a button that allows the subjects to send a loud blast of noise to someone wearing headphones. After the test, the researchers determine whether the experimental group displayed more aggression than the control group, which most often is the case.[7]

In laboratory experiments, participants are assigned randomly to the experimental and control groups. Random assignment is used to ensure that there are no a priori differences between the groups, for example, in the extent to which participants are already aggressive. If researchers detect a difference between the groups, that difference can be ascribed only to the effect of media violence. In other words, laboratory experiments have a high degree of internal validity (that is, the ability to establish a causal relationship). The disadvantage, however, of laboratory experiments is that they take place in an artificial environment, and thus lack external validity (the ability to generalize to settings typical of everyday life). For example, delivering a loud blast of noise is certainly not a "standard" form of aggression. Researchers thus can never guarantee that their results will be valid in real-life circumstances.

This problem of external validity can be addressed by the second type of experiment, the field experiment or quasi-experiment. Field researchers often work with existing groups in their own environments, for example, with pupils at a school. A good example of a field experiment was one conducted by Jacques-Philippe Leyens and colleagues.[8] In this study, children living at an institution for juvenile delinquents were shown violent movies every evening for a week while the control group watched neutral movies. Afterward, the researchers found that the children who had watched the violent films were more aggressive than those who had seen the neutral movies. Field experiments are conducted in the subjects' natural environment, giving the results a relatively high degree of external validity. Yet they also have an insurmountable weakness in relation to the effect of media violence: they can never lead to definitive conclusions about causality. It is impossible to say that only the violent movie or game caused the experimental group's aggression; some other factor may have played a role, such as an unforeseen incident of aggression in the group. Field experiments thus have a lower degree of internal validity.

Correlational Research: The Chicken-or-Egg Dilemma

Correlational (also called cross-sectional correlational) studies assume that if media violence stimulates aggression, then children exposed to high levels of media violence will be more aggressive than those who are not. In correlational studies, researchers typically collect data in schools or in families. They ask students or family members a series of questions about the number of violent movies that children see or the number of violent games they play. They also look at how aggressively a child behaves. They do this by observing the child, by asking parents or teachers to evaluate the child's aggression, or by having children fill out questionnaires. The majority of correlational studies indicate that children who are frequently exposed to violent media are somewhat more aggressive than children who are less frequently exposed.[9] The external validity of correlational studies is similar to that of field experiments, but their internal validity is minimal. Correlational studies can establish a relationship between media violence and aggressive behavior, but they cannot demonstrate that media violence causes aggressive behavior. After all, they cannot solve the "chicken-or-egg" dilemma: it is impossible to determine which came first—media violence or aggressive behavior.

Researchers can help compensate for the chicken-or-egg dilemma by conducting causal-correlational, or longitudinal, research. Such research again involves evaluating children's media use and aggressive behavior, but the measurements are conducted at two or more time points. In doing so, researchers can better establish whether media violence exposure may be a precursor to or a consequence of aggressive behavior. While the internal validity of these designs is certainly stronger than that of cross-sectional correlational studies, it remains possible that unmeasured third variables (for example, a child's temperament, peer and family circumstances) may explain potential associations between media violence and aggression.

Leonard Eron and colleagues were the first to investigate the influence of television violence and aggressive behavior in causal-correlational research.[10] They observed a group of eight-year-olds to determine how much they liked watching violence on television and how aggressive they were. Ten years later, they observed the same subjects as eighteen-year-olds. They showed that watching violent movies at the age of eight predicted increased aggressive behavior at age eighteen. There was no suggestion of a reverse correlation; that is, aggressive behavior at age eight did not lead the subjects to watch more violent television programs at eighteen. Some later studies, however, did reveal a reciprocal relationship between media violence and aggressive behavior. These studies showed that media violence influences aggressive behavior, but that aggressive behavior has just as much influence on youth's preference for media violence.[11]

Meta-Analyses

Meta-analyses are studies that use statistical techniques to summarize the results of numerous experimental and correlational studies. Meta-analyses involve entering the statistical effect sizes produced in individual empirical studies into a new database. This database permits researchers to determine an average effect size based on the effect sizes of the studies included in the meta-analysis. Provided they are performed properly, meta-analyses typically gain more respect from the research community than individual empirical studies because they can lead to refinements in scientific theories, show which questions have and have not been addressed in research, and identify new directions for study.[12]

Starting in the 1990s, researchers carried out several meta-analyses on the influence of television, movie, and gaming violence on aggressive behavior. All have shown that media violence consumption is associated with aggressive behavior among youth. The first large-scale meta-analysis, carried out by Haejung Paik and George Comstock, encompassed 217 empirical studies. The researchers found a correlation of $r = .31$ between watching violent movies or television shows and aggressive behavior.[13] Five meta-analyses published in the new millennium concerning the effects of video games on aggressive behavior have similarly shown a positive correlation between violent games and aggressive behavior, with effect sizes ranging from $r = .08$ to $r = .20$.[14] Statisticians consider statistical effects of this size to be small to moderate. The studies on the effects of viewing indirect aggression in the media are still too scarce to justify a meta-analysis, but the empirical studies that have been conducted thus far suggest that viewing indirect aggression can also stimulate both direct and indirect aggression.[15]

Two meta-analyses have studied the correlation between media violence and criminally violent behavior. In Paik and Comstock's meta-analysis, the correlation between media violence and criminally violent behavior was smaller than that between media violence and aggressive behavior ($r = .06$ based on the correlational studies). This result was replicated in a meta-analysis conducted by Joanne Savage and Christina Yancey in 2008.[16] In their study, the meta-analytical correlations between media violence and criminally violent behavior ranged from $r = .06$ in experiments to $r = .12$ in longitudinal research. That said, according to Savage and Yancey, the quality of the approximately thirty included studies varied significantly—which undermined the reliability of their meta-analysis. They concluded that the relationship between media violence and criminally violent behavior has yet to be established, but that this does not mean that such a relationship does not exist. More research is required into this effect, and a clear distinction needs to be made between criminal violence and other aggressive behaviors.

Minor Effects, Major Consequences

Perhaps the largest issue in the field of media violence effects is not whether there is a small-to-moderate effect of media violence on subsequent aggression, but whether this effect is meaningful. A statistically small-to-moderate effect, as found in the existing meta-analyses, can easily lead to misunderstandings in society. That is why it is important to know what such effects mean. A statistically small-to-moderate effect means that there is a small-to-moderate chance of media violence exposure causing aggressive behavior. Based on earlier research, we estimate that 5–10 percent of children are vulnerable to depictions of violence in media.[17] Media violence can have other effects, for example, on fear, hyperactivity, creativity, empathy, or impulsive behavior. These effects are not included in our estimated percentages. The question then becomes one of interpretation: is 5–10 percent of children a sufficiently large fraction of all children to warrant concern and potential public policy changes?

A large body of scholars would argue yes—5–10 percent of the population is large enough to warrant concern, certainly when one considers, for example, that 5 percent of American youth (those younger than nineteen) is roughly equivalent to four million American youth who may be affected by media violence. Or similarly, that 10 percent of youth in the UK is roughly equivalent to 1.5 million youth who may act aggressively as a result of media violence.[18] These scholars further posit that the effects of media violence are cumulative, and when one considers the risks associated with media violence exposure, societal efforts to mitigate these effects are warranted. On the other hand, there are scholars who argue that these estimates are conflated with other risk factors (for example, an aggressive temperament or harsh familial environments).[19] These researchers demonstrate that when holding other risk factors constant, the effect of media violence on aggression is nearly nonexistent. They thus argue that efforts to reduce media violence exposure are misdirected and that, instead, societal efforts should target the "true" risk factors of aggression.

In our own research on media violence and aggression, we interpret the small-to-moderate effect sizes that we usually find for what they are: an aggregate indicator of the relationship between media violence and aggression. We believe that a small-to-moderate statistical effect size may represent two different groups of youth: one that may be strongly influenced by media violence, and another that may be less affected or unaffected. While the group that is strongly influenced is small, it is a minority that we must take seriously; after all, in absolute terms, we could be talking about millions of children worldwide. Simultaneously, we must recognize that most youth are probably unaffected or minimally affected by media violence. It is our role as scholars to provide parents and practitioners with balanced information about media violence effects as well as to counter the moral-panic rhetoric that often accompanies real-world violent tragedies. It is therefore vital for future researchers to investigate which dispositional, developmental, and environmental factors may enhance or reduce children's vulnerability to media violence effects.

Theories: Why Media Violence Can Lead to Aggression

When triangulating the findings from the majority of existing experimental, correlational, and meta-analytic studies, it becomes clear that there exists—at a minimum—a small relationship between media violence exposure and subsequent direct aggression. The question, however, is why this relationship exists. The scientific literature offers several theories to explain the effects of media violence. We discuss five of these theories below. Some of them predominantly explain the short-term effects of media violence (for example, priming and arousal theories), others the longer term (cognitive script and desensitization theories), and yet others both (social cognitive theory).

Social Cognitive Theory

In chapter 3, we introduced Albert Bandura's social cognitive theory. This theory, with its roots in behaviorism and (later) cognitive psychology, posits that children learn behavior in two ways: by direct experience and by observing others. According to this theory, aggressive behavior, like other behavior, is learned. Young children try out behaviors in their social environment and learn which ones are considered appropriate and which are not. They learn that they can bang away with a hammer in the backyard, but that they are not to hit their sibling with that same hammer. By being punished for undesirable (that is, aggressive) behaviors such as hitting their sibling, as well as by being rewarded for desirable behaviors, they learn what is and is not acceptable and how to control their impulses.

Children can also learn aggressive behavior by observing other people's behavior and its consequences. In observational learning of this kind, children do not themselves experience reward or punishment, but watch what happens to others. For example, imagine that a child sees his older brother kick the family dog. When the children's father punishes the brother, the child learns that it is wrong to kick dogs. A different child sees his brother kick the family dog while his friends around him laugh at the yelping dog; that child will acquire a very different set of values. It is not difficult to predict which of the two children is more likely to kick a dog later in life. Every child imitates the role models around him or her. For children, these role models can be found in the family, in their broader social environment, and in the media.

Social cognitive theory (previously known as social learning theory) was developed in the 1960s. Bandura developed and tested his theory in the now-classic "Bobo doll" experiments (see figure 7.1). In one of these experiments, Bandura had a group of preschool-age children watch a movie showing an adult punching and kicking a clownish Bobo doll. As the figure shows, Bobo dolls are life-size plastic dolls with a rounded bottom. They

Figure 7.1. The first experiments on the effects of media violence: original pictures of Albert Bandura's Bobo doll experiments. (Photo courtesy Albert Bandura)

are bottom-weighted so that they always bounce back upright after being knocked down. Bandura divided the preschoolers into three groups. The first group saw the adult male in the movie being rewarded for his aggressive deeds. He was told that he was a "strong champion" and was rewarded with candy and soda. The second group saw the man being punished by being smacked with a rolled-up magazine and told reprovingly "Hey there, you big bully. You quit picking on that clown. I won't tolerate it." In the movie shown to the third group, the man was neither punished nor rewarded for his aggressive behavior. Afterward, all children were allowed to play with the Bobo doll featured in the movie. The children in the rewarded condition imitated more aggressive acts than the children who had seen the man being punished and those who had seen the man that experienced no consequences.[20]

The Bobo experiments, and other comparable studies, tried to explain the process of observational learning, and the importance of whether aggressive behavior in the media is rewarded or punished. Media often portray physical aggression as the only way to resolve problems between people: the "good" guys feel little hesitation about hurting or killing the bad guys, and they are often richly rewarded for their behavior. By depicting aggressive behavior in combination with rewards, social cognitive theory argues that children are more likely to imitate the aggressive behavior they have seen. Furthermore, beyond imitation, Bandura argues that consistent exposure to such content can influence children's opinions about aggression and shape long-term lessons about the appropriateness of aggression.

Of course, not all children who view rewarded media violence will become aggressive. What might explain individual differences in susceptibility to this type of content? In the 1980s, Bandura updated his theory to place a greater emphasis on youth's cognitive and self-regulatory processes. While still focusing on the importance of rewarded behaviors, the updated version of social cognitive theory suggests that children's individual traits (for example, their interest in the content of media, their general level of aggression) and social environment (for example, the attitude toward aggression in the child's home and peer environment) play an equally crucial role in predicting whether a child is likely to imitate rewarded media violence.[21]

Desensitization Theory

While social cognitive theory helps explain both short- and long-term effects of media violence, desensitization theory focuses primarily on the long-term effects of media violence on aggressive behavior. According to desensitization theory, youth who are routinely exposed to media violence become habituated to it, and this eventually lowers their inhibitions to displaying aggressive behavior. In other words, the theory assumes that—over time—youth become used to the constant portrayal of violent incidents in the media. As a result, they find the violent content less ethically problematic. And over time, they become indifferent to violence in their everyday surroundings—for example, feeling less upset when other youth fight in the schoolyard, and feeling less inhibited about acting aggressively.[22]

Indeed, there is evidence to suggest that media violence can dull the responses of children and adults to milder forms of violence (for example, verbal abuse) and more serious ones such as murder. In a study by Daniel Linz and colleagues, a group of young men were shown sexually violent motion pictures for five days in succession. After each showing, the researchers recorded the men's emotional reactions. The more movies the young men saw, the less intense their emotional response became. They no longer found the movies as objectionable as in the beginning; they also did not find them as violent as they did at first, or as insulting to women.[23]

More recently, functional magnetic resonance imaging (fMRI) research has provided evidence to support desensitization. Researchers observed the brain function of boys ages 14–17 in an fMRI scanner while they watched violent film clips. An fMRI scan measures brain activity while a person is performing a task, for example, watching a violent movie. More specifically, it measures oxygen-rich and oxygen-poor blood in different areas of the brain; brighter areas on the images indicate increased oxygen. The argument is that active areas of the brain need more oxygen than less active areas. While the boys viewed the violent film clips, the researchers detected increased oxygen (that is, increased activity) in the brain area assumed to be involved in emotional responses. Interestingly, however, the researchers also found that as the boys saw more violent film clips, the activation diminished. According to the researchers, this was suggestive of a desensitization effect.[24]

Cognitive Script Theory

Like desensitization theory, cognitive script theory focuses squarely on the long-term effects of media violence. The theory focuses on cognitive scripts, defined as mental structures and sequences for routine activities. By three years of age, children have acquired a large number of scripts. For example, they have scripts to describe how they get ready for bed at night (brush teeth, put on pajamas, read a story, turn off bedroom lights, turn on nightlight) or what happens on someone's birthday (birthday cake with candles, singing, presents). Although many activities in life vary from occasion to occasion, their basic structure often remains the same. Our familiarity with the basic structure of activities or events is known as a script.

Our cognitive scripts are shaped by everyday events, but also by media experiences. How can media violence influence our scripts? In entertainment media, characters frequently resolve their interpersonal problems by resorting to aggression. Cognitive script theory argues that, over time, consistent exposure to this routine behavior will create an aggressive script in young media users. In other words, for children who consistently view media content that shows aggression to be a means to solving interpersonal problems, over time their own cognitive scripts will indicate that aggression is a common way to solve problems, and these children therefore become more likely to use aggression to solve problems in their everyday life. Cognitive script theory assumes that it takes some time for scripts to form, and so it predicts that aggressive, media-induced scripts that arise in early childhood will stimulate aggressive behavior later in life.[25]

To date, several studies have been guided by cognitive script theory and have supported predictions arising from it—including a now-classic longitudinal study by Rowell Huesmann and colleagues that examined television violence exposure at ages six and ten and adult aggressive behavior fifteen years later. Using both archival and interview data, the researchers demonstrated a longitudinal association between media violence and later aggression—which was particularly pronounced for those viewers who identified with the television characters and perceived the content to be realistic.[26]

Priming Theory

Like cognitive script theory, priming theory borrows heavily from cognitive constructs such as scripts and schemata. Schemata are, like scripts, clusters of related concepts in our brains that underpin how we interpret experiences. Scripts consist of one or more schemata associated with a specific routine activity or event. But rather than focusing on long-term effects, priming theory attempts to explain the short-term effects of media violence exposure. Priming theory assumes that the human brain consists of associative networks. Each network is made up of a multitude of nodes (for example, thoughts, ideas, emotions, actions) that are stored in our memory. When an external stimulus (such as a movie scene) stimulates a certain node in an associative network, it may also prime (activate) many other conceptually related nodes.

Leonard Berkowitz posits that media violence exposure may activate certain aggressive nodes such as feelings of pain or frustration, which in turn may activate related nodes such as anger, revenge, and combativeness. In Berkowitz's view, the aggressive nodes evoked by the media need not be conceptually identical to the observed media content. Because of the brain's associative network, observed media content can engender a complex set of associations consisting of aggressive ideas, emotions, and actions.[27] According to priming theorists, exposure to violent content primes nodes that have a conceptual relationship to violence, and as a result, aggressive nodes in the brain become temporarily more accessible.

A study by Brad Bushman highlights how priming works. Bushman divided participants into two groups. One group watched a nonviolent film clip, and the other watched a clip from *Karate Kid III*. Afterward, participants were asked to identify whether a set of letters was a real English word or a nonword. Participants were told to press a button as quickly as possible when the letter formed an English word. Half of the English words had aggressive connotations, and the other half did not. Results showed that the participants who watched the *Karate Kid III* clip had faster reaction times to aggressive words than did the students who saw the nonviolent clip, whose reaction times for aggressive words were the same as for nonaggressive words. In other words, participants who saw the violent clip seemed to recognize aggressive words more quickly. According to Bushman, that was because the violent film had made certain violent nodes temporarily more accessible.[28]

Importantly, while priming theorists generally focus on the temporary or short-term effects of media violence, the theory posits that short-term effects can eventually lead to long-term change. Initially, a stimulus in the environment (such as watching *Karate Kid III*) may make an aggressive node temporarily more accessible. This temporary priming, however, can lead to long-lasting effects. Specifically, if certain aggressive nodes are repeatedly primed by a stimulus in our environment, the theory posits that our brain will become increasingly likely to call on these nodes when attempting to understand and interpret media violence. As a result, the aggressive nodes can become chronically accessible, leading to long-term effects of media violence.

Excitation Transfer Theory

Like priming theory, excitation transfer theory attempts to explain the short-term effects of viewing media violence. It assumes that children become physically aroused while watching depictions of violence. This arousal is purely a physical response: increased respiration, elevated heart rate, higher glucose levels, and more active sweat glands. At the most basic level, the theory argues that the physical arousal provoked by a disturbing depiction of violence does not die away as soon as the movie or program ends. Instead, the arousal functions as a sort of energizer of behavior after viewing—serving to intensify behavior after media use.[29] The physical arousal experienced while watching certain types of violent movies may thus cause children to remain agitated afterward, and they will express this agitation in their play and their dealings with other children. Many movies and games combine violence with action, speed, and stirring music. According to excitation transfer theory, children are likely to remain agitated after seeing these movies or playing these games, and as a result, they may play or act aggressively toward others after this media use.

General Aggression Model

Each of the five theories discussed above offers a plausible explanation for how media violence may stimulate aggressive behavior. Unfortunately, we do not know which theory best describes reality. It may be that they are all more or less correct for particular types of media violence and particular types of youth. In 2002, Craig Anderson and Brad Bushman worked to unite these existing theories under a new model—the General Aggression Model (GAM).[30] This model encompasses almost all the aforementioned theories on media violence. Moreover, it identifies individual, environmental, and situational factors that may interact to influence three potential routes to aggression: cognitive (for example, aggressive scripts), affective (hostile feelings), and physiological (increases in heart rate). In doing so, the GAM highlights how we process media violence in our brains, how that processing can lead to aggressive behavior, and who is particularly susceptible to media violence.

Effects Are Neither Universal Nor Uniform

While researchers often talk about media violence as though it is a homogenous entity, the reality is that media violence takes many different forms. A documentary containing violent scenes that is meant to inform viewers cannot be compared with a movie in which a character attacks his enemies with a chainsaw. In other words, it is not difficult to predict that the effects of viewing *Schindler's List* will differ from those of *Terminator Genisys*. Research has shown that five contextual features of media violence increase the likelihood of aggressive behavior. They are summarized in table 7.1.[31]

Table 7.1. Contextual features of media violence that may increase aggression

Contextual Feature	*Effect*
Perpetrators are appealing.	The effects of media violence are heightened if the perpetrators are appealing and invite children or adolescents to identify with them.[a]
Violence is rewarded.	Role models or heroes are often rewarded for their violent acts.[b] When they receive compliments or win the admiration of their beloved, they communicate that violence pays and that it is a successful way of resolving conflicts.[c]
Violence is justified.	The media often depicts violence on the part of the good guys as justified. It is meant to help or protect someone, or to save the world. Children are much less perturbed by justified violence than unjustified, senseless violence.[d] It is justified violence, in particular, that increases aggression.
Violence has no consequences.	The consequences of violence (pain, wounds) are rarely depicted in children's television shows.[b] These portrayals of violence increase aggression because they cause children or adolescents to believe that they do not need to take violence seriously.
Violence is arousing.	Media violence that leads to physical arousal stimulates aggression.[e] When violence is combined with action and stirring music, young children in particular may become agitated and display aggressive behavior afterward.

Source: [a] Haejung Paik and George Comstock, "The Effects of Television Violence on Antisocial Behavior: A Meta-Analysis," *Communication Research* 21, no. 4 (1994).

[b] Barbara J. Wilson et al., "Violence in Television Programming Overall," in *National Television Violence Study 2,* ed. Center for Communication and Social Policy (Thousand Oaks, Calif.: Sage, 1998).

[c] Albert Bandura, *Social Foundations of Thought and Action: A Social Cognitive Theory* (Englewood Cliffs, N.J.: Prentice-Hall, 1986).

[d] Marina Krcmar and Patti M. Valkenburg, "A Scale to Assess Children's Moral Interpretations of Justified and Unjustified Violence and Its Relationship to Television Viewing," *Communication Research* 26, no. 5 (1999).

[e] Craig A. Anderson et al., "Violent Video Game Effects on Aggression, Empathy, and Prosocial Behavior in Eastern and Western Countries: A Meta-Analytic Review," *Psychological Bulletin* 136, no. 2 (2010).

Developmental, Dispositional, and Social Vulnerability

While these contextual features of media violence are important, it is also important to remember that just as media violence is not homogenous, neither is the audience. It is reasonable to expect, for example, that children growing up in highly violent homes or in violent neighborhoods may experience media violence differently from peers growing up in safer homes or communities. In fact, research has shown that three global factors can increase or decrease a relationship between media violence and aggression, namely, developmental factors (for example, age or cognitive development), dispositional factors (an aggressive temperament), and social factors (an aggressive social environment).

Research suggests that media violence seems to affect younger children more than older ones, and children under the age of seven are the most vulnerable.[32] One reason for this is that younger children interpret violence in animated movies and cartoons just as seriously as realistic media violence. They cannot comfort themselves with the thought that what they are witnessing is imaginary, and this inability prevents them from distancing themselves from what they see. Another reason is that younger children have a harder time than older ones in regulating their emotional and physical arousal. They quickly experience arousal while watching action-packed cartoons and movies, which helps explain why media violence effects are particularly pronounced in this age group (see also chapters 4 and 5).

Research has also shown that boys are more affected by media violence than girls. Most researchers believe this is because boys are more interested in media violence than girls, thus increasing the likelihood of their being influenced by it.[33] Research also indicates that youth who have an aggressive temperament and a heightened need for sensation are more vulnerable to negative effects of media violence. Violent media content more often aligns with the dispositions of these youth, and as a result of this congruity, their processing of violent content is more fluid and aesthetically pleasurable—which in turn may lead to amplified media effects.[34]

Finally, while development and disposition are crucial factors to consider when studying media violence effects, the social setting in which youth develop is just as important. In particular, researchers have found that when children or adolescents see things in the media that resemble their everyday lives, they are especially susceptible to media effects (often referred to as a resonance effect).[35] In the case of media violence, youth who live in a social environment that rejects violence may well learn aggressive behavior from the media. But because their environment imposes severe sanctions on aggression, they will not be inclined to put what they have learned into practice. Alternatively, for youth living in an environment where violence is treated as an acceptable behavior, it becomes much more likely that they will accept the messages contained in violent media. For example, our own research has demonstrated that media violence had a significant effect only on teens growing up in high-conflict families.[36] Similarly, other researchers have shown that children who are confronted by violence in their daily life, for example, in the form of bullying, are more vulnerable to the effects of media violence on aggression than are their peers whose lives are less violent.[37]

Conclusion

Despite decades of investigation, researchers are still asking questions about the influence of media violence on youth. In recent years, there has been more recognition that not all media violence leads to aggressive behavior. Scholars increasingly are asking how the context of aggression in the media (for example, whether it is justified or rewarded) influences effects, and how and when viewing indirect aggression (spreading rumors, trying to get others to dislike a peer) leads to effects. As the field continues to progress in sophistication, we hope to see increased efforts to understand the antecedents and multiple consequences of different types of violent media exposure. It is only through such work that we can refine our theories and develop better predictions about how, for whom, and why media violence effects occur.

It would be convenient to offer a simple yes-no answer to the question whether media violence leads to particular types of aggression, but this chapter has demonstrated that such an easy answer does not exist. Multiple meta-analyses demonstrate that, in general, media violence has a statistically small-to-moderate effect on subsequent direct aggressive behavior, an effect particularly pronounced among younger children, boys, children with an aggressive temperament, children with an increased need for sensation, and children that develop in harsh homes or peer environments. In other words, not all children who consume violent media content will experience increased aggression—either immediately or in the long term.

Some scholars argue that these effects are too small to be important and that rather than focusing on media violence as a predictor of aggression, we should focus on risk factors with more robust associations with aggression. We, however, believe it is equally important to identify the effect of media violence—particularly by identifying which youth are most vulnerable to media violence. With a growing array of movies, TV shows, and games available, and with digital entertainment becoming increasingly privatized, there is a greater likelihood than ever before that children will be exposed to media violence at an early age. Only if we can understand who is most vulnerable to these effects can we develop adequate initiatives to counteract or prevent this group from experiencing undesirable effects of media violence.

8

MEDIA AND EMOTIONS

> "It's long," said the Knight, "but very, VERY beautiful. Everybody that hears me sing it—either it brings TEARS to their eyes, or else—"
>
> "Or else what?" said Alice, for the Knight had made a sudden pause.
>
> "Or else it doesn't, you know."
>
> —Lewis Carroll, *Through the Looking-Glass* (1871)

We can all remember a time when a movie brought tears to our eyes, when a suspenseful television show made the hairs on our arms stand up, when a terrifying movie replayed itself in a nightmare, when we bent over laughing during a comedy, and when a video game made our heart race as we feverishly tried to defend ourselves from impending death. These and other examples highlight what we know to be true—entertainment media can evoke powerful emotions in youth (as well as adults). In this chapter, we take a look at this emotional pull. How is it that entertainment media can make children and teens fearful, agitated, and even sad—all while they know they are seeing fictional content? And does the experience of emotion differ across childhood, or is it, perhaps, more universal? To answer these and other questions, we review key theories on emotion and discuss the role of child development in the experience of media-induced emotions, using fear as a case study. Finally, we review the tragedy paradox: why do we often enjoy watching horror movies and tearjerkers even though they make us feel afraid or sad?

Why Fiction Evokes Emotions

In recent decades, researchers have grown increasingly interested in children's and teens' emotional responses to media entertainment. On the one hand, this increased interest reflects the fact that beginning in the 1980s, the field of psychology began to pay closer attention to emotions. On the other hand, it reflects the changing entertainment media landscape. Thanks in part to technological developments, entertainment media have become more realistic, dramatic, and shocking. This is true of adult-directed content as well as content that targets children and adolescents. And with this increasingly realistic, dramatic, and shocking content, entertainment media are increasingly able to evoke powerful emotional responses in audiences. The question is why. Although it is easy to see why viewers may experience emotional responses such as fright, joy, or anger when watching nonfictional content (for example news, documentaries), it is a bit more challenging to understand why *fictional* content can similarly evoke intense emotions in youth (as well as adults). After all, this content is not real—so why do users seem to experience it as such? Psychological theories of emotion help us answer this question.

The Law of Apparent Reality

Psychological theories of emotion assume that people's emotional responses to a stimulus depend on the reality status of that stimulus. We immediately feel frightened when we hear a fire alarm, but if the alarm turns out to be false, our fears melt away. If we hear that a loved one is sick, we feel shock and sadness. If the doctor's diagnosis turns out to be incorrect, our sadness is lifted. The intensity of our emotions is related to how real we perceive the threat to be. Nico Frijda incorporated this emotional process into a psychological law that he called the "law of apparent reality."[1] According to this law, emotions are elicited by events that individuals regard as real, and the intensity of their emotions corresponds to the degree to which they experience the events as real.

While the law of apparent reality is plausible, it precludes the notion that people can feel emotions while watching fictional entertainment. Take the example of the science fiction movie *Alien,* in which a man writhes in pain just before a baby monster explodes out of his chest. There is nothing even remotely realistic about the scene. Nevertheless, it rouses strong fear responses in viewers. Why do audiences not respond to such fictional depictions as they would to a false fire alarm? In a follow-up to his initial theory, Frijda suggested that viewers see entertainment media depictions as real events that take place in an imaginary world. They fail to spot incongruities and ignore any evidence in the film that the events are not real. They willingly suspend their disbelief. Importantly, however, they can only do this if they perceive the film to be realistic enough to allow it.

Paul Harris has given a more elaborate explanation for "aesthetic emotions," or the emotional responses we have to fictional media content. According to Harris, viewers can consume fiction in two ways. First, they can do so in the default mode, by ignoring any information about the film's reality status that would dampen their emotions. In the default mode, viewers experience emotions not because they believe the content is real, but because—as Frijda had proposed—they leave any information about the content's reality status out of their assessment. Alternatively, Harris suggests that there are some situations in which viewers do assess the reality status of the media content. They may do this consciously, for example, while watching depictions of torture or other scenes that they find too upsetting. To protect themselves, they discount such scenes by telling themselves that the torture is "fake." They may also do so unconsciously—for example, because the acting is unconvincing. In both cases, viewers disengage emotionally from the movie. Whether their emotional distancing is conscious or unconscious, they start to question the reality status of the content, and their corresponding emotional responses diminish.[2]

An Evolutionary Explanation

Although both Frijda and Harris offer plausible explanations about why we experience aesthetic emotions, their ideas have never been tested. In addition, no one has ever examined why audiences frequently consume fictional entertainment in the so-called default mode, in which they experience the emotions. Harris offers an evolutionary explanation for this process. At a certain point in prehistory, human beings developed the capacity to use language. Initially, they probably used language only to communicate about the present, for example, to point out an edible plant or to coordinate a group hunt. With time, humans began to convey information obtained at other times and in other places. They began to rely on eyewitness accounts. Sometimes these accounts concerned emotionally charged events, for example, a woman relating how her son had died in excruciating agony after eating a certain fruit. To understand these accounts, the listeners had to form mental images of the fruit and the serious implications of eating it. They also had to feel the emotions that went along with his horrendous experience.

What if this secondhand information had left our ancestors emotionally numb, and they had responded emotionally only if they themselves had experienced the situation being described to them? Human social relationships would have remained extremely limited, and we would have been incapable of heeding other people's warnings. We would not be able to anticipate the dangers that others point out to us. After all, a warning is meant to scare listeners so that they avoid the same accidents or mistakes. The human ability to form mental images of secondhand information, together with the ability to empathize with others, has had enormous implications for human evolution. Harris believes that our emotional engagement with fiction is a legacy of our use of language and our ability to picture in our minds what someone else is experiencing. Our emotional response to entertainment media is said to be the small "evolutionary price" that we pay for our interest in and emotional receptiveness to eyewitness accounts.[3]

Feeling Fright

Although there are many exemplars of media content evoking different emotions (joy, anger, sadness, etc.) among young audiences, research on the effects of media-induced fear on youth is perhaps some of the most extensive. Frightening media thus serve as an excellent case study for evaluating how emotion-inducing media influence youth. Entertainment media designed to evoke fear have a relatively long history. For example, in the 1950s, comic strips—once highly popular among (male) adolescents—began to include horror elements. This turned out to be a highly lucrative addition. Even the first monochrome television images could not compete with the macabre, brightly colored graphics and blood-soaked tales of horror comics.[4] Shortly thereafter, the film industry started to take note of the popularity of horror content. *The Curse of Frankenstein* in 1957, for example, led to a series of low-budget movies in which the camera no longer panned away from blood and horrific scenes. After several years, the limited success of these films got the attention of renowned filmmakers such as Alfred Hitchcock. In 1960, Hitchcock released *Psycho,* which is generally recognized as a turning point in the production of horror movies. The overwhelming success of *Psycho* led to a flood of imitations, with Hitchcock's prestige legitimizing the arrival of a type of horror movie featuring macabre murders and realistically depicted mutilations.[5]

The emergence of the horror genre brought with it numerous anecdotes of extreme fear experienced by audience members. For example, the summer that *Jaws* was released, some American newspapers reported that beaches were virtually devoid of bathers. They speculated that people stayed away because they were afraid of being ripped apart by a horrendous great white shark. The infamous scene in *Psycho* in which Janet Leigh is murdered in the shower similarly left its mark. The urban legend goes that never before or since have transparent shower curtains been as popular as they were when *Psycho* was playing in movie theaters.

With the increasing development of (often youth-targeted) entertainment media designed to induce fear, it is not surprising that researchers began to ask questions about how media can induce fear among young audiences. Defined as an immediate response to a real or imaginary danger, fear is accompanied by feelings of physiological unease and by physical responses such as sweating and a pounding heart. Fear is a normal, adaptive response that we require for survival. If we did not experience fear, what would stop us from crossing a street without looking for cars or from swimming in waters with a strong riptide? In other words, from a survival perspective, fear can be healthy. But some of the consequences of media-induced fear are arguably less healthy. For example, among youth, consequences of media-induced fear include sleep problems, depression, and posttraumatic stress.[6]

Of course, not all youth experience media-induced fright, nor does all content induce fright in its audience in the same way. In earlier chapters, we noted that child development is one of the strongest predictors of youth's media preferences. Importantly, child development has also been shown to be a strong predictor of the emotions that children and teens experience when consuming media content. Media-induced fear, in particular, is highly related to development. While the youngest children (under two years of age) typically experience little fear from media content and instead tend to fear concrete objects and situations (strangers, having their mother disappear), by the preschool years, media can and do evoke significant fear among their users.[7]

Ages 2–7: Crocodiles under the Bed

Child-targeted entertainment programs such as *The Lion King*, *Frozen*, and *Monsters Inc.* can induce intense fright reactions in young viewers. Several developmental reasons explain these reactions. First, during this period of cognitive development, children learn how to make "if this, then that" predictions. At the same time, their premature cognitive level makes it challenging for them to consistently discern imaginary from real content. This combination of nascent predictive skills and continued trouble in separating fantasy from reality means that virtually everything is possible in the mind of toddlers and preschoolers. In this "everything is possible" world, imaginary threats can become incredibly scary. Fears of "monsters hiding in closets," "crocodiles hiding under beds," and "ghosts in the bathroom" may lead to many sleepless nights for children (and their parents). In fact, the most prevalent fear among toddlers and preschoolers is a fear of large animals (they might eat you up) and insects (they might walk on you). More than 80 percent of five- and six-year-olds indicate that they are afraid of either an animal or an insect. The second most common fear is a fear of monsters. Other common fears include the dark, doctors or dentists, deep water, heights, and everything that looks odd or moves suddenly.[8]

Harris suggested that adults can control their emotional reactions to media content by acknowledging that the content is not real. But because everything is possible to children at this age, they are unable to control their emotional reactions by reassuring themselves that what they are viewing is "just pretend." As a result, a good deal of media content—especially media content that includes upsetting characters (for example, Sid in *Toy Story*) or situations that are impossible in real life (such as the snow monster in *Frozen*)—can be very frightening to young children. In fact, early research suggests that nearly 62 percent of children at this age have experienced fear (sometimes long lasting) after exposure to certain media content.[9]

While the inability to separate fantasy from reality plays a key role in explaining why young viewers often experience media-induced fear, their perceptual boundedness also contributes to this fear induction.[10] As mentioned in chapter 4, children at this age focus much more heavily on perceptual information than on less visible information, such as the role or motives of a character. For example, a character that looks scary but in fact has a positive demeanor will be judged as scary—regardless of his or her psychological attributes. As a result, children at this age often experience extreme fear of scary-looking characters, regardless of their role and motivations. It explains why they fear not only Sid, the legitimately mean character in *Toy Story,* but also Genie, the good-natured genie in Disney's *Aladdin.* Anyone who has seen *Aladdin* knows that Genie is a friendly and helpful character. Nevertheless, he frightens many young children because what strikes them are his grotesque features and how he explodes out of the lamp and spreads across the entire screen. In other words, even if a character has no evil intentions, a scary-looking character can easily frighten a young child.[11]

Finally, characters that demonstrate transformations can also induce fear. As discussed in chapter 4, children at this age struggle with the ability to understand transformations. Transformations are often relied upon in media productions for this young audience. For example, part of the appeal of the superhero genre is that the transformation from human to superhero seems almost magical, and young children often say that the human character is different from his superhero form. Yet researchers have shown that transformations in which a relatively benign character suddenly becomes grotesque looking can be particularly fear inducing for young audiences. This explains why a program like *The Incredible Hulk* (featuring a male scientist who transforms into a large green-skinned creature that helps people) frightens many young children. In fact, this show was found to be so frightening for children that *Mister Rogers' Neighborhood* (an American educational television program) aired a special segment to try and explain the Hulk's motives and costume to young viewers.[12] Indeed, as the following recollection shows, children can experience significant and lasting fear from exposure to characters that transform from pleasant to scary looking.

> When I was 5, I was terrified of *The Incredible Hulk*. That man changing into the Hulk has left a long-lasting impression on me. When in bed at night, I would insist on leaving the door open. I was petrified that the Hulk would come into my room with those white eyes of his. This fear lasted several months. When I see *The Incredible Hulk* on television now, it just cracks me up.
> *Student, female, 21, about* The Incredible Hulk[13]

In all, the existing research on media-induced fear in this audience shows that youngsters can experience fear after viewing and using media. For children between the ages of two and seven, this fear seems to stem from their difficulty in separating reality from fantasy, their perceptually bounded judgments, and their inability to understand transformations. The question then becomes how can we limit these fearful experiences? For media producers, this involves limiting the use of fearful characters and scenes in media content designed for this audience. It also involves informing parents about potentially fearful scenes so that they can implement strategies to offset fear. For example, although cognitive reassurance strategies (telling children, "This content is not real") have been shown to be largely ineffective for this age group, noncognitive reassurance strategies such as fast-forwarding through a particularly frightful scene, holding the child on the lap, or giving the child his or her cuddly toy have been shown to be effective.[14] If parents view content ahead of time or with their young child, the fearful emotions that media content may (unintentionally) induce can be prevented or mitigated.

Ages 7–11: Earthquakes and Burglars

From about age seven, children's fear of imaginary threats declines. In fact, by the time they are eight, their self-reported fear of monsters has declined by nearly half.[15] This decrease does not, however, mean they are not experiencing fear. Indeed, this group of youth reports more media-induced fear than their younger peers. Perhaps not surprisingly, given their increasingly concrete-operational thinking abilities, this age group begins to show fear of getting sick, suffering physical harm, and losing people they love. They now are frightened by concrete, realistic threats such as accidents, kidnappings, burglaries, and bombings. As the following quotation highlights, frightening (adult-directed) content can cause lasting fear.

> I don't remember the title of the movie, but there was a plague of ants in a town. Everything, people and animals, even elephants were being attacked and eaten. First the arms. Then the head and finally the body. Running was futile . . . Afterwards I often dreamed that I was being crushed by something that grew ever larger, just like the group of ants that got bigger and bigger. My aversion to insects may well be because of this film. Even a single ant on the kitchen work top will start my heart pounding.[16]
> *Student, female, 25*

Despite the numerous fearful experiences that youth of this age report, they (perhaps somewhat paradoxically) also report enjoying scary content. For example, the Canadian classic *Are You Afraid of the Dark?*—a television program in which young teens share ghost stories around a campfire—was such a commercial success that it was revived for a second iteration. Similarly, programs such as *The Grim Adventures of Billy and Mandy* and *R. L. Stine's The Haunting Hour* as well as movies such as the Harry Potter franchise have also experienced commercial success with this audience. Given that youth of this age enjoy scary media content, and yet report experiencing (sometimes long-lasting) fear from it, researchers have asked what types of strategies may help offset this fear. Results indicate that cognitive reassurance strategies are reasonably effective, thanks to children's ability to distinguish between reality and fantasy.[17] For example, youth of this age report that telling themselves that the content is not real ("That's not blood, it's just ketchup") as well as talking to their parents about the content are effective ways to reduce media-induced fear.

Ages 12 and Up: Horror Movies, Wars, and the Greenhouse Effect

In chapter 6, we discussed how adolescence is a period in which the brain's dopamine system changes. When adolescents have an exhilarating experience, their dopamine levels (that is, the pleasure reward system of the brain) shoot up higher than the same experience would induce in children and adults.[18] As a result of this change, teens often seek exhilarating experiences—which frequently include horror-based films, television, and games. Indeed, teens are much more interested than their younger peers in horror content, and they experience media-induced fear more positively.[19] Given this preference, it is unsurprising that the commercial market is filled with entertainment content designed to get teens' dopamine system flowing—television programs such as *Supernatural, The Originals,* and *Teen Wolf,* and movies such as *The Gallows* and the *Scream* franchise.

Of course, movies and television programs are not the only way that adolescents find horror. In fact, for (male) teens in particular, the video game market equals or surpasses movies and television programs as a source of frightening content. In general, games are probably even more effective than television or movies at arousing intense emotions. Movie viewers typically have no control over what happens. Their fear and other emotions are evoked mainly by the movie's shock effects and grotesque images, and by their own feelings of empathy with characters. Games are like movies in that respect, but differ in the amount of control that players have over what happens. Unlike movies, games may suddenly put players in control of threatening situations over which they previously had no power. Gamers are therefore in a constant state of heightened vigilance and engagement, since they might have to respond instantly to a threat at any moment.[20]

Many games, including survival horror games such as *Silent Hill* and *Amnesia: The Dark Descent,* make use of the first-person perspective, which means that the player sees everything through the eyes of the controlled game character and explores all the highways and byways in the game as that character. Other horror games use the third-person perspective, in which the player sees the body of the controlled game character. For example, in so-called over-the-shoulder games, the player is positioned directly behind the character. In both types of games, a gamer's experience of intense emotional engagement can be recalled long after gameplay subsides:

> You know, somewhere . . . in the remake of Part 1 for the GameCube console—I remember this so well—there was this corridor with all kinds of mirrors. At a certain point I saw something or someone moving in a mirror off in the distance. I didn't know whether it was a zombie or a curtain blowing in the breeze, but it was something. The shitty thing was that I had to go down

> that corridor to get anywhere, so I sat there giving myself a pep talk, telling myself "Go on, walk down that fucking corridor!" It turned out to be nothing . . . That was a big relief, but three seconds later I heard something crash through a door behind me, and there was this grunting, snorting zombie running at me. I almost died of shock on the spot and had to pause the game to give myself a chance to recover.
> *Student, male, 22, reflecting on playing* Resident Evil[21]

When it comes to the types of content that elicit fear, teens continue to fear many of the same things they did during middle childhood. But with their increased ability to think abstractly, they also fear abstract subjects that are neither visible nor tangible, for example, political issues, economic issues, wars, and nuclear weapons (see also chapter 6). This is well illustrated in a study by Joanne Cantor and colleagues, in which they investigated children's and adolescents' responses to a made-for-TV movie titled *The Day After*. The movie dramatized the fallout of a nuclear attack on a small town in the United States. Results indicated that, after viewing, adolescents were significantly more distressed and fearful than their younger peers.[22] The researchers argued that the movie's emotional impact came mainly from speculation about the possible destruction of Earth, an abstract concept beyond children's comprehension. The ability to perceive danger depends in part on a person's knowledge and experience. Both children and adults find an animal attack frightening because it invokes instinctive human responses to rapid advances, sudden or odd movements, and loud noises. Abstract threats such as a nuclear war, however, require a certain level of abstract thinking, which develops only in adolescence (see also chapter 6).

Why We Like Fears and Tears

There are legitimate concerns associated with children's fright reactions to media (for example, anxiety, sleep challenges). But we know that many children and teens enjoy the thrill of being scared. Many of us can similarly recall enjoying tearjerkers such as *Titanic* and *Atonement*. Although it may seem paradoxical, the need to witness violent, fight-inducing, or tragic events is deeply rooted in human nature. We need only recall the popularity of the gladiator spectacles in Roman amphitheaters two thousand years ago. The gladiators—most of them prisoners or slaves—fought battles to the death against one another or wild animals. In many cases, they were ripped apart by lions or crocodiles while tens of thousands of spectators roared with excitement.

The Tragedy Paradox

Why do we enjoy watching scary or sad events, whether in real life or in the media? There are few things as paradoxical as watching scary or sad events. On the one hand, movies and television programs can scare us badly or make us feel very sad. At the same time, we often enjoy this experience. Indeed, the sadder or scarier a movie or show is, the more some of us enjoy it.[23] Philosophers call this phenomenon the tragedy paradox, which seems to apply to both adults and children. For example, in one of our studies more than 50 percent of children who reported being scared by media content in the past year simultaneously also reported "kind of liking" scary scenes, and nearly 8 percent said they "really like" quivering in front of the screen.[24] This tragedy paradox is particularly common among boys and teens, who more frequently seek sensation in their daily life.[25]

The tragedy paradox has puzzled scholars and philosophers for centuries. Ancient Roman poets such as Lucretius marveled at the tragedy paradox: "Pleasant it is, when over a great sea the winds trouble the waters, to gaze from shore upon another's great tribulation; not because any man's troubles are a delectable joy, but because to perceive you are free of them yourself is pleasant."[26] In other words, Lucretius believed that humans need to experience tragedy because it makes them acutely aware of their own good fortune. Nearly two millennia later, the social psychologist Leon Festinger called this process downward social comparison, theorizing that people can feel better about themselves or their situations by comparing them to a person or situation that is ostensibly "worse off."[27]

Excitation Transfer Theory

Although downward social comparison offers a plausible explanation for the tragedy paradox, Dolf Zillman, a media psychologist, is credited with developing a theoretical account, which he called excitation transfer theory, to help explain the tragedy paradox. Although we first came across this theory in our discussion of media violence effects (chapter 7), excitation transfer theory was developed to explain why people enjoy viewing frightening media content.[28] The theory assumes that every emotion (fear, anger, or pleasure) brings about the same state of physical arousal. While that arousal may vary in intensity, its quality is essentially the same for each emotion. The theory further assumes that when two physically arousing events occur in succession, the arousal caused by the first event may intensify the arousal caused by the second.

What does this have to do with media entertainment? If we view something frightening, for example, a murder scene, then our fear response puts us in a state of physical arousal. Once the frightening scene ends, perhaps because the victim escapes, we feel another emotion, relief. Because we are still in a state of heightened physical arousal when experiencing relief, and because that arousal is transferred to the new emotion, the sense of relief is especially intense. In other words, people who are scared by something in media entertainment will feel an even greater sense of relief and satisfaction when the danger has passed. Excitation transfer theory posits that it is precisely the arousal-intensified sense of relief that makes viewing frightening and violent content strongly appealing.

It's Not Just Chills and Thrills—There Is Meaning Too

Although excitation transfer theory offers some theoretical input about why we enjoy the tears and fears that media can bring, media psychologists have continued to grapple with understanding the role of emotions in viewers' selection and experience of media entertainment. For example, a good deal of research in the 1990s looked at the opportunities offered by media entertainment for escapism and mood management. Proponents of escapism suggested that people sought out entertainment in order to feel happy and help them forget their everyday troubles for a while. Mood management theorists extended this idea, positing that audiences were constantly trying to regulate their mood in order to maximize a good mood (such as pleasure) and minimize a bad one (such as sadness).[29] People who feel exhausted might select comedic entertainment in hopes of improving their mood, while those feeling particularly stressed might opt for more soothing content.

Both escapism and mood management theory have their roots in the principle of hedonism. Hedonism is a doctrine in ethics that posits pleasure as the highest form of well-being. According to the hedonic principle, people have an innate drive to rid themselves of bad moods and to maintain or put themselves in good moods.[30] The hedonic form of well-being involves having pleasurable experiences (for example, watching a funny movie or eating an enjoyable meal). Although this hedonic perspective seems reasonable, when escapism and mood management theory were tested empirically, researchers found that hedonic motives did not explain entertainment choices to the extent that had been imagined. For example, it turned out that sad people were inclined to select tragic as well as humorous movies, and to enjoy them equally.[31] And how could such horror-genre blockbusters as *Paranormal Activity* or *The Exorcist* possibly put viewers in a good mood? Similarly, how could tragic films such as *The Champ* or *Atonement* elevate one's mood? Choosing to watch these films is surely not in line with the hedonic principle that entertainment should be pleasurable.

If audiences do not select media entertainment purely for its thrills and chills or for its hedonic offerings, then why do they enjoy the tears and fears that media offer? The answer, media psychologists now believe, lies in the principle of eudaimonia. Eudaimonia involves the quest to be a better person, to have a meaningful life in accordance with one's values. Rather than view entertainment media as purely fulfilling hedonic needs, entertainment media can also fulfill eudaimonic needs. Scholars suggest that it is better to conceptualize our entertainment choices along both a hedonic and a eudaimonic dimension.[32] Hedonic and eudaimonic forms of well-being are complementary rather than contradictory. Eudaimonic well-being may precede or co-occur with hedonic well-being. After all, people who strive to live meaningful lives are often also better able to enjoy every moment. Both forms of well-being are important to a healthy development.[33]

How can eudaimonic motives explain the appeal of frightening or tragic entertainment? Scholars now believe we are probably drawn to such types of entertainment because they give us ample opportunity to reflect on our lives and to improve our sense of eudaimonic well-being.[34] Our eudaimonic well-being can, in turn, improve our hedonic sense of well-being (enjoyment or pleasure). We do that, first of all, in the manner described by Lucretius two thousand years ago, through downward social comparison. Seeing the misery of others helps us appreciate how well life is treating us. We have not lost any family members, we are healthy, we are not being cheated on by our beloved or threatened by devils or other monsters. Downward social comparison with a fictional character's suffering may increase our feelings of happiness, self-esteem, and enjoyment.

Entertainment media need not rely on downward comparison to cause us to reflect on our current state. Our sense of empathy alone may cause us to feel what victims are feeling and to sympathize with the situation in which they find themselves. This combination of empathy and sympathy can result in an enhanced appreciation of our own relationships, parents, children, and lovers, and in an increased sense of happiness, self-esteem, and enjoyment. Self-reflection during or after frightening or tragic entertainment—whether the result of downward comparison, empathy, or sympathy—is unlikely to increase our sense of hedonic well-being directly, but may do so indirectly, through our eudaimonic well-being.[35]

It seems plausible, then, that audiences select media entertainment to fulfill both hedonic and eudaimonic motives. This explains why they may select comedies that make them laugh, tearjerkers that make them cry, horror stories that make them scream, and thrillers that make them cling to the edge of their seats. On the one hand, the joy experienced while watching comedies, or the intense relief experienced during horror films (via excitation transfer), may fulfill hedonic motives (pleasure seeking). On the other hand, the despair that sad or tragic entertainment can elicit may fulfill the need for meaningfulness. And it is quite possible for media entertainment to fulfill hedonic and eudaimonic needs simultaneously.

What does this mean for children's use of media? Most of the work, to date, has focused on the hedonic and eudaimonic needs of adults.[36] To date, there is no comparative work with younger audiences. Given the developing cognitive and social-emotional skills of children, it seems possible that hedonic needs may be more pronounced at earlier ages, and that during adolescence, as youth increasingly understand their selves and the world around them, eudaimonic needs may take precedence. This is not to suggest that hedonic motives decrease with development, but rather that by adolescence, teens may be expressing need for content that can meet both their hedonic and their eudaimonic needs. Research that evaluates the developmental trajectory of hedonic and eudaimonic needs during childhood and adolescence is an important next step for understanding media and emotion in this field.

Teaching Emotions

Thus far, this chapter has taken the stance that media entertainment can evoke powerful emotions from its audiences and that, paradoxically, these emotions, even the negative ones, serve reciprocally as a strong motive for the use of media entertainment. What our discussion has omitted, however, is the recognition that media can teach (young) audiences emotions as well as evoke them. Consider a scene from the American version of *Sesame Street* featuring Jon Hamm (Don Draper in *Mad Men*) and the monster Murray:

> J: Murray, how are you?
> M: You know what? I'm good, but I'm a little confused.
> J: Okay, what are you confused about?
> M: Well, emotions, Jon. I heard about all of these new emotions and I don't know what they are!
> J: Well, maybe I can help you.
> M: You can help me with emotions?! You know about emotions?!
> J: I know a lot about emotions.
> M: Oh my goodness! Okay, that is awesome! . . . Okay, what does it mean to feel guilty?
> J: Guilty. That's not a very good emotion. You don't want to have that emotion sometimes. . . . It means that you feel sad because you did something that you shouldn't have done.[37]

The scene goes on with Jon Hamm explaining and dramatically acting out guilt, frustration, and amazement. It is hard to imagine a scene such as this one not influencing how its young viewers understand and express emotions.

Although research on whether and how youth may learn emotions from media is relatively limited, the existing work suggests that educational media can help children understand their feelings and how to express them. For example, American school-age children who viewed children's educational programs reported learning how to overcome fears, how to label feelings, and how to use interpersonal skills such as sharing, respect, and loyalty.[38] Other researchers found that a media diet consisting primarily of prosocial children's programming (for example, programming that models nonviolent conflict resolution, empathy, and recognition of emotions) enhanced the social and emotional competence of children ages 3–7.[39] And interviews with teens from seventeen countries have shown that media entertainment can support their emotional competence, that is, their ability to express their inner feelings and to recognize and respond constructively to emotions in themselves and others.[40]

Emotional Relationships with Media Characters and Personalities

A considerable body of work on the relationship between media and emotions has focused on the power of parasocial relationships with media characters or personalities. Parasocial relationships are the illusory, one-sided, emotionally tinged relationships that youth and adults develop with such characters or personalities.[41] Such relationships mimic the development of traditional interpersonal relationships in at least two ways. First, they are most likely to start if media users share specific attributes with the character or personality, such as age, gender, and certain preferences. Second, they are, just like traditional interpersonal relationships, used to fulfill certain fundamental human needs, such as the need for attachment and the need for companionship.

Parasocial relationships have been shown to improve children's learning from media characters. For example, in an experiment by Alexis Lauricella and colleagues, toddlers viewed two characters who separately taught them a seriation task (in this case, nesting cups). One of the characters, Elmo, is iconic in American culture and very popular among this age group. The other, Dodo, was new to the subjects. Children were better able to learn the seriation task from Elmo than from Dodo. But after children were given Dodo toys to play with, their ability to learn from Dodo improved.[42] A later study by this research group showed that children's learning from Dodo was greatest when they showed stronger parasocial relationships with the character.[43]

Parasocial relationships are appealing to adolescents in the throes of identity formation and increasing detachment from parents. Parasocial relationships offer teens valuable information for developing gender role identities and emerging sexual and romantic scripts. The one-sidedness of such relationships may provide adolescents with idealized figures with whom they can identify without the risk of rejection. For example, the development of a crush on a boy band like One Direction may give teenage girls the opportunity to develop their sexual identity in a safe environment that they can control. Moreover, parasocial relationships like these may strengthen adolescents' feelings of being part of a clique or subculture (see chapter 6). For example, when one of the members of One Direction, Zayn Malik, left the band in 2015, millions of teenage girls around the world united through social media to share their sadness and sorrow. The inevitable lack of knowledge about some aspects and traits of the media character or personality may stimulate teens to superimpose idealized attributes onto the character or personality that especially cater to their own developmental needs.[44]

Media and Emotions in the Twenty-First Century

While no one anticipates that television and movies will fade from popularity anytime soon (although how and where content is consumed is changing), the twenty-first century is likely to bring with it new questions when it comes to youth, media, and emotions. Take, for example, video games. The detailed customization of avatars combined with the three-dimensional and virtual-reality possibilities of games can make players feel as though they are truly in the game. Yet at present, it remains unclear how this highly realistic gameplay may influence emotional experiences. If Paul Harris is right that we use the reality status of a media production as a means of dampening our emotional experiences, twenty-first-century games may induce incredibly deep emotional experiences among their users, both young and old. It is no surprise that researchers are now asking more questions about our emotional responses to mediated entities other than television characters. These questions concern emotional responses to avatars in games, responses to the interactive technology we may use in our phones (e.g., Siri), and the increasingly popular use of social robots.

Indeed, one-sided parasocial relationships with mediated characters are becoming increasingly two-sided, and twenty-first-century researchers will likely ask what such relationships mean for the development of emotional competence among youth and adults. Take, for example, Paro. Paro is a Japanese therapeutic robot that resembles a fluffy baby seal. It includes built-in sensors that allow it to respond to someone's touch or speech by moving its eyes and head and making baby-seal-like sounds. It also reacts to its name. Paro has been brightening the lives of elderly dementia patients and autistic children for many years.

A growing body of research suggests that it is not only elderly patients or autistic children who respond to social robots as if they were real. Rather, such responses reflect a universal human tendency to treat computers and robots like people, for example, by being polite and cooperative and by ascribing humor, aggression, gender, and other personal traits to them. Byron Reeves and Clifford Nass described this tendency in the 1990s in their media equation theory.[45] They argued that our interactions with computers and new media are fundamentally social, just like our interactions in real life. These responses and interactions are automatic and inevitable, and they take place despite our being aware that computers are nothing more than cables and processors. A striking depiction of this human tendency is found in the movie *Her* (2014), in which the lonely Theodore Twombly (Joaquin Phoenix) falls in love with Samantha (Scarlett Johansson), an intelligent computer operating system personified by a female voice.

If the media equation theory is valid for computers and new media, it is very likely that we also ascribe human traits to social robots, which are three-dimensional and tangible. And in fact, early research supports this premise. In one study, young adults were given ten minutes to play with Pleo, a small (50 × 20 cm) rubber dinosaur robot (see figure 8.1). Like Paro, Pleo displays happiness when petted and emits sounds that presumably resemble those of a baby dinosaur. He even begins to cry if he is placed in a dark box. After ten minutes of play, half the participants watched a video in which a whimpering Pleo was tortured (beaten, kicked), while the remaining half saw a clip in which Pleo was treated kindly (petted, fed).

The participants who watched the torture clip displayed more physiological arousal and experienced more negative emotions, and more empathy

Figure 8.1. If we see someone hurt Pleo the robot dinosaur, our brain responds as if a human were being hurt. (John B. Carnett/Getty Images)

toward Pleo, than the subjects who viewed the clip in which Pleo received kind treatment.[46] In a follow-up to this study, the researchers investigated the extent to which such strong responses to Pleo's torture could be observed in fMRI scans. They also compared the responses of those who saw Pleo's torture to the responses of participants viewing a clip of a person being tortured in the same way. The viewers of both clips displayed similar activation patterns in their limbic system, a set of brain structures that support emotions, empathy, and other functions. This follow-up study, one of the first of its kind, suggests that our tendency to react emotionally to fictional characters may indeed be hardwired in our brains.[47]

Conclusion

Media are designed, in part, to evoke emotions from their audiences. For children and adolescents, these emotional responses can be intense and long lasting. Responses to violent and fright-inducing entertainment, for example, can continue to elicit stress for years afterward. And while cognitive strategies can help offset these problematic consequences, these strategies tend to be ineffective for younger children, who struggle with separating fantasy from reality. Moreover, all types of reassurance strategies are challenged by the inherent appeal of these same media. Through the process of excitation transfer, media entertainment that can frighten or upset its users can also bring about intense feelings of relief—thereby fulfilling hedonic (pleasure-seeking) and eudaimonic needs.

Should we be concerned? Yes and no. On the one hand, frightening and tragic media entertainment may lead to problematic outcomes for youth, and certainly those who are developmentally unprepared for it. Yet, the same types of media entertainment can provide children with an important stepping-stone for identity development and the development of emotional competence. The key to balancing the negative and positive consequences of emotionally tinged media entertainment likely involves merging developmentally appropriate media content with developmentally appropriate intervention strategies. Helping youth select entertainment that they are able to process, and teaching them to use strategies to offset negative consequences, will better equip them to use entertainment media as an effective channel for identity development and the development of emotional competence.

9

ADVERTISING AND COMMERCIALISM

> So the philosophy becomes cradle to grave: Let's get to them early. Let's get to them often. Let's get to them as many places as we can get them. Not just to sell them products and services, but to turn them into lifelong consumers.
>
> —Enola Aird

As the epigraph shows, beginning at very young ages, children are considered an important consumer market. But why? In this chapter, we discuss why youth are commercially interesting and why marketing seems to be targeting children at ever-younger ages. In particular, we show how children represent three markets—a primary market, a market of influencers, and a future market—and discuss the implications of being a threefold market for children's socialization as consumers. How do brand awareness and brand loyalty develop in early childhood? How does children's development influence their consumer behavior? Following this, we evaluate whether advertising is effective among these young consumers. To what extent does the commercial environment that surrounds youth influence them? We contextualize these questions by highlighting what the youth market looks like today, noting sophisticated digital developments and discussing efforts to counter the potential negative consequences of advertising.

Children as Consumers

Youth have become an increasingly important commercial target group in recent decades. While marketers in the 1990s were interested in learning how to reach children as young as five, today they try to reach even younger audiences. Why has this cradle-to-grave approach become a mantra in marketing circles? Why are youth so commercially interesting? The most likely explanation is that marketers have realized that rather than representing one market, youth simultaneously represent three markets: a primary market, a market of influencers, and a future market.

Children as a Primary Market

To begin with, children are—like adults—a primary market, a more or less distinct customer group interested in and able to afford specific products. More than ever before, children have ample discretionary money available to them. For example, more than 60 percent of American youth receive an allowance (typically beginning at eight years of age), and the amount of their allowances increases through primary school and high school.[1] Although specific amounts vary significantly across countries, nearly half of all children receive money for making good grades in school or for doing household chores (for example, walking the dog or washing the family car). By adolescence, this money is often coupled with earnings from small jobs such as babysitting or lawn care. For example, American children and teens receive on average about eight hundred dollars a year for allowance (excluding money from outside employment). With more than forty million youth between the ages of eight and eighteen in the United States, we are talking about more than thirty billion discretionary dollars annually—a serious primary market indeed.

How do children develop into full-fledged consumers? To answer this question, it is most useful to turn to theories of consumer socialization, the spontaneous process in which children develop the skills, knowledge, and attitudes that they need in order to operate as consumers. Although there is no generally accepted definition of consumer behavior, many definitions share four components. A consumer is capable of taking action to fulfill his or her needs and preferences; choosing and purchasing a product; evaluating a purchase and comparing it with alternatives; and understanding the social and cultural significance of the product.

Taking Action to Fulfill Needs and Preferences

To qualify as a primary market, children need to be able to express needs and take action to fulfill them. Children are born with particular needs and preferences for tastes, colors, and sounds. Initially, they mainly express these needs and preferences reactively, by indicating whether they like or dislike a certain product. By the time they reach about two years of age, children become more active in expressing their needs and preferences. They begin to request products that they come across in their environment—and pester their parents to buy them. Moreover, as many parents can attest, this pestering sometimes takes the form of "store wars," in which parents and children have heated battles regarding which objects will (and will not) be placed in the store shopping cart.

These store battles tend to increase until children are six years of age, after which they typically decline. Developmentally, this curvilinear pattern (increase followed by decrease) of parent-child disputes is plausible. Children are able to ward off temptation and delay gratification only after they reach five or six years of age. Before then, such abilities are much more limited or nonexistent. As the now-classic "marshmallow experiment" (see chapter 11) has repeatedly shown, when younger children see something tasty, they are usually powerless to resist it. Parents can draw toddlers' and preschoolers' attention away from enticing products by giving them a toy to play with, but it is only when children have learned effective strategies of their own (around five or six years old) that they are able to resist temptation and delay gratification.[2]

In addition to their improved ability to delay gratification, children's persuasive strategies for getting what they want from their parents typically become more sophisticated as they get older. Whereas younger children often use coercive strategies to convince their parents (nagging, tantrums, etc.), by about age five, children increasingly use more advanced persuasive strategies, such as arguing, bargaining, buttering up, eliciting pity, and even telling lies ("But Mom, all the kids in my class are allowed to eat chips!"). These more sophisticated persuasive attempts result in fewer parent-child disagreements than occur with younger children. And it should be no surprise that older children (nine to twelve years old) are twice as successful at persuading their parents to buy a particular product in the supermarket as younger children (three to five years).[3]

Choosing and Purchasing a Product

Around age five, children start to buy things on their own, which is a second important prerequisite for a member of a primary market. Initially, parents supervise the process of selecting and paying for an item in a store. Research suggests that nearly 75 percent of five-year-olds purchase something in the presence of their parents. By the time children are eight, most have made a purchase with their parents there.[4] At that age, according to James McNeal, approximately half of children make more or less regular trips to the store to buy something on their own. They usually go to a nearby store or supermarket to which they can walk safely.[5] And by the time they are teenagers, nearly 70 percent use a savings account, checking account, debit card, or credit card.[6]

Evaluating and Comparing Purchases

In addition to expressing preferences and being able to select and make purchases, a third prerequisite of becoming a full-fledged consumer involves knowing how to evaluate products and compare alternatives. To do this, one must have the critical ability to assess a product's suitability and quality. Young children (toddlers, preschoolers, young primary school children) do not have this ability. As discussed in chapters 4 and 5, they often center their attention on one or two details of a product. As a result, they typically have trouble taking in multiple product details at once, a skill necessary for proper evaluation. By around age eight, however, children start to scrutinize every product that attracts their attention, down to the last detail, and to compare it with other products.

As discussed in chapter 5, this process of decentration results in critical evaluations of media content—critiquing it for poor acting, lack of humor, and other undesirable characteristics. Advertisements are not exempt from children's critical gaze. Unlike younger children, who see commercials mainly as appealing entertainment, children from about the age of eight can be extremely skeptical of commercials. In this period, they begin developing the ability to grasp multiple perspectives, and with this understanding, they begin to comprehend that advertising is meant to persuade them to buy a certain brand, a realization that may further increase their skepticism.[7]

Understanding the Social Significance of Consumer Behavior

Finally, the ability to function as a full-fledged consumer requires an understanding of the social and cultural aspects of consumer behavior. This understanding, which coincides with adolescence, involves the ability to frame products or brands within the social, cultural, and economic contexts of specific individuals and groups. Hip-hop fans and emo enthusiasts wear clothing from different brands, and goths look decidedly different from hipsters. Adolescents develop the skills to assess products and brands within the social context of their cliques or subcultures. They learn their groups' norms, and the ways they differ from the norms of other groups and subcultures. They learn that certain subcultural differences are associated with differences in social, cultural, and economic status. They express their identity in large part through what they consume. Through the clothes they wear, the music they listen to, the movies they see, and their activity on social media, they show who they are and are not, what they find important, and how they want others to view them. This final developmental prerequisite of consumer behavior occurs in a period that has been named the reflective stage.[8]

Children as Influencers

Children are attractive as consumers not only because they form an important primary market but also because they have a sizable influence on family purchases. Besides influencing what groceries end up in the family home, they influence the family's choice of restaurants, vacation destination, and even the model of the new family car. This increasing influence of youth on family purchases began in the 1970s, and has since increased quite steadily.[9] One of the main reasons for this shift, scholars believe, is that families have moved from an authoritarian style to a more authoritative parenting style. Until the 1960s, the most common parenting style was authoritarian, in which parents demanded obedience and respect from their children. When parents spoke, for example, children were expected to be quiet and listen. In today's families, parents value their children's input and encourage them to speak up. Understanding, equality, and compromise are now paramount. Modern families have fewer fixed rules. Family members negotiate family decisions and act in accordance with the outcome.

Children influence their parents' purchases both directly and indirectly. Direct influence occurs when they ask for or demand a product, hint that they want something, or make a recommendation. And these direct requests happen often, particularly among young children. For example, research in the United States showed that when at the grocery store with their parents, four- to six-year-olds request a certain product every two and a half minutes.[10] Similarly, work in the Netherlands found that children between three and five years old request a product, on average, once every four minutes.[11] These direct requests are relatively successful. Studies have shown that with very young children (around age two), parents acquiesce about 14 percent of the time. By the time their children are about five years of age, this number increases to roughly 50 percent—and estimates are even higher if "postponed concessions" are included; after all, parents do not always give in to their children immediately, but may do so after a period of time has passed.[12]

The number of product demands declines once children reach the age of seven. This does not mean that they have less influence on family purchases. On the contrary, numerous studies show that children have more influence on family purchases as they get older.[13] One explanation for this seeming paradox is that older children are more likely than younger children to influence their parents indirectly. Indirect influence occurs when parents account for their child's wishes and preferences when making purchases for the child. Many parents buy their children's favorite brands, without prompting, when shopping because they know precisely which brands their children prefer and want to do something nice for them.[14]

Children as Future Customers

Finally, children also represent a third important market—they are the adult customers of the future. Research shows that adults tend to remain loyal to many brands that they favored as children. Manufacturers that manage to capture a young child's attention have a very good chance of gaining his or her enduring loyalty as a consumer. Thus, fostering customer loyalty via brand preference at an early age is a key aim for marketers. Through experience with products, such as shopping with parents, children learn about brands and improve their brand awareness, for example, their recognition and recall of brand names. But for marketers, brand awareness is only half the battle—they ultimately aim for brand preference and customer loyalty.

Brand preference seems to develop very early in life. In fact, research has shown that approximately two-thirds of children between three and six years old "often" or "almost always" ask their parents for specific brands.[15] For example, starting around two years of age, children tend to prefer peanut butter featured in frequent commercials over the same peanut butter packaged as an unknown brand. They also think the branded peanut butter tastes much better than the same peanut butter without the label.[16]

These findings, and others like them, indicate that children start developing brand preferences at a very young age. What is unclear, however, is the extent to which their preferences remain stable as they get older. There have been only a few studies on brand loyalty among children, and their results are inconsistent. Some authors say that children's preferences change significantly during childhood but stabilize in adolescence. One study, for example, found that more than half of thirty-year-olds still purchased the brands that they used when they were sixteen.[17] Another study showed, however, that brand loyalty applied only in the case of certain products and brands. For example, preferences for some products (such as soft drinks) and brands are formed during childhood and are rather stable, but preferences for products and brands that develop only during or after adolescence are less stable than advertisers might wish.[18] Adolescents seem to be most loyal to "intimate" products, such as deodorant, shampoo, and contact lens solution, whereas products and brands they use to express their identity in their clique or subculture, such as fashion labels, are less likely to induce feelings of loyalty.[19]

The Changing Commercial Environment

In the past, advertisers relied largely on intuition when designing marketing campaigns for children. But as the focus on youth as budding consumers has increased, the marketing world has come to depend heavily on market research. This research has led to a world in which youth are surrounded by marketing efforts. They come across these marketing efforts while watching their favorite television shows, perusing their favorite magazines, and listening to their favorite bands on Spotify. Youth now find commercial content appearing within their favorite programs (product placement), on their sports uniforms (brand sponsorship), and online in the form of viral video clips, advergames, banners, and more. And at an ever-increasing rate, advertisers are beginning to embrace cross-platform marketing—using a combination of different platforms—to reach youth.

A striking example of this integrated marketing is the international "AHH Effect" campaign that Coca-Cola launched in 2013. As the name suggests, the purpose of the campaign was to intensify the "AHH effect" in teens when they pop open a can of Coca-Cola. In addition to television commercials, the campaign included dozens of sites with URLs that differed only by the number of *H*s they contained. According to the Coca-Cola Company, the campaign provided adolescents a large variety of "snackable" digital content, such as quick YouTube videos and online casual games. It also relied on cross-promotions (promotional tie-ins involving two or more companies) starring famous teen idols, and used social media to encourage adolescents to design their own digital content.[20]

With such a flooded commercialized environment, it is reasonable to ask how these efforts might be influencing young people. Does watching an average of twenty-eight television commercials an hour (an estimate found in Europe, the United States, and China) influence youth? And if so, how?[21] Put another way, how are the more than twenty-five thousand ads that youth see each year influencing them?[22] In what follows, we evaluate the effect of advertising on youth, discussing not only how advertising may affect this audience, but also the role of development in this process.

Advertising Effects

Advertising agencies ask themselves daily which commercials are most effective for which products and in which medium. Although these agencies have undoubtedly gathered valuable information about the effects of advertising, such findings are not typically publicly available, because of their competitive information. As a result, published research on the effects of advertising usually involves academic studies.

Academic research on the effects of advertising has a broader aim than commercial research because it seeks to investigate whether and to what extent advertising is harmful to children and teens. Such research generally distinguishes between two broad types of advertising effects: intended and unintended. Intended advertising effects are the effects that advertisers try to achieve, for example, to increase youth's brand awareness, to influence their brand preferences, or their purchase intentions. The unintended effects of advertising include undesirable side effects. Researchers investigating unintended effects focus on questions such as whether advertising makes children more materialistic, whether it leads to parent-child conflict, or whether it encourages unhealthy eating habits. Academic research investigating advertising effects has typically looked at the effects of television advertising, although more recent work has begun to address newer advertising formats such as those found in video games and online.[23]

Intended Advertising Effects

To date, nearly one hundred academic studies have been published concerning the intended effects of advertising on youth. These studies generally focus on brand awareness, brand attitude and preferences, and children's purchase intentions.

Brand Awareness

Children start to become brand aware at a very young age. Marketers know that children as young as two connect the brands they see in advertising with brands they see in stores.[24] But is it truly advertising that explains this brand awareness? Are children who watch more commercials, for example, more brand aware than other children? Researchers have explored this question through both correlational and experimental studies, defining brand awareness as both brand recognition and brand recall.

Overall, the existing academic work shows that increased advertising exposure is responsible for increased brand recognition. In correlational studies, researchers typically establish how much television children watch and how many brands children can correctly identify when they are presented with a brand logo, brand character, or packaging. All of these correlational studies have shown that children who consume more television recognize more brand logos and brand characters than do other children.[25] Similarly, work with teens has shown that advergames (i.e., games especially designed to promote a specific product) increase brand recognition—particularly among those youth who find the game appealing.[26]

Experimental studies on brand recognition point to similar results. Carole Macklin, for example, had four- and five-year-olds watch three commercials, one for candy, one for breakfast cereal, and one for chewing gum. After watching just one commercial, 61 percent of the four-year-olds and 65 percent of the five-year-olds recognized the breakfast cereal brand.[27] In another study, nine- and ten-year-old girls watched commercials for two diet soft drink brands and two lipstick brands. It took only a single viewing of the commercials for the diet soft drink to increase the subjects' brand recognition from 28 percent to 88 percent.[28] The pre- and post-viewing difference for the lipstick commercial was insignificant, but that was due to a ceiling effect: all the girls had already scored 100 percent on brand recognition, whether or not they had just watched the commercial.

The results of research into brand recall, that is, the extent to which children are able to correctly generate and retrieve a brand name in their memory, seem to be age specific. Both the correlational and experimental studies suggest that advertising can influence brand recall, but only that of adolescents. For example, in one correlational study, researchers asked younger children (between the ages of four and twelve) to list as many brands of toothpaste (and other products) as they could. Although most of the brand names that the children listed were for heavily advertised products, the relationship between television viewing and brand recall was not significant.[29] In a study involving children of up to eight years of age, researchers similarly found a correlation between television viewing and brand recognition, but not brand recall.[30] A study among late adolescents (fifteen- to eighteen-year-olds), however, did yield a positive relationship between television viewing and brand recall.[31]

The results of experimental research on brand recall generally concur with those of correlational research. For example, in one study, seven- and eight-year-olds and eleven- and twelve-year-olds watched a recording of the British version of *American Idol* in which the researchers had digitally inserted product placements. Half of each age group saw unhealthy branded food products (for example, Pepsi and Cheetos), and the other half saw healthy branded food products (Milk 2 Go, Dole fruit cups). The older children recalled more brand names than the younger ones. In both age groups, recall was particularly pronounced for the unhealthy brands, which may be due to the fact that most children were more familiar with the unhealthy than the healthy brands.[32]

Brand Attitudes and Preferences

Research on brand attitudes and preferences asks whether advertising can foster a positive attitude in children toward advertised brands (brand attitude) and whether they prefer certain brands to others (brand prefer ences). It is much more difficult to influence attitudes and preferences than recognition and recall. As discussed earlier in this book, even the very youngest children have distinct tastes. Many factors shape brand attitudes and preferences, including age, gender, media preferences, family environment, and susceptibility to peer and subculture influence. All of these factors predict children's selective exposure to advertising and, as a result, the impact of advertising on their brand attitudes and preferences.

Research on children's brand attitudes and preferences began in the 1970s. In a correlational study, 755 children were asked how often they had seen a certain commercial for a Snoopy pencil sharpener as well as much how they liked the commercial and the pencil sharpener. Results indicated a significant positive correlation between exposure to the commercial and attitudes toward the sharpener. Interestingly, additional analyses revealed that whether the children liked the commercial had a greater influence on their preferences than the number of times that they watched it.[33]

A large number of experiments have also investigated the effects of advertising on brand attitude and preference.[34] Almost all of these studies involved showing children one or more commercials and then asking them how much they liked the advertised brands. For example, in one study, half of a group of seven- to ten-year-olds watched a videotape that included a commercial for Clearasil, and the other half watched the videotape without the commercial. Those who saw the commercial had a more positive brand attitude than those who did not. The effect was greater among girls, and occurred only with children who were unfamiliar with the Clearasil commercial.[35] Girls evidently found a commercial for acne treatment more relevant than boys at that age, perhaps because they entered puberty earlier and were more concerned about their appearance than boys.

In a comparable study, girls ages 9–10 watched a taped interview with Steven Spielberg. Half of them also viewed two lipstick commercials that had been inserted into the interview, whereas the other half viewed two diet soft drink commercials. A preliminary study had shown that the girls were interested in lipstick but not in the diet soft drink. The study revealed that the lipstick commercials had a positive influence on the girls' brand attitude, whereas the soft drink commercials had no effect.[36]

These studies and others like them indicate that advertising can positively influence brand attitude and brand preference—but this influence is not guaranteed. Instead, the extent to which youth find the advertising appealing or find the marketed content relevant and interesting to them can greatly enhance or reduce the effects. Children who find a commercial message appealing—particularly because it highlights content that is relevant and interesting to them—seem to ascribe a more positive attitude and a stronger brand preference to the marketed brand. On the other hand, when the content is unappealing or seems inapplicable, brand appeal and preference are unaffected.

Purchase Request Behavior

While brand awareness and brand appeal are important, advertisers ultimately want children to purchase their brands. Since children do not always have the opportunity to buy things for themselves, and since assessing purchase behavior can be quite complex, researchers often gauge "purchase intention" by looking at what children ask their parents to buy for them. A considerable body of research has addressed purchase request behavior, but far fewer studies have looked at the relationship between advertising and such behavior.

In a notable study that took place during Christmastime, young children were asked what they wanted Santa Claus to bring them. During the same period, the researchers studied which commercials were being aired on television and the frequency of children's television exposure. Results indicated that children who were exposed to more commercials had significantly more of the advertised products on their wish lists.[37] Other studies exploring the correlation between advertising and request behavior have similarly shown that children who are exposed to more commercial messages ask their parents for products more often.[38] Importantly, these findings are not limited to younger children. Several studies have shown that commercial messages increase purchase intention among teens, particularly when these messages rely on content that they deem appealing.[39]

Experimental studies have likewise focused on purchase behavior. In one study, a group of three- to five-year-olds and their mothers watched a cartoon into which food commercials had been inserted. Another group of the same size watched the same cartoon but without the commercials. Afterward, the mothers took their children grocery shopping. The group of children who had watched the cartoon with the commercials asked for products more often than the group of children who had not.[40] Similarly, in an experiment on the effect of product placement, children watched a scene from the movie *Home Alone*. Half the children were shown the scene with a product placement by Pepsi, and the other half without a product placement. Afterward, the children were given a choice between a can of Coca-Cola and a can of Pepsi. Sixty-two percent who had seen the product placement chose Pepsi, as opposed to 42 percent of the children who were not exposed to the Pepsi product placement.[41]

Unintended Advertising Effects

Advertisers have clear goals for the content they create. They want their target audience to know who they are, to find their brands appealing and preferable to competitive brands, and ultimately to purchase them. And while, overall, the literature indicates that advertisers are able to meet these goals among youth, there are unintended consequences of advertising that they typically pay less attention to. Academic researchers, however, have often asked about these unintended consequences, paying particular attention to materialism, parent-child conflict, and unhealthy eating.

Materialism

Consumer cultivation theory, an adapted version of George Gerbner's cultivation theory, assumes that advertising promotes ideas and values that differ from our own experience of the world. If we are frequently exposed to the ideas and values promoted in advertising, we will gradually adopt them as our own. According to this theory, advertising communicates the ideology that ownership is important and that it gives us access to beauty, happiness, success, and other desirable qualities.[42] Given this proposition, scholars have asked whether advertising does in fact lead to increased materialism among youth.

Overall, the research indicates that advertising increases materialism among youth. For example, most of the existing correlational work has shown a positive relationship between advertising and materialistic attitudes in children and adolescents. Like most effects of media, the correlations are small to moderate, varying from r = .13 to r = .32.[43] Most of these studies, however, could not solve the chicken-or-egg dilemma (see chapter 7), which means that they could not decisively assess whether exposure to advertising leads to materialism or whether materialistic children pay more attention to advertising. A recent longitudinal study by Suzanna Opree and colleagues, suggests that direction of the relationships points more from advertising to subsequent materialism than the other way around.[44] This finding has been supported by experimental research showing that advertising can be a cause of materialistic values of children and adolescents.[45] But as with most other media effects, it is plausible that not all children are equally susceptible to the effects of advertising as a source of materialism. Up to now, no research has shown which children are particularly vulnerable to the effects of advertising on materialism. This is an important question for future research.

Parent-Child Conflict

As we discussed, advertising may encourage children's purchase request behavior. This is an expected, intended effect of advertising. But if children make too many requests or are too demanding, parent-child conflicts may arise, which we regard as an unintended effect of advertising. Thus far, at least five correlational studies have examined the relationship between television advertising and parent-child conflicts, and each one found that exposure to advertising correlates with a rise in parent-child conflict.[46]

The same findings are supported by one of the few experiments examining the effect of advertising on parent-child conflicts. In this experiment, two groups of four- and five-year-olds watched a videotape of a television program for preschoolers. One of the videotapes included a commercial for an appealing toy, while the other videotape did not. Afterward, the children were asked which product they preferred, a tennis ball or the toy featured in the commercial. The researchers added that their mothers preferred the tennis ball. Children who had viewed the videotape that included the commercial were more than twice as likely (46 percent) to go against their mother's wishes as children who had not (21 percent).[47]

Overweight and Obesity

Overweight and obesity in childhood have become a worldwide crisis. The World Health Organization reports that worldwide obesity has more than doubled since 1980, among adults and youth. For example, nearly forty-two million children under the age of five were overweight or obese in 2013.[48] If current trends continue, this number is expected to rise to seventy million by 2024.[49] And while the increases have been particularly dramatic in developing countries, developed countries have experienced similarly high rates of growth. For example, 29 percent of boys and 30 percent of girls younger than twenty in the United States are overweight or obese, as are 26 percent of boys and 29 percent of girls in the UK, and 34 percent of boys and 29 percent of girls in Greece.[50] Children who are overweight (10–20 percent higher than normal weight) or obese (20 percent or more above normal weight) are a matter of grave concern for public health officials, since these conditions can lead to diabetes, cardiovascular disorders, joint problems, depression, and many other health issues.

Unhealthy food—fast food, soft drinks, potato chips, candy—accounts for a large proportion of the products being marketed to children. In the United States, researchers have found that nearly 25 percent of all ads targeting youth focus on unhealthy content. And of this content, nearly 90 percent feature products that are high in fat, sugar, or sodium.[51] In another worrisome finding, a cross-national study carried out in eleven countries on three continents reported that between six in the morning and ten at night, children watch an average of twenty-eight commercials an hour, five of which advertise unhealthy food products.[52] These high percentages are the reason why people often hold advertising responsible for the epidemic of overweight and obesity among children. As unhealthy foods become increasingly marketed online, public concern has grown, leading to numerous investigations into the relationship between advertising and overweight or obesity in childhood.

Researchers have posited three potential hypotheses to explain why advertising may lead to large weight gains in youth.[53] The first is the advertising-effect hypothesis, which states that exposure to food advertising incites a longing to eat. The second hypothesis is the activity-displacement hypothesis, which states that media use is displacing more active pursuits like playing outside and sports, which help in the fight against obesity. The third is the "grazing" hypothesis, which suggests that children are more likely to snack when watching television. The media themselves often promulgate the idea of snacking and viewing. As figure 9.1 shows, photographs or movies showing children or families watching television together frequently feature a bowl of potato chips or popcorn.

Researchers have found support for all three hypotheses. Dutch researchers showed that the time children spent watching commercials was correlated with an unhealthy diet, supporting the advertising-effect hypothesis. This result was also supported by a study of American youth that

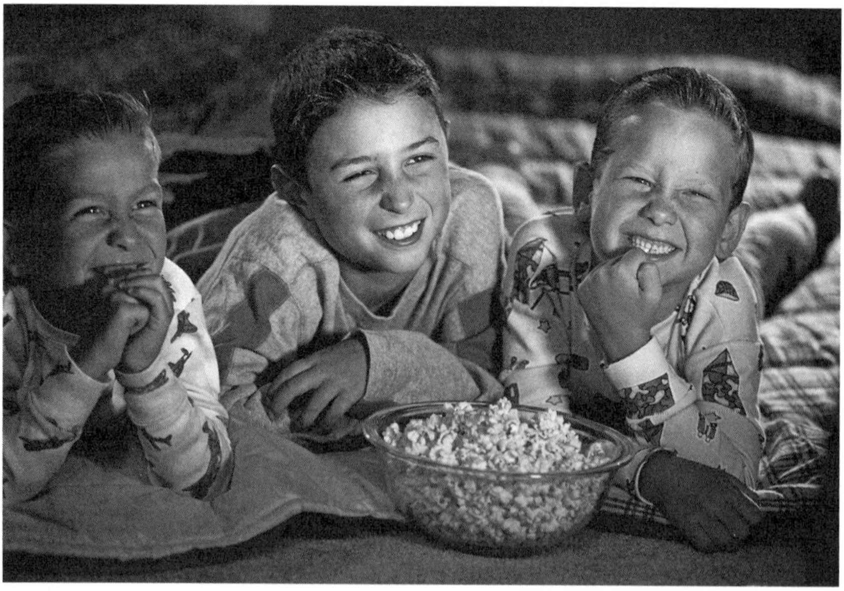

Figure 9.1. In media portrayals, television viewing and snacking seem to be inextricably connected. (Brand X Pictures/Thinkstock)

found a positive longitudinal relationship between exposure to soft drink and fast food advertising and consumption of these foods.[54] In the same Dutch study, the activity-displacement hypothesis was supported, too: children's television viewing time was found to be negatively related to playing outside, which suggested that television viewing displaced more active pursuits. Finally, support for the grazing hypothesis comes from a study showing that children increased their consumption of snacks when watching a cartoon episode with commercials that promoted unhealthy foods.[55]

All in all, most studies have shown that advertisements for unhealthy food can lead to unhealthy eating, excess weight, and obesity, although the reported effect sizes are typically small. An important explanation for these small effects is the complexity of the causes of obesity. Although advertising for unhealthy food products has increased dramatically in recent decades, children's physical, social, educational, and commercial environments have also changed significantly. Children are less physically active today because they seek their entertainment mainly indoors, in their bedrooms. Parenting styles have changed, and today's parents are much more likely to agree to their children's requests.[56] And many stores display candy, potato chips, and other "fun food" products on lower shelves, where children can easily spot them and select them when they go shopping with their parents. All in all, today's children grow up in an "obesogenic environment" in which they easily consume too many calories or get too little exercise, which makes it extremely difficult to pinpoint the unique effect of advertising on the growing obesity trend.

Child Development and Advertising Effects

Thus far, we have seen that youth are affected by advertising, but the role of development has been largely omitted from this conversation. The one exception is research on the effect of advertising on brand recall, which suggests a smaller effect on younger children than older children. That said, we know from earlier chapters that development is a key predictor of media consumption and media effects, and so we would expect that development also matters when it comes to the effects of advertising.

Indeed, there is convincing work to suggest that young children are more susceptible to the effects—intended and unintended—of advertising than older children. In particular, research has established that advertising has a greater effect on younger children's brand attitude, request behavior, parent-child conflicts, and obesity. Younger children are also more likely than older children to think highly of an advertised brand if they enjoy a commercial for that brand.[57] Unsurprisingly, then, advertisers are particularly keen to produce attractive commercials for young children. Younger children are more likely than older children to make purchase requests of their parents in response to appealing commercials. This is largely because young children, who have less experience with products, are less likely to subject them to systematic and critical evaluation. For example, they are not yet capable of weighing the advantages and disadvantages of an advertised brand and comparing it to another brand—which is key to reducing or mitigating advertising effects.

This process of weighing the advantages and disadvantages of an advertised brand is an important aspect of advertising processing. In general, advertising—like entertainment—can be processed in different ways. To explain advertising processing, scholars have developed models such as the elaboration likelihood model of Richard Petty and John Cacioppo[58] and the heuristic-systematic model of Alice Eagly and Shelly Chaiken.[59] In 2010, Moniek Buijzen and colleagues adapted these adult-focused models for a study of how children process advertising.[60] Like the adult models, this youth-focused model assumes that under certain circumstances, children process advertising systematically and critically (systematic processing), under other circumstances superficially (heuristic processing), and under yet other circumstances, unconsciously and automatically (automatic processing). Thus far, work with this model indicates that young children mostly tend to process advertising heuristically and automatically, that is, without thinking critically or considering counterarguments. Older children and adolescents, however, are able to rely on more systematic processing, at least when they are motivated to do so.

Development helps explain these age-related differences in advertising processing. Specifically, compared with older children, younger children are less experienced and have less domain-specific knowledge that they can draw from when evaluating advertising. They are thus less likely than older children to recognize when a claim in a commercial is exaggerated or unrealistic. Younger children are also less capable than older children of developing counterarguments when confronted with advertising.[61] This inability to systematically process advertising is particularly true of newer advertising formats (e.g., product placements, advergames) because the concealed content in these formats requires that viewers first consciously identify the content before they can begin to counter it.

Countering Advertising Effects with Advertising Literacy?

It seems reasonable to argue that advertising has intended and unintended consequences for youth, and that its effects are particularly pronounced among younger children and children for whom the advertised content is strongly relevant or appealing. For marketers, these findings—particularly those associated with intended effects—are encouraging. Yet many parents, caregivers, and public policy advocates are concerned about these effects. These concerned parties often question whether marketing to this younger audience is ethical, citing research that shows that children under the age of eight do not understand the persuasive intent of advertising, that is, they lack the ability to understand that advertising is meant to persuade and sell. At the same time, these parties express concern about the unintended effects of advertising and believe that efforts must be taken to help offset these effects.

Although it might seem that knowledge of persuasive intent would be sufficient to buffer negative effects by encouraging systematic and critical processing, the reality is not that simple. Otherwise, none of us would be affected by advertising. The assumption that persuasion knowledge and a certain level of cognitive development offer sufficient defense against the effects of advertising is based on a simplistic model. After all, commercials make cognitive as well as emotional appeals, and our ability to regulate our emotions with cognition (knowledge and understanding) is not always optimal. Even though we know a movie is not real, it can still make us feel scared, sad, or happy. Similarly, even though youth (or adults) know that an advertised snack being promoted to them is unhealthy, they may still feel a strong urge to eat it.

Why does this occur? Why is it that youth (and adults) are persuaded and seemingly fooled by commercials whose claims they know to be unrealistic? The answer to this question is somewhat similar to our account of the law of apparent reality (see chapter 8), which explains why viewers feel emotions and desires when watching fictional media entertainment. Like entertainment, advertising often appeals to our emotions and social needs. As with our responses to media entertainment, we may ignore skeptical thoughts that would blunt our desire for advertised brands. Moreover, sometimes we simply do not mind being persuaded, especially if the product or brand has relevance for us.

That said, some researchers believe that increased efforts to heighten consumers' advertising literacy might help buffer some of the ill effects of commercial messages. These researchers have shown that helping youth engage in critical thinking about the message (for example, recognizing the persuasive intent) can help reduce advertising effects.[62] Of course, such processes are possible only with older children (about age eight and up, which coincides with the acquisition of persuasion knowledge) and adolescents—youth who are cognitively able to engage in such processing. Yet it is important to recognize that while critical thinking can defend us against the influence of advertising, it does not necessarily do so. Advertising communicates emotions, and emotions cannot always be controlled by knowledge and understanding. Thus, while media's youngest audiences are the most susceptible to advertising effects because they lack the ability to engage in cognitive defense strategies, older youth are not automatically protected by virtue of their advanced cognitive development. Older youth might have more cognitive tools with which to defend themselves, but getting them to use these tools is an entirely different story.

Conclusion

In this chapter, we explained why children have become such an important target group for advertisers, and why it is so lucrative to start marketing to them while they are still in the cradle. Children represent three markets (a primary market, a market of influencers, and a future market), and marketers are eager to capitalize on each one. Given the increased commercialization of childhood, it comes as little surprise that multiple studies have shown that children and adolescents are indeed affected by advertising.

Advertising can increase brand awareness, brand appeal, and product requests. Further, as a robust literature attests, advertising produces unintended effects—increased materialism, parent-child conflicts, and a heightened risk of overweight and obesity. These effects are particularly pronounced among younger children, who lack the cognitive abilities yet to defend themselves against advertising. And for older youth (and adults) who have these abilities, advertising literacy is often insufficient to blunt the effects of advertising.[63]

So, where does this leave us? To argue for a ban on advertising to the youth market is neither realistic nor reasonable. We live in a consumer society in which advertising plays a key role. But academic researchers can work to identify ways to limit the potential ill effects of advertising. Those efforts might include working with public policy officials to limit advertising that targets the youngest age group, or working with companies to encourage them to consider self-regulation. Moreover, working with youth to identify ways to help them effectively manage the huge amount of advertising they are confronted with is also a worthwhile direction. Taking a multidimensional approach to an issue as important as youth-targeted advertising is likely the best way to balance the needs of marketers with those of youth.

10

MEDIA AND SEX

> The first picture which stands out in my memory is "The Sheik" featuring Rudolph Valentino. I was at the impressionable and romantic age of 12 or 13 when I saw it, and I recall coming home that night and dreaming the entire picture over again; myself as the heroine being carried over the burning sands by an equally burning lover. I could feel myself being kissed in the way the Sheik had kissed the girl. I wanted to see it again, but that was forbidden; so as the next best thing my friend and I enacted the especially romantic scenes . . . She was Rudolph and I the beautiful captive, and we followed as well as we could remember the actions of the actors.
>
> —Movie autobiography of an adolescent girl

The passage quoted in the epigraph dates from 1933, when sex in the media was primarily implicit, merely suggested, in the same way that bloody or violent acts usually took place off camera. Now, however, onscreen sex is more accessible than ever before. Sexual media content is no longer relegated to television, movies, magazines, and games. Nowadays, typing "free sex" into a Google search box yields more than one million hits in less than a second. With only a few more clicks, you can quickly enter a world of explicit videos of "hot teenage girls," MILF porn, and much more. More than any other media format, the Internet has brought sexual media content to the masses in an affordable, accessible, and anonymous manner. It is no wonder that many teens, who are in the middle of developing their sexual identities, look for sex online. And it is no wonder that there is concern about the potential consequences for these teens. Are these concerns justified? What is the influence of this vast quantity of easily accessible sex and porn on adolescents? What are the characteristics of online sex and porn, and how do these influence adolescents' ideas about sexuality and gender roles? In this chapter, we discuss the research into the effects of sex and porn on adolescents' sexual beliefs, sexual attitudes, and sexual behavior.

Sexualization and Pornification

Since the first decade of the twenty-first century, the terms "sexualization" and "pornification" have become household words. This is due, first, to the increased accessibility of digital porn and the societal concerns associated with this accessibility. And second, it is a result of a series of books about the sexualization of women such as the best sellers *Female Chauvinist Pigs: Women and the Rise of Raunch Culture*, by Ariel Levy (2007); *Pornified: How Pornography Is Damaging Our Lives, Our Relationships, and Our Families*, by Pamela Paul (2005); and *Girls Gone Skank: The Sexualization of Girls in American Society*, by Patrice Oppliger (2008). These books, along with a massive report about the sexualization of girls issued by a task force of the American Psychological Association, have helped ensure that sexualization and pornification have become prominent fixtures on the political and social agenda.[1]

But what exactly is meant by "sexualization" and "pornification"? "Pornification" is most typically defined as the "increasing occurrence and acceptance of sexual themes and explicit imagery in popular or mainstream culture." While there are numerous definitions for sexualization, the APA report offers perhaps the most encompassing definition, explaining that "sexualization occurs when (1) a person's value comes only from his or her sexual appeal or behavior, to the exclusion of other characteristics; (2) a person is held to a standard that equates physical attractiveness (narrowly defined) with being sexy; (3) a person is sexually objectified—that is, made into a thing for others' sexual use, rather than seen as a person with the capacity for independent action and decision making; and/or (4) sexuality is inappropriately imposed upon a person."[2]

Not all four conditions need be satisfied, according to the APA report authors, for sexualization to be present. Instead, any of these conditions represents a form of sexualization. The fourth condition, according to the authors, is particularly relevant for children. Why? Everyone—girls, boys, men, women—can be sexualized, but if children are confronted with sexualization, it is often not something they have chosen, and thus it is being imposed on them. The report provides several examples of the sexualization of children: a five-year-old child in a T-shirt with the word "flirt" on it, readers of a magazine for teenage girls being advised to lose weight in order to appear more attractive to boys, and a woman in an ad who is posed provocatively but dressed as a girl with pigtails and lacy ruffles.

Although the term "sexualization" has become fashionable, neither the expression nor the phenomenon is new. At the dawn of psychoanalysis in the early twentieth century, "sexualization" was used to describe people's feelings with regard to erotic objects. And indeed, if we place sexualization in a historical context, as proposed by the sociologist Cas Wouters, there have been several shifts in sexualization as sexuality moved from public to private and back to public again. According to Wouters, the trend toward increasing sexualization in the twentieth century was mainly a response to more than two centuries of "desexualization," that is, the elimination of sex from the public sphere.[3] In the early sixteenth century, everyone, young and old alike, spoke freely about sex. Children were not hidden away when their parents (and other adults) had sex, and instead learned quickly that sex was a normal aspect of adult relationships. Through the end of the nineteenth century, however, this attitude gradually changed toward an increasing prudishness that forced youth (and adults) to repress their sexual desires. This desexualization reached its peak in the Victorian era, when sex and anything evoking eroticism were taboo in public. Until the end of the nineteenth century, there was a societal aversion to public displays of affection and physical contact.

This desexualization process gradually reversed itself in the twentieth century. People dealt with each other less formally, and emotions could be expressed again. Child rearing and the relationships between parents and children were focused more on love and affection. This process accelerated in the 1920s and again in the 1960s and 1970s, the decades of collective emancipation.[4] Indeed, since the 1970s, it has become more widely accepted for people to express their sexual desires and interests in public. Some scholars believe that entertainment media have played a key part in shifting sex back from the private to the public realm. This shift parallels a similar one in entertainment media, which have increasingly come to rely on reality content—lifestyles, exposés, and confessions, a phenomenon that Brian McNair has named the "striptease culture."[5]

Sexual Messages in Media

As noted, many scholars believe that media played a key role in shifting sex from the private domain to the public. In fact, the APA task force report specifically argues that media provide some of the most pronounced messages of sexualization and pornification for youth today.[6] The question is, what do these sexual messages look like? Content analyses offer useful insight into the sexual and pornographic messages that youth consume, but these analyses often suffer from two challenges. First, nudity is often conflated with sex; much of this work has been conducted in the United States, where the approach to sex is more conservative than that found in, say, northern Europe. Second, it is often hard to pinpoint the difference between porn and "normal" sex.

Many vain attempts have been made to distinguish between sex and porn, a distinction nicely expressed in the famous statement by U.S. Supreme Court justice Potter Stewart in 1964, which has since been abridged to "I can't define pornography, but I know it when I see it." Stewart wrote this conclusion in *Jacobellis v. Ohio*, a decision denying a motion by the State of Ohio to ban the French film *Les Amants* (1958) on the grounds that it contained obscene material. In Potter's view, *Les Amants* was not obscene.

It is still difficult to clearly separate porn from sex in mainstream entertainment. One of the causes is—indeed—the increased presence of sex in the public sphere. The heated debate sparked by *Les Amants* six decades ago is an apt illustration of how our standards about sex have shifted. *Les Amants* was the first film in history to show a woman (Jeanne Moreau) commit adultery and not be punished. For its time, the black-and-white film had unusually "explicit" love scenes in a boat, a bed, and a bathtub (see figure 10.1). The French director François Truffaut (who did not direct the film) called it "the first love night in the cinema." By standards of that time, many viewers considered this content pornographic—so much so that the U.S. Supreme Court was asked to vote on whether it was legal for the State of Ohio to ban the film.

Figure 10.1. The movie *Les Amants* (1958), featuring Jeanne Moreau, led to heated debates around the world because of its alleged obscenity. By contemporary standards, the movie seems rather innocent. (Ullstein Bild/Getty Images)

By today's standards, however, very little in the film is offensive or shocking. *Les Amants* contains almost no nudity, and the "sex" in it is primarily implicit, merely suggested, in the same way that bloody and violent acts usually took place off camera at the time. Thus, while content analyses can provide us with useful information to ascertain what is in media content, it is important to consider these messages (and the critical reactions to these messages) within their broader cultural and historical contexts.[7]

Sex Entertains, Sex Sells, and Females Lose

Much of the content-analytic work on sexual media messages has sought to identify how much "sex" is present in entertainment media, as well as how these messages are tied to gender roles. While some of this work has looked specifically at youth-targeted content, other work has looked more generally at the entertainment media landscape. Defining "sex" broadly as sexual language and other references to sex, the majority of content analyses indicate that it is commonplace in entertainment media, whether aimed at a general audience or teens. For content aimed at a general audience, Dale Kunkel and colleagues showed that in the late 1990s, 56 percent of all American TV shows had sexual content, a figure that rose to 75 percent in 2005.[8] Similarly, an analysis of the top-grossing films between 1950 and 2006 showed that 80 percent of them contained at least some sexual content.[9] These high rates were not restricted to American media. British researchers analyzing more than one hundred episodes of soap operas that were popular with young British viewers found that 79 percent of them contained some form of sexual content, and that sexual talk occurred more frequently than sexual behavior.[10]

In teen-specific content, sexual content is equally or more prevalent. For example, most teen-targeted films that appeared from 1980 to 2007 contained a significant amount of sexual content. This content typically took the form of passionate kissing and sexual dialogue; implied intercourse and intimate touching occurred less often.[11] Interestingly, the percentage of sexual content in television programs is higher in those that feature teenage characters than in those that feature adult characters.[12] And remarkably, this difference seems to hold true for teen-targeted novels, which are replete with sex-related information—including passionate kissing, romantic ideation, and sexual intercourse.[13] It seems that sex does entertain this age group.

That said, across the entertainment content spectrum, content analyses show that girls and women are nearly always the losers. First, women and girls are present less frequently than men and boys. An analysis of youth programs in twenty-four different countries, including more than nine thousand programs from across the United States, the United Kingdom, Germany, Israel, Brazil, and India, found that—on average—male characters outnumbered female characters two to one.[14] This imbalance in favor of the male sex also applies to other media such as games and films.

More worrisome, though, is that when females do appear in entertainment media, they are depicted as caricatures of femininity. Since the late 1980s, even in relatively innocent cartoons, the depictions of female characters are sexier than those of their predecessors. Compared with earlier Disney heroines such as Snow White and Cinderella, contemporary characters such as Ariel (the Little Mermaid), Pocahontas, and Jessica Rabbit feature deeper cleavage, less clothing, and sexier appearances.[15] And this increased sexualization is not limited to television and film content. In video games, it is becoming increasingly commonplace to depict women in bikinis, with exaggeratedly huge breasts and round buttocks. Similarly, in music videos, which often contain sexual content, women are frequently objectified—presented in a subordinate role while their bodies (or parts of them) are emphasized.[16] Women serve mainly as decoration, rather than as core characters, in these videos.

Although the literature makes the point that girls and women are often the "losers" in media content, there is an important caveat to these findings—namely, that most of these studies have originated from within the feminist tradition. Thus, they concentrate heavily on the stereotypical roles of women and girls. As a result, we know significantly less about how boys and men are represented in the media. There are indications that boys and men are portrayed just as stereotypically as females, with broad shoulders and narrow hips (the "V shape," which almost no male has), the obligatory six-pack abs, and an overemphasis on sexual "performance." But we know far less from content analyses about stereotypical male representation.[17]

While media entertainment is most often the topic of concern when it comes to sex, it is important to recognize that the advertising industry also relies heavily on sexualized media content to sell products, and has done so for some time. In fact, the first "sex" advertising dates back to 1871, when a naked woman was used to (successfully) sell Pearl tobacco. Soon after, other tobacco makers jumped on board—placing scantily clad women on their packaging and advertisements—making "sex sells" an often-repeated mantra in the advertising world.[18]

Today, youth are unlikely to be confronted with explicit sex in advertising, but it is commonplace for them to be confronted with implicit sexual advertising messages.[19] And just as in entertainment media content, women are again the losers. For example, ads for many products (for example, makeup, fashion) tell female youth that they need these products in order to increase their physical or sexual attractiveness—thereby objectifying the female body. For many other products, the female body is used as a prop to attract attention and sell a product. Indeed, a content analysis of the advertisements on twenty popular websites for adolescents, mostly for teen girls (for example, Seventeen and CosmoGirl), showed that the majority of advertisements (82 percent) zoomed in on or emphasized physical attractiveness (62 percent).[20]

Sex Goes Digital

While much of the work on sexual media content has focused on more traditional forms of entertainment and advertising, the digital revolution has dramatically changed this landscape. Adolescents frequently encounter sexual content online. In the Netherlands, 40 percent of boys and 15 percent of girls ages 12–14 have deliberately sought out sex online in the past half year. These percentages increase quickly with age. By seventeen, more than 60 percent of boys and 20 percent of girls have deliberately searched for sexual content online. And these data reflect only their deliberate, conscious searches. Teens also often accidentally stumble on online sex. Indeed, 61 percent of boys ages 12–14 reported having accidentally come across sex while online (compared with 45 percent of girls). By seventeen years of age, such accidental hits have increased to 74 percent for boys and 59 percent for girls.[21] These estimates are consistent with trends found in other industrialized countries.[22]

When it comes to online sexual media content, the most frequently researched area is porn. This is not surprising. Thanks in part to the improvement of digital access and increased bandwidth, the porn business has grown into one of the World Wide Web's most profitable sectors. Audiovisual porn is now mainstream, and anyone can make, upload, and share porn online. And thousands of people do. Amateur porn is now a strong competitor to professional porn. In professional porn, paid actors who meet the criteria of particular "ideal" body types perform a scripted scenario. In amateur porn, performers do not necessarily have ideal shapes and "act" mainly for their own enjoyment. But whether online porn is made in a professional studio or in someone's bedroom, its consumers appreciate its "triple A" quality: it is anonymous, accessible, and affordable—ideal for teenage brains and budgets.[23]

So what are teens seeing when they are confronted with, or seek out, online porn? Most content analyses of professional heterosexual porn indicate that sex in such porn is depicted mainly as a physical, recreational activity between temporary partners. As in the messages in entertainment and advertising content, women are portrayed mainly as passive beings whose role is to provide physical satisfaction to men. Porn typically follows the standard pornographic script, which begins with fellatio and ends with the male orgasm.[24] Recently, Marleen Klaassen and Jochen Peter investigated whether the rise of amateur porn had led to an increase in messages that counter those presented in professional porn. In their work, they analyzed four hundred of the most popular video clips on four popular erotic sites (305 professional, 95 amateur). And "popular" videos were popular indeed: the most popular video clip had been viewed fifty-three million times.[25]

Since some researchers believe that amateur porn is a reaction to the stereotypical and unrealistic depictions of sex in professional porn, Klaassen and Peter expected amateur porn to present less gender inequality than professionally produced porn. This turned out not to be the case. In both amateur and professional porn, women were "instrumentalized" more than men, that is, their body parts were used for sexual gratification more often than those of men. More than 30 percent of the analyzed video clips featured close-ups of women's body parts, whereas only 7 percent of the clips zoomed in on men's body parts.

The most astonishing difference between the two types of porn was seen in the initiation of sex. In professional porn, men and women initiated sex with about the same frequency. But in amateur porn, men initiated sex significantly more often than women did. Moreover, although in professional porn about as many women as men had sex for their own pleasure, in amateur porn this ratio was significantly skewed toward men. Amateur porn presented women significantly more often in lower social or professional positions, and whereas both forms of porn presented women as subordinate, this disparity was much more dramatic in amateur content.

So what does this all mean? First, contrary to expectations, amateur porn presents content that is even more stereotypical and regressive than that found in professional porn. Perhaps amateurs allow themselves to be guided by a naïve and conservative porn script—that is, their ideas about how porn should look—when creating the content. Alternatively, it may also be that professional content is beginning to change its representations of women as a result of cultural shifts. For example, professional pornography may be responding to the growing popularity of MILF (mother I'd like to fuck) porn, in which women in their forties and in higher social or professional positions initiate sex, whereas amateur porn may be slower to alter the classic pornographic script. In either case, it seems that teens are increasingly likely to encounter strongly stereotypical messages in amateur porn.

Sexy Media Effects

Unsurprisingly, along with evaluating the amount and types of sexual media content that youth come across, scholars have asked what the effects of exposure to this content might be. Many scholars take the position that sexual media content has a negative influence on adolescents' sexuality. They argue that sex in entertainment media provides youth with an unrealistic and distorted picture of sexuality, and that most youth are not mature enough to put this distorted picture into perspective. Other scholars think that media serve as a kind of "super peer" for youth: teens may turn to the media for ideas and norms about sexuality that are unavailable in their peer group or that strengthen existing ideas and norms in this group.[26] In both cases, the likelihood that the distorted sexual content will affect them increases.

Some scientists take the potential negative effects of sex in entertainment media less seriously. They argue that youth—particularly girls—are seen by other researchers as too vulnerable, when in fact their agency is much greater than we assume. These self-aware girls are quite capable of recognizing unrealistic and distorted sexual images and of rejecting them.[27] Finally, a handful of researchers believe that sexual content can positively influence young people's sexuality.[28] Some of these scholars suggest, for example, that media can educate young people about sexual issues such as sexually transmitted diseases and pregnancy.[29]

What is the truth? Are adolescents affected by sexual media content? And if so, how? How are their sexual cognition (thoughts and beliefs), emotions, or behavior affected? A growing number of studies have tried to answer these questions. But attempting to study youth and sexual messages is complicated. To investigate the effects of sexual media content on children and adolescents is particularly difficult, because, ethically, researchers cannot confront children with, or even ask them about, sexuality and pornography. As a result, the existing research tends to focus on adolescents thirteen and over, even though developmentally it would be more informative to begin at a younger age—before sexual identities begin to unfold.

Studies into the effects of sexual media content rely on different theories to explain how the content might influence adolescents. The most notable ones are Bandura's social cognitive theory, Steele and Brown's media practice model, Valkenburg and Peter's differential susceptibility to media effects model, and Gerbner's cultivation theory.[30] Recall from chapter 2 that cultivation theory states that if viewers are regularly exposed to ideas from the media world (by, for example, consistently consuming messages that treat females as sex objects), they will gradually internalize these ideas. Whereas this theory helps explain how a distorted media world might influence teens, it does not pay much attention to individual differences that might explain why some teens would be more (or less) influenced by sexual entertainment content.

The remaining theories acknowledge such individual differences. These models predict how and when, and for which adolescents, sexual media content has stronger or weaker effects. Their most important principles are that sexual media consumers are active in their processing of sexual media, and that their use of sexual media content is predicted by numerous dispositional factors (for example, sexual maturity and identity) and social factors, such as friends and parents. Like other contemporary media effect theories, they assume that the influence process is reciprocal: the use of sexual media content is usually both the cause and the effect of youth's sexual cognitions, emotions, and behavior.

Effects on Sexual Cognition

Much of the research on the influence of sexual media content has asked how such content might influence teens' sexual cognition—their knowledge and beliefs about sex and sex-related matters. Sexual cognition includes knowledge about sexual scripts (that is, ideas about how sexual encounters normally proceed), sexual techniques, and concrete matters such as how to use a condom. But it also encompasses beliefs about sex and gender roles. For example, do teens believe that commitment should be present before two people have sex, or do they believe that sex is purely recreational and does not require love? Do teens see women as sex objects and men as being "driven" by sex? Do they believe that a sexy-looking woman is "looking for sex"? These and other beliefs fall under the umbrella term "sexual cognition."

In general, the literature indicates that exposure to sexual media content influences the sexual cognition of youth. American research, for example, has found that the more contact teens have with sexual media content, the more they view sex as a recreational, commitment-free pastime.[31] Similarly, research with Dutch teens has found that increased exposure to online sex is associated with more liberal and recreational ideas about sex. In particular, teens with a higher exposure to online sex are more likely to view sex as a game between two casual partners, with physical satisfaction as the primary goal. Thus, teens with increased exposure to online sex are more likely to believe that having more than one sexual partner at a time is acceptable and that it is less important for sex to occur in the context of a romantic relationship.[32]

Exposure to online sex can also influence teens' beliefs about gender roles. Researchers have found that for boys, surfing the Web for erotic content is positively associated with traditional ideas about gender roles (for example, the endorsement of the beliefs that men are sex driven and that women are sex objects).[33] Extending this work, other researchers have found that the relationship between exposure to online sex and gender beliefs is reciprocal. Specifically, teens (boys and girls) who believe that women are sex objects are more likely to go looking for online sex. Their exposure to this online content, in turn, reinforces their gender-related beliefs.[34]

To date, the negative effects of sexual media content pervade the academic literature. That said, there is growing recognition that sexual media content may positively influence sexual cognition.[35] Take, for example, a now-classic study by Rebecca Collins and colleagues featuring the American television series *Friends*. During one episode, viewers learn that one of the characters (Rachel) is pregnant because of condom failure. After the episode aired, 506 American teens were interviewed about their condom knowledge. Results indicated that viewers had significantly better understanding than nonviewers about condoms, including the risks and consequences of condom failure.[36]

This study by Collins and colleagues shows the powerful role of media as an educator. It also highlights the opportunities of entertainment media for sharing important health-related messages with teens. Yet at the same time, it underscores teens' susceptibility to sexual media content. Numerous content analyses have shown that entertainment media present an unrealistic and distorted picture of sex. We know that teens who believe that sexual media content is realistic are more susceptible to the effects of such content.[37] While estimates suggest that about 60 percent of teens believe that sex in porn is not the same as sex in real life, this means that about 40 percent do take sexual media experiences as seriously as real-life ones.[38] Efforts to help teens understand the differences between sex in the media and in reality are therefore certainly worthwhile. Moreover, interventions to counter the sexual media culture that surrounds teens are an important next step.

Effects on Arousal and Emotions

Compared with the relatively large literature on sexual cognition, the work on sexual emotions is more limited. Sexual emotions include physiological reactions, such as sexual arousal, and the feelings that adolescents can experience during and after seeing sex in media, such as pleasure, disgust, satisfaction, or insecurity. Although sexual emotions are an integral part of theoretical models to explain how people react to sexual media content, research to test these models is lacking. This is mostly due to the ethics associated with researching arousal or sexual emotions among children and teens. There is, however, at least one study on the influence of sexual media content on sexual arousal. This work, which was conducted by Wendell Dysinger and Christian Ruckmick, was part of the well-known Payne Fund Studies, which were published in 1933 (see chapter 3).[39] Perhaps the ethical review boards of that time, if they existed, were less strict than they are today.

In their study, Dysinger and Ruckmick showed sad, scary, and erotic films to children (ages 6–11), adolescents (ages 12–18), and adults, both in the lab and in the cinema. To measure arousal, they used a galvanometer (an instrument no longer in use) to measure moisture on the skin. The degree of moisture, or conductivity, is an indication of the degree to which physiological arousal is occurring; it can indicate emotions such as fear and sexual desire, too. In comparison with adolescents and adults, children reacted to all types of films with more arousal—except erotic films, to which they, strikingly, reacted with hardly any physiological arousal whatsoever. Physiological response to erotic films occurred only in those older than about ten years of age. This finding makes sense. It is likely that erotic content was largely "over the heads" of younger children, and it is only after the onset of puberty that teens experience arousal and emotional responses to such content.

In more recent research, using a self-report longitudinal survey, Jochen Peter and Patti Valkenburg investigated to what extent Dutch teens and young adults (ages 13–20) experience pornography as arousing. Results indicated that teens, particularly boys, experience it as arousing.[40] Girls appeared to be more ambivalent in their emotional responses to erotic and pornographic material. Although girls experienced porn as arousing, they sometimes also found watching it to be shameful. They seemed to distance themselves more than boys from the lack of intimacy in porn and the fact that porn is so clearly presented from a male perspective.[41] In another study, Peter and Valkenburg found that exposure to online porn was associated with increased feelings of sexual insecurity. This effect held for both sexes, although it was more pronounced among girls.[42]

Beyond these studies, the remaining (limited) work on emotional responses has concentrated on the sexual satisfaction of adolescents. This work has shown that exposure to sexual media content (particularly online porn) can negatively influence the sexual satisfaction of both boys and girls.[43] Interestingly, this relationship appears reciprocal. Adolescents who are less satisfied with their sex lives watch more porn, and this porn makes them even more unsatisfied. This effect is particularly prominent among teens who have less experience with sex and teens whose friends are also less sexually experienced.

Effects on Sexual Behavior

While cognition and emotions are clearly important, parents and practitioners are most interested in understanding whether exposure to sexual media content influences sexual behavior. Research on the effects of sexual media content on sexual behavior typically focuses on the age at which adolescents start having sex and on sexual risk behavior related to unprotected sex, teenage pregnancy, and STIs (sexually transmitted infections).

Although only a handful of studies have investigated sexual behavior, all agree that exposure to sexual media is associated with an increased incidence of sexual behavior.[44] For example, one American study revealed that early exposure to sexually explicit media increased the likelihood of teens having oral sex and sexual intercourse two years later.[45] In another American study, researchers similarly found that teens who often consume sexual media content are more likely to engage in sexual activity. But, interestingly, they also found that sexually active adolescents are more likely to expose themselves to sexual media content. Thus, the relationship between exposure to sexual media content and sexual behavior appears to be reciprocal: sexually active teens are more likely to consume sexual media content, and this exposure, in turn, increases their likelihood to progress in their sexual behavior.[46] Finally a Flemish study found that the use of online porn was associated with a higher likelihood of initiating sex. But this result held only for adolescents in early puberty. Among older adolescents, online porn use was related with a lower likelihood of initiating sex.[47]

While it seems clear that exposure to sexual media content can influence sexual behavior, it is less clear whether it influences sexual risk behavior. For example, some studies find no effect on teen pregnancy and the rates of STIs, but others do find such effects.[48] Most of these studies, however, were conducted in the United States, and thus are difficult to generalize to the rest of the world. The United States is more conservative about sex education than other developed countries, and it is at the top of the list of developed countries for teen pregnancy rates.[49] For example, a Swiss study found no effect of sex in the media on teen pregnancies.[50] Similarly, a Dutch study found no effect of exposure to online porn on teens' condom use or their participation in casual sexual encounters.[51] Yet an American study found that sexting (sending and sharing sexual photos online) was associated with risky sexual behaviors, namely, having concurrent sexual partners and more past-year sexual partners.[52] While more work is needed to obtain a clearer picture of the relationship between sexual media and risky sexual behavior, these findings suggest that cultural values influence how youth process and are influenced by sexual media messages.

Conclusion

Adolescents are growing up in an environment replete with sexual messages. In movies, games, advertisements, or Google searches, teens are frequently confronted with sexual media content. Unfortunately, much of this media content presents a view that is unrealistic and stereotypical—often treating women as mere sex objects and men as sex seekers. Over time, these distorted messages can influence teens' sexual cognition, emotions, and, in some cases, sexual risk behavior.

It should be emphasized that the longitudinal relationships between sexual media content and sexual cognition, emotions, and behavior are often reciprocal. For example, adolescents who begin having sex earlier seek out sex in the media at an earlier age. Both behaviors, after all, are expressions of the same phase in their sexual development: seeking sexual media content gives these interested adolescents new ideas and contributes to their sexual experiences at an earlier age.

We also see that not all adolescents are equally susceptible to the effects of sexual media content. Boys and girls do not seem to differ appreciably in their susceptibility to the effects of sexual media content, but other factors do seem to increase susceptibility. Some effects of sexual media content seem to hold particularly for adolescents in early puberty. Other effects, especially cognitive ones, seem to hold more for teens who believe that the media's representation of sex is realistic and who are less sexually experienced. More research is needed to better identify which youth are especially susceptible to the potentially negative effects of sexual media content, and how media education may serve as a protective factor for these susceptible youth.[53]

Finally, while continued efforts to understand the negative consequences of sexual media content exposure are crucial, it is also important to realize that sexual media content can serve as a positive role model for children and teens today. Thus far, the studies on positive effects are promising—showing, for example, delay of sexual initiation, improvement in condom self-efficacy, increased knowledge of sexual risks, and even removal of sexual references from social media profiles.[54] In the future, we hope to see more work designed to evaluate how media can support the development of healthy sexual knowledge, sexual self-confidence, and tolerance of sexual diversity.

In an era when sexual media is omnipresent, when teens are becoming "senders" of sexual media content (for example, via sexy selfies; also see chapter 13), and when sexual content is available at the touch of a button, it is imperative for scholars to continue to ask questions about who is affected by this content, why this influence occurs, and whether and when such effects may be troublesome. As with media violence, this issue is not a black-and-white debate about whether a particular type of media content has effects on teens. It is time to move way from a public debate characterized by a competition between parties with traditional or liberal ideas about human behavior, and move toward a more balanced approach that addresses the crucial questions discussed in this chapter.

11

MEDIA AND EDUCATION

> "Hold your tongue!" added the Gryphon, before Alice could speak again.
> The Mock Turtle went on:
> "We had the best of educations—in fact, we went to school every day—"
> "*I've* been to a day-school, too," said Alice; "you needn't be so proud as all that."
> "With extras?" asked the Mock Turtle, a little anxiously.
> "Yes," said Alice, "we learned French and music."
> "And washing?" said the Mock Turtle.
> "Certainly not!" said Alice indignantly.
> "Ah! Then yours wasn't a really good school," said the Mock Turtle in a tone of great relief.
>
> —Lewis Carroll, *Alice's Adventures in Wonderland* (1865)

Thus far, we have highlighted the darker side of media use, such as the effects of media violence on aggression or the effect of sexual media content on sexual behavior. In this chapter, we turn to its sunny side, focusing on the positive effects of educational media—media designed to support youth's development. Today, there are more platforms for educational media content than ever before. And while researchers have long identified the effectiveness of educational television, the potential for other educational platforms is still being understood. We begin with a short account of the history of educational media, along with statistics on the use of educational media in the family. We then discuss several effects of educational media content. For example, does educational content stimulate academic skills, such as literacy and numeracy? Can it facilitate social-emotional learning by promoting characteristics such as empathy, willingness to share, and self-regulation? And can it help children be more imaginative and creative? The chapter concludes with a discussion of future directions for the field of educational media.

Where It All Began

Educational media, particularly educational television, secured its place in history with the arrival of *Sesame Street* in 1969. At its time revolutionary, *Sesame Street* was developed to help prepare preschool children (ages 2–5) for elementary school, particularly children from low-income and minority backgrounds. *Sesame Street* was not the first children's series to embed education into humor and entertainment. Other series at the time, such as *Captain Kangaroo* (1955–84), were based on the same formula. What distinguished *Sesame Street* was its use of empirical research as an integral part of the production process. In its design, *Sesame Street* relied (and continues to rely) on the input of in-house experts on child development, learning, and media. In doing so, it has become an exemplar of how to incorporate academic insight into educational programming. By being both entertaining and research driven, *Sesame Street* permanently changed the landscape of educational media.[1] Today, the series airs in more than 140 countries, either in its standard version or in culturally adjusted forms.

From its inception, the core aim of *Sesame Street* has been to foster the school-readiness skills of preschool children. School-readiness skills encompass not only academic learning, such as letter and number recognition, but also social-emotional learning, such as friendliness, cooperation, and acceptance of diversity. Although the founders of *Sesame Street* included social-emotional learning goals in their initial concept, in the early years they focused primarily on academic learning. They took seriously the opinions of parents and educational experts, and in the early 1970s, these groups identified academic learning as the greatest need among children from low-income and minority backgrounds (the target group of the series).[2]

In the 1990s, the curriculum of *Sesame Street* underwent a structural shift in the direction of social-emotional learning. A different view of education was emerging at the time. Evidence began to appear that academic success was a function not only of academic skills, but also of healthy social-emotional development. Studies showed, for example, that children who have difficulty controlling their negative emotions or who cannot get along with their teachers or classmates do poorly in school.[3] As a result of these and other similar studies, child psychologists began to acknowledge the importance of both academic and social-emotional skills in predicting school success. Moreover, along with this shift, parents changed their views on social-emotional learning, which they regarded as equal, rather than secondary, to academic learning.

Sesame Street's approach to formally include academic and social-emotional curricula in its content slowly spread to the educational media genre more generally. Developers and researchers agreed that educational media could be used to stimulate academic and social-emotional learning. This trend toward a more encompassing definition of learning could be seen in educational media legislation at the time. For example, in the United States, the 1996 guidelines of the Children's Television Act introduced the so-called three-hour rule requiring that public broadcast stations air, at a minimum, three hours a week of children's educational or informational television. To be considered educational or informational, programs could meet children's cognitive-intellectual or social-emotional needs.[4]

Educational Media Use at Home

In the new millennium, educational media have become a fixture in children's media diets. American children ages 2–10 now spend about an hour a day with educational media, with comparable estimates in other industrialized countries.[5] Moreover, ever-younger children now use educational media. Whereas two decades ago, children began to watch television at around two and a half years of age, today's children start watching at around four months.[6] In fact, children under the age of two now use screen media (television, DVDs, tablets) for an average of an hour a day.[7]

What might explain this acceleration in (educational) media use in early childhood? First there have been increased marketing efforts directed toward the youngest age group. As noted in chapter 1, since the resounding success of *Teletubbies* in 1997, commercial conglomerates have set their sights on the "diaper demographic." For example, shortly after *Teletubbies*, Baby Einstein products (videos, toys, etc.) were introduced to the public and soon became a multimillion-dollar business, which was sold to Disney in 2001. In 2003 came the birth of Baby TV—a twenty-four-hour-seven-day-a-week television channel, which is now available in more than a hundred countries. And most recently, a deluge of infant- and toddler-targeted educational apps have appeared on the market, with Apple's educational app store, for example, currently featuring more than eighty thousand apps to choose from.

Ramped-up marketing efforts to parents are not the only explanation for the increase of educational media use in early childhood. In many Western countries, policies have also started to put more emphasis on so-called informal learning in early childhood. Informal learning is the kind of learning that occurs spontaneously and playfully outside school. As discussed in chapter 2, today's parents want the best for their children, including the benefits of educational media in the home. Many parents see educational media as an easy and accessible means of providing their children with experiences that can give them a leg up in life.[8] And the more that parents believe in the value of educational media content, the higher the likelihood that their children will have access to this content at home.[9]

Although educational media are now a common part of early childhood, the use of such media seems to decrease as children grow older. For example, whereas two- to four-year-olds spend slightly more than an hour a day using educational media, eight- to ten-year-olds are estimated to spend only forty-two minutes a day with such content.[10] Moreover, the percentage of educational media content in overall media use drops significantly with age: for two- to four-year-olds, it is 78 percent, whereas for eight- to ten-year-olds, it is 27 percent.[11]

The substantial drop-off in educational media use among older children is not clearly understood. It may reflect the fact that as children enter formal schooling, they have less discretionary time for educational media use because of homework and extracurricular activities. And from that point on, parents may be less likely to promote educational media for older children. Another explanation is that fewer successful educational media options are available for older children. In research on touch-screen technology, this phenomenon has been referred to as the "app gap," highlighting the challenges that developers face in creating educational media content for an audience that is increasingly critical of such content.

Finally, the downtrend in older children's educational media use may simply reflect their declining interest in such content. Often referred to as the "spinach syndrome," this term refers to what happens to children by about five years of age, as they begin to reject anything that is supposed to be good for them (see chapter 5). Children become less interested in "teachy-preachy" content and instead prefer real-life content that addresses social and emotional themes. Older children and teens seem to be mainly interested in prosocial content dealing with social-emotional themes, such as friendships, cooperation, and altruism.[12]

Learning from Educational Media

Public concerns about the negative effects of media on children are of long standing. Implicit in these concerns is the notion that children and teens can learn from media. And if we subscribe to the notion that media content can teach youth negative lessons, it stands to reason that it can teach positive lessons too. As Joan Ganz Cooney, one of the founders of *Sesame Street,* famously noted, "It is not whether children learn from television, it is what they learn, because everything children see on television is teaching them something."[13]

The goals of educational media vary significantly, but most have attempted to support youth's academic skills, social-emotional learning, or creativity. Our focus here is on educational media used in the home as tools for informal learning. We do not review the effects of such media in the classroom or in other formal learning situations. Although research on the positive effects of media is not as robust as that on their negative effects, this growing field has thus far compellingly shown that under certain conditions, educational media content can bolster both the academic and social-emotional development of youth.

One of the key aspects of educational media effects involves an understanding of how they occur. How do children and teens learn from television and other media? Several scholars have attempted to explain educational media effects, most notably Albert Bandura (social cognitive theory), Shalom Fisch (the capacity model), and Katherine Buckley and Craig Anderson (the general learning model). Each theory makes predictions about the conditions under which the skills, attitudes, and behaviors portrayed in educational media will be replicated in and transferred to other circumstances.

Social Cognitive Theory

Just as social cognitive theory has been used to explain how violent content may translate to increased aggression among children, it has also been used to explain how children may benefit from educational media content. As discussed in chapter 7, social cognitive theory predicts that children are more likely to learn from a model in the media if they are able to identify with the model or if they perceive the model to be similar to themselves. According to the theory, children are more likely to adopt behavior from a model that is rewarded than from a model that is punished. Moreover, by observing models, children learn not only how to imitate the rewarded behavior but also how to extract abstract behavioral rules that they can adapt in future situations. For this kind of observational learning to occur, attention to the model and its behavior is critical. Attention can be enhanced by specific characteristics of the model (attractiveness, popularity in the group, sense of humor) and predicted by differences between the children (their developmental levels, prior experiences, preferences).[14] Social cognitive theory has provided important insight into how media can positively influence children and adolescents.[15]

The Capacity Model

Shalom Fisch developed his capacity model to explain how children extract and comprehend educational content from narrative educational media. His model proposes that educational media (particularly television) contain two forms of content: a narrative (story line) and the embedded educational content. Central to the model is the supposition that children's working memory is limited, and that the cognitive demands of the embedded educational content should not exceed the resources available in working memory.

In the processing of educational media, cognitive demands are said to come from processing the narrative, processing the embedded educational content, and the distance between the two content types. When the educational content and the narrative are tangential to each other, the two parallel comprehension processes compete for children's limited resources in working memory, which may result in impaired comprehension of the educational content. But when the educational content is integral to the narrative, comprehension of the educational content is expected to improve.

Like social cognitive theory, the capacity model predicts that characteristics of the content (for example, program pace, direct questions from a character to the child) and of the child (for example, developmental level) may lead to more efficient processing and increased comprehension.[16] And like social cognitive theory, it has been used successfully to predict children's learning from educational television.[17]

The General Learning Model

Buckley and Anderson's general learning model was developed to explain the effects of prosocial video games. It is in many ways comparable to the general aggression model discussed in chapter 7. According to Buckley and Anderson, many features of video games make them excellent teachers. For example, games easily attract attention; they are highly motivating; they allow people to actively participate instead of passively watch; they show all steps necessary to perform a specific behavior; and they allow repetitive practicing.

The general learning model posits that prosocial media, in which the characters (or players in games) help one another, can increase both short- and long-term prosocial behavior. This can occur via a cognitive route, in which the prosocial game content primes identical prosocial scripts or schemas. It can occur via an emotional route, too, for example, when players form emotional attachments to characters or avatars, which in turn improves their learning.[18] As with social cognitive theory and the capacity model, there is evidence to support the predictive value of the general learning model.[19]

Educational Media and Academic Skills

Can children learn academic skills from educational media? Can they, for example, learn letters, numbers, and geometric forms? Can they learn how to classify objects, reason logically, and solve problems? Yes, they can, but whether that happens depends on the content, the child, and the social environment. It was pointed out in earlier chapters that media effects depend on a host of developmental, dispositional, and social factors. The same is true for the effects of educational media. One of the most important of these factors is children's developmental level, particularly the (mis)-

match between their developmental level and the difficulty of media content.

Infants and Toddlers

The question whether young children can benefit from academically enriching media content brings us to one of the hottest debates in the educational media landscape—whether children under the age of two can learn at all from media. In chapter 4, we came across the video deficit hypothesis, which reflects a compelling body of research showing that infants and toddlers learn less from video than from real-life experiences—a phenomenon that seems to dissipate at around age three. Although it is not entirely clear what accounts for the video deficit, scholars have suggested that very young children are not able to transfer information portrayed in a two-dimensional space to a three-dimensional space. In addition, they have suggested that audiovisual media may not properly direct young children's attention, since the video deficit seems to apply to young children's interpretations of picture book illustrations as well as to television.[20]

There are two important provisions to the video deficit hypothesis. First, although infants and toddlers may learn less from a model in the media than from a real-life model, that difference does not mean they are not learning anything from the former. It just means that for very young children, real-life models are better teachers than mediated models. Second, although evidence for the video deficit is convincing, recent studies have demonstrated that the video deficit can be reduced or even neutralized—particularly in the context of literacy and mathematics education. For example, research has shown that repeated viewing of educational content can limit the video deficit.[21] Similarly, the video deficit can be reduced when the child is familiar with a character in the program.[22] And finally, new work with apps indicates that interactive features that draw children's attention to the educational information promote learning.[23]

Equally interesting, the video deficit seems to disappear if an adult provides additional information to the child in order to help with learning. Such parental encouragement is known as parental mediation or, in Vygotskian terms, as scaffolding. Lev Vygotsky, a Russian developmental psychologist, made a distinction between the problems a child can solve by himself or herself (actual development) and problems she or he can solve with help from an adult (potential development). The space between what children can achieve alone and what they can achieve with the support of a competent other is known as the zone of proximal development. Through parental mediation of educational media content, adults can help children bridge this zone and, in the case of infants and toddlers, nullify the video deficit.[24]

Thus, while there is robust evidence to suggest that very young media users are better able to learn from real-life models than from media models, it is clear that both specific content characteristics and parental scaffolding can mitigate this video deficit. If these factors are taken into account, educational media can teach infants and toddlers literacy skills (such as language acquisition) and mathematical skills (such as seriation).

Preschoolers and Older Children

Although there are a handful of studies on the effects of educational media on academic skills among older children and teens, the majority of existing work has concentrated on early childhood. More than 1,000 studies have, for example, examined the influence of *Sesame Street* on young children's early academic skills, and the vast majority have demonstrated its ability to support young children's learning.[25] In fact, in 2013, Marie-Louise Mares and Zhongdang Pan conducted a meta-analysis to identify the effectiveness of the international coproductions of *Sesame Street*. Working with data from more than ten thousand children across fifteen countries, their meta-analysis revealed significant positive effects of the program on literacy and numeracy, knowledge about health issues, and social reasoning.[26]

Sesame Street, however, is not the only program that has been shown to support early academic skills. Experimental research with *Super Why!*, an animated literacy-based American educational television show, found that children ages 3–6 who watched the program for eight weeks outperformed their nonviewing peers on nearly all literacy outcomes.[27] Similarly, work with the American program *Between the Lions* found that children ages 6–8 who watched the program for four weeks had better word recognition and reading test scores than nonviewers.[28] These effects were particularly pronounced among children moderately at risk for literacy deficits.

Similar benefits of educational television content on academic skills have been found for a host of other programs, including *Barney and Friends*, *Dragon Tales*, *Blue's Clues*, and *Pinky Dinky Doo*. These programs were designed with the explicit intent to support academic skills, and they all relied on a combination of desk and field research to help ensure that the content met these goals.[29] And impressively, watching such programs in early childhood has longer-term benefits: a longitudinal study by Daniel Anderson and colleagues revealed that adolescents who had watched many educational programs as preschoolers had higher grades in school, read more books, and placed more value on achievement than their nonviewing peers.[30]

The few studies on educational media effects among older children and teens have likewise found positive effects. For example, research on the American program *Cyberchase,* a show designed to support mathematical skills, revealed that among eight- to nine-year-olds, viewers' problem-solving skills improved more than those of nonviewers after four weeks of watching the show.[31] Similarly, evaluations of two popular science-based programs targeting older children (*The Magic School Bus* and *Bill Nye the Science Guy*) revealed that, compared with nonviewers, viewers demonstrated increased understanding of scientific concepts and the process of scientific discovery.[32] Overall, the literature provides persuasive evidence that children can—and do—learn academic skills from educational media.

Educational Media and Social-Emotional Skills

When people use the term "educational media," it is common to immediately think of content that supports traditional academic skills, such as literacy or numeracy. Indeed, most publications that rely on this term typically refer to *Sesame Street*'s influence on early academic skills and contextualize educational media within these contours. But as the founders of *Sesame Street* believed in the 1970s, media can teach more than academic skills. Educational media are equally suited, and perhaps even better suited, to teach social-emotional skills.

Despite the potential of educational media to promote social-emotional learning, research on this issue is scarce, particularly among young children. But a growing body of work has looked at media support for social-emotional development among older children and adolescents. Thus far, this work has focused on the role of media in supporting prosocial behavior (helping, friendliness, altruism) and other expressions of social-emotional learning, such as social competence and self-regulation.

Prosocial Behavior

In the 1950s, 1960s, and 1970s, classic American family shows such as *Lassie* (1954–74) and *The Waltons* (1971–81) were among the most popular programs on television. Content analyses at the time revealed that these and other similar programs often contained prosocial portrayals of helping, friendliness, and altruism.[33] And these programs increased children's prosocial behavior. For example, in an early study, Joyce Sprafkin and colleagues demonstrated that children who viewed an episode of *Lassie* in which the protagonist helped the dog (Lassie) were more likely to help an animal presumed to be in distress than children who saw an episode devoid of this scene.[34]

By the 1980s, these kinds of programs were being slowly replaced by cartoons or animated productions such as *Teenage Mutant Ninja Turtles*, which turned out to be immensely popular among children.[35] These series were highly profitable. Production was relatively cheap, and the animated characters traveled well across different cultures. As a result, their licenses could be readily sold to other countries. It was not until passage of the Children's Television Act in the United States that American developers were forced to refocus their efforts on educational content that expressly supported children's informational or social-emotional development.

Soon after, the children's media landscape saw a range of content emerge that was said to meet children's social-emotional needs. Much of this content lived up to the letter rather than the spirit of the law (for example, there were claims that the cartoon *The Jetsons* taught about the future). That said, the Children's Television Act did lead to an influx of content designed to support prosocial behavior.[36] For example, Disney's *Doug* was an animated program following the life of a socially awkward preteen as he managed typical preteen situations and emotions, such as trying to fit in, bullying, and (platonic) romantic relationships.

Along with this influx of prosocial programming, a multitude of studies have investigated whether and how prosocial media content contributes to prosocial behavior. Prosocial behavior in these studies refers to positive interactions such as friendly play or peaceful conflict resolutions, altruism (sharing, offering help), and stereotype reduction (changed attitudes and beliefs toward the opposite gender or other ethnicities). Most of these studies have focused on the effects of television. In 2007, Marie-Louise Mares and Emory Woodard conducted a meta-analysis to assess the effects of prosocial television exposure on prosocial behavior. Their results revealed that children who watched more prosocial content exhibited more prosocial behavior. They also showed that these effects increased sharply during early childhood and peaked around age seven, after which they declined throughout the tween and teen years.[37]

Mares and Woodard believe that the peak around age seven implies that younger children may not yet fully understand prosocial content on television, and may especially have difficulty extracting the prosocial messages in prosocial television. But the peak around age seven also implies that the effectiveness of prosocial programs declines after that age. A possible explanation for this age-related decline might be that the television programs included in Mares and Woodard's meta-analysis were less attuned to the developmental level of older children, and were therefore not sufficiently appealing to them (see the moderate discrepancy hypothesis in chapter 4). If more age-appropriate and appealing programs had been used in the empirical studies included in their meta-analysis, the effects of prosocial programs might have been more pronounced among older children.

Several recent studies confirm that appealing and age-appropriate prosocial content can lead to prosocial effects among older children and teens. For example, Dutch researchers recently showed that tweens' and teens' watching of an episode of a teen-targeted news program featuring prosocial action for UNICEF led to more donations to UNICEF than watching an episode without the modeling of prosocial action.[38] Similarly, a series of studies by Douglas Gentile and colleagues, conducted across three age groups (tweens, teens, adults) in three countries, found that playing prosocial video games such as *Chibi Robo!* increased players' prosocial behaviors.[39]

Social Competence and Self-Regulation

We have now seen that educational media content can teach prosocial behavior, but can it teach other social-emotional skills? Can it teach children self-regulation? And can it teach social competence (that is, the ability to adapt positively to other persons and situations)? Perhaps as a result of the promising findings of studies on prosocial content, developers have begun looking at whether other social-emotional lessons can be taught through the media. We have seen, for example, an influx of apps meant to help children learn about emotions more generally, such as *Daniel Tiger's Grr-ific Feelings, Inside Out: Storybook Deluxe,* as well as apps designed specifically to encourage empathy, such as *Peppy Pals.* Even Disney's Pixar has gotten in on the action; its movie *Inside Out* focuses on how a young girl's emotions (joy, fear, sadness) conflict when she moves with her parents from the Midwest to San Francisco.

Empirical research to confirm the effectiveness of content that addresses emotional and social competence is scarce but promising. Studies thus far have focused on young children. For example, Dimitri Christakis and colleagues devised an intervention in which a group of parents were encouraged to expose their children to high-quality educational programming such as *Sesame Street, Dora the Explorer,* and *Super Why!* After six and twelve months, the children in the intervention families showed higher levels of social competence than did children in the nonintervention families.[40]

A separate line of research in the area of social-emotional development indicates that educational media can also help support young children's self-regulatory skills (that is, the ability to resist impulses and temptations that keep them from achieving their long-term goals). Children younger than eighteen months of age are incapable of self-regulation. Ask any little one to wait before enjoying a cookie, and you will quickly see the request is futile. By about two years old, children begin to learn how to resist temptation and repress unwanted behavior (see also chapter 4). Thus, it is around this age when efforts to support self-regulatory abilities can be particularly beneficial, and it was for this reason that *Sesame Street* decided to build self-regulation into its aims for the 2013–14 season.

Sesame Street's Cookie Monster is the perfect character to teach children self-regulation. After all, just as the show's viewers struggle with resisting delicious treats, so too does Cookie Monster (see figure 11.1). And just like his viewers, Cookie Monster often needs a little help with self-regulation. An experimental study by Deborah Linebarger investigated whether Cookie Monster could indeed teach children self-regulation. She exposed fifty-nine preschoolers in their homes to several clips featuring Cookie Monster rehearsing self-regulation strategies. Children's self-regulation was measured with the marshmallow test, a classic delay-of-gratification task

Figure 11.1. Cookie Monster is the perfect character to teach young children self-regulation. (© 2015 Sesame Workshop. All rights reserved. Photo credit: Sesame Workshop)

in which children get the option to eat one marshmallow immediately or to wait for fifteen minutes in order to get two marshmallows. Viewers of the Cookie Monster clips were able to wait on average nearly four minutes longer than nonviewers.[41]

Creativity

While there is growing evidence that educational media can support children's academic and social-emotional development, can they also foster children's creativity? All parents want to see their children grow into creative adults. Creativity is an ability that is well regarded in society. Multinationals spend loads of money to teach their staff how to think creatively or innovatively. Creativity, which is sometimes called creative imagination or divergent thinking, is the ability to generate novel or unusual ideas. In young children, creative thinking is typically expressed in their imaginative play, the play in which they transcend reality by acting "as if."[42]

One of the clearest findings from studies of creativity is that adults who are creative tend to come from families that provided them with a favorable background for the development of intellectual abilities.[43] Since environmental forces in childhood can affect later creative achievement, one might therefore expect that media use could be a socializing factor with a great potential to influence creativity. A considerable body of research has been designed to demonstrate that screen media use can be detrimental to creativity and imaginative play, but far fewer studies have been done to evaluate whether educational media use can support imaginative play and creativity.

In 2012, Patti Valkenburg and Sandra Calvert reviewed the existing literature to identify whether and when media support children's creativity and imaginative play.[44] In their review, they tried to identify whether the existing literature provided support for the stimulation hypothesis. This hypothesis states that well-designed educational media can enrich the store of ideas from which children can draw when engaged in imaginative play or creative tasks. More specifically, it posits that children pick up characters and events in these media, transform and incorporate these into their play and products of creativity, and as a result, the quality or quantity of their play and creative products is improved.

In all, their review provided support for the stimulation hypothesis. Several experimental studies with young children indeed show that educational television programs such as *Mister Rogers' Neighborhood*, *Barney*, and *Dora the Explorer* can promote imaginative play.[45] Similarly, longitudinal evidence indicates that the viewing of educational television during early childhood predicts increased creativity during adolescence.[46] And interestingly, nearly 80 percent of parents in an American survey reported that their children "sometimes" or "often" engage in imaginative play based on something they saw in educational media.[47]

Although research on the effects of television on creativity is limited, research on the role of interactive media in creativity is even scarcer. A study by Linda Jackson and colleagues found that twelve-year-olds who frequently played games scored higher than their nonplaying peers on a figural subtest in the Torrance Tests of Creative Thinking in which children are supposed to make a drawing using a curved line.[48] Researchers in an experimental study attempted to gather evidence on the relationship between the creative app play of children ages 8–10 and their creativity.

Their study revealed that developmentally appropriate creative apps improved children's engagement with content and increased its appeal for them. They did not find effects of app use on creativity, though, which, according to the researchers, may have been a result of children's limited exposure to the content.[49]

In an era when children can design avatars, when they can experiment with identities in cyberspace, and when they can play games that allow them to construct homes, cities, and landscapes, the potential benefits of interactive media on creativity seem vast. Indeed, app sales indicate that creative apps become increasingly popular throughout childhood—with tweens in particular gravitating to this form of content. As digital gaming comes to demand ever-more creative solutions to gameplay, and as creativity emerges as a key factor for twenty-first-century success, an emphasis on fostering creativity is certainly an important direction for interactive media.

Program Characteristics and Child Characteristics Matter

Overall, the evidence that educational media can support children's academic knowledge, social-emotional learning, and creativity is convincing. It is important to recognize, however, that theories of educational media effects make the point that such benefits are, in large part, contingent on program characteristics and child characteristics. Although a complete review of characteristics that might enhance children's learning from educational media is beyond the scope of this chapter, several key factors warrant attention.

Program Characteristics

Unless children pay attention to the content of educational media, they will be unable to comprehend the embedded lessons. According to the moderate discrepancy hypothesis (introduced in chapter 4), the media content most likely to attract and sustain attention is content that differs moderately from what children know and understand. Content that is too easy quickly leads to boredom and decreased attention, and content that is too challenging leads to frustration and decreased attention. Careful attention to content complexity is thus crucial when designing (educational) media content.

It is important that media developers consider the developmental needs of their target users in order to find the sweet spot of content complexity. For younger children, comprehension increases when producers rely on a simple, prototypical story line that clearly states causal linkages between the successive story events.[50] For this age group, comprehension is enhanced when the educational content is explicitly modeled (that is, every step is clearly demonstrated). And finally, comprehension is enhanced when advance organizers are used. Advance organizers are cues presented early in the program to alert viewers to particular subject matter. Such organizers can help orient younger children by identifying which content will be central to the story.[51] For older children, most program characteristics of this type are too simple. A developmentally appropriate story line for older children and teens violates some of the rules of the prototypical story (for example, by using flashbacks, a more complex chain of events, or multiple story lines), and relies on a balance of explicit and implicit modeling of the embedded educational lessons.

While the appropriate degree of content complexity is crucial, other program characteristics can enhance children's learning from media, too. For example, researchers have found that repetition of the educational lesson in varied ways helps children understand and apply the content more successfully. This use of varied repetition is effective with younger children as well as tweens and teens. For younger children, repetitive exposure to the same media content can be an effective means of supporting learning. For example, an American study using the animated program *Blue's Clues* revealed that preschool children who viewed the same episode repetitively showed improved problem-solving strategies compared to children exposed to a single viewing.[52] Both forms of repetition—within the program or through repeated exposure to the program—help draw attention to the embedded lessons.

Along with repetition, developers can use participatory cues to draw children's attention and encourage their comprehension of embedded educational content. Participatory cues involve asking children to respond to questions or building in pauses to allow children time to respond to these questions.[53] The well-known American preschool program *Mister Rogers' Neighborhood* was among the first shows of this type to include such participatory cues. In games and apps, participatory cues are more self-evident, since they can easily call on their users to interact with the educational content. Participatory cues provide children with time to reflect on the content and to engage with the lessons, a type of interaction that is particularly important for younger children, whose information-processing capacity is relatively limited. Research indicates that participatory cues in educational media can facilitate learning, imaginative play, and creativity.[54]

While a variety of program characteristics can support learning, at the end of the day, it is entertainment that matters most. If media content is not appealing to a target group, it will be ignored. Unfortunately, the entertainment aspect of educational media all too often fails. So much care is given to the educational message that attention on how to deliver the message is slighted. A simple "drill and kill" app designed to teach mathematics misses out on critical entertainment opportunities. Similarly, throwing dozens of historical facts into a television program without an entertaining narrative discounts the greatest capability of television—to tell stories.

From a programmatic perspective, it is therefore crucial that developers consider what appeals to a target audience. One particularly important element in educational media is the use of characters. Typically, the lead characters drive the educational lesson. These characters often serve as social role models, depicting, for instance, how to help others, how to generate creative responses, and how to delay gratification (as we saw in the case of Cookie Monster). If such characters are done right, children are more likely to develop parasocial relationships with them (see chapter 8), in which case the likelihood of learning is greatly enhanced.[55]

Child Characteristics

Program characteristics work in tandem with child characteristics to predict effects. This means that when developing (educational) media content, developers must clearly define and understand their target audience. As has been argued throughout this book, children's development is the most important factor to consider when reflecting on educational media content. Children's developmental capabilities will influence not only what content they find moderately discrepant (and thus appealing) but also the extent to which they can comprehend and recall this content.

Just as it is developmentally inappropriate to attempt to teach a three-year-old about algebra, it is equally inappropriate to attempt to teach teens about letter recognition. As the moderate discrepancy hypothesis states, the most appropriate content will be content that is slightly different from what a child already knows.

That said, there are other audience characteristics that producers should keep in mind when creating educational media content. When working with educational media that contain story lines, it is important to consider children's understanding of story schema (the set of expectations about the internal structure of stories that makes comprehension and recall of the narrative more efficient).[56] Research has shown that children who have a more advanced story schema process narratives more easily and, as a result, have more cognitive resources available to process the embedded educational content.[57] Similarly, if children are familiar with the content (the program, the characters, the setting), they are better able to learn the educational lessons.[58]

What might this look like in practice? Consider an episode of the preschool program *Blue's Clues* entitled "Bugs." During the design phase of this episode, the program developers envisioned a scene in which the main characters were in a jungle looking for bugs. But the show's educational consultants felt that the concept "jungle" might be too unfamiliar to American preschoolers and, therefore, not moderately discrepant. Ultimately, the designers changed the scene into an expedition in which the main characters explored a backyard, looking for bugs that preschoolers might find in their own environment.[59] In this way, by capitalizing on a familiar backyard (rather than an unfamiliar jungle), developers allowed children to devote greater cognitive resources to attending to and learning the educational content.

Conclusion

Perhaps the most important conclusion of this chapter is that just as today's youth can learn negative lessons from media content, they can (and do!) learn positive lessons. When developmentally appropriate educational content merges with entertainment content, children and teens can benefit. Younger children, in particular, seem to benefit from the academic, social-emotional, and creative lessons that media can offer. There are benefits for tweens and teens too, particularly when it comes to prosocial and social-emotional learning. By capitalizing on the power of narrative entertainment, educational media can play an incredibly powerful role in supporting the development of youth.

In addition, this chapter has shown that there remain at least two gaps in our knowledge of the effectiveness of educational media. First, the educational media landscape for youth is quite unbalanced. While infants, toddlers, and preschoolers have a range of options at their (and their parents') disposal, options become more limited as children enter middle childhood and beyond. Given the potential benefits of educational media beyond the early childhood years, efforts to develop educational media that appeals to older children and teens seem worthwhile.

It can be done. Numerous one-off examples in the health communication literature show how blending entertainment and education can be an effective means of educating teens and adults about a range of topics. Similarly, there has been considerable growth in "serious games" aimed to foster academic and social-emotional learning. The next chapter shows that these games, which predominantly focus on older children and teens, have the potential to bridge the age gap in educational media use. While there is no simple recipe for success, a key point for the future of educational media lies in identifying how to create successful educational media content for older children and teens.

A second gap is our lack of knowledge of how educational media content works. There is evidence that it can support beneficial outcomes, but empirical efforts to explain these effects are still scarce. Evidence is emerging about the ways in which programmatic and child characteristics can predict learning—but this knowledge is far behind what theories on the effects of educational media tell us. We know that differences in children's development, disposition, and social environment influence how they experience media and how media affect them. If we can identify which children are most likely to benefit from educational media, and why, our ability to create effective content for youth will dramatically improve. And, in doing so, so will our ability to capitalize on an easy and affordable means of supporting the development of youth today.

12

DIGITAL GAMES

> Why are there games? Why do we, biological entities capable of creating poetry, climbing mountains, and splitting the atom, spend so much time playing games, especially when playing these games often conflicts with our basic human needs: to sleep, to feed ourselves, to communicate with our spouses?
>
> —Simon Egenfeldt-Nielsen, Jonas H. Smith, and Susana P. Tosca, *Understanding Video Games* (2013)

Why do we play digital games? What makes them deeply attractive and, for some, seriously addictive? Although digital games were once considered the domain of a small, clearly defined demographic of young men, today they are a mainstream pastime for young and old, male and female. How have games managed to occupy such a significant share of our leisure time? Do games affect us, and if so, how? Do they, as some suggest, positively influence spatial skills and, perhaps, intelligence? Or do they, as others fear, hinder our physical and emotional development? And if these effects occur, for whom do they occur? These key questions of game studies, a new research field concerned with the use, appeal, and effects of digital games, are ones this chapter will address.

How It All Began

The human need to play games is as old as Methuselah. Indeed, people in ancient Egypt played at least one game that we know about, called Senet, a board game assumed to be comparable to backgammon. And while analogue games still have a prominent place in daily life, the rise of digital technology has permanently changed our game experience. According to books on the history of digital gaming, the story begins in Boston in 1961, in the basement of a lab at the Massachusetts Institute of Technology (MIT). A small passionate group of geeks conceived of a science-fiction game in which players had to torpedo their opponent's spaceship. At the time, computers had very limited capacity and capabilities, making these ideas just that—ideas. Yet, shortly thereafter, the MIT lab obtained access to the cutting-edge technology of the PDP-1—a computer with monitor (see figure 12.1). This was, quite literally, a game changer. In 1962, one of the geeks—Steven Russell—turned this dream into a reality with the birth of *Spacewar!*[1]

Although *Spacewar!* represented a crucial starting point in the history of digital games, it was ten years later, in 1972, that Magnavox transformed gaming with the introduction of a home video game console (the Magnavox Odyssey). A few years later, in 1975, Atari released *Pong*—a primitive Ping-Pong game in which two white bars representing paddles hit a square ball.

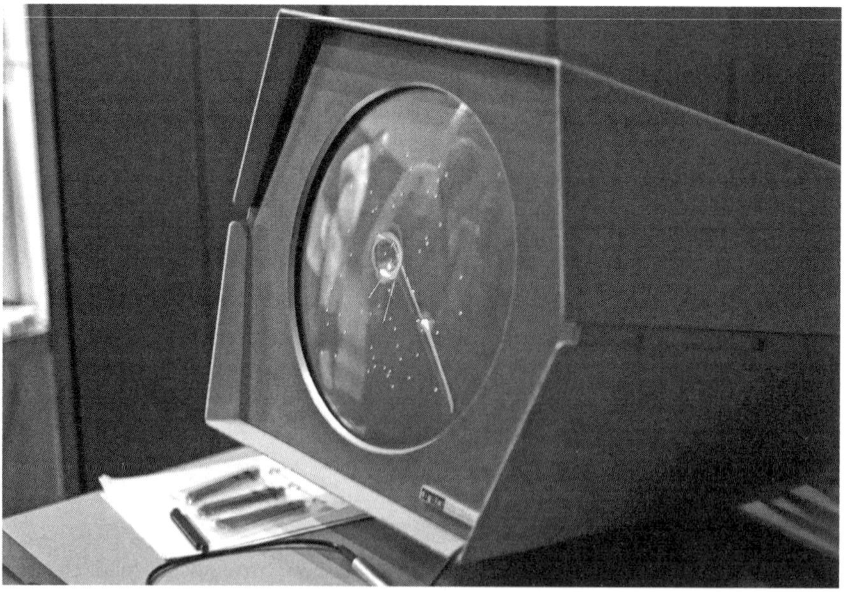

Figure 12.1. The PDP-1 monitor was used for playing *Spacewar!* in 1962. The computer used with this monitor was the size of a truck. (Joi Ito, MIT Media Lab)

Pong was a tremendous success, and it permanently moved video games from the arcade into the home. Soon after, second-generation video game consoles (containing microprocessors) pervaded the market. Games came on cassettes, meaning that more than one game could be played on a console. Many games at the time were adaptations of arcade games such as *Space Invaders* and *Pac-Man,* and like *Pong*, they were hugely successful. By the end of the 1970s, dozens of factories all over the world were manufacturing video games.

In the early 1980s, the console market collapsed. From 1983 to 1985, revenues of the game industry dropped almost one hundred percent. The public seemed to have had enough of video games, too few good games were being produced, and a need for something new arose. And then in 1985, Nintendo introduced its NES (Nintendo Entertainment System) in America, and one year later in Europe. Almost instantly, this game console became a worldwide rage. The NES came standard with the video game *Super Mario Bros.,* which featured an Italian plumber (Mario) trying to save a beautiful princess from a giant turtle-like monster. Mario became the symbol of video game culture, giving the market a boost that has continued to today.

Not surprisingly, the success of NES and *Super Mario Bros.* soon gave rise to formidable rivals, especially Sega Genesis, with its icon *Sonic the Hedgehog* and *Mortal Kombat,* a two-player battle game known primarily for its photorealistic characters committing excessive violence. Interestingly, although *Mortal Kombat* could be played on Nintendo consoles too, only the Sega version featured blood. It was mostly the blood, the legend goes, that helped *Mortal Kombat* grow into one of the most successful games for the third generation of consoles. In time, Sony's PlayStation became an important competitor of Nintendo, as did the home computer, which was capable of delivering better graphics than console games.

Beginning in the 1990s, innovations in game hardware and software followed each other in rapid succession. Unable to keep up with the ruinous competition, some initially successful console manufacturers, including Atari, were forced to close their doors. And while these doors closed, other opportunities emerged. In particular, the "16-bit age" brought three-dimensional games onto the gaming landscape. The first was *Wolfenstein 3D* in 1992, which was soon followed by *Doom,* an extremely successful "first-person shooter" for home computers. *Doom,* one of the first games with a multiplayer function, allowed players to form a team or play against each other. Gamers could even modify the conditions of the game itself, providing them more control and freedom of movement. These new functions led to more intense involvement by gamers, as illustrated by this "vintage" interview from 1995:

> Yeah, I do really get involved in a computer game . . . Sometimes playing Doom is so scary that I just . . . that my heart really goes bonk-bonk-bonk . . . that I really think 'oh shit' and sometimes I just think I don't want to be playing this! Like in Doom, there was a room . . . you had to play in the dark, the only thing you could see was gunfire from the mouth of the other guy's gun and then you could shoot at that and then you heard him screaming so you could tell if you'd hit him or not. That was it, I said, I'm not playing this and I found the code that turned the light on.
>
> *Boy, age 14*[2]

After *Doom,* 3-D games became mainstream. New generations of consoles, with better and more realistic graphics, followed each other in rapid succession. The release of the Wii U in 2012, PlayStation 4 in 2013, and Xbox One in 2013 reflected what is now the eighth generation of video game consoles. While bloggers often foreshadow an upcoming ninth generation of consoles, most experts believe that the eighth generation will be around for a while. For now, developers seemed to have refocused their efforts on mobile platforms that host other types of games, most notably casual games (for example, *Candy Crush*) and freemium games such as *Clash of Clans.*[3] Along with this refocusing, game developers seem to have reconsidered their target groups: Video games are no longer the domain of a clearly defined segment of young men. The age of the traditional gamer has been extended in two directions: to toddlers and preschoolers, among whom "edu-apps" are booming, and to seniors, among whom casual and brain games are thriving.

What Is a Game?

Although the history of gaming highlights how digital games came to have a prominent spot in our everyday media landscape, just exactly what constitutes a game continues to be somewhat of an enigma. For example, *Tetris*, *Assassin's Creed*, and *SimCity* are games, but their playing situations and objectives are wildly different. In classic *Tetris*, or in one of its countless clones, the idea is to fit geometric figures into each other, leaving as few spaces as possible. Tetris has clear rules and goals. But unlike *Assassin's Creed* or *SimCity*, it has no story line or imaginary world. *Assassin's Creed* is an action-adventure stealth game that takes place in a fictitious historical setting in which the main objective is to commit a murder without being observed. In the *SimCity* franchise, the player must build and manage a city while maintaining the happiness of its citizens and keeping a stable budget.

From the beginning, the industry has attempted to classify games according to genre. Initially, this was relatively simple, since most early games were action games. But along with the technological advancements that characterized gaming in the 1990s came a boom in other game genres. Websites such as Gamespot.com identify more than thirty genres; AllGame (a former databank for games) suggested that there were fifteen main genres, which could be divided into more than 130 subgenres, including action puzzle games (such as *Angry Birds*), 3-D real-time strategy games (such as *Myth*), and brain games (such as *Mind Quiz*).[4]

Most games released today combine several genres, and therefore genre classification tends to result in an oversimplified representation. We will nonetheless make an attempt to classify games by using the system devised by Simon Egenfeldt-Nielsen and colleagues. These researchers claim that the most meaningful classification system should be based on the success criteria of types of games.[5] They discuss, for example, the differences between *Tetris* and *Myst*. To play *Tetris* successfully, a player must first and foremost have good spatial awareness and be able to quickly determine the consequences of the decisions he or she has to make. *Myst* is a first-person adventure in which the gamer must investigate the disappearance of several characters in an unfamiliar world. To play *Myst* well, a gamer must have good problem-solving abilities and deductive reasoning. On the basis of the analysis of Egenfeldt-Nielsen and colleagues, we distinguish three global game genres: action games, strategy games, and process-based games.

Action Games

The action game is the oldest game genre. Most video games released in the 1970s and '80s were action games. Classic platform games also belong to this genre, since they usually contain a great deal of action. In platform games, the gamer jumps and fights through different levels (platforms). The aim is to skillfully arrive at the end of each level and, ultimately, the end of the game. The *Super Mario* game series falls into this category, as do first- and third-person shooter games such as *Grand Theft Auto* and racing games, which are primarily about evading opponents and surviving hazards such as collapsing bridges and tunnels. In addition, fighting games such as *Street Fighter* fall into this category. Success in playing action games requires fine motor skills and excellent hand-eye coordination. These are the games in which players must not think for too long, but act quickly.[6]

Strategy Games

In strategy games, players must use logical and deductive thinking (à la Sherlock Holmes), and strategic insight. Winning at these games requires carefully balancing large amounts of information and signals from various sources. In particular, users must consider the consequences of several potential strategic decisions and then use their knowledge of the system and rules to make their decision. Favorite strategy games include *Command & Conquer, Warcraft,* and *League of Legends.* Other examples include *Monkey Island* and *Myst,* along with single-player role-playing games that focus heavily on solving puzzles (for example, *Fire Emblem*).

Process-Based Games

Although researchers have long thought that conflict and competition are essential game elements, process-based games have proved that these elements are not as important as we might have thought. Process-based games provide the player a system to play with rather than a predefined goal to achieve.[7] Examples of process-based games include massively multiplayer online role-playing games such as *World of Warcraft,* as well as economic and social simulation games in which a player's task is to construct or manage a city, farm, or household. Process-based games have no consistent criteria for success, although the rewards make it clear which outcomes are positive. Players aim to reach higher levels in *World of Warcraft,* manage a successful city in *SimCity,* or play with every aspect of life in *The Sims.* Simulation games such as *Flight Simulator X* and *Train Simulation,* in which the object is to imitate a real situation as well as possible, belong to this genre, too. These simulations differ from economic and social simulation games, in which creatively simulating reality is most important. In simulation games, the object is to mimic reality in detail, for example, by landing a passenger airplane perfectly.

Why Do We Like Games?

Like other entertainment media, gaming has a universal attraction for young and old alike. And as with other entertainment media, research on the attraction to and reasons for gaming is inspired by two theories: selective exposure theory and uses-and-gratifications theory. The foundation of both theories is that people's dispositions (e.g., beliefs, needs, and motives) lead them to use certain media types or content. Both theories have been used to examine and understand different types of gamers. To date, research by Christopher Klug and Jesse Schell suggests that nine player archetypes can be identified by their primary motives for playing games. The nine archetypes and their main motives for gaming are shown in table 12.1.[8]

These nine player archetypes are not mutually exclusive. Most gamers seem to be a combination of archetypes and thus have more than one motive for playing games. In addition, the motives of the archetypes may have different emphases in different games. For example, the same person can be a competitor who wants to win in *Unreal Tournament 4* as well as a craftsman who enjoys playing *Candy Crush.* These archetypes can be helpful for trying to understand why games are so appealing. If there are different player archetypes, there must be different needs that gaming can fulfill. In other words, by reflecting on these archetypes, we can obtain a better sense of the motives behind gameplay.

Table 12.1. Nine player archetypes

Archetype	*Plays digital games . . .*
Competitor	to be better than other players
Explorer	to experience the boundaries of the play world, to discover first what others do not know yet
Collector	to acquire the most stuff through the game
Achiever	to improve, to rise in the rankings over time, to attain the most championships over time
Joker	to have fun, mainly, and to enjoy the social aspects of gaming
Director	to be in charge, to orchestrate events
Storyteller	to create or live in an alternate world and build a narrative out of that world
Performer	to put on a show
Craftsman	to build, solve puzzles, and engineer constructs

Source: Christopher Klug and Jesse Schell, "Adolescents and the Appeal of Video Games," in *Playing Video Games: Motives, Responses and Consequences,* ed. Peter Vorderer and Jennings Bryant (Mahwah, N.J.: Erlbaum, 2006).

A consideration of the player archetypes makes it clear that there are at least six motives for gaming: competition, overcoming challenges, obtaining control, exploration, social motives, and physiological arousal. Like the player archetypes, these motives are not mutually exclusive, which implies that they can, and do, co-occur. For example, action games may simultaneously meet a gamer's need to overcome challenges and to achieve physiological arousal, while playing a strategy game may, for some, be motivated by a need to obtain control and to interact with peers.

The motive that most people first think of when it comes to gameplay is competition. The competition motive, frequently espoused by boys, reflects the desire to win, to improve one's scores, and to measure oneself against other gamers. Digital games often allow for competition against the system itself or against others. The competition motive is no different from motives for many traditional sports, which are also often about competition and winning.

While the competition motive is most focused on the desire to win, gameplay can be motivated as well by a desire to overcome challenges. Most game researchers agree that a good game is one that continually challenges the player within his or her abilities. A good game is one that is neither too hard nor too difficult, but is instead "pleasantly frustrating" (this idea is akin to the moderate discrepancy hypothesis, introduced in chapter 4).[9] When a game is pleasantly frustrating, the gamer continues to play as the game increases in difficulty. In doing so, the game offers the player at every level a difficult but not insurmountable challenge. This, in turn, enhances the likelihood of the player entering a state of flow, which can be accompanied by intense feelings of satisfaction.[10]

Unlike "lean back" entertainment such as movies or television programs, games can fulfill one's need for control. In some games, players can influence the direction of the narrative, the difficulty of the game, and even the appearance of the game and avatars. Players often indicate that "control" is a key reason for gameplay, emphasizing the possibility of being able to affect gaming outcomes. Among youth, particularly those struggling with their own physical or emotional development, the possibility of games to fulfill their need for control is especially experienced as pleasant.

Somewhat related to control, for some players, the many exploratory opportunities in games are particularly motivational. In this context, games—particularly process-based games—offer players the chance to take on identities and roles and to live out particular fantasies. Games strongly appeal to players' curiosity. Unlike lean-back entertainment, which stimulates curiosity mainly by temporarily withholding information, games appeal to players' curiosity by requiring them to answer problems or puzzles that are often indispensable to continued play.

Games can also fulfill important social needs. And while the stereotypical notion of the lonesome nerd may be the first image that comes to mind when thinking about gaming, in fact, gaming has become an important social activity—particularly for teens. Thanks to technological developments, players no longer need to share a couch in order to play games together. Indeed, gamers will often spend extra money on systems that provide multiplayer functionality. In strategy and process-based games, for example, teens often develop a shared reality with other players and form close ties with other gamers, sometimes even communicating in a special language that they have invented together. Games and gaming can have important symbolic functions in teens' cliques and subcultures, just like fashion and sports. For example, teens often will not purchase games until they have been "approved" in their cliques or subculture. And teens who acquire a game earlier or master it better than others are more likely to have a high status among their peers.[11]

Finally, games can fulfill physiological needs by providing players a rush of excitement during gameplay. Gamers such as this fifteen-year-old often describe their experiences with games as exciting, explosive, and fun: "The first time I played *Dragon Ball*, I don't know what, I was sitting there pushing these buttons . . . I was doing special moves . . . I'm, like, I didn't know I could do that . . . I don't know where it came from . . . the adrenaline."[12] The pleasure experienced while gaming is often explained by excitation transfer theory (see chapter 8).[13] Several elements of games, such as their speed and obstacles, help ensure that gamers' excitement and arousal increase. If the tempo slows down or the obstacle is surmounted, the player feels relief. This relief, similar to the relief felt after watching a fearful scene in a horror movie, is experienced intensely because the gamer is still in a heightened state of physical arousal. The enjoyment of games, from the combination of confronting obstacles and not knowing whether they can be overcome, is said to resemble the experience of spectators watching a thrilling competitive sport.[14]

Do Girls Like Games Too?

Although we have an understanding of why young people in general are motivated to play digital games, the notion exists that girls do not like digital games or, at a minimum, find them less appealing than boys do. And in fact, it has repeatedly been shown that boys and men are the predominant players of games. In the 1980s, for example, data indicated that boys spent three times as much time playing games as girls did—with market data similarly indicating that males purchased about three-fourths of the video games. But these sex differences seem to be shrinking somewhat, with recent estimates suggesting that adolescent boys and men now spend about twice as much time playing games per day as do their female counterparts.[15]

Why has the gender gap in gaming decreased? The answer can be found, in part, by taking a historical look at the trends in games and gaming. In the 1980s, the video game market was dominated by action games with virile men as main characters. Many games did not have female characters at all; if they did, their female characters were beautiful princesses or helpless victims who had to be saved by the hero. With such offerings, it is not surprising that girls were not attracted to digital games. Even today, the action-game genre clearly appeals less to girls and women than to boys and men.

In the early 1990s, the large differences in game use between boys and girls were considered a serious problem. The ability to work with computers was becoming indispensable at the time, and it was assumed that games were the portal to the adult world. People feared that the gaming gap between boys and girls would continue to grow, threatening to put girls at a disadvantage later in life. In part as a result of these concerns, by the mid-1990s, game manufacturers had begun to make concerted efforts to appeal to girls. Initially, they did this by reversing the traditional role patterns. By the end of the 1990s, for example, female protagonists featured in about 15 percent of games.[16]

A well-known game with a strong female heroine at the time was *Tomb Raider*. It featured Lara Croft, an archeologist with a prominent bosom who was able to effortlessly shoot down all manner of bloodthirsty men and monsters. Although the game did seem to appeal to a small group of girls, it was the hearts of boys that the scantily clad Lara Croft won by the millions. *Tomb Raider* completely reversed the female-as-victim stereotype. The female was the hero. This dichotomy—female as either killer or victim—remained in place for the majority of violent video games on the market in the 1990s. Not surprisingly, both roles offered girls too few opportunities for role-model identification, and so the games experienced little success with the female population.[17]

In the period when the killer female was introduced, gaming companies also tried to design other sorts of games to entice female players. The industry reasoned that females might be avoiding digital games because of their violence. As a result, the market soon saw an influx of nonviolent female-headed games that were heavily advertised and brightly packaged in pink and purple. But these nonviolent games fared no better with girls. A likely explanation is that violence and action have always been inextricably linked in games. Once the violence was taken out of the games, the action disappeared as well, and so the games simply became boring.[18]

Interestingly, one game released in 1996 became extremely popular among female players: *Barbie Fashion Designer.* The enormous success of this game could not be ascribed to the lack of violence or the presence of a female main character. After all, many other, less successful Barbie games were also female headed and nonviolent. So what might explain the success of this particular game? The success of this game, it seems, lies in its combination of realism, the femininity of the leading character, and the creative tasks it contained. In *Barbie Fashion Designer,* girls design clothes for Barbie—an activity compatible with the imagination and play themes of elementary school girls. Like adult women, girls prefer meaningful interaction and are less fond of the kind of competition that boys greatly enjoy.

As noted above, sex differences in the amount of time spent gaming are significantly smaller now than they were in the 1980s. The game industry is working to become better at attracting the other half of their target group. For example, some action games seem to have become less gender stereotypical than those from the 1980s and 1990s. Even Lara Croft has changed considerably. She now has more humanlike proportions and is fully clothed, albeit in skintight pants and a tank top. And these initiatives of the industry may have been effective. For example, data we are collecting in the Netherlands indicate that five- to eight-year-old boys on average play only seven minutes more a day than girls (30 versus 23 minutes; see chapter 5). These subtle sex differences in early childhood become larger in early adolescence. In the same study, ten- to fifteen-year-old boys spent more than twice as much time per day as girls on games (105 versus 45 minutes). It is worth noting, though, that teen girls nowadays spend on average much more time gaming than adolescent boys did in the 1980s. Moreover, if we compare the total screen time of boys and girls (including their Internet and social media use), sex differences disappear.[19]

Although the overall screen time of boys and girls does not differ much in adolescence, their preferences for game genres differ dramatically. Table 12.2 shows teenage boys' and girls' top five favorite games. The only game on both lists is *Minecraft. Minecraft* is an ingenious process-based game whose goal is to create or decorate objects with blocks. There are relatively few traditional game features in *Minecraft.* For example, it lacks levels (that is, the rewards that make a player want to continue playing). The player must invent many of the details himself or herself, alone or together with

Table 12.2. Top five favorite games among ten- to fifteen-year-olds, by gender, 2014

	Boys	*Girls*
1	*Minecraft*	*Candy Crush*
2	*Call of Duty*	*The Sims*
3	*Grand Theft Auto (GTA)*	*Just Dance*
4	*Fifa*	*Subway Surfers*
5	*League of Legends*	*Minecraft*

Source: Unpublished data from a study by Patti M. Valkenburg, supported by a grant from the European Research Council

friends. Moreover, the social functions of the game are extensive. Numerous YouTube clips contain role-playing scenarios, instructions, etc. The versatility of the game may be the reason why it appeals to teens of both sexes. They can express and exploit their own interests and exercise individual creativity.

In addition, table 12.2 shows that as in the 1980s, teenage boys prefer violent games such as *Grand Theft Auto (GTA)* and *Call of Duty. GTA* is a controversial game; it is a parody of American society, but understanding the parody requires knowledge that younger teenagers often lack. In most countries, *GTA,* which contains a significant amount of violence, is considered inappropriate for children and adolescents. Although a small percentage of girls like to play violent games, most girls opt for casual games such as *Candy Crush,* dancing games such as *Just Dance,* or simulation games such as *The Sims.* Thus, while the gender gap in time spent playing games (and, more generally, in time spent with interactive media) may be shrinking, gender still dramatically influences game preference. It is not so much that girls do not like games, but rather that their genre preferences differ from those of boys.

Effects of Gaming

Academics have long been fascinated by the phenomenon of play. Play seems to be an integral part not only of Homo sapiens (our "wise" species), but also of other mammals, and even of some birds and reptiles. This trans-specific quality of play suggests that it has an important evolutionary function. By imitating adults and playing at hunting or gathering food, young individuals of a species learn how to survive in a hostile world. Play is important for humans' cognitive, emotional, and social development. Children who play extensively have a better chance of growing into creative adults than those who do not. Playing helps them to explore the boundaries of social behavior, to understand other perspectives, and to learn to control emotions (as when they win or lose).[20]

The functions of traditional play have been well documented. But as traditional play is increasingly supplanted by digital gaming, the question arises whether digital gaming is as good as traditional forms of play for child development. Opinions on this issue are divided. Proponents of gaming usually cite its positive effects, such as improved hand-eye coordination and spatial awareness, and the potential for playing with others. Opponents maintain that games take too much time from other activities, including traditional play, homework, reading, and sports, implying that digital gaming is inferior to these activities. These critics stress the addictive potential of games. Research on gaming is evolving. Thus far, most of it has dealt with the effect of violent games on aggressive behavior (see chapter 7). Here we focus on the burgeoning literature on other physical, cognitive, and social-emotional effects of digital gaming.

Physical Effects

The popular press is replete with articles focusing on the negative physical effects of video gaming. In the 1990s, we heard about "Nintendo thumb," a repetitive-stress-injury-like ailment associated with popular controllers of the time. Similarly, as mobile phones and tablets entered the media landscape, neologisms such as "Blackberry thumb," "WhatsAppitis," and the "computer hump" were used to describe maladies said to be caused by making repetitive movements with the thumbs and by sitting hunched over for too long.[21] Although mass media hyperbole makes it hard to know how much stock to put into these concerns, some studies suggest that excessive computer use and gaming can lead to lower-back problems and neck or shoulder pain.[22] In fact, studies have shown that adolescents ages 14–18 who sit at a screen four to five hours a day are more likely to have neck and shoulder problems.[23] If a player ignores the pain and does not take steps to improve his or her posture, back deformities can result.

Children's backs seem to be analogous to bonsai trees: if they are constantly pushed in one direction, they will grow in that direction.[24]

It is important to recognize that these physical phenomena are not caused by games themselves. They are caused by too many repeated movements, by sitting or working in the same position for too long, or by a combination of the two. It is a reality, however, that adolescents spend a significant portion of their day sitting. A recent Irish study indicated that teen girls spend nearly twenty hours a day sitting or lying down.[25] Because of the problems associated with prolonged sitting, sitting is now considered a serious side effect of screen media use.[26] In fact, the lament "sitting is the new smoking" is often made by health care practitioners. On the one hand, these findings highlight the importance of teaching children to alternate gaming or other sedentary activities with physical exercise. On the other hand, they highlight an opportunity for the gaming industry to combat the usual sedentary nature of gaming. And there are already efforts to do so—with an influx of so-called exergames targeting both children and adults.

Exergames require players to physically move in order to advance the game. Depending on the game, the movement can vary from relatively little effort to moderate or even vigorous effort. Meta-analytic work indicates that the energy expenditure of exergames is similar to that of more traditional physical exercise.[27] For example, in *Dance Dance Revolution,* players must mimic dance patterns displayed onscreen to popular music—and the movements increase in complexity and speed during gameplay. In *Zombies, Run!* (a mobile phone app), the player is challenged to run away from zombies as fast as possible and to seek refuge in one of humanity's last remaining outposts. And in the Nintendo Wii game *Punch-Out!!*, the player must try to physically punch an opponent, and to dodge and duck the opponent's punches, in a classic boxing game.

Research into the effects of these and similar exergames is still in its infancy, but the scant evidence seen thus far indicates that such games—rather than promoting sedentary behaviors and negative health effects—may be an effective means of fighting obesity and promoting a healthier lifestyle. Interestingly, this benefit seems to be particularly true for teens who play these games cooperatively rather than competitively. Cooperative play may foster a team bond, which in turn may increase teens' motivation to persist during a physically demanding game.[28]

Cognitive Effects

While the physical effects of gaming, particularly the negative ones, tend to make most media headlines, gaming's cognitive effects have also received increased attention in recent years. Cognitive effects of games focus on knowledge, comprehension, and learning. Research in this area often falls under the umbrella term "serious gaming," which has come into vogue during the new millennium but was coined in 1970.[29] Conversations about serious gaming most often occur along with discussions of classroom education. Why is this? Modern educational theories are based on the principle that learning is most effective when it is active, experience based, and problem based, and when it offers immediate feedback—all features that digital games can offer. Scholars have thus begun to ask what role gaming may have in the classroom. Can it replace the teacher, or, perhaps more realistically, augment teacher instruction? Can it serve as a tool for more personalized education? Or does its inclusion in the classroom, as some teachers fear, result in students' belief that all learning must be fun?

To date, there have been a number of studies on the effects of games in the classroom. Overall, they indicate that gaming can have an important place in the classroom. For example, a meta-analysis of 129 studies revealed that students' knowledge of subjects such as biology and history increased with the use of games in the classroom.[30] Similarly, a review of more than 300 studies found evidence for the benefits of gaming on language learning and history (but less so for science and math knowledge).[31] Serious games seem to be particularly effective for learning when they are augmented by other instruction methods and when youth engage in cooperative play.[32] Findings like these suggest that serious gaming may be a valuable addition to classrooms. That said, researchers must still tackle many questions when it comes to serious gaming. We need more research on the longer-term effects of serious games, on the types of games most likely to support learning, and on the types of children most likely to benefit from games in the classroom.[33]

The cognitive effects of gaming can be seen also in the home environment. Research in this area started in the 1980s, spurred by the often-cited book *Mind and Media* by Patricia Greenfield.[34] Hundreds of studies have since been published on the effects of games on intelligence, spatial awareness, multitasking, inhibitory control (the ability to repress unwanted information), working memory (the ability to temporarily store information), and visual processing (the ability to quickly spot targets, objects, or changes). In a recent meta-analysis, Kasey Powers and colleagues summarized the effects of these studies.[35] The analysis suggests that gaming has a positive effect on most cognitive skills—particularly on intelligence and spatial awareness. And these effects do not seem to be limited to a specific genre. Instead, a variety of game genres—including the often-maligned action games—seem to offer cognitive benefits.

Intelligence

One of the hottest topics in gaming and cognition is intelligence. Games appeal strongly to our problem-solving abilities. Does this mean that the more we play games, the more intelligent we become? It was long thought that intelligence, or "cognitive ability," was a quality inherited from one's parents and was therefore unchangeable, or at least difficult to change. Thanks to heredity research, we now know that only about half of children's intelligence can be explained by hereditary factors.[36] This means that environmental factors play a significant role in the development of intelligence. In chapter 2, we mentioned the Flynn effect—the term used to describe the strong increase in youth's intelligence test scores over the last six decades. As discussed, this increase is mainly found on intelligence tests of fluid intelligence, which involves the capacity to think logically and solve problems in novel situations, independent of acquired knowledge.[37] Since the tasks to measure fluid intelligence often resemble those in games, it is not surprising that researchers suspect that gaming is one cause of the increase in fluid intelligence scores.[38]

If gaming is indeed responsible for the increase in fluid intelligence that has been observed among youth, then frequent gamers should score higher than occasional gamers on this type of intelligence. Several studies have investigated this assumption. In the meta-analysis of Powers and colleagues, studies were divided into two types: quasi-experiments that compared existing groups of heavy and light gamers, and true experiments (brain-training studies) that measured gamers' intelligence after they have had some game training. Some of the brain-training studies used games specially designed for the studies, and others use existing commercial games, such as *Tetris*, *Rise of Nations*, or *Counter-Strike*.

The quasi-experiments demonstrated that heavy gamers scored higher on intelligence tests than light gamers or nongamers.[39] But these studies suffer from the chicken-or-egg problem. They cannot rule out the explanation that intelligent adolescents are more likely to play video games. The true experiments, which are able to control for causality, yielded mixed results. The studies using commercially available games showed no effect of gameplaying on intelligence scores.[40] But the studies using specially designed games did find an effect. For example, Susanne Jaeggi and colleagues found that after a month of game training, children scored higher than before on two fluid intelligence tests.[41] This effect primarily held for children who were interested in the game, and who felt less frustration as the game increased in difficulty. This result is consistent with media effects theories that argue that media are most likely to have effects on media users who have a particular interest in a medium or its content.

Spatial Awareness and Hand-Eye Coordination

Much of the success of human evolution has depended on our being able to orient ourselves in an environment, to navigate, and to remember the shapes of visual objects, and such skills remain essential in today's world. Unsurprisingly, spatial awareness is a form of intelligence that is part of virtually all intelligence tests. Everyone needs it for tasks like putting the right lid on a pot or finding the way home. And specialized professionals such as surgeons, airline pilots, and architects greatly rely on spatial awareness. Hand-eye coordination is the ability to immediately and correctly react with one's hands to what one sees. For dentistry, watchmaking, and other professions that require fine motor skills, good hand-eye coordination is a must.

Spatial awareness and hand-eye coordination are essential for gaming. A gamer has to remember and manipulate objects and be able to move his or her character or avatar. Perhaps it is not that surprising, then, that both quasi-experiments and brain-training studies have shown that gaming has a positive effect on spatial awareness and hand-eye coordination.[42] These effects are found for both youth and adults, and across myriad game genres—although they seem particularly robust for games that rely on spatial visualization performance.[43]

The effects of gaming can be seen in the brain, too. For example, in a brain-training study, forty-eight students were randomly assigned to one of two experimental conditions: half were passive controls (they did not play any games), and half played *Super Mario 64* on a Nintendo DS for at least thirty minutes a day over a period of two months.[44] The gameplayers had to navigate through a virtual world and collect items. After the two-month period, the brains of all participants were scanned. The gamers had more gray matter in their right posterior hippocampus, an area of the brain that plays a role in spatial processing and navigation. In addition, gray matter had grown in the dorsolateral prefrontal cortex and the cerebellum. According to the researchers, these areas play a role in integrating sensory information with behavioral intentions, which are necessary for hand-eye coordination.

Social-Emotional Effects

What do you think of when you think of a gamer? Most often, the stereotypical image that comes to mind is a socially incompetent, pimply-faced nerd who neglects his friends, withdraws to his darkened bedroom, and becomes progressively more isolated. This image took hold in the 1980s, when gaming was dominated by teenage males. And yet even in gaming's earliest days, this image was inaccurate. For example, in 1985, American research demonstrated that playing video games brought parents and children together and seemed to have a positive influence on family relationships.[45] Similar findings emerged in other countries as well. For example, an Australian study showed virtually no differences in social adjustment between adolescents who frequently played games and those who played rarely. In fact, gamers actually reported feeling more attached to other family members and peers than did nongamers.[46] And in a study of more than 1,200 *World of Warcraft* players, 67 percent of respondents (teens and young adults) listed social reasons as a key motivation for gameplay. The great majority of the players noted that *World of Warcraft* provided them with opportunities to maintain existing relationships with their family and friends and to form new friendships.[47] Indeed, rather than isolating young people from the offline world, gaming seems to provide them with important additional opportunities to form friendships and maintain family relationships.

Game Addiction

Although games may provide youth with opportunities for social development, they have certain features that keep children and adolescents glued to their screens. This fascination for digital games could be seen even in the early days of digital games. In 1984, for example, researchers demonstrated that children who had received a new video game would rather play their new game than do anything else. But for most gamers, the infatuation soon wore off. After a few weeks, the frequency with which they played games had dropped back to the level before receiving the new game.[48]

A small group of children and adolescents, however, remain under the long-term spell of gaming. These youth find it incredibly difficult to stop playing, they become restless if they cannot play anymore, and they can think of nothing besides their game. Moreover, they often sacrifice other important activities, such as homework, sports, and family meetings, in order to play. This small group is often referred to as pathological gamers or, in popular parlance, game addicts. Pathological gaming is characterized by continued obsessive and excessive gaming that the player cannot control, despite the problems it causes.[49]

For a long time, there has been a debate among psychiatrists about whether pathological gaming should be recognized as a true addiction. Traditionally, addictions were legitimate only if they involved the abuse of substances such as alcohol or drugs. Later, substance-related addictions were joined by behavioral, or nonsubstance, addictions, such as gambling. Since 2013, pathological gaming has been included as a tentative behavioral addiction in the latest version of the *Diagnostic and Statistical Manual of Mental Disorders* (*DSM-5*), the handbook that psychiatrists use to make diagnoses. *DSM-5* calls it Internet gaming disorder (IGD). A diagnosis of IGD is based on nine criteria, including preoccupation, tolerance, deception, and conflict (see table 12.3). Gamers who meet at least five of the nine criteria in the course of a year can be considered disordered gamers.

Given the increasing preponderance of digital games, it is unsurprising that the last few years have seen a deluge of research on the prevalence of game addiction as well as the identity of the addicts.[50] Data from 2014 indicate that approximately 5 percent of adolescents (ages 13–19) meet five or more of the nine criteria for game addiction and thus can be classified

Table 12.3. Criteria for Internet gaming disorder

Criterion	*In the past year . . .*
Preoccupation	have there been periods when all you could think of was the moment that you could play a game?
Tolerance	have you felt unsatisfied because you wanted to play more?
Withdrawal	have you felt miserable when you were unable to play a game?
Persistence	were you unable to reduce your time spent playing games after others had repeatedly told you to play less?
Escape	have you played games so that you would not have to think about annoying things?
Problems	have you had arguments with others about the consequences of your gaming behavior?
Deception	have you hidden the time you spend on games from others?
Displacement	have you lost interest in hobbies or other activities because gaming was all you wanted to do?
Conflict	have you experienced serious conflicts with family, friends, or partners because of gaming?

Source: Jeroen S. Lemmens, Patti M. Valkenburg, and Douglas A. Gentile, "The Internet Gaming Disorder Scale," *Psychological Assessment* 27, no. 2 (2015).

as gaming addicts. These estimates are up somewhat from 2009, when 4 percent of adolescents were classified as game addicts. This increase can be explained in part by an increase in gaming addiction among girls. The study conducted in 2009 showed that virtually no girls were addicted to gaming, while 4 percent of girls were found to be gaming addicts in 2014.[51] This increase may have to do with the emergence of game genres that are just as attractive to girls and women as they are to boys and men.

Interestingly, while gaming has many positive social effects on children and teens, many of these social benefits decrease or even reverse when gaming becomes pathological. In a longitudinal study of Dutch teens, researchers demonstrated that lonely teens more readily become pathological gamers and that this pathological gaming behavior exacerbated their loneliness.[52] In other words, these pathological gamers fit the stereotype of lonesome nerds with no offline friends. Similar work in Singapore found that children who had lower social competence and greater impulsivity were more likely to become game addicts. And this addiction subsequently led to increased depression, anxiety, and social phobias (as well as decreased school performance).[53]

Conclusion

As digital media increase in their portability and accessibility, they will continue to become an inextricable part of the lives of young people. Along with this, the audience for these games will be increasingly filled with both males and females of all ages. This trend is not surprising. Youth have been playing games since the dawn of time, and although games are increasingly moving to the digital realm, youth's desires and motivations for gameplay have not changed that much. They continue to look to games as a way to fulfill their need for competition, to surmount challenges, to obtain control, and to engage socially with others.

The question, then, is not why youth (and adults) play games, but whether we should be concerned about the effects of gameplay. As the research discussed in this chapter suggests, gaming is generally a healthy activity for youth. Gamers seem to have a larger working memory, better spatial skills, and improved familial and peer relationships. Moreover, when used in the classroom, gaming is related to deeper learning, particularly when used in combination with traditional instruction by a teacher. Additionally, playing exergames is linked with healthier physical well-being among youth, particularly when played in cooperative situations. Overall, today's games go far beyond *Pac-Man,* a rather straightforward test of hand-eye coordination. They revolve around creativity, perseverance, patience, pattern recognition, and complex problem solving—skills that are expected to be crucial for twenty-first-century success.

Yet the promise of gaming comes with important concerns that should not be disregarded. Extensive sedentary gaming has been linked with physical problems. Moreover, some children and adolescents can become aggressive and agitated from violent gameplay (see chapter 7), and others, particularly lonely teens, can become pathological gamers and, as a result, experience physical and social-emotional problems. In other words, many of the games that can result in positive effects can also lead to troublesome outcomes. This paradox is a challenging one—do we encourage gaming or not?

As with other media effects, the answer should lie in a combination of understanding the child, the game content, and the social context of gameplay. As discussed in chapter 7, not all violent games make all children violent. Similarly, only a small minority of teens are prone to gaming addiction. And for both aggression and addiction, certain risk factors can increase susceptibility to these effects. As we have highlighted throughout this book, the effects of media (including games) depend on a variety of dispositional, developmental, and environmental factors.

In all, it seems reasonable to conclude that for the majority of children and teens, gaming can play a positive role in their physical, cognitive, and social-emotional development. A minority of them may be susceptible to the negative effects of gameplay—and for these children and teens, we need research that helps identify who they are and how we can prevent or mitigate negative effects early on.

13

SOCIAL MEDIA

> It has only been five years or so that I have noticed that people, and young people in particular, seem to have two faces: a private face that reveals how they really feel, and a public face, which they use to present themselves to the outside world and bring to perfection on YouTube and Facebook. Only it seems like this public face is becoming increasingly important, as if putting it on has become an instinct; almost like an evolutionary development that enables people to survive in today's society.
>
> —Rineke Dijkstra (2010)

Never before have youth had so many opportunities to bring their self-presentation to perfection. They can, for example, endlessly edit their digital profiles and selfies before they post them on the Web or send them to friends. Does this ability make them more self-aware, as the photographer Rineke Dijkstra observes? Or does it turn them into narcissists? In recent years, a great variety of social media has seen the light of day in rapid-fire succession. Even a juggernaut like Facebook must do its utmost to ensure that it does not lose its young users to emerging apps such as Snapchat and Instagram. These developments raise a great many questions. Does the use of social media lead to superficial relationships and loneliness—or does it boost self-esteem and social skills? What effects does extensive media multitasking have on youth? Does it make them lose their ability to concentrate and contemplate? In this chapter, we present the latest scientific research on the role of social media in teens' lives.

The Smartphone Generation

With the increasing affordability of smartphones, we are witnessing a dramatic change in how youth access and use media technologies and content. Nearly 75 percent of American teens ages 13–17 have or had access to a smartphone.[1] Data across seven European countries (the UK, Denmark, Italy, Romania, Ireland, Portugal, and Belgium) have similarly demonstrated the quick penetration of smartphones among teenagers.[2] And this growth is not limited to the teen audience. In 2011, global smartphone penetration per capita was 10 percent; in 2018, it will reach 37 percent.[3] These figures demonstrate that in just ten years, from 2006 to 2016, the smartphone has penetrated virtually all strata of global societies. This speed of penetration by a new technology is unprecedented. The telephone, for example, took nearly seventy years to reach the same rate of penetration, while the Internet took nearly sixteen years.

The breakthrough of the smartphone to the wide public began with the BlackBerry Pearl in 2006, which was followed by the iPhone 2G in 2007—which soon became the fastest-selling gadget in history. Today, smartphones appear in every aspect of daily life. More than any other media device, smartphones are inextricably linked with the use of social media (media with which users share information with one another through text, audio, photos, videos, or blogs). The portability, power, and connectivity of the smartphone have resulted in a generation of youth (and adults) that are truly "phono sapiens."[4] Indeed, it seems that Steve Jobs's hyperbolic statement upon introducing the iPhone in 2007 ("This will change everything") was not all that hyperbolic.

In Lewis Carroll's *Through the Looking-Glass,* the Red Queen tells Alice, "*Here,* you see, it takes all the running *you* can do, to keep in the same place." The analogy of this statement to today's social media landscape is compelling. In the world of social media, everything is rapidly new and rapidly old. One of the dangers that this poses is that the usage data in a book are long outdated before it is published. In this chapter, we have included the latest data available. Nevertheless, while writing this chapter, we saw new apps looming on the horizon. Indeed, authors of academic books often try to avoid including social media usage percentages, or they apologize for referring to outdated apps and services, as danah boyd did in *It's Complicated* (2014): "Social media is a moving landscape; many of the services that I reference throughout this book may or may not survive. But the ability to navigate one's social relationships, communicate asynchronously, and search for information online is here to stay. Don't let my reference to outdated services distract you from the arguments in this book."[5]

Like boyd, we may refer to research on social media that are no longer in existence, or to websites that, by the time this book is published, no longer exist. Nonetheless, the findings of these studies still have relevance. Specific sites and services change continually, but the possibilities for social interactions remain the same. Their transience requires us to discuss social media at a higher, somewhat abstract level. This is what many social media researchers have begun to do by looking not at social media platforms per se, but instead at the more general affordances of social media.

The Seven Affordances of Social Media

Coined in 1979, the concept of affordance is used to describe the possibilities that objects in our environment offer us.[6] The affordance of a chair, for instance, is that you can sit on it. Of course, you can also use a chair for other purposes, for instance, as a step to get something from a top shelf or as a place to rest your feet. But those are unintended affordances—possibilities observed or selected by a user, but not intended by the designer. In recent years, the affordance concept has turned up in communication research. Here, affordances are the possibilities that (social) media offer their users. An affordance of social media, for example, is that we can be reached at any place and at any time. Affordances are important, since—as we will demonstrate—they help explain the enormous appeal of social media as well as their effects. Social media are characterized by at least seven affordances that are relevant to adolescents' developmentally induced needs. These are summarized in table 13.1.[7]

The appeal of social media for adolescents can, in part, be explained through one or more of these affordances. But to understand how these affordances may explain this appeal, it is important to recall the specific developmental needs of adolescence. As discussed in chapter 6, the key objective in adolescence is the development of autonomy—the capacity to

Table 13.1. Affordances of social media that may enhance teens' perceived control

Affordance	*The possibility for users to . . .*
Asynchronicity	communicate when it suits them, in real time (synchronously) or delayed (asynchronously)
Identifiability	decide to which degree content is anonymous or linked to their true identity
Cue manageability	show or hide visual or auditory cues about the self while communicating
Accessibility	easily find information and contact other persons
Scalability	choose the size and the nature of their audience
Replicability	copy or share existing online content
Retrievability	store and later retrieve posted content

Source: danah boyd, "Social Network Sites as Networked Publics: Affordances, Dynamics and Implications," in *A Networked Self: Identity, Community, and Culture on Social Network Sites*, ed. Zizi Papacharissi (New York: Routledge, 2010); Jochen Peter and Patti M. Valkenburg, "The Effects of Internet Communication on Adolescents' Psychological Development," in *The International Encyclopedia of Media Studies: Media Psychology / Media Effects*, ed. Erica Scharrer (San Francisco: Wiley-Blackwell, 2013).

independently make decisions and act on the basis of what is deemed personally important or useful. To attain autonomy, adolescents must first form a stable identity (a clear idea of who they are and who they want to become). Additionally, they must develop the ability to experience and share intimacy and, therefore, the skills required to form friendships and relationships. And finally, they must discover who they are sexually; that is, they must learn what their sexual identity is, how to control their sexual desires, and how to maintain healthy sexual relationships.

To successfully complete these huge tasks, adolescents have to learn two communication skills: self-presentation and self-disclosure. Self-presentation is the presenting of aspects of identity within the normative standards of a certain audience. Self-disclosure is the sharing of intimate information, also according to the normative standards within a certain group. Adolescents should, for example, not reveal too much about themselves during initial conversations, but not be tight lipped either. Too much or too little self-disclosure hinders the formation and maintenance of friendships and other social relationships.[8]

Self-presentation and self-disclosure require practice. Through self-presentation, adolescents practice certain roles in front of a varying audience. By using the feedback that they receive on their self-presentation, they are able to validate their beliefs and behavior and to integrate them in their identity. Similarly, practice in self-disclosure helps them determine what is correct and appropriate within contexts and groups. Appropriate self-disclosure enhances the forming of close friendships and romantic relationships. This happens through the norm of reciprocity: if one party tells something personal, the other is inclined to tell something personal in return. This reciprocal, tentative exchange of increasingly personal information forms the basis of intimate friendships and romantic relationships.[9]

While previous generations of teens acquired dexterity in self-presentation and self-disclosure primarily offline, the smartphone generation prefers to rely on social media to help with the development of these skills. In fact, one in three adolescents prefers to talk through social media rather than face-to-face when it comes to love, sexuality, and things that embarrass them.[10] Moreover, recent American data indicate that the vast majority of teens indicate that social media helps them feel more connected with their friends' feelings and daily lives.[11]

What might explain why adolescents strongly prefer to communicate via social media, even about intimate matters? In short, this preference is due to the affordances of social media, which give adolescents an enhanced sense of control—or, more accurately, the illusion of control.[12] The affordances give them the impression that they are able to determine with whom, how, and when they interact, and whether they should or should not reveal their identity. This sense of control, in turn, makes them feel more secure and self-assured on social media than in offline situations. And this sense of control is particularly important in adolescence, because adolescents, on their way toward autonomy, can feel uncertain about numerous things.

How do the affordances of social media give teens a sense of control and security? This is best explained via theories about privacy. A sense of control and security is central to virtually all definitions of privacy. When we read about social media and privacy in the newspapers, it is mostly about issues such as privacy settings or the misuse of personal information. Such reports, however, deal only with one form of privacy: informational privacy. Informational privacy describes the extent to which people can control the amount and content of their personal information that is being distributed.[13] Contrary to what some believe, most teens are well aware of the dangers that social media pose to their informational privacy.[14]

Why, then, do teens (and adults) keep posting all sorts of information about themselves on social media that form a threat to their privacy? This contradictory behavior is referred to as the privacy paradox: just like adults, most teens know perfectly well that social media threaten their privacy, and they are often uncomfortable with it, but do not act accordingly. The privacy paradox is best understood when one accepts a broad definition of privacy. In our view, the privacy paradox focuses too much on informational privacy when there is another type of privacy that may better explain teens' (and adults') online behavior. That form of privacy is referred to as psychological privacy—our possibility to control when, what, to whom, and how we share something about ourselves.[15]

Although most affordances of social media may decrease informational privacy, they may increase psychological privacy. To a much greater degree than offline communication, social media allow users to control when, what, and how they express themselves, and to whom. And this is particularly relevant to teens, who, more so than adults, define privacy as the control of what, when, and with whom they communicate when they are out of sight of their parents and siblings. Seen in this light, the privacy paradox is less paradoxical than it might seem at first. The affordances of social media may decrease teens' informational privacy, yet provide them with enhanced psychological control over their communication and allow them to demonstrate their autonomy—which helps explain the immense appeal of social media for teens.[16]

Each of social media's seven affordances, in its own way, can boost teens' perceived sense of control and, therefore, their sense of psychological privacy. Asynchronicity, for example, offers teens the possibility to choose when they communicate. They can ponder for hours or days exactly which photograph they want to post. They can also do it synchronously, though, and with astonishing speed—for instance, in Snapchat, where they exchange photos that show up for a maximum of ten seconds. This rapid synchronous communication heightens teens' sense of control, in this case, their ability to always stay in direct contact with their friends.

While not a standard affordance of popular social media sites such as Facebook or Instagram, visual anonymity is an important attribute of virtual worlds and certain websites (for example, self-help sites and sites for homosexual teens). On these websites, visual anonymity can provide teens the opportunity to explore their identity by interacting with others. Perceived anonymity enhances their illusion of control and security, which in turn enhances the likelihood that teens will share personal information on these sites. Similarly, adolescents can choose whether they show (or emphasize) certain visual or auditory cues about themselves while communicating. This possibility of cue manageability may enhance their perceived sense of control and, in this case, the way they present themselves online.

The accessibility of information can likewise add to teens' sense of control. Never before have adolescents been capable of finding such a huge amount of information related to the development of identity, intimacy, and sexuality. They can look up information about their idols, make online friends, and find support in self-help groups. Moreover, thanks to the scalability of (most) social media, teens can choose for themselves the audience with which they communicate. And they can do so for each social media tool separately, for instance, by using WhatsApp to communicate with intimate friends, and Facebook and Twitter for group contact.

Finally, the replicability and retrievabilty of communication add to adolescents' sense of control. With a single click on the "share" button or a reply to all, they can reach all their "friends." What is more, even after they have been away for weeks, they can still answer their messages—for anything posted online stays there. On Facebook alone, nearly 350 million photos are posted online daily, and they will remain online forever.

Theories of Social Media Effects

Estimates suggest that the majority of teens throughout the Western world spend some time with social media daily, so it is not surprising that scholars have been carefully investigating the effects of social media use on teens' development.[17] These studies are often influenced, in part, by theories of computer-mediated communication (CMC). CMC theories focus on discovering the differences between face-to-face communication and CMC. They revolve around the question whether, and how, certain CMC characteristics, such as its anonymity or its lack of nonverbal cues, influence the quality of the interpersonal communication. Do these characteristics make CMC more intimate, more uninhibited, or more aggressive than face-to-face communication? Do CMC partners get different impressions from each other than face-to-face partners do? Do they find each other more (or less) attractive?

The first cluster of CMC theories originated in the 1970s, long before the Internet came into our lives. These rather pessimistic theories tried to compare "lean" text-only CMC with the "rich" communication of face-to-face settings. In doing so, they tried to explain, for example, why CMC led to less intimacy and more uninhibited behavior.[18] In the early 1990s, a new cluster of theories emerged that took a more optimistic view of CMC. At that time, e-mail and the Internet became widely available for personal use. Joseph Walther's social information processing theory became particularly influential at the time. It explained how CMC partners could gradually overcome the limitations of CMC by creatively employing strategies to send and understand social and emotional messages. In this way, given enough time and message exchanges, CMC partners could develop intimacy levels comparable to those found in face-to-face communication.[19]

In the second half of the 1990s, Walther extended his perspective with an even more optimistic theory, which predicted that CMC messages could lead to greater intimacy than face-to-face communication. According to his hyperpersonal communication model, CMC encourages people to optimally present themselves, for instance, by pretending to be kinder and more beautiful than they are. Meanwhile, the recipients of these optimized self-presentations are free to fill in the blanks in their impressions of their partners, which may encourage them to idealize these partners. In doing so, CMC relationships could even become hyperpersonal—that is, more intimate than offline relationships.[20]

The focus of early CMC theories on anonymity and limited nonverbal cues fit well in the 1990s and the first half of the 2000s, when CMC was predominantly text-based and typically took place in anonymous chat rooms or newsgroups. By contrast, most Web 2.0 applications, such as Twitter (2006), Facebook (2006), WhatsApp (2009), Instagram (2010), Snapchat (2011), and Vine (2012), rely on both textual and audiovisual channels. Therefore, it has become less relevant to compare specific CMC applications with one another or with face-to-face communication. In fact, these changes in technologies have led to a new theorization about social media effects.[21]

CMC theories, like many traditional media effects theories, are rooted in a reception model. That is, both types of theories assume that media or technologies have a unidirectional impact on recipients. And in both types of theories, it is too often forgotten that users of social media can simultaneously be *both* recipients and senders of communication.[22] With the easy use of cameras, editing software, and distribution channels, everyone can be both a sender and a recipient of digital content. Long before the advent of Web 2.0, it had been observed that consumers of media content were becoming producers of this content, too, a phenomenon for which the now somewhat obsolete term "prosumers" was coined.[23]

Another issue that has received too little attention in both types of theories is that the production and distribution of media content may have effects not only on its recipients, but also on the senders. Adolescents might influence their peers by the photos they post on Instagram, but the act of producing and sharing these photos might also affect themselves. This phenomenon, in which our beliefs and behavior exert an influence on ourselves, has been referred to as an expression effect.[24] An expression effect occurs when a sender internalizes the behavior that she or he shows or the beliefs that she or he discloses, so that his or her own self-concept or behavior changes. The behavior or message does not have to be publicized; its creation alone may lead to expression effects. By merely writing a blog, for instance, without posting it, we could improve our memory, feel better, or come to terms with an emotional experience.

Expression effects are best explained via Daryl Bem's self-perception theory, which postulates that people like to be consistent in their beliefs, attitudes, and conduct.[25] Faced with inconsistencies, people experience cognitive dissonance, which generates an unpleasant internal tension. Typically, we believe that our behavior is the result of our beliefs and attitudes. For instance, if we believe that strength training is good for us, we are more likely to act accordingly (and thereby go to the gym). But this process may also run the other way: we can alter our beliefs and attitudes by observing our behavior in retrospect. For example, if we fail to go to the gym for several weeks, we might conclude that strength training is rather boring and may not be so important after all.

Research into expression effects in online environments is surprisingly scarce. The affordances of social media provide users with an opportunity to experiment with forms of behavior that can influence their self-concept. This is rather surprising. After all, consider the selfie phenomenon. Recent estimates suggest that millions of selfies are posted on social media daily, and teens heavily partake in this activity. We know that teens take (and retake) selfies until they find the image that they want to represent themselves in a particular moment. It is reasonable to imagine that, over time, the taking, retaking, and posting of selfies (a social media behavior) may influence not only the recipients of these selfies but also the selfie takers' self-perception. In other words, the effects of social media use on teens' social-emotional and cognitive development are likely a two-way street.

Social-Emotional Effects of Social Media

Given the main goals of social media, it makes sense that the vast body of research on the effects of social media has focused on social-emotional consequences. This literature has tried primarily to understand how social media influence teens' identity, intimacy, and sexuality—in other words, the three pillars needed for the development of their autonomy. When it comes to identity formation, researchers have studied four related constructs: self-concept clarity, self-esteem, self-awareness, and narcissism. Studies of intimacy have focused on the sunny side of intimacy, friendships and connectedness, and on its darker side, cyberbullying. Finally, research on sexuality has focused on sexual self-expression as well as stranger danger.

Self-Concept Clarity

An important task in adolescence is to form a stable identity. To measure the stability of our identity, researchers often rely on the idea of self-concept clarity. Self-concept clarity is the degree to which our beliefs about our identity are clearly defined and stable.[26] There are two contrasting hypotheses about the effects of social media use on self-concept clarity. The fragmentation hypothesis claims that because it is very easy for teens to experiment with their identity online, they are faced with too many different views online. As a result, they may experience confusion and difficulty in integrating all these new views into their (already fragile) identity. On the other hand, scholars have suggested that social media may improve self-concept clarity because the many different views that teens encounter online can serve as a model and sounding board while they develop and corroborate their identity.

Thus far, research into the influence of social media on self-concept clarity has yielded mixed effects. Some studies have shown that a high degree of Internet use (thus, not exclusively social media) corresponds to lower self-concept clarity.[27] But this negative relationship disappears when teens' loneliness and shyness is accounted for—both of which apparently play a larger role in the development of self-concept clarity than Internet use.[28] More recently, work by Katie Davis demonstrated the nuances of social media effects. Specifically, Davis found that teens who use the Internet to talk with their friends experience stronger self-concept clarity, whereas teens who use the Internet primarily to experiment with their identity (which occurs far less frequently) experience weaker self-concept clarity. This does not necessarily mean that online experimentation is problematic; instead, it indicates that it can be problematic for teens who use the Internet almost exclusively for experimentation.[29] These findings are a good example of an expression effect: adolescents differ in the way they use social media, and these differences predict the effects that they experience.

Self-Esteem

Self-esteem is the degree to which we value ourselves. Human beings, young and old, have a universal need to maintain their self-esteem at the same level or, preferably, to increase it. There are two main predictors of self-esteem: the feeling that we have control of our environment, and the approval that we hope to get from that environment.[30] Social media offer teens both, by providing numerous possibilities for control and positive feedback (for example, Facebook's "like" button). These two functions of social media are particularly important in adolescence, since this is the time when self-esteem is most sensitive to environmental influences and most subject to fluctuations.

Studies have looked into the relationship between online communication and self-esteem. Most of these, especially the studies that focused on blogs and profile sites, indicate that online communication increases adolescents' self-esteem. For example, American teens experience a greater sense of control when posting online profiles and blogs. This (perceived) control, in turn, is linked with increased self-esteem.[31] Similarly, research with Dutch teens revealed that managing one's profile on a social network site leads to increased self-esteem. How? Adolescents who create an online profile seem to use feedback from their peers about these profiles to adjust and optimize their profiles, which leads to even more positive feedback. In this way, through improved feedback and their own communicative behavior, adolescents manage to enhance their self-esteem.[32]

But it is not at all roses and sunshine on social media. Indeed, while most teens receive primarily positive feedback online, roughly 7 percent receive mainly negative online feedback.[33] For these teens, unsurprisingly, social media use is linked with a decrease in self-esteem. In the same vein, other research has shown that the positive effects of social media use on self-esteem are limited to "normal" use—not to abnormal or compulsive use.[34] Finally, the benefits of social media on self-esteem are most pronounced for those who use social media to connect with their close friends.[35] Overall, then, it seems that for most adolescents, social media are conducive to supporting self-esteem, but for a minority, social media are problematic.

Self-Awareness

The chapter epigraph quotes the photographer Rineke Dijkstra, who has noticed that young people are increasingly skilled in putting on a public face. This observation refers to a personality characteristic that we call self-awareness. There are two types of self-awareness, private and public. Private self-awareness is our tendency to pay attention to the inner aspects of our identity. Public self-awareness is our attention to the way we are perceived by others. Individuals with strong public awareness are very good at predicting how others will respond to them and adjusting their self-presentation accordingly.[36]

Some research backs up Dijkstra's observation. Adolescents who are more active on social media have greater public self-awareness than their less active counterparts. They have more Facebook friends, post more photos on social media, and have a greater tendency to reply when they receive comments on those photos.[37] It is important to recognize, however, that these studies used correlational designs, which do not allow for cause-and-effect inferences: social media may increase public self-awareness, but it may also be the case that teens with greater public self-awareness use social media more extensively. In truth, the relationship is likely a circular one—as is often the case with media use and personality characteristics. Personality characteristics lead to certain types of media use, which subsequently enhance these personality characteristics.

Narcissism

A high degree of public self-awareness is an important characteristic of narcissism. Narcissists are excessively preoccupied by others' opinion of them, and they will go to great lengths to be positively assessed. Narcissism is a personality trait that all people have to some degree. At its extreme, it is a psychiatric disorder that occurs in 1–2 percent of the population.[38] Narcissists have a complex range of symptoms. They have an inflated self-image and overblown self-confidence. They are vain, they overestimate their talents and feats, and they expect these to be admired. They have little empathy, they can exploit their environment, and they become arrogant or aggressive if they do not get their way.

Freud coined the term "narcissism." It is derived from the Greek myth of Narcissus, a handsome youth who fell in love with his reflection in a pool of water and eventually starved to death because he could not tear himself away from gazing at his image. Freud's concept of narcissism took on a highly negative connotation in the late 1970s after the appearance of Christopher Lasch's best seller *The Culture of Narcissism*. Today, in part thanks to the new symbol of narcissism, the selfie, narcissism is receiving renewed attention in both scholarly debate and the popular press.

There have been indications that youth today are more narcissistic than earlier generations, as claimed in alarming publications such as *The Narcissism Epidemic* by Jean Twenge and Keith Campbell.[39] Like public self-awareness, the increase in narcissism has often been linked to social media use.[40] But there is an important caveat for the interpretation of these findings. Perhaps most importantly, we should ask ourselves whether (and when) narcissism is a negative trait. Some psychologists argue that narcissism, on a modest scale, is conducive to self-development. Indeed, research among adults suggests that narcissism goes together with many positive characteristics, including self-esteem, assertiveness, and extraversion, and our own research on teens indicates a positive relationship between narcissism and self-esteem.[41]

These relationships between narcissism and positive personality traits highlight why we should interpret research into the relationship between social media use and narcissism with care. Healthy doses of self-esteem, assertiveness, and extraversion, after all, are regarded as positive traits, whereas narcissism is not. A modest dose of narcissism is probably adaptive, functional, and beneficial to social well-being. Too much, on the other hand, leans toward pathology and is harmful. Thus, before we decide whether social media use is cause for concern when it comes to narcissism, it is important for the research field to make a distinction between normal and pathological narcissism.[42]

Friendships and Connectedness

In 1998, newspaper headlines around the world were quick to highlight the results of one of the first studies on Internet use and friendships. The study, conducted by Robert Kraut and colleagues, indicated that Internet users (teens and adults) had fewer social bonds and were lonelier than nonusers. To explain their results, the researchers suggested that the time spent communicating online was displacing time that would have otherwise been spent with friends offline. As a result, the quality of offline friendships decreased and Internet users became lonelier.[43] The negative findings by Kraut and colleagues were replicated in several other studies in the late nineties.[44]

These first negative results fit well with the state of Internet access at the time. In those days, it was impossible to maintain existing contacts through the Internet, because very few of those contacts were online. In one of the studies, only 11 percent of the adolescents had Internet access. This meant that their online contacts were for the most part separate from their offline contacts. Online communication in those days was limited to chatting in anonymous chat rooms or newsgroups. It is therefore not surprising that Kraut and colleagues found negative effects of loneliness, since online communication at the time was mostly with strangers, appealing to people who lacked something in their offline environment.

Today, that situation is completely different. Since the rise of Web 2.0, virtually everyone is online. Displacement effects are less likely to occur, because adolescents have significantly more opportunities than before to maintain their existing relationships through social media. Moreover, newer social media applications encourage users to communicate with their existing friends, and that is what teens most typically use them for. Unsurprisingly, recent studies into the effects of online communication have found that online communication leads to increased (rather than decreased) social involvement.[45]

What might explain these positive results? Why might social media be linked with improved social relationships? Longitudinal research suggests that social media invite adolescents to share intimate feelings with their offline friends, for instance, about love, sex, and things they would be somewhat embarrassed to discuss offline. This is due to the affordances of social media, which, as discussed, foster teens' perception of social and psychological privacy. Just like offline self-disclosure, online self-disclosure between friends engenders closeness and intimacy, and eventually strengthens friendships. By disclosing something personal to a friend, we invite the friend to share something personal with us. This mutual and gradually more intimate self-disclosure is how friendships and romantic relationships are formed and maintained. It seems that especially for teens, this norm of reciprocity takes place online as well as offline.[46]

Cyberbullying

While it seems that social media use can play a healthy role in teens' social and emotional development, there are some important caveats to these findings. One particular problem is cyberbullying. Cyberbullying takes place when online applications are used to insult, exclude, or in any other way hurt others. As with offline bullying, cyberbullying is not an incidental, one-time attack, but comprises purposeful and repeated aggressive actions by individuals or groups, against which the victims cannot easily defend themselves.

There are numerous estimates of the proportion of adolescents who have been cyberbullied; figures range from 1 percent to 53 percent. This wide variation is mainly due to differences in the definitions of cyberbullying. When adolescents are asked whether they have "ever" received a nasty message, the researchers (unsurprisingly) find a higher prevalence than when adolescents are asked whether they have received such a message in the past month. Cyberbullying is about repeated forms of online aggression against victims who are unable to defend themselves. If we base our estimates on this definition, cyberbullying is found far less frequently. In a large-scale study by Sonia Livingstone and colleagues, which included participants from twenty-five EU countries, 6 percent of the nine- to sixteen-year-olds reported that they had been bullied on the computer, and 3 percent on their mobile phone, whereas 13 percent stated that they had been bullied offline (see figure 13.1).[47]

Cyberbullying occurs particularly often between the ages of thirteen and fifteen, and although boys, in general, bully more than girls do offline, boys and girls seem to have an equal share in online bullying. If differences are found, it is the girls who cyberbully the most. And despite worries that cyberbullying has increased with the mass use of smartphones, its prevalence

Figure 13.1. About 9 percent of teens, boys and girls, report having been bullied online in the past year. (ClarkandCompany/iStock)

seems to have remained relatively stable—continuing to occur less frequently than offline bullying.[48]

Cyberbullying is a troubling and undesired side effect of the affordances of the social media. The affordances lead to an increased chance of engaging in uninhibited behavior, and of the impact of that behavior being less visible. They afford greater ease in distributing bullying communications and enhance their visibility among a wider audience. And they enhance the permanence and indelibility of such communications.[49] Perhaps not surprisingly, online and offline bullying are correlated. This means that children and teens who are bullied online more often become victims of offline bullying. Both types of bullying go together with the same problems, such as social anxiety and depression. Efforts to help prevent cyberbullying and counter its effects continue to be an important area for research and public policy.

Sexual Self-Exploration

Besides influencing the development of identity and intimacy, the affordances of social media affect adolescents' sexuality. As we saw in chapter 10, adolescents routinely use the Internet to learn about sex and sexual identity. In addition, they routinely use social media to obtain advice about sexual issues or to discuss the moral, emotional, and social aspects of sex. This applies in particular to gay and bisexual adolescents. Homosexuality still cannot be freely discussed in some circles.[50] But it is not just gay and bisexual adolescents who are relying on social media to explore their sexuality. More than ever before, increasing numbers of teens are turning to social media as a means of expressing their sexuality. This is particularly evident through two related phenomena: sexting and the sexy selfie.

Along with the rise of smartphone-based social media, sexting has gained wide interest. "Sexting," a portmanteau word formed from "sex" and "texting," refers to the sending or posting of sexual messages, photos, or videos via a smartphone or any other electronic device. Studies investigating the prevalence of sexting among teens have yielded mixed results; some suggest prevalence limits as low as 2 percent, and other estimates are closer to 10 percent.[51] In general, it seems that sexting occurs more frequently among older adolescents. And while the public often perceives that girls sext more often than boys, this pattern seems to be country dependent, with several studies reporting equal sexting rates for boys and girls.[52]

Sexting seems primarily motivated by self-presentation. Adolescents sext in order to be found sexy, to get attention, to flirt, and also because they think it is funny.[53] There is a consensus that the exchange of sexual information between young couples in love is part of normal sexual development. If, however, this exchange happens online, where it is easily accessible, scalable, replicable, and retrievable, it can become risk behavior. But is it as problematic as is often suggested in popular media? On the one hand, longitudinal research suggests that sexting may precede sexual intercourse in some teens, but it does not predict sexual risk behavior such as having sex with multiple partners or having sex without a condom.[54] On the other hand, the negative peer perceptions that can result from sexting warrant concern because such perceptions may subsequently harm teens' social-emotional health. In particular, girls are judged harshly whether they sext ("slut") or not ("prude"), while boys typically do not experience such criticism.[55]

Related to sexting is the more specific phenomenon of the sexy selfie. The sexy selfie typically consists of sexy poses rather than nude or seminude body displays, which are more typical of sexting (see figure 13.2). Interestingly, sexy selfies have consequences not necessarily for the sender of the pictures but rather for their recipients. Specifically, teens who are exposed to sexy selfies via social media are more likely than teens who are less exposed to such selfies to subsequently initiate sexual behavior.[56] The researchers suggest that as a result of repeatedly seeing sexy selfies via social media, teens may start to believe that sexual activity is common in their peer group and may feel increased pressure to engage in sexual activities. Given the relative newness of sexting and the sexy selfie, however, it may take some time before we can conclude whether these phenomena represent normal parts of teens' sexual development or, instead, indicate maladaptive sexual development and warrant concern.

Stranger Danger

The same social media that provide teens with an opportunity to express their sexuality via sexting and sexy selfies makes them vulnerable to sexual grooming and offline sexual abuse. Sexual grooming occurs when someone approaches a child or a teen with the intent of eventually initiating offline sexual contact. A groomer usually starts by striking up an online friendship,

Figure 13.2. Repeated exposure to "sexy selfies" can stimulate sexual initiation among teens. (Corbis)

which he (it is generally a man) slowly steers toward offline sexual abuse. Whenever there is a case of grooming, the press covers it extensively. Nonetheless, although grooming is among the most highly reported online sexual allegations, research in several countries has demonstrated that its prevalence in these countries is low.[57] Sexual abuse is still committed more often by offline acquaintances than online strangers.

The teens who are the most vulnerable to grooming are girls and gay boys. Furthermore, teens who are uncertain about their sexual identity, who were abused as children, and who have already demonstrated offline risk behavior are also particularly vulnerable. Although estimates vary by country, an EU Kids Online report found that 30 percent of children and adolescents have made contact "in the past twelve months" with a person whom they knew only from the Internet.[58] Nine percent of these respondents arranged a face-to-face meeting with these "strangers," who, in most cases, turned out not to be strangers, but friends of friends. One percent of them looked back on the offline meeting with an unknown person as an unpleasant experience. Although 1 percent is a small proportion, we of course should take it very seriously. Such experiences may have very painful or even tragic consequences for children and teens. It is also important to recognize that it can be very difficult for children and teens to properly gauge when online contacts pose a threat, because groomers generally use extremely complex and sophisticated tactics. Here is an important task for educators—identifying ways to make youth aware of these dangers and ensuring that they are sufficiently "social media literate" when it comes to interacting with unknown others.

Cognitive Effects of Social Media

While researchers initially paid attention mainly to the social-emotional consequences of social media for teens, there has been a recent influx of research on their cognitive consequences. The affordances of Web 2.0 services—particularly their ever-extending accessibility—has led researchers to ask about the potential effects of social-media-driven media multitasking on adolescents' cognitive skills. Along with these concerns have come heated debates about whether youth (and adults) are becoming dumber and experiencing "digital dementia" as a result of a world that increasingly relies on bite-size chunks of information.

Media Multitasking

A deluge of studies since 2010 have looked at the impact of media multitasking—using multiple media at the same time. Media multitasking has increased markedly since the advent of Web 2.0. In the 1990s, 16 percent of adolescents used different media at the same time. The percentage today is almost double.[59] With media literally in the palms of many teenagers, these estimates are hardly shocking. Although most media multitasking occurs when teens read and simultaneously listen to music, the combination of watching television and using social media plays a close second. It has become quite common for teens (and adults) to watch television on one screen while simultaneously using social media to comment on the program, dodge the commercials, or stay in touch with friends and other viewers.

There are two main explanations for the dramatic uptick in media multitasking. First, changes in the traditional media landscape increasingly call on media consumers to be able to multitask while consuming the content. Take, for example, gaming. For most of today's games, successful gameplay requires the gamer to multitask—to keep an eye on all sorts of visual information at the same time. Similarly, many of today's television programs assume some level of multitasking. On news programs, banners carrying headlines or summaries scroll at the bottom or on the side of the screen as the announcer gives information about a separate, often unrelated story. More than ever before, designers are creating products that challenge us to divide our attention.

Related to this is the second, more important explanation for the meteoric rise in media multitasking: the smartphone. Smartphones accustom us to ingest what *Wired* magazine calls "fast entertainment"—the continuous stream of bite-size entertainment that comes our way through Twitter, Instagram, and YouTube. This steady flow of images, videos, music, and words, particularly when delivered to our palms instantaneously, is said to capitalize on our collective need to quickly consume great quantities of entertainment and information.[60]

One of the growing concerns about this "fast entertainment" world is that as youth become acculturated to the continual switching of activities and attention, they will eventually lose the ability to concentrate. Research on this topic has usually focused on whether media multitasking can alter our cognitive control. "Cognitive control" is an umbrella term for the mental processes that relate to result-focused behavior, such as paying sustained attention to relevant information, ignoring irrelevant information while concentrating (response inhibition), efficiently switching between tasks (task switching), and storing task-relevant information in working memory. We need cognitive control for virtually any task that requires focus and concentration, and so the threat of decreased cognitive control is worrisome.

Several studies on the relationship between youths' (and young adults') media multitasking and cognitive control have looked at different aspects of cognitive control. Meta-analytic research by Winneke van der Schuur and colleagues reveals that media multitasking is negatively related to sustained attention, which implies that teens who more often engage in media multitasking are less able to concentrate on relevant tasks.[61] Media multitasking was unrelated to other aspects of cognitive control, including response inhibition, task switching, and working-memory capacity. In fact, one study found that fervid media multitaskers switch between tasks more efficiently than their less ardent counterparts.[62] This result makes sense. Media multitaskers continually switch between tasks when they multitask, so they have the opportunity to practice task switching.

There are, however, important limitations to most of the research published thus far in this area. The meta-analysis of van der Schuur and colleagues noted that the majority of work to date has relied on a correlational design. This means that it cannot rule out the reverse explanation, namely, that teens who are less able to concentrate are inclined to multitask more often. As is often the case in media effects research, a reciprocal relationship may be at work: adolescents who cannot focus properly on certain tasks are more likely to increase their media multitasking, which in turn worsens their ability to focus.

It is also important to note that the relationships that have been found are statistically small—suggesting that they do not hold true for all adolescents. It remains unclear, however, for whom these findings are most applicable. None of the existing studies have established which adolescents media-multitask more (or less), or which adolescents are more (or less) susceptible to the negative effects of media multitasking. There are great individual differences in this respect, and sorting them out should be a priority—an undeveloped land for follow-up research.

"Shallow" Thinking and Digital Dementia

Popular books such as *The Shallows: What the Internet Is Doing to Our Brain* (2011), by Nicholas Carr, have increased interest in whether social media can harm our capacity for concentration and contemplation as well as our ability to store and recall information. Such books often argue that by continually reading snack news and being distracted by the pop-ups and alerts of smartphone apps (for example, a like on Facebook, a retweet on Twitter), we are losing our capacity to focus and think deeply. As Carr noted:

> What the Net seems to be doing is chipping away my capacity for concentration and contemplation. Whether I'm online or not, my

> mind now expects to take in information the way the Net distributes it: in a swiftly moving stream of particles. Once I was a scuba diver in the sea of words. Now I zip along the surface like a guy on a Jet Ski.
>
> . . . When I mention my troubles with reading to friends, many say they're suffering from similar afflictions. The more they use the Web, the more they have to fight to stay focused on long pieces of writing. Some worry they're becoming chronic scatterbrains.[63]

Another assumption in books such as Carr's is that the great accessibility of digital information is making us mentally lazy. In an increasingly Googleable world, we no longer need make an effort to store information in our memories. The Internet has, as it were, become our external memory, and thus we no longer need to train our own. As a result, our own memory functions will decline over time. This process of memory deterioration has been termed "digital dementia" by the German psychiatrist Manfred Spitzer: "The brain shrivels up because it is no longer tapped. Stress destroys brain cells, and newly grown brain cells do not survive, as they are not being used. Digital dementia is, in essence, an increasing inability to fully use, and control, intellectual performance."[64]

To substantiate claims of digital dementia, authors such as Spitzer provide examples of behavior change. For example, none of us are likely to memorize telephone numbers any longer, since they are stored on our smartphones. Similarly, we have become less skilled at arithmetic, for we have calculators readily at our disposal. These examples appeal to us, since many of us do indeed not know any telephone numbers by heart, not even our own sometimes. We also have to acknowledge that we are not as good in mental arithmetic as we used to be, because if we need to add or multiply a string of numbers, we grab a calculator. But do these new habits lead to shallow thinking? Is Google making us stupid, as Carr and others assume?[65]

In truth, the scientific evidence presented by authors of these popular texts is meager, relying on a handful of brain-based studies. For example, they often cite a study by Eleanor Maguire and colleagues in which researchers found that the hippocampi of experienced London taxi drivers contained more gray matter than those of a control group without driving experience.[66] They also often rely on a study by Gary Small and colleagues to support the shallow-thinking assumption. Observing fifty-five adults, these researchers showed that compared with inexperienced Internet users, experienced users exhibit significantly more brain activity when conducting an online search task.[67] Both studies reveal that learning goes hand in hand with structural or functional changes in brain areas. But they do not establish that these changes are related to a shallow information processing or to a deteriorating working memory. In other words, interesting and valuable as these findings might be, they are not evidence that the Internet is turning its users into shallow thinkers suffering from digital dementia.

Thus, although popular assumptions claim that today's socially mediated world is creating a population of shallow thinkers, there is insufficient scientific evidence to back up this assertion. It is true that social media have led to an increase in media multitasking. It is also true that ardent media multitasking is linked, among adolescents and young adults, with a decreased ability to focus.[68] This deficit, however, is an effect not of social media per se, but instead of a specific form of social media use. Incidentally, it would be strange if no relationship whatsoever had been found between media multitasking and the ability to focus. After all, taken in combination, media multitasking and focusing are a contradiction in terms. They are as incompatible as water and oil, or light and darkness.

Similarly, despite the headlines, there is no scientific evidence that today's socially mediated world is making teens less intelligent and more apt to experience digital dementia. If there are any indications for a relationship between media usage and intelligence, it is a positive rather than negative one. As mentioned earlier in the book (chapters 2 and 12), several authors have attributed the Flynn effect (the rise in measures of fluid intelligence) to our quick and complex media environment.

And although many of us do not invest effort in memorizing phone numbers or other information, there is no reason to suggest that this is due to decreasing intelligence. When people are asked to type trivial information, such as "The eye of an ostrich is bigger than its brain," and they are told that they can retrieve the exact information later, they no longer make an effort to remember that information.[69] This is not because their working memory has deteriorated, but because they do not want to memorize things if they see no reason to do so. We no longer memorize telephone numbers not because we are getting dumber, but because we no longer see the relevance of it. And by not doing so, we reserve time and space for more important or complex things. As Clive Thompson noted, "Our ancestors learned how to remember; we'll learn how to forget."[70]

Conclusion

Virtually all teens use some form of social media today. While these social media continue to change—yesterday's MySpace becomes today's Instagram—their enduring appeal is that they provide teens (and adults) with an easy means of communicating with known and unknown others. The research discussed in this chapter is limited to the teen audience. This is primarily due to the fact that social media use by children is typically not legally permitted, although the social media landscape is quickly changing. Within the next few years, as technologies advance and legal policies change, it is likely that we will see an uptick in social media use among children—and a related increase in research on the topic.

As highlighted in this chapter, the affordances of social media are what make social media so appealing. These affordances appeal to a strong, developmentally induced need for control and autonomy among adolescents, allowing them to determine what, with whom, when, and how they communicate. The affordances offer an important explanation of the positive role that social media play in the social-emotional development of teens. They may foster teens' self-concept clarity, self-esteem, and self-awareness. They may provide teens with important opportunities for developing friendships, and offer them a space for experimenting with their sexuality and sexual self-presentation.

But as with other media, there is a dark side of social media use, which warrants attention. In particular, social media use is associated with the risk of cyberbullying and sexual grooming. Although, thankfully, these behaviors occur very infrequently, they remain important areas for continued concern and investigation. Similar worries about sexting and sexy selfies call for more scholarly attention to helping teens identify how to manage social media in a healthy and safe way.

In general, the negative effects of social media use on social-emotional development seem to depend on how teens use social media. If teens use social media to maintain existing contacts, which is what most of them do, overall effects seem positive. But if they use social media primarily to communicate with strangers, or if they create unusual profiles and thereby evoke negative responses, the effects are negative. This implies that to a certain extent, adolescents shape their own social media use and its effects. Until now, such so-called expression effects have not received much attention in the social media literature, yet they are likely the best way to understand the social-emotional effects of social media use.

And while social media use has most often been studied in conjunction with social-emotional development, there is growing anxiety that today's mediated world of bite-size information and multitasking may be hindering teens' cognitive development. The scientific evidence suggests that alarm bells may be premature. Fervid media multitasking, which frequently accompanies social media use, is indeed associated with poorer concentration. Yet no scientific evidence to date supports the claim that the causal direction runs from media multitasking to concentration problems. It is possible that teens with concentration problems are more inclined to media-multitask. In addition, no convincing evidence supports the claim that media multitasking is problematic for other cognitive outcomes, or that today's young people are becoming dumber or suffering from digital dementia. If anything, it seems that teens may be displaying improved intelligence when compared with previous generations.

Accessibility, scalability, and retrievability are important affordances of the Internet and social media. Without any effort, we can find a former classmate online or Google the name of an actor that is on the tip of our tongue. Thanks to the smartphone, we can easily call for help if we feel unwell on the road or if the car breaks down. And it is reassuring to know that our children and loved ones can reach us when they need to. The same affordances, however, come with caveats. In the smartphone era, it is more difficult—for everyone—to focus and to resist temptations. The affordances of social media require users to practice a certain agency so that they reap the benefits and avoid the risks of social media use. For youth, and especially young teens, parents, caregivers, and practitioners come into play here. With their help, today's youth can benefit from these affordances in a healthy and safe way.

14

MEDIA AND PARENTING

> Pedagogy must be oriented not to the yesterday, but to the tomorrow of the child's development.
> —attributed to Lev Vygotsky

Hundreds, perhaps thousands of studies ask whether and how media affect children and teens. As we have seen throughout this book, these studies show that media use can have a positive or negative influence on how children and teens think and behave. But as also has been noted throughout this book, media use does not occur in a vacuum. Many forces can influence media effects on children and teens, including their developmental level, dispositions, and environment. In this chapter, we home in on the environment by focusing on the power of the parent. We discuss how parenting styles differ and what many consider as the most effective form of parenting. With this in mind, we then discuss media-specific parenting for different age groups, highlighting specific media-related issues that parents are faced with as children get older. For example, should parents allow their youngest children to use media? How can parents prevent or mitigate the negative influences of violence in the media during childhood? Why is it so difficult to get teens to put down their cell phones? And what can be done about it?

Parenting in the Twenty-First Century

Parenting has never been easy. The literature is replete with examples of the difficulties that parents face in raising their children to become successful adults. Yet today's parents seem to be facing an unusually complex road. When asked about their experiences, most parents lament that parenting in the twenty-first century is harder than ever before. For example, only 11 percent of American parents feel that raising children is easier than it used to be, and 68 percent feel it has become harder.[1] Similarly, in a study of Dutch parents, nearly 20 percent of mothers and 15 percent of fathers indicated they sometimes had doubts about whether they could successfully raise their children. Over half felt that parenting was more difficult than they had imagined it would be.[2]

One of the many challenging aspects of parenting is to find a way to balance the nurturing side of parenting with its strict side. Indeed, this balance is a core aspect of most parenting theories. And when it comes to this balance, researchers have found that parenting in which warmth and responsiveness are combined with clear and consistent rules—referred to as authoritative parenting—is most beneficial for child development.[3] Authoritative parents formulate rules for their children's behavior that are developmentally appropriate, explain why these rules are necessary, ask their children for input when formulating rules, and consistently enforce the rules they set.[4] In short, they provide structure within a warm and loving relationship. Children raised with authoritative parents do better in school, are more successful later in life, and are happier.[5]

Authoritative parenting has been shown to work better than an authoritarian style—a style that prevailed through the 1950s and is characterized by strict rules and little warmth. It also works better than a permissive style—in which parents are warm but provide little structure. This is because authoritative parenting, compared with authoritarian and permissive parenting, is more effective at promoting and supporting the development of children's self-regulation. As noted in chapter 11, self-regulation reflects the ability to resist impulses and temptations that keep us from achieving our long-term goals. It implies, for example, that we limit our intake of junk food and alcohol so that we can stay healthy; that we resist taking a swipe at a boss or a loved one if they make an annoying remark; and that we turn the smartphone to silent or off when we need to finish homework or other tasks.

Self-regulation is one of the most important predictors of success in life.[6] People who struggle with self-regulation are, compared with successful self-regulators, at a greater risk of succumbing to behaviors that lead to problems such as obesity, substance abuse, spiraling debt, and unwanted pregnancy. The mission of authoritative parents is to help children slowly but surely accept and internalize the rules and requirements of their environment and society at large. This internalization is best achieved when parents communicate rules and requirements in a way that promotes the child's autonomy, that is, the degree to which children feel that their choices and behavior come from their free will.[7] Authoritative parents stimulate their children's internalization of rules, and by doing so, they gradually teach their children how to regulate their behavior autonomously and voluntarily.

This voluntary self-regulation does not come about by itself. Adhering to most of the rules parents impose on their children, such as cleaning up their rooms, doing their homework, turning off a video game or the Internet, is not fun, meaning that children will not spontaneously obey their parents. Instead, children's initial compliance comes from an extrinsic motivation, that is, either to avoid punishment or to please their parents. When parents raise their children authoritatively—by setting rules that take the child's perspective seriously, and by providing convincing arguments for these rules—children's extrinsic motivations will likely turn into intrinsic ones. And when this happens, children will have internalized these rules and feel that they follow them voluntarily, which ensures that they can rely on their own self-regulatory skills.

Setting Boundaries Does Not Mean Being Harsh

Discussions of authoritative parenting often raise the question of how to set boundaries. Most theories about parenting assume that parents are calm and rational when it comes to raising their children, particularly when it comes to setting and enforcing boundaries. In practice, however, parents do not always manage to stay calm and rational. Any parent can think of a time when their child's resistance to boundary setting tested their patience. Just imagining a child throwing a temper tantrum in a store is enough to get one's heart pumping a bit faster. Authoritative parenting requires considerable self-regulation from parents. They must be able, and want, to see things from the child's perspective, keep their emotions under control, and be patient and tolerant with their child's behavior rather than indifferent, angry, or pushy.

This is no easy task. Indeed, providing the "warm environment" aspect of authoritative parenting is relatively easy for most parents. But setting and consistently enforcing rules can be difficult. Some parents, especially those with a higher education, find it a challenge to set and enforce rules because they wrongly associate rules with harshness and a lack of warmth.[8] Other parents may feel too busy or too tired to enforce the rules they set. And still others may find it difficult to discipline their children in public because they feel they are being watched and are afraid that others will think they are bad parents.

Equating the enforcement of rules with a lack of warmth is a common misunderstanding among today's parents. Inconsistent enforcement takes several forms. Parents may, for example, give into a temper tantrum at the supermarket if the child kicks and screams long and loudly enough. Or parents may be unwilling to punish their child at the moment she or he misbehaves, because they are too tired or have visitors, but plan to punish the child more severely the next time. Although understandable, these forms of inconsistent enforcement can have negative outcomes, including increased conflict in the family and problem behaviors in children. Inconsistent parenting stimulates resistance and recalcitrance in children, a phenomenon known as psychological reactance.[9] Psychological reactance is incompatible with, and thus interferes with, the internalization of rules and requirements and, as a result, with the development of children's self-regulatory skills.

Media Management in the Family

Not all rules are equally difficult to enforce. Few parents have trouble reprimanding a child who tells a lie or steals something from the refrigerator. But other parenting issues can be more difficult to resolve. The most difficult limits for parents to enforce are rules about media use, particularly teens' media use. Setting rules in this area is even more difficult than setting limits on going out at night, handling money, smoking, drinking alcohol, or taking drugs (see figure 14.1).

Figure 14.1. Restricting media use, especially for teens, is a challenge for many parents because restriction can easily lead to boomerang effects. (iStock)

Why is this? Why do parents find themselves face-to-face with such a struggle when it comes to media use? Because, it seems, children and teens are less tolerant of parental inference with media use than they are with other domains of parenting. According to Judith Smetana, the effectiveness of parental discipline seems to depend strongly on the degree to which children consider their parents' authority legitimate.[10] In her social domain theory, she distinguishes between three domains of parenting: the moral, the conventional, and the personal.

The moral domain deals with problems such as lying and stealing. Most children and teens find parental interference in this domain legitimate: it is never okay to lie or steal, not even if it goes unnoticed. Thus, parents are "allowed" to punish if they discover transgressions within this domain. Children are also relatively tolerant of interference in the conventional domain, which involves matters such as table manners and doing homework, things that are "part of the game" and thus are normal within society. Children are less tolerant, however, of parental interference in the personal domain, which includes matters such as clothing, friends, and media use.

Personal-domain issues are those that involve children's individual preferences and choices, and thus are not questions of good versus bad, or what is "normal," as is the case in the other domains. With young children, this domain is mostly about clothing. Any parent can attest to the fights that can ensue if a child is made to wear certain clothes against his or her wishes. With older children and teens, the personal domain is more extensive and includes friendships and media use. Older children and teens see parents as having no right to meddle in these personal matters. Prohibitions imposed on personal-domain matters, especially with teens, can quickly lead to reactance or even to a boomerang effect (a result opposite from the one the parents intended).

Regulating media use is thorny not only because children are intolerant of interference in the personal domain, but also because parents are more ambivalent, confused, or insecure about regulating this area than they are with other parenting issues. In the last few years, new communication technologies have supplanted one another at breakneck speed. What is new today is old tomorrow. In most families, the status of media has shifted from a small and incidental aspect of leisure time to a thoroughly embedded means of social interaction, in and outside the family. More than ever before, media play a functional role in the family by regulating household routines, facilitating family members' communication, and even physically organizing family members within the house.[11]

According to Lynn Clark, author of *The Parent App*, the newest generation of mobile media has solved some parental dilemmas but exacerbated others. On the one hand, mobile media are a low-threshold way to enable family members to keep in contact with one another. They also make it easier for parents to follow their children's activities and social contacts. On the other hand, mobile media can cause great concern and fear for parents, for example, because these media occupy much of their children's attention, or because they offer children numerous opportunities to display (sexual) risk behavior at an early age.[12]

No unequivocal research-based answers have been found for many of the questions that parents ask about their children's media use. For example, there is no clear-cut answer to the question of how much media use is "enough" or "too much." Meanwhile, parents are faced with many often-conflicting ideas about media and their effects on their children, a lack of consensus that can easily make them feel insecure.[13] Publications about the effects of media on children have traditionally been divided into utopian and dystopian discourses. Both schools of thought assume that technology influences all individuals equally under all circumstances: either positively, for utopians, or negatively, for dystopians. In truth, neither approach does justice to the complex and nuanced reality of today, in which children react in a variety of ways to media, sometimes even contrary to what developers expected or hoped for. These great differences in children's susceptibility have significant implications for how parents approach and manage media.

Parental Mediation in the Twenty-First Century

Parental mediation refers to all the actions of adults aimed at making children media literate. In particular, it is about encouraging children to set limits on their media use, and to use media safely, selectively, and judiciously. Research on parental mediation began in the 1980s, when screen use was mostly limited to watching television. This strand of research traditionally distinguishes among three parental mediation styles: restrictive mediation (limiting time or content), active mediation (explaining and evaluating content), and co-viewing (watching television together without discussing the content).[14]

When television was children's dominant screen use, researchers assumed that co-viewing would implicitly protect children from negative media influences and encourage them to learn from media. But research soon showed that co-viewing is not always effective. For example, when parents watch violent media content with their children, they can inadvertently give children the impression that they approve of violent content. In doing so, they may stimulate rather than restrain undesirable consequences of this kind of viewing. In the same vein, co-viewing of educational content can be beneficial because it similarly gives children the impression that the content is important, which may bolster the likelihood of learning effects.[15]

With the rise of digital and mobile media, however, parental mediation has required reconsideration. Today's children and teens are senders as well as recipients of media content, and it is important for parents to consider both roles. And thanks to the mobility of media, youth spend more and more time with media in their private spaces, out of their parents' sight, a phenomenon that has been called the bedroom culture. These developments have significant implications for parental mediation. Previously, the term "parental mediation" primarily elicited the idea of mediation, that is, parental interventions in the media content that reached their children. In the last few years, we have seen a shift from mediation to proactive media monitoring, that is, the supervision of what children are doing with media, and with whom, how, and when they are doing it.[16]

The term "proactive," when used to describe media monitoring, comes from research on general parenting strategies. Proactive monitoring means that parents keep an eye on their children.[17] Parents may wonder who their children's friends are, whether they use alcohol, and where they go when they go out. Proactive monitoring is an essential element of parenting. Children of parents who do not monitor proactively are, compared with their actively monitored peers, at a greater risk for problem behaviors such as sexual risk taking and excessive alcohol or drug use.[18] Modern parenting theories make it clear that general proactive monitoring is most effective when it is a two-way process—namely, when children are willing to share their needs and experiences with their parents.[19] Seen in this light, proactive monitoring is a characteristic not of parents per se, but of the relationship between parents and children.

This same reciprocal process applies to proactive media monitoring, which is most effective when the strategies are based on children's developmentally induced needs and experiences. For example, even in infancy, children differ greatly in their responses to media. A boy who develops a fascination with an aggressive media hero and imitates him all day, sometimes dangerously so, will likely require closer monitoring than a boy who shows no interest in those kinds of media heroes. Effective proactive media monitoring occurs when parents establish strategies for their children's media use, are aware of their children's media consumption, are willing to reflect on their children's needs and experiences, and are willing, if needed, to update and alter their strategies to best map them onto their child's needs and experiences. It likely comes as little surprise that both general proactive monitoring and proactive media monitoring occur in authoritative families more often than in other types of families.[20]

Restrictive and Active Proactive Media Monitoring

There are two kinds of proactive media monitoring: restrictive and active. Restrictive monitoring can occur in several ways. Parents can restrict certain types of media content ("You can play *Minecraft*, but not *Grand Theft Auto*"), the time children spend on various media ("no more than one hour of gaming"), or the place of media in the family ("no computer in the bedroom"). These kinds of limits are classified as restrictive monitoring. Restrictive monitoring of media use is an essential part of parenting. Media are like a large bag of potato chips to children; they eat all of them unless their parents prevent it.

Research indicates that restrictive media monitoring is not always effective. In general, it seems to work better with younger children than older children. In fact, it can be so counterproductive with teens that they will show reactance against any recommendations that they consider to be interfering with their autonomy. For example, if a parent forbids them to interact on social media, their reactance may drive them to show more instead of less risky behavior on the Internet. That said, certain strategies (discussed later in this chapter) can increase the effectiveness of restrictive monitoring, even with teens.

Active monitoring is different from restrictive monitoring. Active monitoring is understood as communication from parents before, during, or after their children's media use that has the aim of reinforcing or weakening media's potential effects. Active monitoring is most typically characterized as factual or evaluative. Factual monitoring involves all communication geared to increasing children's critical media skills, such as supplying additional information about production techniques (for example, camera work or special effects) or explaining that the violence, advertising promises, or pornography in the media does not match reality. Evaluative active monitoring, on the other hand, refers to parents' attempts to reinforce or weaken media influence by communicating their own opinions or judgments about media content or issues. In this way, parents try to counterbalance the undesirable standards and values in the media with which their children are confronted.[21]

The effectiveness of active monitoring has been demonstrated in several studies. It can make children less susceptible to the influence of media violence. It can also increase learning from educational media, lead to more positive attitudes toward minority groups, and increase children's interest in the arts and culture.[22] In addition, active monitoring reduces the probability of teens showing risk behavior online and visiting sites that promote drug use.[23]

When Child Development and Proactive Media Monitoring Meet

As has been noted throughout this book, age is one of the strongest predictors of children's media use and the subsequent effects of media on children. Very young children exhibit preferences for media different from those of their teen counterparts, and as we have highlighted, each group is affected quite differently by media. It is logical, then, for age to influence the issues that parents experience when it comes to media monitoring.

In the remainder of this chapter, we highlight three issues that are relevant for parenting children in three age groups. These issues serve as exemplars for other potential issues that parents face throughout childhood and adolescence. We first discuss the literature on whether parents should allow their babies and toddlers to look at screens at all. Second, at around five, some children, especially boys, acquire an interest in violent media, and we discuss how parents can mitigate or nullify potential negative effects of media violence. Finally, we discuss the literature on effective strategies for managing teens' media use, particularly their smartphone use.

Babies, Toddlers, and Screen Time

Babies and toddlers differ considerably in their interest in screen media. Some are not drawn to them at all, while others cannot be torn away from them. Observational research has shown that the differences in their interest in television are huge. While playing with toys, some babies look at a television screen only twice in ten minutes, while others look no fewer than sixty-one times in the same ten minutes. And remarkably, these viewing patterns are quite stable. The same considerable differences between babies at six months are still observable at twelve and twenty-four months.[24] It is clear that media use habits are formed at an early age.

In the last ten years, children under the age of two have dramatically increased the amount of time they spend with media.[25] As discussed in chapters 4 and 11, this is due both to the emerging focus on the "diaper demographic" by commercial conglomerates and to an increased emphasis by parents on the importance of informal learning in early childhood. As a result of the frenzied attempts by marketers to reach ever-younger children in the front of a screen, parents have (understandably) felt increasingly unsure about whether and how much media content is okay for their littlest ones and what their media monitoring should look like. In the literature, parents' intentional efforts to expose their children to media that are educational or (at least) attuned to their developmental level has been named foreground media exposure.

While we have seen a sizable growth in children's foreground media exposure, in recent years increased attention has also been paid to children's unintentional media exposure, often referred to as background media exposure. Background media exposure typically involves media content that is intended for adults but that children are exposed to simply by being in the room where others are watching it. This type of exposure seems to be particularly prevalent among very young children, possibly because parents (or older siblings) believe that very young children are unaffected by such content, assuming that it is mostly over their heads. Unfortunately, this supposition appears to be wrong. Background media exposure has been linked to several negative outcomes in young children, including lower sustained attention during playtime, lower-quality parent-child interactions, and weaker executive function.[26] Considering that recent estimates suggest that American children under two are exposed to an average of 5.5 hours of background television per day, efforts to help parents manage background media use are certainly warranted.[27]

Media Guidelines of Pediatricians

Partly in response to these media-related issues pertaining to very young children, countries around the world have published guidelines to help parents manage media for infants and toddlers. The American Academy of Pediatrics (AAP) was among the first, issuing in 1999 a policy statement cautioning parents against allowing any media use for children under the age of two.[28] Following this recommendation, which the AAP republished in 2011, several other countries, including Australia, France, and the Netherlands, clamped down on screen use by young children. Yet these recommendations seem to have had little effect. As noted earlier, in many countries, the very youngest viewers have experienced increases—not decreases—in media exposure.[29]

Why would the AAP and others have such strict guidelines for children under two? Initially, the AAP and others argued that exposing very young children to media, even educationally oriented foreground media, would result in their experiencing fewer beneficial activities such as playing outside, reading, and imaginary play. This perspective was bolstered, in part, by two studies—one in 2004 by the pediatrician Dimitri Christakis and colleagues, and one in 2007 by Frederick Zimmerman and colleagues. These studies indicated that watching television in toddlerhood and early childhood resulted in delayed language development and in attention problems.[30] With these findings in hand, along with research that demonstrated that infants learn better from humans than media (the video deficit; see chapter 11), it is understandable why such cautious recommendations emerged.

Unsurprisingly, the studies by Christakis and Zimmerman stirred up worldwide debate. Perhaps because of this extensive attention, both studies were reanalyzed by other researchers after publication—a phenomenon that seems to be increasing in the social sciences. In one reanalysis, the correlation between television viewing and attention problems found by Christakis and colleagues was significant only in young children who watched seven or more hours of television a day.[31] In other words, the relationship held for only an exceptional group of children.

Similarly, the results found by Zimmerman and colleagues regarding children's language development could not be replicated. In fact, a reanalysis by other researchers detected a nonsignificant correlation (that is, no relationship) between watching baby videos or DVDs (such as Baby Einstein) and language development, and a positive relationship between watching educational media (such as *Sesame Street*) and language development.[32] As discussed in chapter 11, this latter result is in line with a multitude of studies showing that educational media can stimulate children's cognitive and social-emotional development.

Time to Rethink Media Guidelines?

Is it time to rethink the AAP's recommendations on screen use by young children? On the one hand, there is relatively robust evidence of the undesirable effects of background media use on very young children, which underscores the AAP recommendations. On the other hand, both key studies on the use of foreground media that influenced the AAP's initial media recommendations have been largely overturned. Moreover, as discussed in chapter 11, there is robust evidence for the beneficial effects of educational foreground media on children's cognitive and social-emotional development. And as also discussed in chapter 11, increasing evidence suggests that the video deficit can be reduced or nullified through parental scaffolding and certain program characteristics, such as repetition and familiar media characters. Finally, these encouraging results go together with an overwhelming array of educational touch-screen apps for children under two, many of whose designs have the potential to reduce the video deficit.

Christakis, the lead author of some of the research that inspired the AAP statement (and a member of the AAP commission that drafted the statement) believes it is time to reconsider the guidelines. In an opinion piece in *JAMA Pediatrics*, he stated that the 1999 AAP policy statement could not have taken into account the development of apps for tablets, which have been on the market only since 2010. According to Christakis, educational apps are more comparable to construction toys like blocks than to the passive activity of watching television or DVDs. In his opinion piece, Christakis noted that a child will never say, "I can do it!" while watching television, but will do so while playing with edu-apps.[33] Moreover, he notes that touch-screen educational apps have several important characteristics that can promote, rather than suppress, child development. Table 14.1 lists some of these characteristics of educational apps.

Based on this analysis, Christakis now believes that "the judicious use of interactive media is acceptable for children younger than the age of two years."[34] Furthermore, based on the sleep-wake cycles of children under two, he advises a maximum screen time of thirty to sixty minutes a day. Interestingly, in the fall of 2015, one year after Christakis's opinion piece appeared, the AAP announced that it was in the process of revising its

Table 14.1. Features of educational apps that may foster learning

Feature	*Benefit*
Reactivity	Responds to what a child does
Interactivity	Asks for a response from the child
Customizability	Allows for adaptation to characteristics of the child such as age, sex, and preferences
Progressivity	Increases in difficulty as the child masters the material
Social facilitation	Promotes shared use by adults and children, which increases the probability of scaffolding

Source: Dimitri A. Christakis, "Infants and Interactive Media Use—Reply," *JAMA Pediatrics* 168, no. 10 (2014).

guidelines for children and screens. The AAP now recognizes that not all screen time before age two is detrimental for child development. It is likely that the revised guidelines will make a distinction between educational and developmentally appropriate foreground media use, on the one hand, and developmentally inappropriate and background media use on the other hand.

Christakis's advice regarding screen time for children under the age of two is a usable guideline. But for very young children, exposure to screens, even educational ones, can soon become too much. Therefore, as parents work to manage their young children's media use, it is important for them to rely on active and restrictive parental monitoring to achieve a media diet that balances quality and quantity. This means that media should be one of many possible activities, and not children's main activity. It is also important to realize that parents who set limits on screen time must have the means and opportunity to offer their children alternative activities. In families where these alternatives are lacking, educational media may well be the best thing that can happen to these young children.

Childhood and Media Violence

As children begin to enter childhood, their media interests change, and opportunities and concerns associated with these media interests change as well. A deluge of educational media awaits this age group, and so opportunities for parents to bolster their children's academic and social-emotional skills increase (see chapter 11). That said, by the time children reach about age five, parents are also increasingly faced with the task of mitigating negative media effects that can result from their children's changing media preferences. In particular, children, especially boys, start to take an interest in media violence at around age five. As discussed in chapter 7, we know that an estimated 5–10 percent of children are especially susceptible to the effects of media violence on aggression. Besides boys in general, children with an aggressive temperament and children under seven are most vulnerable to the influence of media violence on aggression. Exposure to media violence can affect more than children's aggression. It can also stimulate restlessness and, in some children, make it more difficult for them to participate in imaginary play and creative activities.[35] Finding ways to combat the effects of media violence is therefore a crucial aspect of parental media monitoring during childhood.

Restricting Violent Media

Parents have several ways to combat the effects of media violence. With restrictive monitoring, parents can consider an outright ban on watching or playing certain violent films or games. This strategy is effective with young children, but the likelihood of reactance increases sharply throughout childhood. Nevertheless, many parents do not want their children or preteens playing games like *Grand Theft Auto*, which is rated for adults in most countries.

Although banning violent media, especially violent games, is not always easy, especially when a child's friends are allowed to play the game, the ban will be most effective if parents impose it in a way that promotes the child's autonomy and if they consistently enforce the rule. In practice, this means that parents must consider their children's perspective ("but all my friends have that game"), present alternative games, and involve the children in decision making. Media rating systems can help in this. For example, the European rating system for games describes *Grand Theft Auto V* as follows: "Contains strong language, extreme violence, multiple motiveless killings, and violence towards defenseless victims." In families in which a ban on media content is imposed in an authoritarian way or in which the ban is not consistently enforced, family conflict and antisocial behavior among preteens increase.[36]

Factual and Evaluative Strategies

In addition to restrictive techniques, parents can consider employing active media monitoring, factual or evaluative, to help offset the consequences of media violence. Factual strategies emphasize the unrealistic nature of violent entertainment or call attention to the formal mechanisms of such entertainment (stunts, camera work, etc.). Factual strategies are often part of formal media education programs that aim to develop critical viewing skills in children. Evaluative strategies, on the other hand, aim to stimulate negative beliefs or attitudes about media violence. Instead of explaining the mechanisms behind media productions, adults attempt to influence children's beliefs, attitudes, and behavior, for example, by expressing negative opinions about media violence.

Evidence for the effectiveness of factual monitoring for mitigating media violence effects is inconsistent: some studies show benefits, and others show no effect or even boomerang effects. For example, in a study by Amy Nathanson and Mong-Shan Yang, children from five to twelve years old watched a film with violent content, but were told that the events in the film were not real and that the characters in it were only actors playing parts. With the youngest children (five- to eight-year-olds), they found a positive effect of this commentary on the children's ideas about violence. But with the nine- to twelve-year-olds there was a boomerang effect. The authors argued that this boomerang effect likely occurred because older children were already well aware that violence in films is staged, and therefore they may experience an adult's explanation about this as simplistic or even pedantic.[37]

Research on evaluative monitoring is a bit more optimistic. Specifically, this research has shown that children who view violent media content with an adult who explicitly disapproves of the violence are less likely to be violent themselves or to tolerate violent behavior. For example, in a classroom experiment, children watched an episode of *Batman* along with their teacher. The teacher made neutral remarks to half of the children, and comments of disapproval to the other half (for example, "Fighting is bad"). In the latter group, he suggested solving the problem in the film in another way (for example, "It's better to go get help"). After the viewing, children who had heard the disapproving comments were less likely to think it was okay to steal, hit people, or cause people pain, compared with the children in the neutral-commentary group.[38]

Follow-up work on evaluative monitoring, however, suggests that the benefits of evaluative monitoring occur only if the adult watching with the child stays with him or her after the film is over. If the adult leaves the room, the child is just as likely to imitate the violent acts as children who did not receive evaluative commentary.[39] This finding is in line with theories about children's moral development. Children five to eight years old rely mostly on the judgments of external socialization agents to regulate their behavior. Only later in their development do they use internalized behavioral norms to do so.

Which Active Strategy Works Best?

The question then becomes which of the two active strategies, factual or evaluative, is most effective at counteracting the effects of negative media (specifically, media violence) in childhood? Unfortunately, little research has compared the two strategies. Most studies have examined the influence of either factual or evaluative monitoring. A handful of studies have looked at the combined effects of both strategies, but in these studies it is difficult to isolate the unique influence of each strategy. Nathanson is one of the few who has compared the unique effectiveness of both strategies.[40] Her work suggests that evaluative strategies in general work better than factual ones, because factual strategies are more likely to result in reactance and boomerang effects than evaluative ones. Factual strategies, while capable of increasing children's critical thinking skills, do not fully protect children against the influence of media—something we saw to be true also in the case of advertising effects and the fear effects of media. Knowing that something is not realistic is no guarantee that the child will be resistant to the influence on his or her emotions or behavior. Although we know that a film is "only pretend," it can still make us afraid, sad, or agitated. Other studies, on youth and adults, show that knowledge of the reality level of media content is often insufficient to combat its influences.

Managing Media Use during the Teen Years

As children enter the teen years, parents face an uphill battle in managing media use. Teens become increasingly sensitive to criticisms about their media use. More than ever before, they see media as part of their personal domain—and thus something that should be off limits to parental oversight. At the same time, teens' cognitive and social-emotional development makes them particularly likely to engage in risky online behaviors, to struggle with limits, and to place a greater value on peers than on parents or other family members. In doing so, they are particularly likely to consume risky media content and to experience media addiction or addictive-like tendencies. Thus, for parents of teens, one of the biggest challenges is to find ways to ensure their teens' media use is safe and well balanced.

In recent years, media-specific parenting has become progressively more complex. One key reason for this is that communication technology has gotten closer and closer to us. The devices with which we communicate have moved from the desktop (on our desks) to the laptop (in our bags) to the smartphone (in our pockets), and are now appearing on our wrists. While the smartphone is a boon for coordinating activities within families and for offering peace of mind to parents, an important shadow side of the smartphone is that it quickly gets too close to us. Most smartphone-based apps are deliberately designed to continually disturb us.[41] Apps depend on advertising income, and they obtain such income only when they can entice enough people into using their product. Thus, apps compete for our attention with a cacophony of pop-ups, alerts, vibrations, and beeps,

And we, youth and adults alike, often have trouble ignoring this cacophony of alerts. The uncontrollable urge to respond to these alerts is a normal human instinct. We are hardwired to be curious about information coming our way. According to the neuroscientist Jaak Panksepp, we all have a built-in reward system that encourages us to be "seekers." Exciting experiences stimulate our brains to produce dopamine, as does seeking them out.[42] The alerts from social media give users a long series of mental mini rewards, thus constantly providing a small energy boost. This experience is said to be analogous to what a gambler feels with every new card dealt on the table.[43] The influence of these rewards is powerful and difficult to resist, and they can inculcate habits that we find very hard to change.

The temptations of the smartphone, challenging for many adults to resist, are considerably greater for teens. Many teens have great difficulty ignoring the alerts.[44] This succumbing to the allure of alerts is due, in part, to teens' growing need for intimacy. With this age group more than any other, the smartphone appeals to a deep-seated need to be in continual contact with friends. Beyond this, teens are more vulnerable than other age groups to the rewards triggered by the alerts. The production of dopamine in adolescence differs from that in childhood or adulthood, which, as noted in chapter 6, translates to increased interest in exciting or potentially exciting events and behaviors.[45]

The Shadow Sides of Smartphones

For parents, the fight against the smartphone can be a difficult one. As discussed in the previous chapter, smartphones, and their social media uses in particular, have many positive influences on teens' development. But the smartphone also brings with it several shadow sides. Excessive smartphone use, a common complaint by parents, can prevent teens from getting sufficient sleep. Intense back-and-forth communication before bedtime can enhance physical arousal, and it can disturb deep (slow-wave) sleep, or REM (rapid eye movement) sleep, which is needed to recover physically and mentally from the day's events. After being up late on a smartphone, teens may wake up tired and irritable and, as a result, experience concentration problems during the day.[46]

In addition to interfering with sleep, excessive smartphone use leaves teens too little time during the day to relax. The smartphone ensures that they always have something to do, whether in the doctor's waiting room, while waiting for a bus, or, for some, on the toilet. In the last few years, reports have shown that it is not good for our well-being to have every second of our waking hours be filled in this way. Besides a good night's rest, we need a good day's rest, some downtime when we can daydream, think things over, or just listen to the birds singing. This idle time is necessary for us to process our impressions, memories, and thoughts.

In his book *Autopilot: The Art and Science of Doing Nothing*, Andrew Smart suggests that the chronic stimulation that results from being continually reachable on the smartphone may be harmful to our mental health. Incessant immersion in smartphone-based activities interferes with reflection, emotional well-being, creativity, and even our ability to be truly social. In the Eastern tradition, the idea of stopping the mind's "chatter" for a short while has been accepted for thousands of years, and according to Smart, it is high time that we in the Western world give it some thought.[47]

As noted in the previous chapter, the smartphone is intricately connected to social media. Indeed, part of the draw of the smartphone is its ability to connect with others at all times of the day. Even for many adults, ignoring social media for a prolonged period requires a considerable amount of self-regulation. But this effort is even greater for teens. Most children have the opportunity to develop their self-regulation skills with the help of their parents. By the age of nine, they are usually able to balance their impulses. But this balance is easily disturbed by the many new urges that result from pubertal development, which place a heavy demand on self-regulatory abilities. Therefore, it is precisely in this phase that teens need their parents to help them set and maintain boundaries, not only for their smartphone use, but also for many other temptations of the teen years.

As with all humans, teens' ability to self-regulate is not exhaustive. Self-regulation is often compared with a muscle. Just as exercising for too long leaves muscles drained, the ability to self-regulate decreases when it becomes exhausted—fatigue, strain, and stress can all use up our abilities to regulate our behavior.[48] Teens battle fatigue and stress every day, which alone is enough to deplete their self-control muscle rapidly. The probability of depletion is even greater if, on top of all this, teens are not getting enough sleep at night or enough idle time during the day. The question then becomes what, exactly, can parents do? How can they help their teens, even if they do not want help? Thus far, the literature makes two key points: help prevent habit formation, and restrict in an autonomy-supportive way.

Preventing Habit Formation

The first tactic—preventing habit formation—is one that parents can begin working toward early. Habits are behaviors that we learned consciously and that became automatic through repetition. Habits in our everyday lives include how we brush our teeth, tie our shoes, or park our cars. Nearly half of our media use seems to be habitual.[49] Some people may read the news every morning with breakfast, others might check their e-mail as soon as they arrive at work, and others might watch a series on Netflix before they go to bed. We have habits for a good reason. Once habits are formed, they save us time and energy, since actions that previously required conscious thought can now be performed automatically. In the longer term, our habits help ensure that energy is left for tasks that require thinking and self-regulation.[50]

Once formed, habits are difficult to break. Thus, if parents hope to prevent teens from forming the habit of being reachable at all times via media, the best approach is to help them form healthier media habits early on—in other words, be proactive. One way that parents can do this is to set a good example and to behave themselves according to the standards they set. Children whose parents smoke are twice as likely to start smoking, even if their parents are critical of smoking and try to prevent their children's initiation.[51] Likewise, it is difficult for parents to set rules for teens' social media use if the parents ignore their own rules.

Another proactive way to prevent habitual smartphone use is to arrive at agreed-upon policies before the smartphone is purchased. For example, parents can discuss beforehand with their teenage children the types of guidelines that will work best in their familial situation and then come to an agreement about certain house rules. Such house rules might include no smartphone use at mealtimes or after a certain time at night, and completely turning off the phone during sleeping hours. The cocreation of these early agreements enhances the probability that teens will feel a personal commitment to stick to the rules.

Autonomy-Supportive Restrictions

One of the challenges that parents face when it comes to helping their teens form healthy media habits is to find ways to do this without eliciting reactance. It is easy to imagine that teens will find ways to sneak smartphone (or other media) use as a means of reacting against restriction guidelines. As noted earlier, media restriction is not always successful. Sometimes it creates the "forbidden fruit" effect, making the restricted behavior even more desirable.[52] How then can parents restrict media use in a way that encourages the formation of healthy media habits and avoids reactance? The answer, it seems, lies not in what parents do but rather in how they do it.

In one of our studies in the Netherlands, we found that if parents restricted media use in a way that supported teens' autonomy, by taking the teen's perspective seriously and developing media guidelines together, family conflict and antisocial behavior among teens were reduced. But if parents took a more authoritarian approach, such as threatening with punishment, or were inconsistent in their enforcement of media guidelines, the reverse was true: family conflict and antisocial behavior increased.[53] In other words, attempting to make teens feel guilty and threatening them with punishment without taking their needs into account can quickly backfire.[54]

Parents of preteens and teens are faced with the often thankless task of helping their children learn to regulate their media behavior. For regulation to be effective, parents must keep in mind that teenagers want to be treated like adults. The regulation of media use can be a struggle, but it is worth the fight. Helping youth develop healthy media habits, particularly in an era of continually available social media, will pay dividends in their later development. Autonomy-supportive strategies, in which parents and teens together form guidelines for media use, work best. Ideally, a conversation about this issue should happen before the media use begins or, at a minimum, before any extreme media use violation occurs. If that happens, the probability that teens will feel some form of personal commitment to the guidelines is increased. And they will then be more likely to keep the agreement they made and to make the transition to the next step: regulating their own behavior.[55]

Conclusion

Parents matter. This is an undeniable fact. How parents raise their children plays a crucial role in how their children develop into adults. Children raised under an authoritative parenting style that balances warmth and structure grow up to be more well adjusted than their peers who grow up in authoritarian or permissive families. Similarly, how parents manage media use in their family can strongly influence child development.

For the youngest children, parents must try to identify whether any media are okay for their children. And if they decide to expose their children to screen media, they have to navigate the burgeoning educational media landscape to find content that meets the needs of their kids. As children get older, they are increasingly confronted with the allure of other content, such as violent content, and as a result, parents must find ways to successfully mitigate such content's potential negative effects. And by the teen years, parents must try to help their teens find a way to regulate their media use—a task that increases in complexity because, in comparison with children, teens less easily tolerate parents' interference in their media use.

As this chapter showed, parents can influence access to and the effects of media content through restrictive and active mediation techniques. Doing so means taking seriously the new challenges of media-related parenting. In the twenty-first century, children and teens send as well as receive media content. Media-related parenting can therefore no longer be confined to the mediation of content that comes to children, but also involves proactively monitoring children and teens as senders of media content, especially if it takes the form of sexting or cyberbullying.

Media have become a main ingredient of teens' social lives. In practice, this means that traditional offline social issues in adolescence (bullying, falling in love, social isolation, and sexuality) have entered the domain of parental media monitoring. And while people often suggest that parents need a sophisticated understanding of new media and technology in order to effectively parent in the twenty-first century, this is largely a misconception. In practice, "new" media-specific parenting issues are typically offline issues in disguise—issues that were at play long before the Internet existed. It is not so much technical knowledge that matters. What matters most is proactive media monitoring, in which parents take the experiences of their children seriously, and in which they help them form the media guidelines that best fit their unique needs.

15

THE END

"Tut, tut, child!" said the Duchess. "Everything's got a moral, if only you can find it."

—Lewis Carroll, *Alice's Adventures in Wonderland* (1865)

In the twenty-first century, media and communication technology have penetrated all levels of society, and they appeal to everyone: infants, children, teens, parents, teachers, practitioners, public policy makers, politicians—everyone. Media and communication technology make for bold headlines in newspapers, and they are hot topics in debates, forums, and congresses. Everyone wants to get a grip on the rapid, large-scale changes in the media landscape. Everyone wants to know what impact media and technology are having on all of us, especially on youth. And everyone wants to understand the dynamics of our network society.

The Network Society

The twenty-first century is, so far, the age of the network society. A society supported by social media networks, which have removed the spatial barriers that traditionally limited our communication, and have changed the world into a global village.[1] In comparison with earlier societies, it is much more difficult to get a grip on the processes at work in a network society. In a network society, values and norms of conduct are less fixed and less shaped by place and social position. For example, in the homogenous societies of the 1950s, relationships were clear and largely predetermined. Father was the breadwinner, Mother was responsible for maintaining the household and raising the children, and children were expected to follow in their parents' footsteps. In many cases, families were part of a religion-defined subculture that influenced their school selection, sports clubs, and much more. Communication was clear and predetermined, occurring either face-to-face or through mass media, and was characterized by a one-way transfer from a sender (such as radio or television) to a receiver.

Whereas society in the 1950s was defined by collectivities (family, neighborhood, religious circle), today's network society revolves around the individual.[2] Every individual member is part of different networks driven by communication technologies. We are familiar with the image of a contemporary family sitting in a restaurant, parents and children glued to their own phones, unaware of one another, and communicating via e-mail, Facebook, WhatsApp, Twitter, Instagram, or Snapchat. In the network society, communication is no longer exclusively face-to-face, but is instead mediated through communication technology. It also no longer exclusively takes place through mass communication, but also through "mass self-communication."[3] Recipients of communication are now also senders of an influential mass of knowledge, entertainment, and opinions.

In a network society, there are fewer absolute rules of behavior than before, and few things are unquestioningly self-evident. In a network society, it is not the social position of the senders but their persuasiveness that predicts their influence and authority.[4] The information flow produced by mass self-communication is infinite. Knowledge is available to everyone; it is produced by everyone; and it is accessible to everyone. The information upon which we base our beliefs comes from everywhere, and the average shelf life of this information is shorter and less predictable than ever before.[5]

In a network society, parents are confronted with a variety of conflicting, often short-lived beliefs about family matters, including, for example, messages about the appropriateness of media in children's lives or about the role that parents "should" play in managing their children's media use—making today's parenting ever more complex. In addition, the network society has resulted in unprecedented freedom for today's youth, and the personalized social media they enjoy requires more intense supervision and comprehensive judgment from parents than any earlier medium.

Without the authoritative rules governing behavior that were once present in collective societies, our identity has become a matter of free choice, which, of course, demands more responsibility and self-regulation than ever before.

This is the context that twenty-first-century families are living in. A context filled with opportunities and challenges. A context in which media and technological innovations are so tightly interwoven that it is hard to see where one stops and the other begins. And this is the context in which twenty-first-century academic research on youth and media is conducted.

Promises and Perils of Youth and Media Research Today

The transition to a network society has, by all accounts, turned research on youth and media on its head—leading to new opportunities and new challenges. Perhaps most obvious is the fact that our object of study has become a moving target. Many of the media and communication technologies that we investigate today are continually changing—often while we try to understand the phenomenon in question. Yesterday's MySpace is today's Instagram. This is especially problematic for the social sciences, because social scientists often need sufficient time to answer questions with appropriate methodological rigor. To establish causal relationships between media use and longer-term outcomes, youth must be followed over several years, and their media use needs to be measured repeatedly. With the rapid and often short-lived developments in the media landscape, such research is far more complicated than it used to be.

Added to this complexity is the fact that youth and media research has always been an interdisciplinary field par excellence. Questions about youth and media are not solely the province of communication scholars or developmental psychologists. Quite the contrary. A successful understanding of youth and media requires knowledge of media developments, child development, family communication, education, and the particular media outcome of interest (aggression, loneliness, friendship quality, etc.). This means integrating knowledge across communication studies, developmental psychology, social psychology, sociology, pediatric medicine, and more.

But interdisciplinary work is challenging. Differing ideas about theories, research designs, and the interpretation of research outcomes must be dealt with. These disciplinary differences complicate the study of youth and media, and it is no surprise that there is not yet a single, all-encompassing theory to connect these disciplines and help explain the relationship between youth and media. Moreover, these different perspectives greatly influence the lens through which the field is viewed. For example, researchers who align themselves with the fields of pediatric medicine or child psychology are confronted more frequently with children struggling with emotional and social problems than are, say, media psychologists or sociologists. It is not surprising then, given their different experiences, that pediatricians and child psychologists are more likely than media psychologists or sociologists to see the dark sides of media and communication technology.[6] As the saying goes, "What you see depends on where you stand."

While the youth and media field is replete with diverging opinions between disciplines, such divides in views also occur within the discipline. This is especially true when it comes to negative effects of media content, such as those of violent media. More than ever before, there are heated debates between scholars about whether media violence leads to aggression among youth. A well-known example of this debate was published in *Psychological Bulletin*. In a piece by Brad Bushman and colleagues, "Much Ado about Something," the authors discussed why findings from meta-analyses on the influence of violent games on aggression were meaningful.[7] In "Much Ado about Nothing," however, Christopher Ferguson and John Kilburn argued that they are not meaningful.[8]

The issue in scholarly debates such as these is not so much that researchers find different results, but rather how differently they interpret the same results. As we showed in this book, meta-analyses on the effects of media on beliefs and behavior usually report small to moderate effect sizes, between $r = .10$ and $r = .20$, with occasional outliers above and below. Some scholars find these effects to be too small to warrant attention. Others, ourselves among them, are of the opinion that we must take such small to moderate effects seriously, since they may indicate that a small group of children and adolescents are particularly susceptible to the effects of media.

Thus, different scholars in the same discipline can have diametrically opposite interpretations of the same research findings. Over a century ago, an anonymous artist drew a picture, later made famous by the psychologist Joseph Jastrow, and again later by the philosopher Ludwig Wittgenstein: the rabbit-duck illusion (see figure 15.1).[9] Some people immediately see a rabbit (or properly, a hare), with its ears on the left. Others immediately see a duck, with its beak on the left. It is impossible to see both the duck and the rabbit at the same time.

Social scientists find themselves in a situation that is comparable to the rabbit-duck illusion. Using the same body of literature, they can discover differing realities and then contradict one another or, what is more serious, talk over one another's heads. Diametrically opposite interpretations of the same information have fueled social science for decades. Yet today's network society, with its proliferation of accessible knowledge, brings this opposition to an entirely new level. For every subject and subarea, no matter how small, an overwhelming amount of research can be found. Whereas fifteen years ago, studies on the cognitive effects of video games could be counted on one's fingers, today there are hundreds of studies and several meta-analyses on the topic.

Figure 15.1. The rabbit-duck illusion: like this image, research findings can elicit multiple, seemingly incompatible interpretations. The first version of this drawing appeared in 1892 in the German magazine *Fliegende Blätter*.

Indeed, while gathering the research for this book, we were often amazed at how much information was available—and simultaneously somewhat apprehensive that in our search, we missed the forest for the trees. This is both a promise and peril of the network society. On the one hand, the impressive (and still growing!) body of knowledge provides fuel for the oppositions housed within and across disciplines. On the other hand, contradiction and criticism have always been the essence of science. They force us to look ever more critically at our research topic and engage with one another's criticisms in order to develop stronger research and achieve better answers. It is also what makes our field more dynamic, more responsive, and more fascinating than ever before.

Plugged In: Learning from the Past, Looking toward the Future

There is no question that we are all plugged in to some extent. We have televisions in our homes, laptops on our desks, tablets in our bags, and smartphones in our pockets. The twenty-first century has enabled us to be always connected, always available, always on. And with this always-connected lifestyle come many questions about what it means for our health and happiness. These questions often focus on youth, since they are typically viewed as highly vulnerable to media effects and are, in fact, growing up almost literally plugged in.

In this book, our goal was to address these questions by contextualizing them within the larger field of media effects. By highlighting the nuanced nature of the relationship between youth and media, we aimed to quell some concerns associated with media while simultaneously highlighting those areas that should be treated with caution. We also aimed to shed light on the opportunities for future work in this field and to recognize the ever-increasing importance of youth and media scholarship in today's network society. To do so, we analyzed a number of key questions that regularly call for the attention of academics and the public at large, such as the effects of violence, sex, advertising, educational media, gaming, and social media.

Perhaps most clearly, *Plugged In* demonstrates that, as Dan Anderson and colleagues rightfully noted in 2001, "Marshall McLuhan appears to have been wrong. The *medium* is not the message, the *message* is the message."[10] Time and time again, we see that the content of media matters. Content that is violent, horrific, or highly sexualized can lead to increased aggressive behavior, fear, and unhealthy sexual attitudes. But in the same vein, content that features academic or prosocial messages can foster academic and social-emotional learning.

Along with issues of content, this book shows that there are other important factors that parents, practitioners, and researchers must pay attention to. We have seen that complex games can increase teens' cognitive skills. And we have seen that social media—when used in a healthy way—can help adolescents build their self-esteem, enhance their peer relationships, and shape their identities. But here too there are risks. For some youth, violent games can lead to aggressive behavior. And for some youth, the use of social media can have important downsides, such as cyberbullying, stranger danger, and sexual risk behavior.

More generally, the adage "There is such a thing as too much of a good thing" rings true when it comes to children's and teens' media use. Indeed, real concerns arise when it comes to excessive media multitasking as well as compulsive gaming or social media use. It is crucial that we bolster the effects of positive media content and mitigate the effects of negative content. We need to help youth learn how to make media a part of their life—but not their entire life. In our always-on, always-plugged-in culture, this will be a key challenge for parents and youth, and for us all.

In addition to highlighting the sunny and dark sides of youth's media use, this book makes the point that while content certainly matters, so too does the audience and the context in which the media use occurs. Perhaps most prominently, we see that media preferences and media effects are highly dependent on children's development. While younger children prefer content that is slow-paced, features fantastical elements, and relies on simple humor, teens prefer fast-paced realistic content that incorporates complex humor and risky elements. Moreover, younger children are more sensitive than older children and adolescents to the effects of media violence, frightening media content, and advertising. Development matters. Development influences not only the media that children consume, but also how are they are affected by this consumption. It is impossible to understand the true relationship between youth and media without considering development.

Beyond development, the research featured throughout this book shows that dispositional and social factors predispose the size and direction of media effects. Effects of media violence show up predominantly among children with an aggressive temperament and an above-normal interest in media violence. In the same vein, sexualized media seem to have negative consequences particularly for teens who become sexually active at a young age and who are particularly interested in sex. Moreover, it is clear that parents play a critical role in enhancing the positive effects of media and combatting the negative ones. These are important findings. They offer a detailed look at who is susceptible to media effects, and make the crucial point that youth's dispositions and their environments help shape media effects. Just as it is impossible to understand the relationship between youth and media without considering development, it is similarly impossible to obtain a true understanding of this relationship without considering relevant dispositional and environmental variables.

It is clear that the youth and media field will need to tackle many more questions in the years ahead. As media experiences continue to become more realistic and responsive, efforts to understand how interactivity influences the effects of media will certainly receive increased attention. For example, do virtual-reality experiences enhance youth's learning about topics such as the solar system or ancient Rome? Do immersive violent games lead to increased arousal and subsequent aggression? Moreover, as media continue to become more ingrained in the daily lives of children and teens, we will undoubtedly ask more questions about media multitasking and social media addiction. And as social media continue their push to become one of the primary ways that youth communicate with peers, scholars will certainly work to understand the opportunities and pitfalls of tomorrow's Facebook.

To answer these questions with the empirical vigor they deserve, it will be crucial for youth and media scholars to continue their march toward more complex theoretical models. The trend in communication studies toward taking a greater interest in individual differences in susceptibility to media effects is in line with similar trends in other disciplines. For example, the medical field is looking at the opportunities of "personalized medicine." In education, personalized learning has been given another boost by developments in communication technologies. And developmental psychology has embraced the dandelion-orchid hypothesis, which states that most children are like dandelions, able to thrive under good and bad environmental conditions, but that a small group of children are like orchids, requiring supportive environments lest they wither or fade.[11]

Of course, investigating how individual differences in development, disposition, and environment affect children's media selection, their processing of media, and the effects of media is no easy task. It is complex, messy, and challenging. But if we understand how and why media use influences youth, which youth are susceptible to positive and negative media effects, and how their social environment can maximize positive media effects and combat negative ones, the answers will be worth the effort. And by all accounts, today's plugged-in generation is most certainly worth the effort.

NOTES

1. Youth and Media

1. Vicky Rideout, *The Common Sense Census: Media Use by Tweens and Teens* (San Francisco: Common Sense Media, 2015).

2. Nico Drok and Fifi Schwarz, *Jongeren, Nieuwsmedia en Betrokkenheid* [Youth, news media, and involvement] (Zwolle/Amsterdam: Hogeschool Windesheim / Stichting Krant in de Klas, 2009).

3. Albert Bandura, Dorothea Ross, and Sheila A. Ross, "Transmission of Aggression through Imitation of Aggressive Models," *Journal of Abnormal and Social Psychology* 63, no. 3 (1961).

4. Marie E. Schmidt et al., "The Effects of Background Television on the Toy Play Behavior of Very Young Children," *Child Development* 79, no. 4 (2008).

5. Robert Kraut et al., "Internet Paradox: A Social Technology That Reduces Social Involvement and Psychological Well-Being?," *American Psychologist* 53, no. 9 (1998).

6. Plato, *Phaedrus,* trans. Harold North Fowler, Loeb Library 36 (Cambridge, Mass.: Harvard University Press, 1999 [1914]).

7. danah boyd, *It's Complicated: The Social Lives of Networked Teens* (New Haven, Conn.: Yale University Press, 2014), 16.

2. Then and Now

1. Philippe Ariès, *Centuries of Childhood: A Social History of Family Life,* trans. Robert Baldick (New York: Vintage, 1962).

2. Linda Baumgarten, *Eighteenth-Century Clothing at Williamsburg* (Williamsburg, Va.: Colonial Williamsburg Foundation, 1986).

3. Ariès, *Centuries of Childhood.*

4. Frank Musgrove, *The Family, Education, and Society* (London: Routledge and Kegan, 1966).

5. Norbert Elias, *The Civilizing Process: Sociogenetic and Psychogenetic Investigations,* rev. ed. (Oxford: Blackwell, 2000).

6. Rita Ghesquière, *Jeugdliteratuur in Perspectief* [Children's literature in perspective] (Leuven, Belgium: Acco, 2009).

7. Ibid.

8. David Elkind, *The Hurried Child: Growing Up Too Fast Too Soon* (Reading, Mass.: Addison-Wesley, 1981).

9. Neil Postman, *The Disappearance of Childhood* (London: Allen, 1983); Joshua Meyrowitz, *No Sense of Place: The Impact of Electronic Media on Social Behavior* (New York: Oxford University Press, 1985).

10. Meyrowitz, *No Sense of Place,* 227.

11. Postman, *Disappearance of Childhood.*

12. Meyrowitz, *No Sense of Place,* 227.

13. Eleanor E. Maccoby, "Television: Its Impact on School Children," *Public Opinion Quarterly* 15, no. 3 (1951).

14. Wilbur Schramm, Jack Lyle, and Edwin B. Parker, *Television in the Lives of Our Children* (Stanford, Calif.: Stanford University Press, 1961).

15. Meyrowitz, *No Sense of Place,* 229.

16. George Gerbner, Larry Gross, Michael Morgan, and Nancy Signorielli, "Living with Television: The Dynamics of the Cultivation Process," in *Perspectives on Media Effects,* ed. Jennings Bryant and Dolf Zillmann (Hillsdale, N.J.: Erlbaum, 1986).

17. Ibid., 18.

18. Erik H. Erikson, *Childhood and Society* (New York: Norton, 1950).

19. Margaret K. Nelson, *Parenting Out of Control: Anxious Parents in Uncertain Times* (New York: New York University Press, 2010).

20. Kim Parker, *The Boomerang Generation: Feeling OK about Living with Mom and Dad* (Washington, D.C.: Pew Research Center, 2012).

21. Margaret Mead, *Culture and Commitment: A Study of the Generation Gap* (New York: Bodley Head, 1970).

22. Jannetje Koelewijn, "Lunchgesprek Met Anna Enquist" [Lunch meeting with Anna Enquist], *NRC Handelsblad,* 12 July 2014.

23. Mead, *Culture and Commitment.*

24. James U. McNeal, *The Kids Market: Myths and Realities* (New York: Paramount, 1999).

25. Stephen Kline, *Out of the Garden: Toys, TV, and Children's Culture in the Age of Marketing Toys and Children's Culture in the Age of TV Marketing* (London: Verso, 1993).

26. Patti M. Valkenburg and Moniek Buijzen, "Identifying Determinants of Young Children's Brand Awareness: Television, Parents, and Peers," *Journal of Applied Developmental Psychology* 26, no. 4 (2005).

27. Mark A. Bellis, Jennifer Downing, and John R. Ashton, "Adults at 12? Trends in Puberty and Their Public Health Consequences," *Journal of Epidemiology and Community Health* 60, no. 11 (2006).

28. Werrett W. Charters, *Motion Pictures and Youth: A Summary* (New York: Macmillan, 1933).

29. James R. Flynn, "Massive IQ Gains in 14 Nations: What IQ Tests Really Measure," *Psychological Bulletin* 101, no. 2 (1987).

30. Jan te Nijenhuis, "The Flynn Effect, Group Differences, and G Loadings," *Personality and Individual Differences* 55, no. 3 (2013).

31. Ibid.

32. James R. Flynn, "Requiem for Nutrition as the Cause of IQ Gains: Raven's Gains in Britain, 1938–2008," *Economics and Human Biology* 7, no. 1 (2009): 23.

33. Jean M. Twenge, *Generation Me: Why Today's Young Americans Are More Confident, Assertive, Entitled—and More Miserable—than Ever Before* (New York: Free Press, 2006); Jean M. Twenge and W. Keith Campbell, *The Narcissism Epidemic: Living in the Age of Entitlement* (New York: Free Press, 2009).

34. Jean M. Twenge, "The Age of Anxiety? The Birth Cohort Change in Anxiety and Neuroticism, 1952–1993," *Journal of Personality and Social Psychology* 79, no. 6 (2000); Lara J. Akinbami, Xiang Liu, Patricia N. Pastor, and Cynthia A. Reuben, "Attention Deficit Hyperactivity Disorder among Children Aged 5–17 Years in the United States, 1998–2009," NCHS Data Brief 70 (Hyattsville, Md.: National Center for Health Statistics,2011).

35. Elisabeth J. Costello, Alaattin Erkanli, and Adrian Angold, "Is There an Epidemic of Child or Adolescent Depression?," *Journal of Child Psychology and Psychiatry* 47, no. 12 (2006).

36. Joel T. Nigg, *What Causes ADHD? Understanding What Goes Wrong and Why* (New York: Guilford, 2006).

37. Laura Pearce and Andy P. Field, "The Impact of 'Scary' TV and Film on Children's Internalizing Emotions: A Meta-Analysis," *Human Communication Research* 42, no. 1 (2016).

38. Sanne W. C. Nikkelen et al., "Media Use and ADHD-Related Behaviors in Children and Adolescents: A Meta-Analysis," *Developmental Psychology* 50, no. 9 (2014).

3. Themes and Theoretical Perspectives

Epigraph: Wilbur Schramm, Jack Lyle, and Edwin B. Parker, *Television in the Lives of Our Children* (Stanford, Calif.: Stanford University Press, 1961), 3.

1. M. L. DeFleur, *Mass Communication Theories: Explaining Origins, Processes, and Effects* (Boston: Allyn and Bacon, 2010).

2. Richard Koszarski, *An Evening's Entertainment: The Age of the Silent Feature Picture, 1915–1928,* vol. 3 (Berkeley: University of California Press, 1994).

3. DeFleur, *Mass Communication Theories.*

4. Charles Darwin, *On the Origin of Species* (London: Murray, 1859).

5. Steven E. Jones, *The Emergence of the Digital Humanities* (London: Routledge, 2013).

6. Hilde T. Himmelweit, Abraham N. Oppenheim, and Pamela Vince, *Television and the Child: An Empirical Study of the Effect of Television on the Young* (London: Oxford University Press, 1958).

7. DeFleur, *Mass Communication Theories.*

8. Werrett W. Charters, *Motion Pictures and Youth: A Summary* (New York: Macmillan, 1933), 16.

9. Edgar Dale, *The Content of Motion Pictures* (New York: Macmillan, 1935).
10. Herbert Blumer, *Movies and Conduct* (New York: Macmillan, 1933).
11. Wendell S. Dysinger and Christian A. Ruckmick, *The Emotional Responses of Children to the Motion Picture Situation* (New York: Macmillan, 1933).
12. Charters, *Motion Pictures and Youth,* 16.
13. DeFleur, *Mass Communication Theories.*
14. Hadley Cantril, *The Invasion from Mars: A Study in the Psychology of Panic* (Princeton, N.J.: Princeton University Press, 1952).
15. Bernard Berelson, "Communication and Public Opinion," in *Communications in Modern Society,* ed. Wilbur Schramm (Urbana: University of Illinois Press, 1948), 112.
16. Elihu Katz and Paul F. Lazarsfeld, *Personal Influence: The Part Played by People in the Flow of Mass Communications* (Piscataway, N.J.: Transaction, 1955); Joseph T. Klapper, *The Effects of Mass Media* (Glencoe, IL: Free Press, 1960).
17. Charters, *Motion Pictures and Youth,* 16.
18. Michael D. Slater, "Reinforcing Spirals: The Mutual Influence of Media Selectivity and Media Effects and Their Impact on Individual Behavior and Social Identity," *Communication Theory* 17, no. 3 (2007).
19. Albert Bandura, *Social Foundations of Thought and Action: A Social Cognitive Theory* (Englewood Cliffs, N.J.: Prentice-Hall, 1986).
20. Richard E. Petty and John T. Cacioppo, "The Elaboration Likelihood Model of Persuasion," in *Advances in Experimental Social Psychology,* ed. Leonard Berkowitz (New York: Academic Press, 1986).
21. Craig A. Anderson and Brad J. Bushman, "Human Aggression," *Annual Review of Psychology* 53 (2002).
22. Patti M. Valkenburg and Jochen Peter, "The Differential Susceptibility to Media Effects Model," *Journal of Communication* 63, no. 2 (2013).
23. Schramm, Lyle, and Parker, *Television in the Lives of Our Children,* 3.
24. Slater, "Reinforcing Spirals."
25. Richard J. Davidson and Sharon Begley, *The Emotional Life of Your Brain: How Its Unique Patterns Affect the Way You Think, Feel, and Live and How You Can Change Them* (New York: Penguin, 2012).
26. Patti M. Valkenburg and Jochen Peter, "Five Challenges for the Future of Media-Effects Research," *International Journal of Communication* 7 (2013).
27. Tom Grimes, James A. Anderson, and Lori Bergen, *Media Violence and Aggression: Science and Ideology* (Los Angeles: Sage, 2008).
28. Jessica T. Piotrowski and Patti M. Valkenburg, "Finding Orchids in a Field of Dandelions: Understanding Children's Differential Susceptibility to Media Effects," *American Behavioral Scientist* 59, no. 14 (2015).
29. W. Thomas Boyce and Bruce J. Ellis, "Biological Sensitivity to Context: I. An Evolutionary-Developmental Theory of the Origins and Functions of Stress Reactivity," *Development and Psychopathology* 17, no. 2 (2005).
30. Schramm, Lyle, and Parker, *Television in the Lives of Our Children,* 3.

4. Infants, Toddlers, and Preschoolers

1. Jean Piaget, *The Construction of Reality in the Child* (New York: Basic Books, 1954).

2. Daniel R. Anderson, Elizabeth Pugzles Lorch, Diane Erickson Field, and Jeanne Sanders, "The Effects of TV Program Comprehensibility on Preschool Children's Visual Attention to Television," *Child Development* 52, no. 1 (1981).

3. Daniel R. Anderson and John Burns, "Paying Attention to Television," in *Responding to the Screen: Reception and Reaction Processes,* ed. Jennings Bryant and Dolf Zillmann (Hillsdale, N.J.: Erlbaum, 1991).

4. Jessica T. Piotrowski and Patti M. Valkenburg, "Finding Orchids in a Field of Dandelions: Understanding Children's Differential Susceptibility to Media Effects," *American Behavioral Scientist* 59, no. 14 (2015).

5. Piaget, *Construction of Reality.*

6. Helmuit Moog, *The Musical Experience of the Pre-School Child* (London: Schott Music, 1976).

7. Anne Fernald, "Four-Month-Old Infants Prefer to Listen to Motherese," *Infant Behavior and Development* 8, no. 2 (1985).

8. Russell J. Adams, "An Evaluation of Color Preference in Early Infancy," *Infant Behavior and Development* 10 (1987).

9. Ellen A. Wartella, Vicky Rideout, Alexis R. Lauricella, and Sabrina L. Connell, *Parenting in the Age of Digital Technology: A National Survey* (Evanston, Ill.: School of Communication, Northwestern University, 2013).

10. Alissa E. Setliff and Mary L. Courage, "Background Television and Infants' Allocation of Their Attention During Toy Play," *Infancy* 16, no. 6 (2011).

11. Holly A. Ruff and Mary K. Rothbart, *Attention in Early Development: Themes and Variations* (New York: Oxford University Press, 2001).

12. Patti M. Valkenburg and Marjolein Vroone, "Developmental Changes in Infants' and Toddlers' Attention to Television Entertainment," *Communication Research* 31, no. 3 (2004).

13. Tiffany A. Pempek, Heather L. Kirkorian, John E. Richards, Daniel R. Anderson, Anne F. Lund, and Michael Stevens, "Video Comprehensibility and Attention in Very Young Children," *Developmental Psychology* 46, no. 5 (2010).

14. Juju Chang, Christine Rakowski, and Daniel Clark, "Toddlers and Tablets: Way of the Future?," ABC News, http://abcnews.go.com/Technology/toddlers-tablets-future/story?id=19332916.

15. Wartella et al., *Parenting in the Age of Digital Technology.*

16. Erik F. Strommen, "Is It Easier to Hop or Walk? Development Issues in Interface Design," *Human-Computer Interaction* 8, no. 4 (1993).

17. Sarah E. Vaala and Robert C. Hornik, "Predicting US Infants' and Toddlers' TV/Video Viewing Rates: Mothers' Cognitions and Structural Life Circumstances," *Journal of Children and Media* 8, no. 2 (2014).

18. Dimitri A. Christakis, "The Effects of Infant Media Usage: What Do We Know and What Should We Learn?," *Acta Paediatrica* 98, no. 1 (2009).

19. Mary L. Courage and Mark L. Howe, "To Watch or Not to Watch: Infants and Toddlers in a Brave New Electronic World," *Developmental Review* 30, no. 2 (2010).

20. Valkenburg and Vroone, "Changes in Infants' and Toddlers' Attention."

21. Henry M. Wellman, *The Child's Theory of Mind,* vol. 37 (Cambridge, Mass.: MIT Press, 1990).

22. Janet W. Astington, *The Child's Discovery of the Mind,* vol. 31 (Cambridge, Mass.: Harvard University Press, 1993), 54.

23. Catherine Carvey and Rita Berndt, cited in ibid., 63.

24. Leona M. Jaglom and Howard Gardner, "The Preschool Television Viewer as Anthropologist," *New Directions for Child and Adolescent Development* no. 13 (1981).

25. Dafna Lemish, "Viewers in Diapers: The Early Development of Television Viewing," in *Natural Audiences: Qualitative Research of Media Uses and Effects,* ed. Thomas R. Lindlof (Norwood, N.J.: Ablex, 1987).

26. Jessica T. Piotrowski, "Participatory Cues and Program Familiarity Predict Young Children's Learning from Educational Television," *Media Psychology* 17, no. 3 (2014).

27. Jerome S. Bruner, "On Cognitive Growth II," in *Studies in Cognitive Growth,* ed. Rose R. Olver and Patricia M. Greenfield (New York: Wiley, 1966).

28. Cynthia Hoffner and Joanne Cantor, "Developmental Differences in Responses to a Television Character's Appearance and Behavior," *Developmental Psychology* 21, no. 6 (1985).

29. Piaget, *Construction of Reality.*

30. Daniel S. Acuff and Robert H. Reiher, *What Kids Buy and Why: The Psychology of Marketing to Kids* (New York: Free Press, 1997).

31. Paul Ekman, "An Argument for Basic Emotions," *Cognition and Emotion* 6, nos. 3–4 (1992).

32. Peter J. LaFreniere, *Emotional Development: A Biosocial Perspective* (Belmont, Calif.: Wadsworth, 2000).

33. Ibid., 178.

34. May L. Halim et al., "The Case of the Pink Frilly Dress and the Avoidance of All Things 'Girly': Girls' and Boys' Appearance Rigidity and Cognitive Theories of Gender Development," *Developmental Psychology* 50, no. 4 (2013).

35. Eleanor E. Maccoby, "Gender and Relationships: A Developmental Account," *American Psychologist* 45, no. 4 (1990).

36. Anne Moir and David Jessel, *Brain Sex: The Real Difference between Men and Women* (London: Mandarin, 1991).

37. Carol L. Martin, "Cognitive Influences on the Development and Maintenance of Gender Segregation," *New Directions for Child Development* 65 (1994).

38. Acuff and Reiher, *What Kids Buy and Why.*

39. Bradley J. Bond and Sandra L. Calvert, "Parasocial Breakup among Young Children in the United States," *Journal of Children and Media* 8, no. 4 (2014): 484.

5. Children

1. Sue Howard, "Unbalanced Minds? Children Thinking about Television," in *Wired-Up: Young People and the Electronic Media,* ed. Sue Howard (London: UCL Press, 1998).

2. Daniel R. Anderson, Elizabeth Pugzles Lorch, Diane E. Field, Patricia A. Collins, and John G. Nathan, "Television Viewing at Home: Age Trends in Visual Attention and Time with TV," *Child Development* 57 (1986).

3. Victoria J. Rideout, *Zero to Eight: Children's Media Use in America* (San Francisco: Common Sense Media, 2013); Ofcom, *Children and Parents: Media Use and Attitudes Report* (London: Ofcom, 2014).

4. Paul E. McGhee, *Humor: Its Origin and Development* (San Francisco: Freeman, 1979).

5. William Kotzwinkle and Glenn Murray, *Walter the Farting Dog* (Berkeley, Calif.: North Atlantic Books, 2001); Tara Gomi, *Everyone Poops* (La Jolla, Calif.: Kane/Miller, 1993).

6. Victoria J. Rideout, *Learning at Home: Families' Educational Media Use in America* (New York: Joan Ganz Cooney Center at Sesame Workshop, 2014).

7. Justin F. Martin, "Children's Attitudes toward Superheroes as a Potential Indicator of Their Moral Understanding," *Journal of Moral Education* 36 (2007).

8. Cynthia Hoffner and Joanne Cantor, "Perceiving and Responding to Mass Media Characters," in *Responding to the Screen: Reception and Reaction Processes,* ed. Jennings Bryant and Dolf Zillmann (Hillsdale, N.J.: Erlbaum, 1991).

9. Ellen Seiter, "Children's Desires / Mothers' Dilemmas: The Social Contexts of Consumption," in *The Children's Culture Reader,* ed. Henry Jenkins (New York: New York University Press, 2006).

10. Dorothy Z. Ullian, "The Development of Conceptions of Masculinity and Femininity," in *Exploring Sex Differences,* ed. Barbara B. Lloyd and John E. Archer (Oxford: Academic Press, 1976).

11. Carol J. Auster and Claire S. Mansbach, "The Gender Marketing of Toys: An Analysis of Color and Type of Toy on the Disney Store Website," *Sex Roles* 67, no. 7 (2012).

12. Moniek Buijzen and Patti M. Valkenburg, "Appeals in Advertising Aimed at Children and Adolescents," *Communications* 27, no. 3 (2002).

13. Daniel S. Acuff and Robert H. Reiher, *What Kids Buy and Why: The Psychology of Marketing to Kids* (New York: Free Press, 1997).

14. Victoria J. Rideout, Ulla G. Foehr, and Donald F. Roberts, *Generation M2: Media in the Lives of 8- to 18-Year-Olds* (Menlo Park, Calif.: Kaiser Family Foundation, 2010).

15. Kristi S. Lekies and Thomas H. Beery, "Everyone Needs a Rock: Collecting Items from Nature in Childhood," *Children, Youth, and Environments* 23, no. 3 (2013).

16. Jackie Marsh, "Young Children's Play in Online Virtual Worlds," *Journal of Early Childhood Research* 8, no. 1 (2010).

17. Keith W. Mielke, "Formative Research on Appeal and Comprehension in *3-2-1 Contact*," in *Children's Understanding of Television: Research on Attention and Comprehension*, ed. Jennings Bryant and Daniel R. Anderson (Hillsdale, N.J.: Erlbaum, 1983).

18. Ranjana Das, " 'I've Walked This Street': Readings of 'Reality' in British Young People's Reception of Harry Potter," *Journal of Children and Media* (2016).

19. Barrie Gunter, Jill L. McAleer, and Brian R. Clifford, *Children's View about Television* (Aldershot, UK: Avebury, 1991).

20. Robert L. Selman, *The Growth of Interpersonal Understanding: Developmental and Clinical Analyses* (New York: Academic Press, 1980).

21. Linda Sheldon and Milica Loncar, *Kids Talk TV: "Super Wickid" or "Dum"* (Sidney: Australian Broadcasting Authority, 1996).

22. Acuff and Reiher, *What Kids Buy and Why.*

23. Patti M. Valkenburg and Karin E. Soeters, "Children's Positive and Negative Experiences with the Internet: An Exploratory Survey," *Communication Research* 28, no. 5 (2001).

24. Tilo Hartmann and Christoph Klimmt, "Gender and Computer Games: Exploring Females' Dislikes," *Journal of Computer-Mediated Communication* 11, no. 4 (2006).

25. Acuff and Reiher, *What Kids Buy and Why.*

6. Adolescents

Epigraph: This quote circulates widely in educational institutions and on the Web; it is an edited compilation of a part of Plato's dialogue *The Republic.*

1. Amanda Lenhart, *Teens, Social Media, and Technology Overview 2015* (Washington, D.C.: Pew Research Center, 2015).

2. These data are based on our ongoing survey study among Dutch teenagers ages eleven to fifteen; our Dutch statistics (gathered in 2014) do not diverge significantly from those reported in other industrialized countries.

3. David C. Sinclair and Peter Dangerfield, *Human Growth after Birth*, vol. 6 (London: Oxford Univiversity Press, 1998).

4. Daniel J. Siegel, *Brainstorm: The Power and Purpose of the Teenage Brain* (New York: Penguin, 2013).

5. Signe Bray, Mark Krongold, Cassandra Cooper, and Catherine Lebel, "Synergistic Effects of Age on Patterns of White and Gray Matter Volume across Childhood and Adolescence," *eNeuro* 2, no. 4 (2015).

6. Eveline A. Crone and Ronald E. Dahl, "Understanding Adolescence as a Period of Social-Affective Engagement and Goal Flexibility," *Nature Reviews of Neuroscience* 13, no. 9 (2012).

7. Daniel S. Acuff and Robert H. Reiher, *What Kids Buy and Why: The Psychology of Marketing to Kids* (New York: Free Press, 1997).

8. American estimates: Victoria J. Rideout, Ulla G. Foehr, and Donald F. Roberts, *Generation M2: Media in the Lives of 8- to 18-Year-Olds* (Menlo Park, Calif.: Kaiser Family Foundation, 2010); Dutch estimates: Hilde A. M. Voorveld and Margot van

der Goot, "Age Differences in Media Multitasking: A Diary Study," *Journal of Broadcasting and Electronic Media* 57, no. 3 (2013).

9. Ann S. Masten, "Humor and Competence in School-Aged Children," *Child Development* 57, no. 2 (1986).

10. Nel Warnars-Kleverlaan, Louis Oppenheimer, and Larry Sherman, "To Be or Not to Be Humorous: Does It Make a Difference?," *Humor* 9, no. 2 (1996).

11. Laurence Steinberg, *Adolescence,* vol. 9 (New York: McGraw-Hill, 2011).

12. Siegel, *Brainstorm.*

13. Natalie Kretsch and Kathryn P. Harden, "Pubertal Development and Peer Influence on Risky Decision Making," *Journal of Early Adolescence* 34, no. 3 (2014).

14. Siegel, *Brainstorm.*

15. Laurence Steinberg, "Risk Taking in Adolescence: New Perspectives from Brain and Behavioral Science," *Current Directions in Psychological Science* 16, no. 2 (2007).

16. Susanne E. Baumgartner, Sindy R. Sumter, Jochen Peter, Patti M. Valkenburg, and Sonia Livingstone, "Does Country Context Matter? Investigating the Predictors of Teen Sexting across Europe," *Computers in Human Behavior* 34 (2014).

17. Angela Huebner, "Teen Social and Emotional Development," in *Families Matter! A Series for Parents of School-Age Youth,* ed. Pat T. Nelson (Neward, Del.: Cooperative Extension, University of Delaware, 2012).

18. Patti M. Valkenburg and Jochen Peter, "Online Communication among Adolescents: An Integrated Model of Its Attraction, Opportunities, and Risks," *Journal of Adolescent Health* 48, no. 2 (2011).

19. Susan Harter, *The Construction of the Self: A Developmental Perspective,* 2nd ed. (New York: Guilford, 2012).

20. David Elkind, "Egocentrism in Adolescence," *Child Development* 38, no. 4 (1967).

21. Jane D. Brown and Carol J. Pardun, "Little in Common: Racial and Gender Differences in Adolescents' Television Diets," *Journal of Broadcasting and Electronic Media* 48, no. 2 (2004).

22. Herbert Blumer, *Movies and Conduct* (New York: Macmillan, 1933).

23. Lenhart, *Teens, Social Media and Technology Overview 2015.*

24. Patti M. Valkenburg, Alexander P. Schouten, and Jochen Peter, "Adolescents' Identity Experiments on the Internet," *New Media and Society* 7, no. 3 (2005).

25. Steinberg, *Adolescence.*

26. Huebner, "Teen Social and Emotional Development."

27. Ibid.

28. Sindy R. Sumter, Patti M. Valkenburg, and Jochen Peter, "Perceptions of Love across the Lifespan: Differences in Passion, Intimacy, and Commitment," *International Journal of Behavioral Development* 37, no. 5 (2013).

29. Sara Magee, "High School Is Hell: The TV Legacy of *Beverly Hills, 90210* and *Buffy the Vampire Slayer,*" *Journal of Popular Culture* 47, no. 4 (2014).

30. Valkenburg and Peter, "Online Communication among Adolescents."

31. Johanna M. F. van Oosten, Jochen Peter, and Inge Boot, "Exploring Associations between Exposure to Sexy Online Self-Presentations and Adolescents' Sexual Attitudes and Behavior," *Journal of Youth and Adolescence* 44, no. 5 (2014).

32. For example, American data similarly indicate that 50 percent of adolescents reported actively seeking sexual content in their media choices; see Amy Bleakley, Michael Hennessy, and Martin Fishbein, "A Model of Adolescents' Seeking of Sexual Content in Their Media Choices," *Journal of Sex Research* 48, no. 4 (2010).

33. Van Oosten, Peter, and Boot, "Sexy Online Self-Presentations."

34. Gary W. Harper, Pedro Serrano, Douglas Bruce, and Jose Arturo Bauermeister, "The Internet's Multiple Roles in Facilitating the Sexual Orientation Identity Development of Gay and Bisexual Male Adolescents," *American Journal of Men's Health* (2015).

35. Aneeta Rattan and Nalini Ambady, "How 'It Gets Better': Effectively Communicating Support to Targets of Prejudice," *Personality and Social Psychology Bulletin* 40, no. 5 (2014); Brian Stelter, "Campaign Offers Help to Gay Youths," *New York Times,* October 18, 2010.

36. Siegel, *Brainstorm.*

37. Steinberg, "Risk Taking in Adolescence."

38. Harter, *Construction of the Self.*

39. Kelly L. Schmitt, Shoshana Dayanim, and Stacey Matthias, "Personal Homepage Construction as an Expression of Social Development," *Developmental Psychology* 44, no. 2 (2008): 496.

40. American estimates: Lawrence B. Finer and Jesse M. Philbin, "Sexual Initiation, Contraceptive Use, and Pregnancy among Young Adolescents," *Pediatrics* 131, no. 5 (2013); for European estimates, see Aubrey Spriggs Madkour et al., "Macro-Level Age Norms for the Timing of Sexual Initiation and Adolescents' Early Sexual Initiation in 17 European Countries," *Journal of Adolescent Health* 55, no. 1 (2014).

41. Melanie J. Zimmer-Gembeck and Mark Helfand, "Ten Years of Longitudinal Research on U.S. Adolescent Sexual Behavior: Developmental Correlates of Sexual Intercourse, and the Importance of Age, Gender and Ethnic Background," *Developmental Review* 28, no. 2 (2008).

7. Media and Violence

Epigraph: *PBS Newshour,* "Can Violent Video Games Play a Role in Violent Behavior," http://www.pbs.org/newshour/bb/social_issues-jan-june13-videogames_02-19.

1. Nancy Rappaport and Christopher Thomas, "Recent Research Findings on Aggressive and Violent Behavior in Youth: Implications for Clinical Assessment and Intervention," *Journal of Adolescent Health* 35, no. 4 (2004).

2. John P. Murray, "Media Violence and Children: Applying Research to Advocacy," in *Child and Family Advocacy,* ed. Anne McDonald Culp (New York: Springer, 2013).

3. Joanne Savage and Christina Yancey, "The Effects of Media Violence Exposure on Criminal Aggression: A Meta-Analysis," *Criminal Justice and Behavior* 35, no. 6 (2008).

4. Ibid., 773.

5. Sarah M. Coyne and John Archer, "Indirect Aggression in the Media: A Content Analysis of British Television Programs," *Aggressive Behavior* 30, no. 3 (2004).

6. See, for example, Sarah M. Coyne, John Archer, and Mike Eslea, "Cruel Intentions on Television and in Real Life: Can Viewing Indirect Aggression Increase Viewers' Subsequent Indirect Aggression?," *Journal of Experimental Child Psychology* 88, no. 3 (2004); Douglas A. Gentile, Sarah Coyne, and David A. Walsh, "Media Violence, Physical Aggression, and Relational Aggression in School Age Children: A Short-Term Longitudinal Study," *Aggressive Behavior* 37, no. 2 (2011).

7. Christopher P. Barlett, Craig A. Anderson, and Edward L. Swing, "Video Game Effects—Confirmed, Suspected, and Speculative: A Review of the Evidence," *Simulation and Gaming* 40, no. 3 (2009); but also see, for example: Christopher R. Engelhardt, Micah O. Mazurek, Joseph Hilgard, Jeffrey N. Rouder, and Bruce D. Bartholow, "Effects of Violent-Video-Game Exposure on Aggressive Behavior, Aggressive-Thought Accessibility, and Aggressive Affect among Adults with and without Autism Spectrum Disorder," *Psychological Science* 26, no. 8 (2015).

8. Jacques-Philippe Leyens, Leoncio Camino, Ross D. Parke, and Leonard Berkowitz, "Effects of Movie Violence on Aggression in a Field Setting as a Function of Group Dominance and Cohesion," *Journal of Personality and Social Psychology* 32, no. 2 (1975).

9. Craig A. Anderson et al., "Violent Video Game Effects on Aggression, Empathy, and Prosocial Behavior in Eastern and Western Countries: A Meta-Analytic Review," *Psychological Bulletin* 136, no. 2 (2010).

10. Leonard D. Eron, L. Rowell Huesmann, Monroe M. Lefkowitz, and Leopold O. Walder, "Does Television Violence Cause Aggression?," *American Psychologist* 27, no. 4 (1972).

11. Michael D. Slater, Kimberly L. Henry, Randall C. Swaim, and Joe M. Cardador, "Vulnerable Teens, Vulnerable Times: How Sensation Seeking, Alienation, and Victimization Moderate the Violent Media Content-Aggressiveness Relation," *Communication Research* 31, no. 6 (2004).

12. As discussed in Savage and Yancey, "The Effects of Media Violence Exposure on Criminal Aggression," meta-analyses may overestimate effect sizes because of problems such as publication bias, the mixed quality of the studies included, and problems with statistical reporting.

13. Haejung Paik and George Comstock, "The Effects of Television Violence on Antisocial Behavior: A Meta-Analysis," *Communication Research* 21, no. 4 (1994).

14. Craig A. Anderson and Brad J. Bushman, "Effects of Violent Video Games on Aggressive Behavior, Aggressive Cognition, Aggressive Affect, Physiological Arousal, and Prosocial Behavior: A Meta-Analytic Review of the Scientific Literature," *Psychological Science* 12, no. 5 (2001); John L. Sherry, "The Effects of Violent Video Games on Aggression: A Meta-Analysis," *Human Communication Research* 27, no. 3 (2001); Christopher J. Ferguson and John Kilburn, "The Public Health Risks of Media Violence: A Meta-Analytic Review," *Journal of Pediatrics* 154, no. 5 (2009); Anderson et al.,

"Violent Video Game Effects"; Tobias Greitemeyer and Dirk O. Muegge, "Video Games Do Affect Social Outcomes: A Meta-Analytic Review of the Effects of Violent and Prosocial Video Game Play," *Personality and Social Psychology Bulletin* 40, no. 5 (2014).

15. Coyne, Archer, and Eslea, "Cruel Intentions on Television"; Gentile, Coyne, and Walsh, "Media Violence, Physical Aggression, and Relational Aggression."

16. Savage and Yancey, "The Effects of Media Violence Exposure on Criminal Aggression."

17. Tom Grimes, James A. Anderson, and Lori Bergen, *Media Violence and Aggression: Science and Ideology* (Los Angeles: Sage, 2008).

18. Anderson et al., "Violent Video Game Effects."

19. Christopher J. Ferguson and John Kilburn, "Much Ado about Nothing: The Misestimation and Overinterpretation of Violent Video Game Effects in Eastern and Western Nations; Comment on Anderson et al. (2010)," *Psychological Bulletin* 136, no. 2 (2010).

20. Albert Bandura, "Influence of Models' Reinforcement Contingencies on the Acquisition of Imitative Responses," *Journal of Personality and Social Psychology* 1, no. 6 (1965).

21. Albert Bandura, *Social Foundations of Thought and Action: A Social Cognitive Theory* (Englewood Cliffs, N.J.: Prentice-Hall, 1986).

22. Ronald S. Drabman and Margaret H. Thomas, "Does Media Violence Increase Children's Toleration of Real-Life Aggression?," *Developmental Psychology* 10, no. 3 (1974).

23. Daniel Linz, Edward Donnerstein, and Steven Penrod, "The Effects of Multiple Exposures to Filmed Violence against Women," *Journal of Communication* 34, no. 3 (1984).

24. Maren Strenziok et al., "Fronto-Parietal Regulation of Media Violence Exposure in Adolescents: A Multi-Method Study," *Social Cognitive and Affective Neuroscience* 6, no. 5 (2010).

25. Brad J. Bushman and L. Rowell Huesmann, "Effects of Televised Violence on Aggression," in *Handbook of Children and the Media*, ed. Dorothy G. Singer and Jerome L. Singer (Thousand Oaks, Calif.: Sage, 2001).

26. L. Rowell Huesmann, Jessica Moise-Titus, Cheryl-Lynn Podolski, and Leonard D. Eron, "Longitudinal Relations between Children's Exposure to TV Violence and Their Aggressive and Violent Behavior in Young Adulthood, 1977–1992," *Developmental Psychology* 39, no. 2 (2003).

27. Leonard Berkowitz, "Some Effects of Thoughts on Anti- and Prosocial Influences of Media Events: A Cognitive-Neoassociation Analysis," *Psychological Bulletin* 95, no. 3 (1984).

28. Brad J. Bushman, "Priming Effects of Media Violence on the Accessibility of Aggressive Constructs in Memory," *Personality and Social Psychology Bulletin* 24, no. 5 (1998).

29. Dolf Zillmann, "Attribution and Misattribution of Excitatory Reactions," in *New Directions in Attribution Research*, ed. John H. Harvey, William Ickes, and Robert F. Kidd (Hillsdale, N.J.: Erlbaum, 1978).

30. Brad J. Bushman and Craig A. Anderson, "Violent Video Games and Hostile Expectations: A Test of the General Aggression Model," *Personality and Social Psychology Bulletin* 28, no. 12 (2002).

31. Paik and Comstock, "Effects of Television Violence on Antisocial Behavior"; Barbara J. Wilson et al., "Violence in Television Programming Overall," in *National Television Violence Study 2,* ed. Center for Communication and Social Policy (Thousand Oaks, Calif.: Sage, 1998); Bandura, "Influence of Models' Reinforcement Contingencies"; Marina Krcmar and Patti M. Valkenburg, "A Scale to Assess Children's Moral Interpretations of Justified and Unjustified Violence and Its Relationship to Television Viewing," *Communication Research* 26, no. 5 (1999); Anderson et al., "Violent Video Game Effects."

32. Paik and Comstock, "Effects of Television Violence on Antisocial Behavior."

33. Ibid.

34. Patti M. Valkenburg and Jochen Peter, "The Differential Susceptibility to Media Effects Model," *Journal of Communication* 63, no. 2 (2013).

35. George Gerbner, Larry Gross, Michael Morgan, and Sylvia Signorielli, "The 'Mainstreaming' of America: Violence Profile No. 11," *Journal of Communication* 30, no. 3 (1980).

36. Karin Fikkers, Jessica Taylor Piotrowski, Wouter D. Weeda, Helen G. M. Vossen, and Patti M. Valkenburg, "Double Dose: High Family Conflict Enhances the Effect of Media Violence Exposure on Adolescents' Aggression," *Societies* 3, no. 3 (2013).

37. Slater, Henry, Swaim, and Cardador, "Vulnerable Teens, Vulnerable Times."

8. Media and Emotions

1. Nico H. Frijda, "The Laws of Emotion," *American Psychologist* 43, no. 5 (1988).

2. Paul L. Harris, *Understanding Children's Worlds: The Work of the Imagination* (Oxford: Blackwell, 2000).

3. Ibid.

4. Ron Tamborini and James B. Weaver, "Frightening Entertainment: A Historical Perspective of Fictional Horror," in *Horror Films: Current Research on Audience Preferences and Reactions,* ed. Ron Tamborini and James B. Weaver (Hillsdale, N.J.: Erlbaum, 1996).

5. Ibid.

6. Laura Pearce and Andy P. Field, "The Impact of 'Scary' TV and Film on Children's Internalizing Emotions: A Meta-Analysis," *Human Communication Research* 42, no. 1 (2015).

7. Eleonora Gullone, "The Development of Normal Fear: A Century of Research," *Clinical Psychology Review* 20, no. 4 (2000).

8. Peter Muris, Harald Merckelbach, Björn Gadet, and Vénique Moulaert, "Fears, Worries, and Scary Dreams in 4- to 12-Year-Old Children: Their Content, Developmental Pattern, and Origins," *Journal of Clinical Child Psychology* 29, no. 1 (2000).

9. Barbara J Wilson, Cynthia Hoffner, and Joanne Cantor, "Children's Perceptions of the Effectiveness of Techniques to Reduce Fear from Mass Media," *Journal of Applied Developmental Psychology* 8, no. 1 (1987).

10. Joanne Cantor and Glenn G. Sparks, "Children's Fear Responses to Mass Media—Testing Some Piagetian Predictions," *Journal of Communication* 34, no. 2 (1984).

11. Joanne Cantor, "Fright Reactions to Mass Media," in *Media Effects,* ed. Jennings Bryant and Dolf Zillmann (Hillsdale, N.J.: Erlbaum Mahwah, 2002).

12. Barbara J. Wilson, "Media and Children's Aggression, Fear, and Altruism," *Future of Children* 18, no. 1 (2008).

13. Unpublished recollection from a study by Patti Valkenburg among Dutch students.

14. Wilson, Hoffner, and Cantor, "Effectiveness of Techniques to Reduce Fear."

15. Muris, Merckelbach, Gadet, and Moulaert, "Fears, Worries, and Scary Dreams."

16. Unpublished recollection from a study by Patti Valkenburg among Dutch students.

17. Wilson, Hoffner, and Cantor, "Effectiveness of Techniques to Reduce Fear."

18. Daniel J. Siegel, *Brainstorm: The Power and Purpose of the Teenage Brain* (New York: Penguin, 2013).

19. Kristen Harrison and Joanne Cantor, "Tales from the Screen: Enduring Fright Reactions to Scary Media," *Media Psychology* 1, no. 2 (1999).

20. Michiel Van Ieperen, "De Aantrekkingskracht Van Horror Films En Horror Videogames" (master's thesis, Utrecht University, 2013).

21. Ibid.

22. Joanne Cantor, Barbara Wilson, and Cynthia Hoffner, "Emotional Responses to a Televised Nuclear Holocaust Film," *Communication Research* 13 (1986).

23. Silvia Knobloch-Westerwick, Yuan Gong, Holly Hagner, and Laura Kerbeykian, "Tragedy Viewers Count Their Blessings: Feeling Low on Fiction Leads to Feeling High on Life," *Communication Research* 40 (2013).

24. Patti M. Valkenburg, *Vierkante Ogen: Opvoeden Met TV En Pc* (Amsterdam: Balans, 1997).

25. Cynthia A. Hoffner and Kenneth J. Levine, "Enjoyment of Mediated Fright and Violence: A Meta-Analysis," *Media Psychology* 7, no. 2 (2005).

26. Lucretius, *On the Nature of Things,* book 2 (c. 50 BCE).

27. Leon Festinger, "A Theory of Social Comparison Processes," *Human Relations* 7, no. 2 (1954).

28. Dolf Zillmann, "Attribution and Misattribution of Excitatory Reactions," in *New Directions in Attribution Research,* ed. John H. Harvey, William Ickes, and Robert F. Kidd (Hillsdale, N.J.: Erlbaum, 1978).

29. "Mood Management: Using Entertainment to Full Advantage," in *Communication, Social Cognition, and Affect,* ed. Lewis Donohew, Howard E. Sypher, and Tory Higgins (Hillsdale, N.J.: Erlbaum, 1988).

30. Ibid.

31. Jinhee Kim and Mary Beth Oliver, "How Do We Regulate Sadness through Entertainment Messages? Exploring Three Predictions," *Journal of Broadcasting and Electronic Media* 57, no. 3 (2013).

32. Mary Beth Oliver and Arthur A. Raney, "Entertainment as Pleasurable and Meaningful: Identifying Hedonic and Eudaimonic Motivations for Entertainment Consumption," *Journal of Communication* 61, no. 5 (2011).

33. Richard M. Ryan, Veronika Huta, and Edward L. Deci, "Living Well: A Self-Determination Theory Perspective on Eudaimonia," *Journal of Happiness Studies* 9, no. 1 (2008).

34. Knobloch-Westerwick, Gong, Hagner, and Kerbeykian, "Tragedy Viewers Count Their Blessings."

35. Ibid.

36. Marie-Louise Mares, Mary Beth Oliver, and Joanne Cantor, "Age Differences in Adults' Emotional Motivations for Exposure to Films," *Media Psychology* 11, no. 4 (2008).

37. At the time of this writing, this clip is viewable at https://www.youtube.com/watch?v=dgMMx5WSd6g.

38. Sandra L. Calvert and Jennifer A. Kotler, "Lessons from Children's Television: The Impact of the Children's Television Act on Children's Learning," *Journal of Applied Developmental Psychology* 24, no. 3 (2003).

39. Dimitri A Christakis et al., "Modifying Media Content for Preschool Children: A Randomized Controlled Trial," *Pediatrics* 131, no. 3 (2013).

40. Maya Götz and Judith Schwarz, "Having and Showing Emotions," *Televizion* 27 (2014).

41. Donald Horton and R. Richard Wohl, "Mass Communication and Para-Social Interaction," *Psychiatry* 19, no. 3 (1956).

42. Alexis R. Lauricella, Alice Ann Howard Gola, and Sandra L. Calvert, "Toddlers' Learning from Socially Meaningful Video Characters," *Media Psychology* 14, no. 2 (2011).

43. Alice Ann Howard Gola, Melissa N. Richards, Alexis R. Lauricella, and Sandra L. Calvert, "Building Meaningful Parasocial Relationships between Toddlers and Media Characters to Teach Early Mathematical Skills," *Media Psychology* 16, no. 4 (2013).

44. David C. Giles and John Maltby, "The Role of Media Figures in Adolescent Development: Relations between Autonomy, Attachment, and Interest in Celebrities," *Personality and Individual Differences* 36, no. 4 (2004).

45. Byron Reeves and Clifford Nass, *How People Treat Computers, Television, and New Media like Real People and Places* (New York: Cambridge University Press, 1996).

46. Astrid M. Rosenthal-von der Pütten et al., "Neural Correlates of Empathy towards Robots" (paper presented at the 8th ACM/IEEE International Conference On Human-Robot Interaction, Tokyo, Japan, 2013).

47. Rosenthal-von der Pütten et al., "Neural Correlates of Empathy Towards Robots."

9. Advertising and Commercialism

Epigraph: Quoted in *Consuming Kids: The Commercialization of Childhood* (2008), directed by Adriana Barbaro and Jeremy Earp.

1. American Institute of CPAs, "What Parents Pay Kids for Allowance," AICPA.org, www.aicpa.org/press/pressreleases/2012/pages/aicpa-survey-reveals-what-parents-pay-kids-for-allowance-grades.aspx.

2. Harriet N. Mischel and Walter Mischel, "The Development of Children's Knowledge of Self-Control Strategies," *Child Development* 53, no. 3 (1987).

3. Moniek Buijzen and Patti M. Valkenburg, "Observing Purchase-Related Parent-Child Communication in Retail Environments: A Developmental and Socialization Perspective," *Human Communication Research* 34, no. 1 (2008).

4. Patti M. Valkenburg and Joanne Cantor, "The Development of a Child into a Consumer," *Journal of Applied Developmental Psychology* 22, no. 1 (2001).

5. James U. McNeal, *Kids as Customers: A Handbook of Marketing to Children* (Lexington, Mass.: Lexington, 1992).

6. Junior Achievement USA, *Teens and Personal Finance*, https://www.junior-achievement.org/documents/20009/36541/2011-Teens-And-Personal-Finance-Poll.pdf/9bcedebc-8920-440b-8cbf-f66f1c153951.

7. Brian Young, *Television Advertising and Children* (Oxford: Clarendon, 1990).

8. Deborah R. John, "Consumer Socialization of Children: A Retrospective Look at Twenty-Five Years of Research," *Journal of Consumer Research* 26, no. 3 (1999).

9. James U. McNeal, *The Kids Market: Myths and Realities* (New York: Paramount, 1999).

10. Joann P. Galst and Mary A. White, "The Unhealthy Persuader: The Reinforcing Value of Television and Children's Purchase-Influencing Attempts at the Supermarket," *Child Development* 47, no. 4 (1976).

11. Buijzen and Valkenburg, "Purchase-Related Parent-Child Communication."

12. Ibid.

13. Ibid.

14. McNeal, *Kids as Customers.*

15. Paul M. Fischer, Meyer Shwartz, John Richards, Adam Goldstein, and Tina Rojas, "Brand Logo Recognition by Children Aged 3 to 6 Years: Mickey Mouse and Old Joe the Camel," *JAMA: The Journal of the American Medical Association* 266, no. 22 (1991).

16. Cynthia F. Hite and Robert E. Hite, "Reliance on Brand by Young Children," *Journal of the Market Research Society* 37, no. 2 (1995).

17. Astrid Middelman and Birgitte Melzer, "The Importance of Brand Preference in Adolescence for Brand Loyalty Later On" (paper presented at the "Seminar on Marketing to Children and Young Consumers: Tactics for Today, and Strategies for Tomorrow," Nuremberg, Germany, 1984).

18. George P. Moschis and Roy L. Moore, "A Study of the Acquisition of Desires for Products and Brands," in *The Changing Marketing Environment: New Theories and Applications*, ed. Kenneth Bernardt et al. (Chicago: American Marketing Association, 1981).

19. Peter Zollo, *Wise Up to Teens: Insights into Marketing and Advertising to Teenagers* (Ithaca, N.Y.: New Strategist, 1997).

20. Common Sense Media, *Advertising to Children and Teens: Current Practices* (San Francisco: Common Sense Media, 2014).

21. Bridget Kelly et al., "Television Food Advertising to Children: A Global Perspective," *American Journal of Public Health* 100, no. 9 (2010).

22. Lucia Moses, "A Look at Kids' Exposure to Ads: Children See a Lot of Marketing Messages, Regardless of Platform," *Adweek,* March 11, 2014.

23. Anna E. Henry and Mary Story, "Food and Beverage Brands That Market to Children and Adolescents on the Internet: A Content Analysis of Branded Web Sites," *Journal of Nutrition Education and Behavior* 41, no. 5 (2009).

24. McNeal, *Kids as Customers;* Patti M. Valkenburg and Moniek Buijzen, "Identifying Determinants of Young Children's Brand Awareness: Television, Parents, and Peers," *Journal of Applied Developmental Psychology* 26, no. 4 (2005).

25. Fischer et al., "Brand Logo Recognition by Children"; Valkenburg and Buijzen, "Young Children's Brand Awareness."

26. Monica D. Hernandez and Sindy Chapa, "Adolescents, Advergames and Snack Foods: Effects of Positive Affect and Experience on Memory and Choice," *Journal of Marketing Communications* 16, nos. 1–2 (2010).

27. M. Carole Macklin, "Do Children Understand TV Ads?," *Journal of Advertising Research* 23, no. 1 (1983).

28. Gerald J. Gorn and Renee Florsheim, "The Effects of Commercials for Adult Products on Children," *Journal of Consumer Research* 11, no. 4 (1985).

29. Scott Ward, Daniel B. Wackman, and Ellen Wartella, *How Children Learn to Buy: The Development of Consumer Information-Processing Skills* (Beverly Hills, Calif.: Sage, 1977).

30. Valkenburg and Buijzen, "Young Children's Brand Awareness."

31. Scott Ward and Daniel B. Wackman, "Family and Media Influences on Adolescent Consumer Learning," *American Behavioral Scientist* 14, no. 3 (1971).

32. Simon Hudson and Charlene Elliott, "Measuring the Impact of Product Placement on Children Using Digital Brand Integration," *Journal of Food Products Marketing* 19, no. 3 (2013).

33. Charles K. Atkin, *The Effects of Television Advertising on Children: Survey of Pre-Adolescent's Responses to Television Commercials; Report no. 6* (East Lansing: Michigan State University, 1975).

34. Dina L. G. Borzekowski and Thomas N. Robinson, "The 30-Second Effect: An Experiment Revealing the Impact of Television Commercials on Food Preferences of Preschoolers," *Journal of the American Dietetic Association* 101, no. 1 (2001).

35. Charles K. Atkin, *The Effects of Television Advertising on Children: Second Year of Experimental Evidence* (East Lansing: Michigan State University, 1975).

36. Gorn and Florsheim, "Effects of Commercials for Adult Products."

37. Moniek Buijzen and Patti M. Valkenburg, "The Impact of Television Advertising on Children's Christmas Wishes," *Journal of Broadcasting and Electronic Media* 44, no. 3 (2000).

38. For a review, see Moniek Buijzen and Patti M. Valkenburg, "The Effects of Television Advertising on Materialism, Parent-Child Conflict, and Unhappiness: A Review of Research," *Journal of Applied Developmental Psychology* 24, no. 4 (2003).

39. Kara Chan, Yu Leung Ng, and Edwin K. Luk, "Impact of Celebrity Endorsement in Advertising on Brand Image among Chinese Adolescents," *Young Consumers* 14, no. 2 (2013); Jyh-shen Chiou, Chien-yi Huang, and Min-chieh Chuang, "Antecedents of Taiwanese Adolescents' Purchase Intention toward the Merchandise of a Celebrity: The Moderating Effect of Celebrity Adoration," *Journal of Social Psychology* 145, no. 3 (2005); Craig A. Martin and Alan J. Bush, "Do Role Models Influence Teenagers' Purchase Intentions and Behavior?," *Journal of Consumer Marketing* 17, no. 5 (2000).

40. Gene H. Brody, Zolinda Stoneman, T. Scott Lane, and Alice K. Sanders, "Television Food Commercials Aimed at Children, Family Grocery Shopping, and Mother-Child Interactions," *Family Relations* 30, no. 3 (1981).

41. Susan Auty and Charlie Lewis, "Exploring Children's Choice: The Reminder Effect of Product Placement," *Psychology and Marketing* 21, no. 9 (2004).

42. L. J. Shrum, James E. Burroughs, and Aric Rindfleisch, "Television's Cultivation of Material Values," *Journal of Consumer Research* 32, no. 3 (2005).

43. Buijzen and Valkenburg, "Effects of Television Advertising on Materialism."

44. Suzanna J. Opree, Moniek Buijzen, Eva A. van Reijmersdal, and Patti M. Valkenburg, "Children's Advertising Exposure, Advertised Product Desire, and Materialism: A Longitudinal Study," *Communication Research* 41, no. 5 (2014).

45. Buijzen and Valkenburg, "Effects of Television Advertising on Materialism."

46. Ibid.

47. Marvin E. Goldberg and Gerald J. Gorn, "Some Unintended Consequences of TV Advertising to Children," *Journal of Consumer Research* 5, no. 1 (1978).

48. World Health Organization, *Obesity and Overweight* (Geneva: World Health Organization, 2015).

49. Commission on Ending Childhood Obesity, *Facts and Figures on Childhood Obesity* (Geneva: World Health Organization, 2014).

50. Marie Ng et al., "Global, Regional, and National Prevalence of Overweight and Obesity in Children and Adults during 1980–2013: A Systematic Analysis for the Global Burden of Disease Study 2013," *Lancet* 384, no. 9945 (2014).

51. Lisa M. Powell, Glen Szczypka, Frank J. Chaloupka, and Carol L. Braunschweig, "Nutritional Content of Television Food Advertisements Seen by Children and Adolescents in the United States," *Pediatrics* 120, no. 3 (2007).

52. Kelly et al., "Television Food Advertising to Children."

53. Moniek Buijzen, Joris Schuurman, and Elise Bomhof, "Associations between Children's Television Advertising Exposure and Their Food Consumption Patterns: A Household Diary-Survey Study," *Appetite* 50, no. 2 (2008).

54. Tatiana Andreyeva, Inas Rashad Kelly, and Jennifer L. Harris, "Exposure to Food Advertising on Television: Associations with Children's Fast Food and Soft Drink Consumption and Obesity," *Economics and Human Biology* 9, no. 3 (2011).

55. Jennifer L. Harris, John A. Bargh, and Kelly D. Brownell, "Priming Effects of Television Food Advertising on Eating Behavior," *Health Psychology* 28, no. 4 (2009).

56. Buijzen and Valkenburg, "Observing Purchase-Related Parent-Child Communication."

57. Elizabeth S. Moore and Richard J. Lutz, "Children, Advertising, and Product Experiences: A Multimethod Inquiry," *Journal of Consumer Research* 27, no. 1 (2000).

58. Richard E. Petty and John T. Cacioppo, "The Elaboration Likelihood Model of Persuasion," in *Advances in Experimental Social Psychology*, ed. Leonard Berkowitz (New York: Academic Press, 1986).

59. Alice H. Eagly and Shelly Chaiken, *The Psychology of Attitudes* (Fort Worth, Tex.: Harcourt Brace Jovanovich, 1993).

60. Moniek Buijzen, Eva A. van Reijmersdal, and Laura H. Owen, "Introducing the PCMC Model: An Investigative Framework for Young People's Processing of Commercialized Media Content," *Communication Theory* 20, no. 4 (2010).

61. Laura Owen, Charles Lewis, Susan Auty, and Moniek Buijzen, "Is Children's Understanding of Nontraditional Advertising Comparable to Their Understanding of Television Advertising?," *Journal of Public Policy and Marketing* 32, no. 2 (2013).

62. Esther Rozendaal, Moniek Buijzen, and Patti M. Valkenburg, "Do Children's Cognitive Advertising Defenses Reduce Their Desire for Advertised Products?," *Communications: The European Journal of Communication Research* 34, no. 3 (2009).

63. Sonia Livingstone and Ellen J. Helsper, "Does Advertising Literacy Mediate the Effects of Advertising on Children? A Critical Examination of Two Linked Research Literatures in Relation to Obesity and Food Choice," *Journal of Communication* 56, no. 3 (2006).

10. Media and Sex

Epigraph: Herbert Blumer, *Movies and Conduct* (New York: Macmillan, 1933). Blumer's study was part of the famous Payne Fund Studies (for a discussion, see chapter 3).

1. American Psychological Association [APA], *Report of the APA Task Force on the Sexualization of Girls* (Washington, D.C.: American Psychological Association, 2007).

2. Ibid., 1.

3. Cas Wouters, "Sexualization: Have Sexualization Processes Changed Direction?," *Sexualities* 13, no. 6 (2010).

4. Ibid.

5. Brian McNair, *Striptease Culture: Sex, Media, and the Democratization of Desire* (East Sussex, UK: Psychology Press, 2002).

6. APA, *Report on the Sexualization of Girls.*

7. Kari Lerum and Shari L Dworkin, "Bad Girls Rule: An Interdisciplinary Feminist Commentary on the Report of the APA Task Force on the Sexualization of Girls," *Journal of Sex Research* 46, no. 4 (2009).

8. Dale Kunkel et al., "Sex on TV 4: A Biennial Report to the Kaiser Family Foundation" (Menlo Park, Calif.: Kaiser Family Foundation, 2005).

9. Amy Bleakley, Patrick E. Jamieson, and Daniel Romer, "Trends of Sexual and Violent Content by Gender in Top-Grossing U.S. Films, 1950–2006," *Journal of Adolescent Health* 51, no. 1 (2012).

10. Rami Al-Sayed and Barrie Gunter, "How Much Sex Is There in Soap Operas on British TV?," *Communications: The European Journal of Communication Research* 37, no. 4 (2012).

11. Mark Callister, Lesa A. Stern, Sarah M. Coyne, Tom Robinson, and Emily Bennion, "Evaluation of Sexual Content in Teen-Centered Films from 1980 to 2007," *Mass Communication and Society* 14, no. 4 (2011).

12. Jennifer Stevens Aubrey, "Sex and Punishment: An Examination of Sexual Consequences and the Sexual Double Standard in Teen Programming," *Sex Roles* 50, nos. 7–8 (2004).

13. Mark Callister et al., "A Content Analysis of the Prevalence and Portrayal of Sexual Activity in Adolescent Literature," *Journal of Sex Research* 49, no. 5 (2011).

14. Maya Götz et al., "Gender in Children's Television Worldwide," *Televizion* 21 (2008).

15. Celeste Lacroix, "Images of Animated Others: The Orientalization of Disney's Cartoon Heroines from the Little Mermaid to the Hunchback of Notre Dame," *Popular Communication* 2, no. 4 (2004).

16. APA, *Report on the Sexualization of Girls.*

17. Shari L Dworkin and Faye Wachs, *Body Panic* (New York: NYU Press, 2009).

18. Barrie Gunter, *Media and the Sexualization of Childhood* (London: Routledge, 2014).

19. Amir Hetsroni, "Three Decades of Sexual Content on Prime-Time Network Programming: A Longitudinal Meta-Analytic Review," *Journal of Communication* 57, no. 2 (2007).

20. Amy Slater, Marika Tiggemann, Kimberley Hawkins, and Douglas Werchon, "Just One Click: A Content Analysis of Advertisements on Teen Web Sites," *Journal of Adolescent Health* 50, no. 4 (2012).

21. Percentages based on ongoing CcaM research by Johanna van Oosten and Jochen Peter among 2,137 adolescents.

22. Amy Bleakley, Michael Hennessy, and Martin Fishbein, "A Model of Adolescents' Seeking of Sexual Content in Their Media Choices," *Journal of Sex Research* 48, no. 4 (2010).

23. Al Cooper, "Sexuality and the Internet: Surfing into the New Millennium," *CyberPsychology and Behavior* 1, no. 2 (1998).

24. Ana J. Bridges, Robert Wosnitzer, Erica Scharrer, Chyng Sun, and Rachael Liberman, "Aggression and Sexual Behavior in Best-Selling Pornography Videos: A Content Analysis Update," *Violence against Women* 16, no. 10 (2010).

25. Marleen J. E. Klaassen and Jochen Peter, "Gender (In)Equality in Internet Pornography: A Content Analysis of Popular Pornographic Internet Videos," *Journal of Sex Research* 52, no. 7 (2015).

26. Victor C. Strasburger, Amy B. Jordan, and Ed Donnerstein, "Health Effects of Media on Children and Adolescents," *Pediatrics* 125, no. 4 (2010).

27. Linda Duits and Liesbet Van Zoonen, "Coming to Terms with Sexualization," *European Journal of Cultural Studies* 14, no. 5 (2011).

28. Lerum and Dworkin, "Bad Girls Rule."

29. Rebecca L. Collins, Marc N. Elliott, Sandra H. Berry, David E. Kanouse, and Sarah B. Hunter, "Entertainment Television as a Healthy Sex Educator: The Impact of Condom-Efficacy Information in an Episode of *Friends*," *Pediatrics* 112, no. 5 (2003).

30. Jochen Peter and Patti M. Valkenburg, "Adolescents and Pornography: A Review of 20 Years of Research," *Journal of Sex Research* 53, no. 4–5 (2016).

31. L. Monique Ward and Kimberly Friedman, "Using TV as a Guide: Associations between Television Viewing and Adolescents' Sexual Attitudes and Behavior," *Journal of Research on Adolescence* 16, no. 1 (2006).

32. Jochen Peter and Patti M. Valkenburg, "Adolescents' Exposure to Sexually Explicit Online Material and Recreational Attitudes toward Sex," *Journal of Communication* 56, no. 4 (2006).

33. Tom F. M. Ter Bogt, Rutger C. M. E. Engels, Sanne Bogers, and Monique Kloosterman, " 'Shake It Baby, Shake It': Media Preferences, Sexual Attitudes and Gender Stereotypes among Adolescents," *Sex Roles* 63, nos. 11–12 (2010).

34. Jochen Peter and Patti M. Valkenburg, "Adolescents' Exposure to Sexually Explicit Internet Material and Notions of Women as Sex Objects: Assessing Causality and Underlying Processes," *Journal of Communication* 59, no. 3 (2009).

35. Jochen Peter, "Media and Sexual Development," in *The Routledge Handbook of Children, Adolescents, and the Media,* ed. Dafna Lemish (London: Routledge, 2013).

36. Collins et al., "Entertainment Television as a Healthy Sex Educator."

37. Autumn Shafer, Piotr Bobkowski, and Jane D. Brown, "Sexual Media Practice: How Adolescents Select, Engage with, and Are Affected by Sexual Media," in *The Oxford Handbook of Media Psychology,* ed. Karen E. Dill (New York: Oxford University Press, 2013).

38. Hanneke de Graaf et al., *Seks Onder Je 25e: Seksuele Gezondheid Van Jongeren in Nederland Anno 2012* [Sex under 25 years: Sexual health among Dutch youth] (Delft: Eburon, 2012).

39. Wendell S. Dysinger and Christian A. Ruckmick, *The Emotional Responses of Children to the Motion Picture Situation* (New York: Macmillan, 1933).

40. Jochen Peter and Patti M. Valkenburg, "Adolescents' Exposure to Sexually Explicit Internet Material and Sexual Preoccupancy: A Three-Wave Panel Study," *Media Psychology* 11, no. 2 (2008).

41. Peter, "Media and Sexual Development."

42. Jochen Peter and Patti M. Valkenburg, "Adolescents' Use of Sexually Explicit Internet Material and Sexual Uncertainty: The Role of Involvement and Gender," *Communication Monographs* 77, no. 3 (2010).

43. "Adolescents' Exposure to Sexually Explicit Internet Material and Sexual Satisfaction: A Longitudinal Study," *Human Communication Research* 35, no. 2 (2009).

44. Rebecca L. Collins, Steven C. Martino, Marc N. Elliott, and Angela Miu, "Relationships between Adolescent Sexual Outcomes and Exposure to Sex in Media: Robustness to Propensity-Based Analysis," *Developmental Psychology* 47, no. 2 (2011).

45. Jane D. Brown and Kelly L. L'Engle, "X-Rated Sexual Attitudes and Behaviors Associated with U.S. Early Adolescents' Exposure to Sexually Explicit Media," *Communication Research* 36, no. 1 (2009).

46. Amy Bleakley, Michael Hennessy, Martin Fishbein, and Amy Jordan, "It Works Both Ways: The Relationship between Exposure to Sexual Content in the Media and Adolescent Sexual Behavior," *Media Psychology* 11, no. 4 (2008).

47. Laura Vanderbosch and Steven Eggermont, "Sexually Explicit Websites and Sexual Initiation: Reciprocal Relationships and the Moderating Role of Pubertal Status," *Journal of Research on Adolescence* 23, no. 4 (2013).

48. For a review of these studies, see Peter, "Media and Sexual Development."

49. United Nations Population Fund, *Motherhood in Childhood: Facing the Challenge of Adolescent Pregnancy* (New York: UNFPA, 2013).

50. Marie-Thérèse Luder et al., "Associations between Online Pornography and Sexual Behavior among Adolescents: Myth or Reality?," *Archives of Sexual Behavior* 40, no. 5 (2011).

51. Jochen Peter and Patti M. Valkenburg, "The Influence of Sexually Explicit Internet Material on Sexual Risk Behavior: A Comparison of Adolescents and Adults," *Journal of Health Communication* 16, no. 7 (2011).

52. Michele L. Ybarra and Kimberly J. Mitchell, " 'Sexting' and Its Relation to Sexual Activity and Sexual Risk Behavior in a National Survey of Adolescents," *Journal of Adolescent Health* 55, no. 6 (2014).

53. Bruce E. Pinkleton, Erica Weintraub Austin, Yi-Chun Chen, and Marilyn Cohen, "The Role of Media Literacy in Shaping Adolescents' Understanding of and Responses to Sexual Portrayals in Mass Media," *Journal of Health Communication* 17, no. 4 (2012).

54. Kylene Guse et al., "Interventions Using New Digital Media to Improve Adolescent Sexual Health: A Systematic Review," *Journal of Adolescent Health* 51, no. 6 (2012).

11. Media and Education

1. John L. Sherry, "Formative Research for STEM Educational Games," *Zeitschrift für Psychologie* 221, no. 2 (2013).

2. Gerald S. Lesser and Joel Schneider, "Creation and Evolution of the *Sesame Street* Curriculum," in *"G" Is for Growing*, ed. Shalom M. Fisch and Rosemarie Truglio (Mahwah, N.J.: Erlbaum, 2001).

3. Joseph E. Zins, Michelle R. Bloodworth, Roger P. Weissberg, and Herbert J. Walberg, *The Scientific Base Linking Social and Emotional Learning to School Success* (New York: Teachers College Press, 2004).

4. Marie-Louise Mares, "Educational Television," in *Sage Handbook of Media Processes and Effects*, ed. Robin L. Nabi and Mary Beth Oliver (Thousand Oaks, Calif.: Sage, 2009).

5. Victoria J. Rideout, "Learning at Home: Families' Educational Media Use in America" (New York: Joan Ganz Cooney Center at Sesame Workshop, 2014).

6. Daniel R. Anderson and Stephen R. Levin, "Young Children's Attention to *Sesame Street*," *Child Development* 47, no. 3 (1976).

7. Ellen A. Wartella, Vicky Rideout, Alexis R. Lauricella, and Sabrina L. Connell, *Parenting in the Age of Digital Technology: A National Survey* (Evanston, Ill.: School of Communication, Northwestern University, 2013).

8. Victoria J. Rideout, Elizabeth A. Vandewater, and Ellen A. Wartella, *Zero to Six: Electronic Media in the Lives of Infants, Toddlers and Preschoolers* (Menlo Park, Calif.: Kaiser Family Foundation, 2003).

9. Matthew A. Lapierre and Sarah E. Vaala, "Predictors of Baby Video/DVD Ownership: Findings from a National Sample of American Parents with Young Children," *Journal of Children and Media* 9, no. 2 (2015).

10. Rideout, "Learning at Home."

11. Ibid.

12. Sandra L. Calvert and Jennifer A. Kotler, "Lessons from Children's Television: The Impact of the Children's Television Act on Children's Learning," *Journal of Applied Developmental Psychology* 24, no. 3 (2003).

13. See the documentary *The World According to Sesame Street*, directed by Linda Goldstein-Knowlton and Linda Hawkins (Los Angeles: Participant Productions, 2006), DVD.

14. Albert Bandura, *Social Foundations of Thought and Action: A Social Cognitive Theory* (Englewood Cliffs, N.J.: Prentice-Hall, 1986).

15. Marie-Louise Mares, Edward Palmer, and Tia Sullivan, "Prosocial Effects of Media Exposure," in *The Handbook of Children, Media, and Development*, ed. Sandra L. Calvert and Barbara Wilson (New York: Wiley, 2008).

16. Shalom M. Fisch, "A Capacity Model of Children's Comprehension of Educational Content on Television," *Media Psychology* 2, no. 1 (2000).

17. Jessica T. Piotrowski, "The Relationship between Narrative Processing Demands and Young American Children's Comprehension of Educational Television," *Journal of Children and Media* 8, no. 3 (2014).

18. Katherine E. Buckley and Craig A. Anderson, "A Theoretical Model of the Effects and Consequences of Playing Video Games," in *Playing Video Games: Motives, Responses, and Consequences*, ed. Peter Vorderer and Jennings Bryant (London: Routledge, 2006).

19. Douglas A. Gentile et al., "The Effects of Prosocial Video Games on Prosocial Behaviors: International Evidence from Correlational, Longitudinal, and Experimental Studies," *Personality and Social Psychology Bulletin* 35, no. 6 (2009).

20. Mary L. Courage and Mark L. Howe, "To Watch or Not to Watch: Infants and Toddlers in a Brave New Electronic World," *Developmental Review* 30, no. 2 (2010).

21. Rachel Barr, Paul Muentener, Amaya Garcia, Melissa Fujimoto, and Verónica Chávez, "The Effect of Repetition on Imitation from Television during Infancy," *Developmental Psychobiology* 49, no. 2 (2007).

22. Alexis R. Lauricella, Alice A. Gola, and Sandra L. Calvert, "Toddlers' Learning from Socially Meaningful Video Characters," *Media Psychology* 14, no. 2 (2011); for a review, see Deborah L. Linebarger and Sarah E. Vaala, "Screen Media and Language Development in Infants and Toddlers: An Ecological Perspective," *Developmental Review* 30, no. 2 (2010).

23. Heather L. Kirkorian, Koeun Choi, and Tiffany A. Pempek, "Toddlers' Word Learning from Contingent and Non-Contingent Video on Touchscreens," *Child Development* (in press).

24. Linebarger and Vaala, "Screen Media and Language Development."

25. Shalom M. Fisch, *Children's Learning from Educational Television* (Mahwah, N.J.: Erlbaum, 2004).

26. Marie-Louise L. Mares and Zhongdang D. Pan, "Effects of *Sesame Street:* A Meta-Analysis of Children's Learning in 15 Countries," *Journal of Applied Developmental Psychology* 34, no. 3 (2013).

27. Deborah L. Linebarger, "*Super Why!* to the Rescue: Can Preschoolers Learn Early Literacy Skills from Educational Television?," *International Journal of Cross-Disciplinary Subjects in Education* 6, no. 1 (2015).

28. Deborah L. Linebarger, Anjelika Z. Kosanic, Charles R. Greenwood, and Nil Sai Doku, "Effects of Viewing the Television Program *Between the Lions* on the Emergent Literacy Skills of Young Children," *Journal of Educational Psychology* 96, no. 2 (2004).

29. For more information about these programs and accompanying studies, see Fisch, *Children's Learning from Educational Television.*

30. Daniel R. Anderson et al., "Early Childhood Television Viewing and Adolescent Behavior: The Recontact Study," *Monographs of the Society for Research in Child Development* 66, no. 1 (2001).

31. Shalom M. Fisch, *The Impact of "Cyberchase" on Children's Mathematical Problem Solving* (Teaneck, N.J.: MediaKidz Research and Consulting, 2003).

32. For a review, see Fisch, *Children's Learning from Educational Television.*

33. Victor C. Strasburger, Barbara J. Wilson, and Amy B. Jordan, *Children, Adolescents, and the Media* (Thousand Oaks, Calif.: Sage, 2009).

34. Joyce N. Sprafkin, Robert M. Liebert, and Rita Wicks Poulos, "Effects of a Prosocial Televised Example on Children's Helping," *Journal of Experimental Child Psychology* 20, no. 1 (1975).

35. Strasburger, Wilson, and Jordan, *Children, Adolescents, and the Media.*

36. Dale Kunkel, "Policy Battles over Defining Children's Educational Television," *American Academy of Political and Social Science* 557, no. 1 (1998).

37. Marie-Louise Mares and Emory Woodard, "Positive Effects of Television on Children's Social Interaction: A Meta-Analysis," in *Mass Media Effects Research: Advances through Meta-Analysis,* ed. Raymond W. Preiss, et al. (Mahwah, N.J.: Erlbaum, 2007).

38. Rebecca N. H. de Leeuw, Mariska Kleemans, Esther Rozendaal, Doeschka J. Anschütz, and Moniek Buijzen, "The Impact of Prosocial Television News on Children's

Prosocial Behavior: An Experimental Study in the Netherlands," *Journal of Children and Media* 9, no. 4 (2015).

39. Gentile et al., "Effects of Prosocial Video Games"; see also Sara Prot et al., "Long-Term Relations among Prosocial-Media Use, Empathy, and Prosocial Behavior," *Psychological Science* 25, no. 2 (2014).

40. Dimitri A. Christakis et al., "Modifying Media Content for Preschool Children: A Randomized Controlled Trial," *Pediatrics* 131, no. 3 (2013).

41. Deborah L. Linebarger, "Lessons from Cookie Monster: Educational Television, Preschoolers, and Executive Function" (Iowa City: University of Iowa, 2014).

42. Patti M. Valkenburg and Tom H. van der Voort, "Televisions Impact on Fantasy Play: A Review of Research," *Developmental Review* 14, no. 1 (1994).

43. Michael D. Mumford and Sigrid B. Gustafson, "Creativity Syndrome: Integration, Application, and Innovation," *Psychological Bulletin* 103, no. 1 (1988).

44. Patti M. Valkenburg and Sandra L. Calvert, "Media and the Child's Developing Imagination," in *Handbook of Children and the Media,* ed. Dorothy G. Singer and Jerome L. Singer (New York: Sage, 2012).

45. Sandra L. Calvert, Bonnie L. Strong, Eliza L. Jacobs, and Emily E. Conger, "Interaction and Participation for Young Hispanic and Caucasian Girls' and Boys' Learning of Media Content," *Media Psychology* 9, no. 2 (2007); for a review of other studies, see Valkenburg and Calvert, "Media and the Child's Developing Imagination."

46. Anderson et al., "Early Childhood Television Viewing."

47. Rideout, "Learning at Home."

48. Linda A. Jackson et al., "Information Technology Use and Creativity: Findings from the Children and Technology Project," *Computers in Human Behavior* 28, no. 2 (2012).

49. Jessica T. Piotrowski and Laurian Meester, "The Opportunities of Creative Apps in Middle Childhood" (paper presented at the 65th Conference of the International Communication Association, San Juan, Puerto Rico, 2015).

50. Fisch, *Children's Learning from Educational Television.*

51. Ibid.

52. Alisha M. Crawley, Daniel R. Anderson, Alice Wilder, Marsha Williams, and Angelo Santomero, "Effects of Repeated Exposures to a Single Episode of the Television Program *Blue's Clues* on the Viewing Behaviors and Comprehension of Preschool Children," *Journal of Educational Psychology* 91, no. 4 (1999).

53. Daniel R Anderson et al., "Researching *Blue's Clues:* Viewing Behavior and Impact," *Media Psychology* 2, no. 2 (2000).

54. Jessica T. Piotrowski, "Participatory Cues and Program Familiarity Predict Young Children's Learning from Educational Television," *Media Psychology* 17, no. 3 (2014); Valkenburg and Calvert, "Media and the Child's Developing Imagination."

55. Calvert et al., "Interaction and Participation."

56. Jean M. Mandler and Nancy S. Johnson, "Remembrance of Things Parsed: Story Structure and Recall," *Cognitive Psychology* 9, no. 1 (1977).

57. Piotrowski, "Narrative Processing Demands and Young Children's Comprehension."

58. For a review of research on the role of familiarity, see Piotrowski, "Participatory Cues and Program Familiarity."

59. Koshi Dhingra, Alice Wilder, Alison Sherman, and Karen Leavitt, "Science on Children's Television: Collaboration, Synergy, and Research," in *Change Agents in Science Education,* ed. Sumi Hagiwara and Koshi Dingra (Rotterdam: Sense, 2006), 137.

12. Digital Games

Epigraph: Simon Egenfeldt-Nielsen, Jonas H. Smith, and Susana P. Tosca, *Understanding Video Games: The Essential Introduction* (New York: Routledge, 2013), 4.

1. Andrew O'Brien, *Little Book of Video Games* (Chelmsford, UK: G2 Entertainment, 2013).

2. Quoted in Lara Ankersmit and Jacomine Van Veen, "Special Moves: Gebruik En Betekenis Van Videospellen" [Special moves: Use and meaning of video games] (master's thesis, University of Amsterdam, 1995).

3. A freemium is an app or game that is available for no cost, and instead relies on in-app purchases to generate income.

4. http://www.allgame.com/genres.php

5. Egenfeldt-Nielsen, Smith, and Tosca, *Understanding Video Games.*

6. Ibid.

7. Ibid.

8. G. Christopher Klug and Jesse Schell, "Adolescents and the Appeal of Video Games," in *Playing Video Games: Motives, Responses and Consequences,* ed. Peter Vorderer and Jennings Bryant (Mahwah, N.J.: Erlbaum, 2006).

9. James Paul Gee, "Learning by Design: Good Video Games as Learning Machines," in *Digital Media: Transformations in Human Communication,* ed. Paul Messaris and Lee Humphreys (New York: Lang, 2006).

10. Arthur A. Raney, Jason K. Smith, and Kaysee Baker, "Adolescents and the Appeal of Video Games," in *Playing Video Games: Motives, Responses and Consequences,* ed. Peter Vorderer and Jennings Bryant (Mahwah, N.J.: Erlbaum, 2006).

11. Ibid.

12. Quoted in ibid., 150.

13. Dolf Zillmann, "Attribution and Misattribution of Excitatory Reactions," in *New Directions in Attribution Research,* ed. John H. Harvey, William Ickes, and Robert F. Kidd (Hillsdale, N.J.: Erlbaum, 1978).

14. Raney, Smith, and Baker, "Adolescents and the Appeal of Video Games."

15. Jeroen S. Lemmens, Patti M. Valkenburg, and Douglas A. Gentile, "The Internet Gaming Disorder Scale," *Psychological Assessment* 27, no. 2 (2015); see also Amanda Lenhart, *Teens, Social Media, and Technology Overview 2015* (Washington, D.C.: Pew Research Center, 2015).

16. Tracy L. Dietz, "An Examination of Violence and Gender Role Portrayals in Video Games: Implications for Gender Socialization and Aggressive Behavior," *Sex Roles* 38, nos. 5–6 (1998).

17. Kaveri Subrahmanyam and Patricia M. Greenfield, "Computer Games for Girls: What Makes Them Play?," in *From Barbie to Mortal Kombat: Gender and Computer Games*, ed. Justine Cassell and Henry Jenkins (Cambridge, Mass.: MIT Press, 2000).

18. Ibid.

19. Results are based on our ongoing longitudinal research among 945 ten- to fifteen-year-olds.

20. Dorothy G. Singer and Jerome L. Singer, *The House of Make-Believe: Children's Play and the Developing Imagination* (Cambridge, Mass.: Harvard University Press, 1995).

21. Inés M. Fernandez-Guerrero, "Whatsappitis," *Lancet* 383, no. 9922 (2014).

22. Solbjørg Makalani Myrtveit et al., "Adolescent Neck and Shoulder Pain: The Association with Depression, Physical Activity, Screen-Based Activities, and Use of Health Care Services," *Journal of Adolescent Health* 55, no. 3 (2014).

23. Paula T. Hakala, Arja H. Rimpelä, Lea A. Saarni, and Jouko J. Salminen, "Frequent Computer-Related Activities Increase the Risk of Neck-Shoulder and Low Back Pain in Adolescents," *European Journal of Public Health* 16, no. 5 (2006).

24. Piet van Loon, pediatrician, cited in *De Volkskrant*, Dutch national newspaper, 7 August 2013.

25. Deirdre M. Harrington, Kieran P. Dowd, Alan K. Bourke, and Alan E. Donnelly, "Cross-Sectional Analysis of Levels and Patterns of Objectively Measured Sedentary Time in Adolescent Females," *International Journal of Behavioral Nutrition and Physical Activity* 8, no. 1 (2011).

26. Hakala et al., "Frequent Computer-Related Activities."

27. Wei Peng, Jih-Hsuan Lin, and Julia Crouse, "Is Playing Exergames Really Exercising? A Meta-Analysis of Energy Expenditure in Active Video Games," *Cyberpsychology, Behavior, and Social Networking* 14, no. 11 (2011).

28. Amanda E. Staiano, Anisha A. Abraham, and Sandra L. Calvert, "Adolescent Exergame Play for Weight Loss and Psychosocial Improvement: A Controlled Physical Activity Intervention," *Obesity* 21, no. 3 (2013).

29. The term "serious" refers not only to cognitive effects but also to social-emotional and health effects; see Clark C. Abt, *Serious Games* (New York: Viking, 1987).

30. Thomas M. Connolly, Elizabeth A. Boyle, Ewan MacArthur, Thomas Hainey, and James M. Boyle, "A Systematic Literature Review of Empirical Evidence on Computer Games and Serious Games," *Computers and Education* 59, no. 2 (2012).

31. Michael F. Young et al., "Our Princess Is in Another Castle: A Review of Trends in Serious Gaming for Education," *Review of Educational Research* 82, no. 1 (2012).

32. Pieter Wouters, Christof van Nimwegen, Herre van Oostendorp, and Erik D. van der Spek, "A Meta-Analysis of the Cognitive and Motivational Effects of Serious Games," *Journal of Educational Psychology* 105, no. 2 (2013).

33. Egenfeldt-Nielsen, Smith, and Tosca, *Understanding Video Games*.

34. Patricia M. Greenfield, *Mind and Media: The Effects of Television, Video Games, and Computers* (Cambridge, Mass.: Harvard University Press, 1984).

35. Kasey L. Powers, Patricia J. Brooks, Naomi J. Aldrich, Melissa A. Paladino, and Louis Alfieri, "Effects of Video-Game Play on Information Processing: A Meta-Analytic Investigation," *Psychonomic Bulletin & Review* 20, no. 6 (2013).

36. Robert Plomin, Nicholas G. Shakeshaft, Andrew McMillan, and Maciej Trzaskowski, "Nature, Nurture, and Expertise," *Intelligence* 45 (2014).

37. James R. Flynn, "Searching for Justice: The Discovery of IQ Gains over Time," *American Psychologist* 54, no. 1 (1999).

38. Patricia M. Greenfield, "The Cultural Evolution of IQ," in *The Rising Curve: Long-Term Gains in IQ and Related Measures*, ed. Ulric Neisser (Washington, D.C.: American Psychological Association, 1998).

39. Powers et al., "Effects of Video-Game Play on Information Processing."

40. Ibid.

41. Susanne M. Jaeggi, Martin Buschkuehl, John Jonides, and Priti Shah, "Short- and Long-Term Benefits of Cognitive Training," *Proceedings of the National Academy of Sciences* 108, no. 25 (2011).

42. Powers et al., "Effects of Video-Game Play on Information Processing."

43. Andrew J. Latham, Lucy L. M. Patston, and Lynette J. Tippett, "The Virtual Brain: 30 Years of Video-Game Play and Cognitive Abilities," *Frontiers in Psychology* 4, no. 629 (2013).

44. Simone Kühn, Tobias Gleich, Robert C. Lorenz, U. Lindenberger, and Jürgen Gallinat, "Playing *Super Mario* Induces Structural Brain Plasticity: Gray Matter Changes Resulting from Training with a Commercial Video Game," *Molecular Psychiatry* 19, no. 2 (2014).

45. Edna Mitchell, "The Dynamics of Family Interaction around Home Video Games," *Marriage and Family Review* 8, nos. 1–2 (1985).

46. Kevin Durkin and Bonnie Barber, "Not So Doomed: Computer Game Play and Positive Adolescent Development," *Journal of Applied Developmental Psychology* 23, no. 4 (2002).

47. Christothea Herodotou, Maria Kambouri, and Niall Winters, "Dispelling the Myth of the Socio-Emotionally Dissatisfied Gamer," *Computers in Human Behavior* 32 (2014).

48. Eric A. Egli and Lawrence S. Meyers, "The Role of Video Game Playing in Adolescent Life: Is There Reason to Be Concerned?," *Bulletin of the Psychonomic Society* 22, no. 4 (1984).

49. Lemmens, Valkenburg, and Gentile, "The Internet Gaming Disorder Scale."

50. For an overview, see ibid.

51. See Jeroen S. Lemmens, Patti M. Valkenburg, and Jochen Peter, "Development and Validation of a Game Addiction Scale for Adolescents," *Media Psychology* 12, no. 1 (2009); Lemmens, Valkenburg, and Gentile, "The Internet Gaming Disorder Scale."

52. Jeroen S. Lemmens, Patti M. Valkenburg, and Jochen Peter, "Psychosocial Causes and Consequences of Pathological Gaming," *Computers in Human Behavior* 27, no. 1 (2011).

53. Douglas A. Gentile et al., "Pathological Video Game Use among Youths: A Two-Year Longitudinal Study," *Pediatrics* 127, no. 2 (2011).

13. Social Media

Epigraph: Interview of Hans Den Hartog Jager by Rineke Dijkstra in the Dutch newspaper *NRC*, 17 December 2010.

1. Amanda Lenhart, *Teens, Social Media, and Technology Overview 2015* (Washington, D.C.: Pew Research Center, 2015).

2. Sonia Livingstone, Leslie Haddon, Jane Vincent, Giovanna Mascheroni, and Kjartan Ólafsson, *Net Children Go Mobile: The UK Report* (London: London School of Economics and Political Science, 2014).

3. See "Smartphone User Penetration as Percentage of Total Global Population from 2014 to 2019," www.statista.com/statistics/203734/global-smartphone-penetration-per-capita-since-2005 (subscription required).

4. See also Vicky Rideout, *The Common Sense Census: Media Use by Tweens and Teens* (San Francisco: Common Sense, 2015); "Planet of the Phones," *Economist*, 28 February 2015, www.economist.com/news/leaders/21645180-smartphone-ubiquitous-addictive-and-transformative-planet-phones.

5. danah boyd, *It's Complicated: The Social Lives of Networked Teens* (New Haven, Conn.: Yale University Press, 2014), 8.

6. James J. Gibson, *The Ecological Approach to Visual Perception* (Boston: Houghton-Mifflin, 1979).

7. These affordances are in part based on danah boyd, "Social Network Sites as Networked Publics: Affordances, Dynamics and Implications," in *A Networked Self: Identity, Community, and Culture on Social Network Sites*, ed. Zizi Papacharissi (New York: Routledge, 2010); and Jochen Peter and Patti M. Valkenburg, "The Effects of Internet Communication on Adolescents' Psychological Development," in *The International Encyclopedia of Media Studies: Media Psychology / Media Effects*, ed. Erica Scharrer (San Francisco: Wiley-Blackwell, 2013).

8. Duane Buhrmester and Karen Prager, "Patterns and Functions of Self-Disclosure during Childhood and Adolescence," in *Disclosure Processes in Children and Adolecents*, ed. Ken J. Rotenberg (Cambridge: Cambridge University Press, 1995).

9. Ibid.

10. Alexander P. Schouten, Patti M. Valkenburg, and Jochen Peter, "Precursors and Underlying Processes of Adolescents' Online Self-Disclosure: Developing and Testing an 'Internet-Attribute-Perception' Model," *Media Psychology* 10, no. 2 (2007).

11. Amanda Lenhart, Aaron Smith, Monica Anderson, Maeve Duggan, and Andrew Perrin, *Teens, Technology, and Friendships* (Washington, D.C.: Pew Research Center, 2015).

12. Patti M. Valkenburg and Jochen Peter, "Online Communication among Adolescents: An Integrated Model of Its Attraction, Opportunities, and Risks," *Journal of Adolescent Health* 48, no. 2 (2011).

13. Sabine Trepte and Leonard Reinecke, "The Social Web as a Shelter for Privacy and Authentic Living," in *Privacy Online: Perspectives on Privacy and Self-Disclosure in the Social Web*, ed. Sabine Trepte and Leonard Reinecke (Heidelberg: Springer, 2011).

14. Mary Madden et al., *Teens, Social Media, and Privacy* (Washington, D.C.: Pew Research Center, 2013).

15. Judee K. Burgoon, "Privacy and Communication," in *Communication Yearbook 6*, ed. Michael Burgoon (New York: Routledge, 1982).

16. Valkenburg and Peter, "Online Communication among Adolescents."

17. Rideout, *The Common Sense Census*. Similar estimates are found in other countries; see, for example, Ofcom, *Children and Parents: Media Use and Attitudes Report* (London: Ofcom, 2014).

18. For a discussion, see Joseph B. Walther, "Theories of Computer-Mediated Communication and Interpersonal Relations," in *The Handbook of Interpersonal Communication*, ed. Mark L. Knapp and John A. Daly (Thousand Oaks, Calif.: Sage, 2011).

19. Ibid.

20. "Computer-Mediated Communication: Impersonal, Interpersonal, and Hyperpersonal Interaction," *Communication Research* 23, no. 1 (1996).

21. Patti M. Valkenburg, Jochen Peter, and Joseph B. Walther, "Media Effects: Theory and Research," *Annual Review of Psychology* 67 (2016).

22. Ibid.

23. Alvin Toffler, *The Third Wave: The Classic Study of Tomorrow* (New York: Bantam, 1980).

24. Raymond J. Pingree, "How Messages Affect Their Senders: A More General Model of Message Effects and Implications for Deliberation," *Communication Theory* 17, no. 4 (2007).

25. Daryl J. Bem, "Self-Perception Theory," in *Advances in Experimental Social Psychology*, ed. Leonard Berkowitz (New York: Academic Press, 1972).

26. Jennifer D. Campbell, "Self-Esteem and Clarity of the Self-Concept," *Journal of Personality and Social Psychology* 59, no. 3 (1990).

27. Moshe Israelashvili, Taejin Kim, and Gabriel Bukobza, "Adolescents' Over-Use of the Cyber World: Internet Addiction or Identity Exploration?," *Journal of Adolescence* 35, no. 2 (2012).

28. Valkenburg and Peter, "Online Communication among Adolescents."

29. Katie Davis, "Young People's Digital Lives: The Impact of Interpersonal Relationships and Digital Media Use on Adolescents' Sense of Identity," *Computers in Human Behavior* 29, no. 6 (2013); see also Valkenburg and Peter, "Online Communication among Adolescents."

30. Susan Harter, *The Construction of the Self: Developmental and Sociocultural Foundations*, 2nd ed. (New York: Guilford, 2012).

31. Kelly L. Schmitt, Shoshana Dayanim, and Stacey Matthias, "Personal Homepage Construction as an Expression of Social Development," *Developmental Psychology* 44, no. 2 (2008).

32. Patti M. Valkenburg, Jochen Peter, and Alexander P. Schouten, "Friend Networking Sites and Their Relationship to Adolescents' Well-Being and Social Self-Esteem," *Cyberpsychology and Behavior* 9, no. 5 (2006).

33. Ibid.

34. Valkenburg and Peter, "Online Communication among Adolescents."

35. Keith Wilcox and Andrew T. Stephen, "Are Close Friends the Enemy? Online Social Networks, Self-Esteem, and Self-Control," *Journal of Consumer Research* 40, no. 1 (2013).

36. Allan Fenigstein, Michael F. Scheier, and Arnold H. Buss, "Public and Private Self-Consciousness: Assessment and Theory," *Journal of Consulting and Clinical Psychology* 43, no. 4 (1975).

37. Jong-Eun Roselyn Lee, David Clark Moore, Eun-A Park, and Sung Gwan Park, "Who Wants to Be 'Friend-Rich'? Social Compensatory Friending on Facebook and the Moderating Role of Public Self-Consciousness," *Computers in Human Behavior* 28, no. 3 (2012); Minsun Shim, Min J. Lee, and Sang H. Park, "Photograph Use on Social Network Sites among South Korean College Students: The Role of Public and Private Self-Consciousness," *CyberPsychology and Behavior* 11, no. 4 (2008).

38. Nikhil Dhawan, Mark E. Kunik, John Oldham, John Coverdale, "Prevalence and Treatment of Narcissistic Personality Disorder in the Community: A Systematic Review," *Comprehensive Psychiatry* 51, no. 4 (2010).

39. Jean M. Twenge and W. Keith Campbell, *The Narcissism Epidemic: Living in the Age of Entitlement* (New York: Free Press, 2009).

40. Larry D. Rosen, *iDisorder: Understanding Our Obsession with Technology and Overcoming Its Hold on Us* (New York: Palgrave Macmillan, 2012); Elliot T. Panek, Yioryos Nardis, and Sara Konrath, "Mirror or Megaphone? How Relationships between Narcissism and Social Networking Site Use Differ on Facebook and Twitter," *Computers in Human Behavior* 29, no. 5 (2013).

41. See also: Robert Raskin and Howard Terry, "A Principal-Components Analysis of the Narcissistic Personality Inventory and Further Evidence of Its Construct Validity," *Journal of Personality and Social Psychology* 54, no. 5 (1988).

42. Otto F. Kernberg, *Severe Personality Disorders: Psychotherapeutic Strategies* (New Haven, Conn.: Yale University Press, 1993).

43. Robert Kraut et al., "Internet Paradox: A Social Technology That Reduces Social Involvement and Psychological Well-Being?," *American Psychologist* 53, no. 9 (1998).

44. For a review, see Patti M. Valkenburg and Jochen Peter, "Social Consequences of the Internet for Adolescents: A Decade of Research," *Current Directions in Psychological Science* 18, no. 1 (2009).

45. For reviews, see Lauren A. Spies Shapiro and Gayla Margolin, "Growing Up Wired: Social Networking Sites and Adolescent Psychosocial Development," *Clinical Child and Family Psychology Review* 17, no. 1 (2014); and Valkenburg and Peter, "Online Communication among Adolescents."

46. "The Effects of Instant Messaging on the Quality of Adolescents' Existing Friendships: A Longitudinal Study," *Journal of Communication* 59, no. 1 (2009); Stephanie M. Reich, Kaveri Subrahmanyam, and Guadalupe Espinoza, "Friending, IMing, and Hanging out Face-to-Face: Overlap in Adolescents' Online and Offline Social Networks," *Developmental Psychology* 48, no. 2 (2012).

47. Reported in: Sonia Livingstone and Peter K. Smith, "Harms Experienced by Child Users of Online and Mobile Technologies: The Nature, Prevalence and Management of Sexual and Aggressive Risks in the Digital Age," *Journal of Child Psychology and Psychiatry* 55, no. 6 (2014).

48. Ibid.

49. Robert Slonje and Peter K. Smith, "Cyberbullying: Another Main Type of Bullying?," *Scandinavian Journal of Psychology* 49, no. 2 (2008).

50. Valkenburg and Peter, "Online Communication among Adolescents."

51. Susanne E. Baumgartner, Sindy R. Sumter, Jochen Peter, Patti M. Valkenburg, and Sonia Livingstone, "Does Country Context Matter? Investigating the Predictors of Teen Sexting across Europe," *Computers in Human Behavior* 34 (2014); Michele L. Ybarra and Kimberly J. Mitchell, " 'Sexting' and Its Relation to Sexual Activity and Sexual Risk Behavior in a National Survey of Adolescents," *Journal of Adolescent Health* 55, no. 6 (2014).

52. Kimberly J. Mitchell, David Finkelhor, Lisa M. Jones, and Janis Wolak, "Prevalence and Characteristics of Youth Sexting: A National Study," *Pediatrics* 129, no. 1 (2012); Baumgartner et al., "Does Country Context Matter? Investigating the Predictors of Teen Sexting across Europe"; Julia R. Lippman and Scott W. Campbell, "Damned If You Do, Damned If You Don't . . . If You're a Girl: Relational and Normative Contexts of Adolescent Sexting in the United States," *Journal of Children and Media* 8, no. 4 (2014).

53. Bianca Klettke, David J. Hallford, and David J. Mellor, "Sexting Prevalence and Correlates: A Systematic Literature Review," *Clinical Psychology Review* 34, no. 1 (2014).

54. Jeff R. Temple and HyeJeong Choi, "Longitudinal Association between Teen Sexting and Sexual Behavior," *Pediatrics* 134, no. 5 (2014).

55. Lippman and Campbell, "Damned If You Do."

56. Johanna M. van Oosten, Jochen Peter, and Inge Boot, "Exploring Associations between Exposure to Sexy Online Self-Presentations and Adolescents' Sexual Attitudes and Behavior," *Journal of Youth and Adolescence* 44, no. 5 (2014).

57. Juliane A. Kloess, Anthony R. Beech, and Leigh Harkins, "Online Child Sexual Exploitation: Prevalence, Process, and Offender Characteristics," *Trauma, Violence, and Abuse* 15, no. 2 (2014).

58. Livingstone and Smith, "Harms Experienced by Child Users."

59. Rideout, *The Common Sense Census.*

60. Nancy Miller, "Minifesto for a New Age," *Wired,* March 1, 2007.

61. Winneke van der Schuur, Susanne E. Baumgartner, Sindy R. Sumter, and Patti M. Valkenburg, "The Consequences of Media Multitasking for Youth: A Review," *Computers in Human Behavior* 53 (2015).

62. Reem Alzahabi and Mark W. Becker, "The Association between Media Multitasking, Task-Switching, and Dual-Task Performance," *Journal of Experimental Psychology* 39, no. 5 (2013).

63. Nicholas Carr, *The Shallows: What the Internet Is Doing to Our Brains* (New York: Norton, 2011), 18.

64. Translated from Manfred Spitzer, *Digitale Demenz: Wie Wir Uns Und Unsere Kinder Um Den Verstand Bringen* (Munich: Droemer, 2012), 312.

65. Nicholas Carr, "Is Google Making Us Stupid?," *Yearbook of the National Society for the Study of Education* 107, no. 2 (2008).

66. Eleanor A. Maguire et al., "Navigation-Related Structural Change in the Hippocampi of Taxi Drivers," *Proceedings of the National Academy of Sciences of the United States of America* 97, no. 8 (2000).

67. Gary W. Small et al., "Your Brain on Google: Patterns of Cerebral Activation During Internet Searching," *American Journal of Geriatric Psychiatry* 17, no. 2 (2009).

68. Van der Schuur et al., "Consequences of Media Multitasking."

69. Betsy Sparrow, Jenny Liu, and Daniel M. Wegner, "Google Effects on Memory: Cognitive Consequences of Having Information at Our Fingertips," *Science* 333, no. 6043 (2011).

70. Clive Thompson, *Smarter than You Think: How Technology Is Changing Our Minds for the Better* (New York: Penguin, 2013).

14. Media and Parenting

1. Institute for Advanced Studies in Culture, *Culture of American Families: A National Survey* (Charlottesville, Va.: Institute for Advanced Studies in Culture, 2012).

2. Freek Bucx, *Gezinsrapport 2011: Een Portret Van Het Gezinsleven in Nederland* [Family report 2011] (The Hague: Sociaal Cultureel Planbureau, 2011).

3. Diana Baumrind, "Parental Disciplinary Patterns and Social Competence in Children," *Youth and Society* 9, no. 3 (1978).

4. Laurence Steinberg, *Adolescence,* vol. 9 (New York: McGraw-Hill, 2011).

5. Ibid.

6. Roy F. Baumeister and John Tierney, *Willpower: Rediscovering the Greatest Human Strength* (New York: Penguin, 2011).

7. Richard M. Ryan and Edward L. Deci, "Self-Determination Theory and the Facilitation of Intrinsic Motivation, Social Development, and Well-Being," *American Psychologist* 55, no. 1 (2000).

8. Margaret K. Nelson, *Parenting Out of Control: Anxious Parents in Uncertain Times* (New York: New York University Press, 2010).

9. Sharon S. Brehm and Jack W. Brehm, *Psychological Reactance: A Theory of Freedom and Control* (New York: Academic Press, 1981).

10. Judith G. Smetana, "Parenting Styles and Conceptions of Parental Authority during Adolescence," *Child Development* 66, no. 2 (1995).

11. See the discussion in Jessica T. Piotrowski, Amy B. Jordan, Amy Bleakley, and Michael Hennessy, "Identifying Family Television Practices to Reduce Children's Television Time," *Journal of Family Communication* 15, no. 2 (2015).

12. Lynn S. Clark, *The Parent App: Understanding Families in the Digital Age* (New York: Oxford University Press, 2013).

13. Ibid.

14. Patti M. Valkenburg, Marina Krcmar, Allerd L. Peeters, and Nies M. Marseille, "Developing a Scale to Assess Three Styles of Television Mediation: 'Instructive Mediation,' 'Restrictive Mediation,' and 'Social Coviewing,' " *Journal of Broadcasting & Electronic Media* 43, no. 1 (1999).

15. Jennifer L. Chakroff and Amy I. Nathanson, "Parent and School Interventions: Mediation and Media Literacy," in *The Handbook of Children, Media, and Development,* ed. Sandra L. Calvert and Barbara J. Wilson (Boston: Blackwell, 2008).

16. Laura M. Padilla-Walker, Sarah M. Coyne, Ashley M. Fraser, Justin Dyer, and Jeremy B. Yorgason, "Parents and Adolescents Growing Up in the Digital Age: Latent Growth Curve Analysis of Proactive Media Monitoring," *Journal of Adolescence* 35, no. 5 (2012).

17. Ann C. Crouter and Melissa R. Head, "Parental Monitoring and Knowledge of Children," in *Handbook of Parenting: Being and Becoming a Parent,* ed. Marc H. Bornstein (Mahwah, N.J.: Erlbaum, 2002).

18. Sarah J. Racz and Robert J. McMahon, "The Relationship between Parental Knowledge and Monitoring and Child and Adolescent Conduct Problems: A 10-Year Update," *Clinical Child And Family Psychology Review* 14, no. 4 (2011).

19. Arnold Sameroff, *The Transactional Model* (Washington, D.C.: American Psychological Association, 2009).

20. Crouter and Head, "Parental Monitoring and Knowledge of Children"; Padilla-Walker et al., "Parents and Adolescents Growing Up."

21. Amy I. Nathanson, "Factual and Evaluative Approaches to Modifying Children's Responses to Violent Television," *Journal of Communication* 54, no. 2 (2004).

22. Chakroff and Nathanson, "Parent and School Interventions."

23. Padilla-Walker et al., "Parents and Adolescents Growing Up."

24. Alissa E. Setliff and Mary L. Courage, "Background Television and Infants' Allocation of Their Attention during Toy Play," *Infancy* 16, no. 6 (2011).

25. Ellen A. Wartella, Vicky Rideout, Alexis R. Lauricella, and Sabrina L. Connell, *Parenting in the Age of Digital Technology: A National Survey* (Evanston, Ill.: School of Communication, Northwestern University, 2013).

26. Marie E. Schmidt et al., "The Effects of Background Television on the Toy Play Behavior of Very Young Children," *Child Development* 79, no. 4 (2008); Amy I. Nathanson, Molly L. Sharp, Fashina Aladé, Eric E. Rasmussen, and Katheryn Christy, "The Relation between Television Exposure and Executive Function among Preschoolers," *Developmental Psychology* 50, no. 5 (2014); Heather L. Kirkorian, Tiffany A. Pempek, Lauren A. Murphy, Marie E. Schmidt, and Daniel R. Anderson, "The Impact of Background Television on Parent-Child Interaction," *Child Development* 80, no. 5 (2009).

27. Matthew A. Lapierre, Jessica Taylor Piotrowski, and Deborah L. Linebarger, "Background Television in the Homes of US Children," *Pediatrics* 130, no. 5 (2012).

28. American Academy of Pediatrics, Committee on Public Education, "Media Education," *Pediatrics* 2 (1999).

29. Wartella et al., *Parenting in the Age of Digital Technology.*

30. Dimitri A. Christakis, Frederick J. Zimmerman, David L. DiGiuseppe, and Carolyn A. McCarty, "Early Television Exposure and Subsequent Attentional Problems in Children," *Pediatrics* 113, no. 4 (2004); Frederick J. Zimmerman, Dimitri A. Christakis, and Andrew N. Meltzoff, "Television and DVD/Video Viewing in Children Younger Than 2 Years," *Archives of Pediatrics and Adolescent Medicine* 161, no. 5 (2007).

31. E. Michael Foster and Stephanie Watkins, "The Value of Reanalysis: TV Viewing and Attention Problems," *Child Development* 81, no. 1 (2010).

32. Christopher J. Ferguson and M. Brent Donnellan, "Is the Association between Children's Baby Video Viewing and Poor Language Development Robust? A Reanalysis of Zimmerman, Christakis, and Meltzoff (2007)," *Developmental Psychology* 50, no. 1 (2014).

33. Dimitri A. Christakis, "Infants and Interactive Media Use—Reply," *JAMA Pediatrics* 168, no. 10 (2014).

34. Ibid., 400.

35. Patti M. Valkenburg and Tom H. van der Voort, "Television's Impact on Fantasy Play: A Review of Research," *Developmental Review* 14, no. 1 (1994); Sanne W. C. Nikkelen, Patti M. Valkenburg, Mariette Huizinga, and Brad J. Bushman, "Media Use and ADHD-Related Behaviors in Children and Adolescents: A Meta-Analysis," *Developmental Psychology* 50, no. 9 (2014).

36. Patti M. Valkenburg, Jessica Taylor Piotrowski, Jo Hermanns, and Rebecca de Leeuw, "Developing and Validating the Perceived Parental Media Mediation Scale: A Self-Determination Perspective," *Human Communication Research* 39, no. 4 (2013).

37. Amy I. Nathanson and Mong-Shan Yang, "The Effects of Mediation Content and Form on Children's Responses to Violent Television," *Human Communication Research* 29, no. 1 (2003).

38. Charles R. Corder-Bolz, "Mediation: The Role of Significant Others," *Journal of Communication* 30, no. 3 (1980).

39. David J. Hicks, "Effects of Co-Observer's Sanctions and Adult Presence on Imitative Aggression," *Child Development* 39, no. 1 (1968).

40. Nathanson, "Factual and Evaluative Approaches."

41. Clive Thompson, *Smarter than You Think: How Technology Is Changing Our Minds for the Better* (New York: Penguin, 2013).

42. Jaak Panksepp, *Affective Neuroscience: The Foundations of Human and Animal Emotions* (New York: Oxford University Press, 1998).

43. Larry D. Rosen, *iDisorder: Understanding Our Obsession with Technology and Overcoming Its Hold on Us* (New York: Palgrave Macmillan, 2012).

44. Ibid.

45. Dustin Wahlstrom, Tonya White, and Monica Luciana, "Neurobehavioral Evidence for Changes in Dopamine System Activity during Adolescence," *Neuroscience and Biobehavioral Reviews* 34, no. 5 (2010).

46. Teija Nuutinen, Carola Ray, and Eva Roos, "Do Computer Use, TV Viewing, and the Presence of the Media in the Bedroom Predict School-Aged Children's Sleep Habits in a Longitudinal Study?," *BMC Public Health* 13, no. 1 (2013).

47. Andrew Smart, *Autopilot: The Art and Science of Doing Nothing* (New York: OR Books, 2013).

48. Baumeister and Tierney, *Willpower.*

49. Robert LaRose, "The Problem of Media Habits," *Communication Theory* 20, no. 2 (2010).

50. Charles Duhigg, *The Power of Habit: Why We Do What We Do in Life and Business* (New York: Random House, 2012).

51. Karl G. Hill, J. David Hawkins, Richard F. Catalano, Robert D. Abbott, and Jie Guo, "Family Influences on the Risk of Daily Smoking Initiation," *Journal of Adolescent Health* 37, no. 3 (2005).

52. Amy I. Nathanson, "The Unintended Effects of Parental Mediation of Television on Adolescents," *Media Psychology* 4, no. 3 (2002).

53. Valkenburg et al., "The Perceived Parental Media Mediation Scale."

54. Ryan and Deci, "Self-Determination Theory."

55. Baumeister and Tierney, *Willpower.*

15. The End

1. Marshall McLuhan, *The Gutenberg Galaxy* (New York: Routledge and Kegan, 1963).

2. Jan Van Dijk, *The Network Society* (London: Sage, 2012).

3. Manuel Castells, *The Rise of the Network Society: The Information Age; Economy, Society, and Culture* (New York: Wiley, 2011).

4. Van Dijk, *The Network Society.*

5. Castells, *The Rise of the Network Society.*

6. Brad J. Bushman, Mario Gollwitzer, and Carlos Cruz, "There Is Broad Consensus: Media Researchers Agree That Violent Media Increase Aggression in Children, and Pediatricians and Parents Concur," *Psychology of Popular Media Culture* 4, no. 3 (2014).

7. Brad J. Bushman, Hannah R. Rothstein, and Craig A. Anderson, "Much Ado about Something: Violent Video Game Effects and a School of Red Herring; Reply to Ferguson and Kilburn (2010)," *Psychological Bulletin* 136, no. 2 (2010).

8. Christopher J. Ferguson and John Kilburn, "Much Ado about Nothing: The Misestimation and Overinterpretation of Violent Video Game Effects in Eastern and Western Nations; Comment on Anderson et al. (2010)," *Psychological Bulletin* 136, no. 2 (2010).

9. The first version of this drawing appeared in 1892 in the German magazine *Fliegende Blätter.* Our thanks to Studio Paul Baars for use of the illustration.

10. Daniel R. Anderson, Aletha C. Huston, Kelly L. Schmitt, Deborah L. Linebarger, and John C. Wright, "Early Childhood Television Viewing and Adolescent Behavior: The Recontact Study," *Monographs of the Society for Research in Child Development* 66, no. 1 (2001).

11. W. Thomas Boyce and Bruce J. Ellis, "Biological Sensitivity to Context: I. An Evolutionary-Developmental Theory of the Origins and Functions of Stress Reactivity," *Development and Psychopathology* 17, no. 2 (2005).

ACKNOWLEDGMENTS

Many people have been extremely helpful in the preparation of this book. First of all, we would like to thank our colleagues at CcaM, the Center for Research on Children, Adolescents, and the Media, for their high-quality comments and suggestions during the writing of the book: Hans Beentjes, Jochen Peter, Susanne Baumgartner, Karin Fikkers, Rinaldo Kühne, Jeroen Lemmens, Annemarie van Oosten, and Sindy Sumter. We also want to thank Monique Vogelzang for her careful handling of the references and other formal issues of manuscript preparation.

Generous colleagues are not limited to one research group or university. Professor Dafna Lemish from Southern Illinois University and several anonymous reviewers provided very helpful and constructive comments. We are indebted to Els Spin, Anne Hodgkinson, and Cecilia Willems, who assisted with translations. And special thanks go to the publication team at Yale University Press—in particular, Kip Keller, for his meticulous eye during the editing process, as well as Jennifer Banks and Heather Gold, who kindly shepherded us through the publication process. We are also very grateful to our dear family and friends, who provided us much needed laughter during the particularly arduous portions of this book. And finally, a different kind of thanks is due to our husbands, Paul van der Heijden and John Piotrowski, to whom this book is dedicated.

INDEX

Numbers in *italics* indicate tables or figures.

AAP. *See* American Academy of Pediatrics
academic skills, 176–77
accessibility, *221*
action games, 200, 204–5
active media monitoring, 252–53, 259–60
active mediation, 250
activity-displacement hypothesis, 152–53
Acuff, Daniel, 56
addiction, games and, 214–16
ADHD, media use and, 26
adolescents: behavior of, 78; communication skills for, 221–22; developmental needs of, 220–21; educational media and, 184; fear-inducing content and, 124–26; gaming and, 206; media use by, 78–79; physical and developmental changes in, 78, 79–80; prolonged sitting by, 209; prosocial content and, 186; public self-awareness and, 229–30; questioning nature of, 81; sexting and, 235; sexuality and, 234–35; sexual media content's effect on, 167; social media's appeal for, 220–24. *See also* early adolescence; late adolescence
adults, television's portrayal of, 17
advance organizers, 191
advergames, 2, 144, 146
advertising: academic research on, 144–45; appeal of, 49, 56; brand preferences and, 147–48; changes in, 2; critical evaluation of, 140–41; effectiveness of, 137; effects of, 144–56; ethics of, 155; gender and, 68; host selling, 5; materialism and, 150; parent-child conflict and, 150–51; processing of, 154–55; purchase request behavior and, 148–49; sex in, 164–65; weight gain and, 151–53
advertising-effect hypothesis, 152–53
advertising literacy, 155–56
aesthetic emotions, 118
affordances, 220–24, 227, 237, 242, 243
age: media monitoring and, 253; as predictor of media use, 39
aggression: contextual features of media violence and, *112;* depiction of, 106–7;

experiments in, 99–101; factors in, 107, 111, 113; indirect, 99, 102; as learned behavior, 105; media violence and, 40, 96–115; problem solving and, 108–9; rewarded, 106–7; risk factors for, 104; studies of, 101–3
"AHH Effect" campaign (Coca-Cola), 144
Aladdin (dir. Clements and Musker), 122
Alone Together (Turkle), 8
amateur porn, 165–67
American Academy of Pediatrics, 5, 254–57
American Psychological Association, 159, 161
Anderson, Craig, 38, 111, 179, 181
Anderson, Daniel, 45–46, 184, 272–73
antiheroes, 17
anonymity, visual, 224
anxiety, media use and, 26
app gap, 178
Apple TV, 2
apps: creativity and, 190; designed to disturb, 261; educational, 7, 178, 256–57; for social-emotional lessons, 187
arousal, 110–13; emotions and, 128; sexual, 34, 170–71
Assassin's Creed, 199
assertiveness, 231
asynchronicity, *221,* 223
Atari, 196, 197
attention, cognitive development and, 46
attention span, 65
audiovisual narratives, 53
authoritarian parenting, 245, 265
authoritative parenting, 245–47, 251
autonomy, 86, 90, 94, 220–22, 246
autonomy-supportive strategies, 265
Autopilot: The Art and Science of Doing Nothing (Smart), 262
avatars, 133
baby apps, 51
Baby Einstein, 21, 177–78
baby media, 5, 6
Baby TV, 21, 178
background media exposure, 254, 256, 257
Bandura, Albert, 4, 38, 105–7, 168, 179
Barbie Fashion Designer, 205
Barney and Friends, 184–85, 189
bedroom culture, 251
behavior: modeling of, 180; sources of, 105
behavior compatibility, 60
behaviorism, 30, 105
Bem, Daryl, 226
Berelson, Bernard, 37
Berkowitz, Leonard, 109–10
Between the Lions, 184
Big Bugs Band, 49
Bill Nye the Science Guy, 184
binary characters, 67
BlackBerry Pearl, 219
blogs, 94
Blue's Clues, 184–85, 193
Blumer, Herbert, 32
Bobo doll experiments, 105–6
Bolton, Frances Payne, 32
Bond, Bradley, 61
books, for children, 10
boomerang effect, 249, 259, 260
boyd, danah, 9, 219–20
brain: associative networks in, 109–10; changes in, for adolescents, 79–81; development of, 7, 84–85; gray matter in, 80–81; research on, 40, 85, 108, 135, 211–13, 240–41; white matter in, 80–81
brand attitudes, 147–48
brand awareness, 145–47
brand preferences, 142–43, 147–48
brand recall, 145–47, 154
brand recognition, 145–46
brands, experimental studies on, 146–48

brand sponsorship, 144
Brown, Jane D., 168
Buckley, Katherine, 179, 181
Buijzen, Moniek, 154
Bulger, James, 97, 98
bullying, 114, 233–34. *See also* cyberbullying
Bushman, Brad, 38, 110, 111, 270

Cacioppo, John, 38, 154
Calvert, Sandra, 61, 189
Campbell, Keith, 230
Cantor, Joanne, 56, 126
Cantril, Hadley, 35–37
capacity model, 179, 180–81
Carr, Nicholas, 239–40
Carroll, Lewis, 219
casual games, 198, 207
causal-correlational research, 101–3
CcaM. *See* Center for Research on Children, Adolescents, and the Media
censorship, 12
Center for Research on Children, Adolescents, and the Media (University of Amsterdam), 7
centration, 56–57, 64
Chaiken, Shelly, 154
characters: preferences for, gender and, 61; transformations in, 122–23
chicken-or-egg dilemma, 101, 150, 212
child development: advertising effects and, 153–55; categories of, 44–45; drivers of, 47; emotions and, 120–21
childhood: changes in, 10, 16–26, 27; concept of, 10, 12–14; erosion of, 14–16; paradox of, 27
children: as consumer markets, 137–43; development of (ages 5–12), 63; educational media and, 12, 183–84; fear and, 121, 123–26; as future consumers, 142–43; gaming and, 206; influencing product purchases, 141–42, 148–49; IQ of, 24; literature for, 14; media for, 10–14, 16; media literacy of, 250; as miniature adults, 11–12, 14–15; money and, 138; moral development of, 260; needs of, 139; physiological response of, to movies, 34; preferences of, 139–40; product purchases by, 140–41; raising of, 12 (*see also parenting entries*); sexualization of, 159–60; social environment for, 12–15; speech in, 50; television's portrayal of, 17; vulnerable vs. empowered, 27
Children's Television Act, 177, 185
Cho, Seung-Hui, 97, 98
Christakis, Dimitri, 187, 255–57
Clark, Lynn, 249
cliques, 89–90, 93, 133, 141, 203–4
Club Penguin, 72
CMC. *See* computer-mediated communication
Coca-Cola, 144
co-figurative culture, 19–20
cognitive ability, 211
cognitive control, 238–39
cognitive development, 45–46, 227, 237–42
cognitive dissonance, 226
cognitive learning, media support for, 52
cognitive psychology, 105
cognitive script theory, 108–9
collecting, 70–72
Collins, Rebecca, 169–70
commercialism, 5, 20–22
commercials. *See* advertising
communication: interpersonal, 224–26; online, 229, 232; synchronous, 223–24; technology for, constant changes in, 269
communication studies, 3–4, 15, 220, 274–75
competition, gaming and, 202
computer-mediated communication, 224–26

computers, treated like people, 134
Comstock, George, 102
concentration, capacity for, and the Internet, 239–40
concrete-operational thinking, 69–71, 81–82, 123–24
conditional media effects perspective, 37–38, 40–41, 43
connectedness, 227, 231–32
conservation tasks, 69–70
consumer behavior, components of, 138–41
consumer cultivation theory, 149–50
consumer socialization, 138
content, significance of, 273
control: attraction of, for youth, 203; self-esteem and, 229; sense of, 222–24
conventional domain, parenting and, 248
Cooney, Joan Ganz, 179
copycat crimes, 97–98
correlational design, 239
correlational studies, 101
Courage, Mary, 49
co-viewing. 250
creativity, 188–90
criminal behavior, factors in, 98
criminal violence, meta-analyses of, 103
Crone, Eveline, 81
cross-platform marketing, 144
cross-sectional correlational studies, 101
crystallized intelligence, 24
cue manageability, *221*, 224
cultivation theory, 17–18, 149–50, 168
cultural studies, 3–4, 7
Culture of Narcissism, The (Lasch), 230
cultures, Mead's typology of, 19–20
cyberbullying, 227, 232–34
Cyberchase, 184

Dahl, Ronald, 81
Dale, Edgar, 32
dancing games, 207
dandelion-orchid hypothesis, 275
Darwin, Charles, 30
Davidson, Richard, 40
Davis, Katie, 228
Day After, The (dir. Meyer), 126
decentering, 70
decentration, 140
desensitization theory, 107–8
desexualization, 160
development, 113, 192, 273–74. *See also* child development
developmental level: media preferences and, 44–47; as predictor of media use, 39, 41, 42
developmental psychology, 45, 46, 274–75
Diagnostic and Statistical Manual of Mental Disorders (*DSM-5;* American Psychiatric Association), 214
diaper demographic, 5, 177, 254
differential susceptibility perspectives, 40–41
differential susceptibility to media effects model (DSMM), 38, 41, 168
digital dementia, 237, 240, 241
Digital Dementia (Spitzer), 8
digital media, sexual content and, 91
Dijkstra, Rineke, 218, 229
disordered gamers, 214–15
disposition, 113, 168; media use and, 39, 41–42
divergent thinking, 188
Doom, 97, 198
dopamine, 84–85, 124–25, 261
Dora the Explorer, 2, 66, 69, 187, 189
Doug, 185
downward social comparison, 127, 130
Dragon Tales, 184–85
drip-drip theories, 17–18
Dr. Seuss (Theodor Geisel), 14
DSMM. *See* differential susceptibility to media effects model
Dysinger, Wendell, 170

early adolescence (ages 12–15): advanced thinking during, 82; content choices of, 83–91; gender modeling and, 87–88; identity and, 88–90; metacognition and, 82; peers and, 88–89; problem-solving and, 82; risk-taking during, 85–86; sexuality and, 90–91, 94; social-emotional development during, 86–91; social media and, 88–89. *See also* teenagers
eating, unhealthy, 149, 151–53
edu-apps, 198
educational media, 175–77, 255–57; academic skills and, 181–84; boredom and, 66; child characteristics and, 192–93; creativity and, 188–90; developmental level and, 192–93; effects of, 179–81; entertainment aspect of, 192; goals of, 179; at home, 177–81; older children and, 178–79; positive lessons from, 179; processing of, 180; program characteristics of, 190–92; prosocial content in, 186; social-emotional development and, 186–87; social-emotional skills and, 184–88
educational programming, 45, 131–32
Effects of Mass Communication, The (Klapper), 37
Egenfeldt-Nielsen, Simon, 199–200
egocentrism, 73–74, 87
Ekman, Paul, 58
Elkind, David, 14–16, 87
emancipation movements, 14
embedded educational content, 180
Émile, ou De l'éducation (Rousseau), 10, 13
emotional competence, 132, 136
emotional contagion, 37
emotions: child development and, 120–21; development of, 57–58; entertainment media and, 116–17; experience of, 116; fiction and, 117–19; human nature and, 119, 126–27; intensity of, 117–18; physical arousal and, 128 (*see also* arousal); sexual, 170; teaching of, 131
empathy, 39, 45, 58, 119, 125, 130
Enlightenment, 12–13
Enquist, Anna, 19
entertainment, motives for, 129–30
entertainment media: changes in, 117; emotions and, 116–17; identity development and, 136; reality content and, 160–61
Erikson, Erik, 18
Eron, Leonard, 101–2
escapism, 128–29
eudaimonia, 129–31
evaluative active monitoring, 252
evaluative monitoring strategies, 259–60
Everyone Poops (Gomi), 66
evolution, 212; language and, 118–19; play and, 207; theory of, 30
excitation transfer theory, 110–11, 127–28, 130, 136, 204
executive functions, 92
exergames, 209
expression effects, 226–28
extraversion, 231
eyewitness accounts, 119

Facebook, 1, 93, 218, 224–26
factual active monitoring, 252
factual monitoring strategies, 259, 260
familiarity, children's preferences for, 57
families: late adolescence and, 93; power balance in, 18–20; structural changes in, 15, 19–20. *See also* parenting styles
fantasy, reality and, 54–55, 64, 113, 121–22, 136
fantasy characters, 54, 55
fast entertainment, 238
fear: limiting or offsetting, 123, 124; media-induced, 119–26
feedback, 51

Female Chauvinist Pigs: Women and the Rise of Raunch Culture (Levy), 159
females: objectification of, 164–66; sexualization of, 163–64
femininity, caricatures of, 163–64
feminist studies, 164
Ferguson, Christopher, 270
Festinger, Leon, 127
fiction: children's understanding of, 64; emotions and, 117–19, 135
field experiments, 99, 100–101
first-person shooter games, 198
Fisch, Shalom, 179, 180
flow, state of, 203
fluid intelligence, 24, 211, 212
Flynn, James, 24–25
Flynn effect, 24, 211, 241
fMRI. *See* functional magnetic resonance imaging
foreground media exposure, 254, 256, 257
formal-operational thinking, 70, 81–82
fragmentation hypothesis, 227–28
Frankfurt School, 3–4
freemiums, 3, 198
Freud, Sigmund, 230
friendships, Internet use and, 227, 231–32
Frijda, Nico, 117–18
functional magnetic resonance imaging, 108, 135
future market, children as, 137, 138, 142–43

GAM. *See* general aggression model
games, 195–96, 199–201. *See also* gaming; video games
game studies, 195
gaming, 216–17; addiction to, 214–16; attraction to, 201–4; categories of, 206–7; changes in, 2–3; in the classroom, 210; cognitive effects of, 210–13; culture of, 203–4; customization of, 133; emotional engagement and, 125–26, 133; first-person perspective in, 125; fostering academic and social-emotional learning, 194; gender and, 68–69, 204–7; hand-eye coordination and, 212–13; horror content and, 125; intelligence and, 211–12; motivations for, 201–4; multitasking and, 238; pathological, 214–16; physical effects of, 207–9; player archetypes, 201–2; players' control over content, 125; prosocial, 181; social adjustment and, 213; social-emotional effects of, 213; social needs and, 203; spatial awareness and, 212–13; technological improvements for, 197–98; third-person perspective in, 125; violence and, 205; young elementary schoolchildren and, 68–69
gender: content preferences and, 72, 75–76; cyberbullying and, 233–34; development and, 59–61; gaming and, 204–7; media preferences and, 87–88; media violence and, 113; sexting and, 235; tragedy paradox and, 127; young elementary schoolchildren and, 67–69
gender roles, 68, 169
gender segregation, 60
general aggression model, 111–12, 181
general learning model, 179
Gentile, Douglas, 186
Gerbner, George, 17–18, 149, 168
Girls Gone Skank: The Sexualization of Girls in American Society (Oppliger), 159
Goebbels, Joseph, 30
Goethe, Johann Wolfgang von, 97
Grand Theft Auto (*GTA*), 207, 252
gratification, delay of, 139, 187–88
grazing hypothesis, 152–53
Greenfield, Patricia, 210

habit formation, prevention of, 263–64
Hamm, Jon, 131
hand-eye coordination, 212–13
Harris, Paul, 118, 121, 133
Harry Potter, 72–73, 123
hedonic principle, 129–30
hedonism, 129
Hitchcock, Alfred, 120
Hitler, Adolf, 30
Hoffner, Cynthia, 56
horror content, 119–20, 124–25
host selling, 5
Huesmann, Rowell, 109
humor, 66; complexity of, 83–84; early adolescence and, 83–84; late adolescence and, 92–93
Hurried Child, The: Growing Up Too Fast Too Soon (Elkin), 14–15
hyperpersonal communication model, 225
hypodermic needle theory, 29–31, 34–36

iBrain (Small), 8
ICA. *See* International Communication Association
identifiability, *221*
identity: components of, 86–88; development of, 136, 227–28; early adolescence and, 88–90; experimentation with, 87–89; parasocial relationships and, 133; social media and, 95, 227–28; subcultures and, 89–90
idle time, need for, 262
IGD. *See* Internet gaming disorder
imaginary audience, 87
Incredible Hulk, The, 122, 123
indirect aggression, 99
infants: educational media and, 182–83; media preferences of, 44; media use by, 48–49, 51–52; screen use for, 253–57; sensory preferences of, 47–49
influencers, children as, 137, 138, 141–42
informal learning, 178, 179, 254
information, accessibility to, 224
informational privacy, 222–23
information processing, 57
Instagram, 224–26
Institute for Propaganda Analysis, 30
intelligence: media usage and, 241; social media's effect on, 237
intended advertising effects, 145–49
interactive media, creativity and, 189–90
interactive technology, 133
interdisciplinary research, 3–4, 269–70
International Communication Association, 7
Internet: affordances of, 243; and capacity for concentration, 239–40; experimenting with, 228; self-concept clarity and, 228; shallow thinking and, 240–41; social effects of, first research on, 6; youth access to, 6
Internet gaming disorder, 214–15
intimacy, 89, 93; computer-mediated communication and, 225–26; social media and, 227; teens' need for, 261–62
introspection, 82
intuition, 92
investigative-orienting system of attention, 49, 51
IPA. *See* Institute for Propaganda Analysis
iPhone 2G, 219
It's Complicated (boyd), 219–20

Jackson, Linda, 189
Jacobellis v. Ohio, 161
Jaeggi, Susanne, 212
Jastrow, Joseph, 271
Jaws (dir. Spielberg), 120
jazz, 29
Jobs, Steve, 219
Journal of Children and Media, 7

Katz, Elihu, 37
KGOL (kids getting older later) phenomenon, 222
KGOY (kids getting older younger) phenomenon, 21, 22
Kilburn, John, 270
Klaassen, Marleen, 166
Klapper, Joseph, 37–38
Kline, Steven, 21
Klug, Christopher, 201
Kraut, Robert, 231–32
Kunkel, Dale, 163

laboratory experiments, 99–100
language, evolution and, 118–19
Lanza, Adam, 96–97
L'Arrivée d'un train en gare de La Ciotat (*The Arrival of a Train at La Ciotat Station;* dir. Lumière and Lumière), 30–31
Lasch, Christopher, 230
Lassie, 185
late adolescence (ages 16–19), 79, 92–94. *See also* teenagers
Lauricella, Alexis, 132
law of apparent reality, 117–18, 156
Lazarsfeld, Paul, 37
lean-back entertainment, 203
Lemish, Dafna, 55
Les Amants (dir. Malle), 161–62
Levy, Ariel, 159
Leyens, Jacques-Philippe, 100
Linebarger, Deborah, 187
Linz, Daniel, 107–8
Livingstone, Sonia, 233
Locke, John, 12
longitudinal research, 101, 109. *See also* causal-correlational research
Lucretius, 127, 130

Macklin, Carole, 146
magical realism, 72–73, 83
magic bullet theory, 29
Magic School Bus, The, 184
Magnavox Odyssey, 196
Maguire, Eleanor, 240–41
mainstreaming, 17
Malik, Zayn, 133
Mares, Marie-Louise, 183, 186
marketing, to youth, 20–22. *See also* advertising
market research, 143–44
marshmallow test, 139, 187–88
massively multiplayer online role-playing games, 200–201
mass media, influence of, 29
mass self-communication, 268
materialism, 149–50
McLuhan, Marshall, 272–73
McNair, Brian, 161
McNeal, James, 140
Mead, Margaret, 19
meaning, interest level and, 46, 49–50
media: age at first use of, 49; changing landscape of, 2, 269; daily use of, 1; developed for youngest viewers, 5–6; educational role of, 169–70; family communication and, 18; fluid intelligence and, 24; influence of, 17–18, 28; journalistic coverage of, 8–9; multitasking with, 237–39, 241; opportunities for use of, 7; pacing of, 83; privatization of, 18–19, 115; rating systems for, 258; repurposing of, 2; as super-peer, 167; teaching about emotions, 131; usage of, and intelligence, 241; youth and, 3–5, 8–9. *See also* new media; *other media listings;* social media
media characters: physical traits in, 56; relationships with, 132–33
media content: production quality of, 73; simplicity of, 55–57
media effects: individual susceptibility to, 40–41; reciprocality of, 42–43, 46, 62; research on, 35, 37, 40, 43;

theories on, 28, 29–30, 37–43, 212, 226
media equation theory, 134
media literacy, 31
media monitoring, 251–57
media practice model, 168
media preferences: changes in, 46–48, 66; fantasy and, 55; gender and, 61; late adolescence and, 92–93
media products, tied to social-emotional development, 58
media psychology, 3–4, 7, 38
media research, 269–70
media-specific parenting, 42, 244
media use: assumptions about, 38; control of, 39; developmental level and, 39; functional role of, in families, 249; habit formation and, 263–64; predictors of, 39, 41; rule-setting for, 247–50, 260–65; safe ages for, 5–6
media violence: aggression and, 40, 96–115; causing physical arousal, 110–11; contextual features of, 111–13; correlational studies of, 101; criminal behavior and, 98–99; effects of, 104–11, 270; exposure to, 258; gender and, 113; habituation to, 107–8; meta-analyses of, 101–3; restricting, 258; social setting and, 114
memory, declines in, 240
meta-analyses, 102
metacognition, 82, 84
Meyrowitz, Joshua, 15–17
Mind and Media (Greenfield), 210
Minecraft, 3, 68, 72, 206–7, 252
Mister Rogers' Neighborhood, 122, 189, 191
moderate discrepancy hypothesis, 46–47, 51, 58, 67, 82–83, 186, 190, 193, 203
moderators, 41–42
mood management theory, 128–29
moral domain, parenting and, 248
Mortal Kombat, 197
movies, 203; analysis of, 32–33; effects of, 29–34, 38; erotic, children's response to, 170–71; horror content in, 119–20; influence of, 88
multitasking, 83
music videos, women's depiction in, 164
Myst, 199–200

narcissism, 4, 25–26, 227, 230–31
Narcissism Epidemic, The (Twenge and Campbell), 230
narratives, older toddlers' interest in, 53–54
Nass, Clifford, 134
Nathanson, Amy, 259, 260
NES (Nintendo Entertainment System), 197
Netflix, 2
Netherlands, commercial television in, 5
network society, 267–69, 271–72
new media: development of, 2; social interaction with, 134
news grazers, 2
newspapers, 12
Nintendo, 197
Nintendo thumb, 208
novels, teen-targeted, 163
nudity, conflated with sex, 161

obesity, 151–53
observational learning, 105–7, 180
One Direction, 133
online profiles, management of, 229
online role-playing games, 76
operational thinking, 52
Oppliger, Patrice, 159
Opree, Suzanna, 150
optimal stimulation, 46
orchid-dandelion hypothesis, 41
orienting features, 49
orienting reflex, 53
over-the-shoulder games, 125
overweight, 151–53

Paik, Haejung, 102–3
Pan, Zhongdang, 183
Panksepp, Jaak, 261
parasocial relationships, 132–34, 192
parental mediation, 182–83, 250–53
parental monitoring, 257
Parent App, The (Clark), 249
parent-child conflict, advertising and, 149, 150–51
parent-child relationships, 15, 19–20
parenting: domains of, 248–49; inconsistency in, 247; media management and, 247–50; in the 21st century, 245–53
parenting styles, 40, 42, 141–42, 244–47
parents, managing children's media use, 253–65
Paro, 134
participatory cues, 191–92
pathological gaming, 214–16
Paul, Pamela, 159
Payne Fund Studies, 24, 31–35, 38, 40, 170
PDP-1, 196
peers: early adolescence and, 88–89; importance of, 67; late adolescence and, 93; media serving as, 167; preadolescents' interaction with, 74–75
perceptual boundedness, 56, 58, 64, 122
permissive parenting, 245
personal domain, 248–49, 260–61
personal fable, 87
persuasion knowledge, 155, 156
Peter, Jochen, 38, 166, 168, 171
Petty, Richard, 38, 154
Piaget, Jean, 45, 47, 52, 54, 56, 64, 69–70, 73–74, 81
Pink Frilly Dress Phenomenon, 59
Pinky Dinky Doo, 184–85
platform games, 200
play, functions of, 207–8
PlayStation, 197
PlayStation 4, 198
Pleo, 134–35
Pong, 196–97
pornification, 159
Pornified: How Pornography Is Damaging Our Lives, Our Relationships, and Our Families (Paul), 159
pornography, 91: arousal and, 171; distinguishing, from sex, 161–62; research on, 165–67
post-figurative culture, 19–20
Postman, Neil, 15–16
Powers, Kasey, 210, 211
preadolescents (ages 8–12): collecting by, 70–71; content preferences of, 72–76; criticism by, 70; development of, 69–70, 73–77; gender and, 75–77; identifying with characters, 74–75; media use by, 70; peers and, 74–75
pre-figurative culture, 19–20
prefrontal cortex, maturation of, 81
preoperational thinking, 52, 64
preschoolers: content preferences for, 55–58; educational media and, 183; egocentrism of, 73–74; fantasy and reality for, 54–55, 113; fear and, 121–23; focus of, 56–57; information processing by, 57; media preferences of, 44
preteens. *See* preadolescents
primary market, children as, 137, 138–41
priming theory, 109–10
print media, childhood and, 16
privacy, 222–23
privacy paradox, 223
private self-awareness, 229
proactive media monitoring, 251–53, 266
problem solving, 92, 182–83, 184
process-based games, 200–201, 203
production quality, 73
product placement, 2, 144, 149

propaganda, 30
prosocial behavior, 184–86
prosocial content, 179
prosocial media, 181
prosocial programming, 185
prosumers, 226
Psycho (dir. Hitchcock), 120
psychoanalysis, 30
psychological privacy, 223
psychological reactance, 247
puberty, 23–24, 79–80, 90
public policy, media violence and, 103–4
public self-awareness, 229–30
purchase intention, 148
purchase request behavior, 148–49

quasi-experiments, 100

rabbit-duck illusion, 271
radio, 29
reactance, 252, 258, 264
realism, gender and, 72
realistic fantasy. *See* magical realism
realistic problem books, 14
reality, fantasy and, 54–55, 113
reality monitoring, 54–55
reassurance strategies, 123, 124, 136
reception model, 226
reciprocality, 42–43, 46, 62, 168, 169, 172, 239
reciprocity, 222, 232
Reeves, Byron, 134
Reiher, Robert, 56
relational aggression, 99
relationships, interest in, 90–91
relief, arousal and, 128
repetition, 57, 191
replicability, *221*, 224
research, reanalysis of, 255
resonance effect, 114
restrictive media monitoring, 252
restrictive mediation, 250
retrievability, *221*, 224
risk taking, 85–86, 92
robots, 133–35
role models, 105, 173, 192, 205
Rousseau, Jean-Jacques, 10, 12–13, 47
Ruckmick, Christian, 170
rules, enforcement of, 246–47
Russell, Steven, 196

Savage, Joanne, 103
scaffolding, 182
scalability, *221*
Schell, Jesse, 201
schemata, 109
Schramm, Wilbur, 16, 38, 43
screen use: for babies and toddlers, 177, 253–57; creativity and, 189; gender and, 206; guidelines for, 254–57
scripts, 109. *See also* cognitive script theory
Sega Genesis, 197
selective exposure theory, 37–38, 201
self-awareness, 25–26, 58, 227, 229–30
self-concept, 86–88, 226, 227
self-concept clarity, 227–28
self-conscious emotions, 58–59
self-disclosure, 221–22, 232
self-esteem, 25–26, 86–88, 94, 227, 228–29, 231
selfies, 91, 227, 230. *See also* sexy selfies
self-perception, 227
self-perception theory, 226–27
self-presentation, 218, 221–22, 235
self-reflection, 130
self-regulation, 184, 186–88, 245–47, 263, 269
sensory preferences, 48
serious gaming, 210
Sesame Street, 66, 131–32, 176–77, 183, 184, 187–88
Setliff, Alissa, 49
sex: in advertising, 164–65; in the public realm, 160–61
sexting, 86, 172, 234–35

sexual behavior, 171–72, 227, 234–35
sexual cognition, 168–70
sexual content, digital media and, 91
sexual grooming, 235–37
sexual insecurity, 171
sexuality: early adolescence and, 90–91, 94; late adolescence and, 94; social media and, 227, 234–35
sexualization, 159–60, 164
sexual media, 158; analyses of, 162–67; children's sexual arousal and, 170; effects of, 167–72; factors in use of, 168; online, 165–66; presence of, 163; sexual behavior and, 171–72
sexual messages, 161–67
sexual satisfaction, 171
sexy selfies, 174, 234, 235, *236*
Shallows, The: What the Internet Is Doing to Our Brain (Carr), 239–40
shared reality, 203
Short, William, 32
SimCity, 199, 201
Sims, The, 201, 207
simulation games, 201, 207
Slater, Michael, 38
Small, Gary, 8, 241
Smart, Andrew, 262
smartphones: affordances of, 243; infants' and toddlers' interest in, 50; multitasking and, 238; and need for intimacy, 261–62; penetration of, 219; rule-setting for, 264; shadow sides of, 262–63; social media and, 263; temptations of, 261–63
Smetana, Judith, 248
Snapchat, 79, 83, 223, 225–26
social aggression, 99
social cognition, 82–84
social cognitive theory, 105–7, 168, 179–81
social competence, 132, 184, 186–87
social-emotional development, 45–46, 52, 58, 73, 179; in early adolescence, 86–91; educational media and, 186–87; social media and, 227–37
social-emotional learning, 176–77
social-emotional skills, educational media and, 184–88
social environment, media use and, 39, 41, 42
social information processing theory, 225
social learning theory. *See* social cognitive theory
social media, 6; adolescents' use of, 79; affordances of, 220–24, 227, 234, 242, 243; appeal of, 242; cognitive effects of, 237–42; developing communication skills through, 222; early adolescence and, 88–89; effects of, 220, 224–27; emergence of, 218; feedback on, 229; identity and, 88–89, 95; ignoring, 263; improved social relationships and, 232; multitasking and, 241; narcissism and, 231; privacy and, 222–23; psychosocial changes and, 25; risky behavior and, 86; scalability of, 224; self-esteem and, 228–29; sexuality and, 227, 234–35; smartphones and, 263; social-emotional effects of, 227–37; stranger danger and, 227, 235–37; usage data for, 219–20; users of, as senders and recipients, 226
social order, 14–18
social robots, 133, 134
social setting, media violence and, 113–14
social smile, 49
Socrates, 8
Sony, 197
Sorrows of Young Werther, The (Goethe), 97
Spacewar!, 196
spatial awareness, 212–13
spinach syndrome, 66, 179

Spitzer, Manfred, 8, 240
Sprafkin, Joyce, 185
Steele, Jeanne R., 168
Stewart, Potter, 161
Steyer, Jim, 96
stimulation hypothesis, 189
stimulus, reality of, 117–18
stimulus-response theory, 29
store wars, 139
story lines, 50, 76, 83, 191
story schema, 193
stranger danger, 227, 235–37
strategy games, 200, 203
striptease culture, 161
Strommen, Erik, 51
subcultures, 89–90, 133, 141, 203–4
superhero genre, 67, 122
Super Mario Bros., 68, 69, 197, 200
Super Why!, 183
symbolic thinking, 52, 54, 55
sympathy, 130

tablets, infants' and toddlers' interest in, 50
technology, changes in, 19, 226
Teenage Mutant Ninja Turtles, 185
teenagers: development of, and social media, 224–27; educational media and, 184; fear-inducing content and, 126; gaming and, 206; habit formation and, 264; managing media use by, 260–65; movies' effects on, 33; as news grazers, 2; prosocial content and, 179, 186; research on, 6–7; self-regulation and, 263; sexual cognition of, 168–70; sexuality and, 234–35; smartphones and, 219, 261–62; social media's appeal for, 223–24; tragedy paradox and, 127. *See also* adolescents
teen marketing, 20–21
teen-specific content, sexual content in, 163
Teletubbies, 5, 21–22, 49, 53, 177
television, 203; activity and, 49–50; brand recall and, 146; different uses of, 2; educational, 131–32; infants watching, 177; multitasking and, 237–38; older toddlers' response to, 55; parent-child relationships and, 16–18; reactive model for viewing of, 45–46; reality distorted on, 16–18; taking childhood away, 16; violence on, studies of, 4, 109; warnings against, 5
Tetris, 199
Thompson, Clive, 242
threats, abstract, 126
Through the Looking-Glass (Carroll), 219
Thurstone, Louis, 32
toddler media, 21–22
toddlers: content interests of, 50, 53–54; educational media and, 182–83; egocentrism of, 73–74; fear and, 121–23; media preferences of, 44; research on, 6–7; screen use for, 253–57. *See also* infants; preschoolers
Tomb Raider, 205, 206
Torrance Tests of Creative Thinking, 189
touch screens, 51, 52
tragedy paradox, 116, 127–31
Truffaut, François, 161
Turkle, Sherry, 8
tweens, 21. *See also* preadolescents
Twenge, Jean, 230
Twitter, 224–26

unintended advertising effects, 145, 149–53
United States, commercial television in, 5
uses-and-gratifications theory, 201

Valkenburg, Patti, 38, 53, 168, 171, 189
values, defining of, 29

van der Schuur, Winneke, 238–39
van der Vlis, Tristan, 97
video deficit hypothesis, 52, 182–83, 256
video game consoles, 197–98
video games: educational aspects of, 181; fluid intelligence and, 25; market for, 197, 198; three-dimensional, 198; women's depiction in, 164. *See also* gaming
Vine, 83, 225–26
violence, rebellion and, 67
violent behavior, 99
virtual worlds, 3, 72
vocabulary, 53, 65
Vroone, Marjolein, 53
Vygotsky, Lev, 182–83

Walter the Farting Dog (Kotzwinkle, Murray, and Colman), 66
Walther, Joseph, 225
Waltons, The, 185
War of the Worlds (Welles), 35–37
War of the Worlds (Wells), 35
Web 2.0, 225–26, 232, 237
Webkinz, 72
Welles, Orson, 35
Wells, H. G., 35
WhatsApp, 79, 224, 225–26
Wii U, 198
wit, popularity and, 84
Wittgenstein, Ludwig, 271
Woodard, Emory, 186
World Health Organization, 151
World of Warcraft, 201, 213
Wouters, Cas, 160
writing, memory loss and, 8

Xbox One, 198

Yancey, Christina, 103
Yang, Mong-Shan, 259
young elementary schoolchildren (ages 5–7): development of, 64; educational media for, 66; formal education for, 65; media preferences for, 66–69; media usage by, 65; peers and, 67
youth: commercialization and, 5; delaying adulthood, 18–19; enjoying fear-inducing content, 124; as market, 20–22; moratorium phase in, 18; surrounded by marketing, 143–44. *See also* adolescents; children; teenagers
youth culture, 14, 19–20
youth research, 269–70

Zillman, Dolf, 127–28
Zimmerman, Frederick, 255
zone of proximal development, 183